Chronicles of the Hudson

THREE CENTURIES OF TRAVEL AND ADVENTURE

ROLAND VAN ZANDT

BLACK·DOME

BLACK DOME PRESS CORP.

RR1, Box 422 • Hensonville, NY 12439 • Tel: (518) 734-6357 Fax: (518) 734-5802

BLACK DOME PRESS CORP.
RR 1, Box 422
Hensonville, NY 12439
Tel: (518) 734-6357
Fax: (518) 734-5802

Library of Congress Catalogue Card Number: 73-152722

ISBN 0-9628523-3-3

Printed in the USA

In Memory of My Daughter Leona

Acknowledgments

I CANNOT HOPE TO THANK all those who have given me help during several years of research and traveling in the Hudson Valley. The staffs of the many estates and mansions that are now open to the public in the valley have been especially courteous and helpful. It is obvious that theirs is a labor of love. The great institutions at the mouth of the Hudson have also lightened the burdens of scholarship and often performed service beyond the call of duty. I distinctly remember with gratitude the staffs of the New York Public Library, the Museum of the City of New York, the Frick Art Reference Library, and the incomparable New-York Historical Society. Of the many individuals who have been generous with time and attention I wish to thank James J. Heslin, Director of the New-York Historical Society, and Edmund E. Lynch, Curator of the Adirondack Museum in Blue Mountain Lake, N.Y. I am also indebted to Maurice K. Kahan of the Sleepy Hollow Restorations, Norman S. Rice of the Albany Institute of History and Art, and Mrs. Robert F. Gay of Rhinebeck, N.Y. I have benefited substantially from the criticism of three anonymous historians, for which I now give thanks, though without disclaiming my responsibility for all remaining imperfections. I extend warm thanks to Pete and May Van Zandt of La Puente, Calif., and to Richard Van Zandt of Laguna Beach—good relatives all—for helping to relieve the tedium of proofreading during the winter months by offering me the haven of their homes in Southern California. For my wife, Leona, veteran of three academic wars, proficient in the mechanics of scholarship as well as the mysteries of sustained enthusiasm and devotion, I reserve my deepest gratitude.

R.V.Z.

Contents

Contents

List of Illustrations

Maps. Drawn by Dorothy deFontaine

Introduction

TO THE TWENTIETH ANNIVERSARY EDITION

As a young city boy growing up in Yonkers, I understood two things about the Hudson: that everything across the river was New Jersey—no matter how far north one travelled—and that the Palisades, the strange, dark vertical shore on the Jersey side, were named for the amusement park that, at the time, sat atop them. In these beliefs, I was like most city kids of the lower river.

My father used to take us to a place he called The Ridge, a promontory which overlooked downtown, the river and the western shore. I was thrilled by the view, by the bustle of the city and its sights—Getty Square, the Carpet Shop, Otis Elevator, the Sugar House—and by the fact that there was a place to stand from which we could see another state.

Some thirty years have passed since. My work life has come to revolve around the Hudson and I have come to see it from many vantages. I am struck by the fact that at one time my orientation was entirely east to west, always directed across the river, viewing a shore that I never paused to think of us as older than I. In these things, I was like most people who chance to view the Hudson.

Roland Van Zandt called his *Chronicles of the Hudson* "an attempt to recapture the primal experience of the Hudson." That primal experience is of the north- and southbound, a younger America whose orientation was the river's breadth *and* length. Travelers negotiated its narrows, rounded its bends, traversed its bays, encountered its peninsulas and islands, entered its ports and, eventually, discovered its Adirondack headwaters. Their journeys were of exploration, settlement, pleasure, exploitation and opportunity—and all that those pursuits imply.

It is almost four hundred years since Robert Juet's 1609 journal of his trip with Henry Hudson, the first of twenty-two accounts of travel on the Hudson River which

Dr. Van Zandt collected for this volume. Yet, much of the primal experience still remains to be enjoyed: the old trail of civilization endures—the Tappan Zee, Dunderberg, Anthony's Nose, Danskammer, Esopus, Kinderhook, Half Moon, Glens Falls. But to follow it we must now buck civilization's flow, often a daunting task. Boat transportation is generally unavailable. The schedules and destinations of train lines are organized around work day commutation. Most travel is by automobile, in some places on arterial highways built upon former river bottom.

And so, for most of us, it is the boundary of the opposite shore rather than the frontier of the next reach that defines our view of the Hudson. At our worst, we take no notice of the river at all.

Roland Van Zandt dearly loved the Hudson and worried for its future. He dearly loved history as well. He knew that the view of ourselves which it offers is unforgiving and unforgetting. Henry Hudson's time was not a simpler or more innocent one, Juet's account makes that clear. And Dr. Van Zandt's careful introductions to each era and each account are characteristically bold and unsentimental. Inevitably he faced the historian's obligation to reflect on his own era. He remained unflinching.

Indeed, the most eloquent of the entries in this volume belongs to Roland Van Zandt himself. You will read it but I am exercising my prerogative to present a bit of it here. It bears rereading.

In his introduction to the final part, "The Age of the Railroad," he writes that modern transportation "permitted millions of people to travel up and down the Hudson Valley without once being aware of the river itself or of the teeming life and history of the past." And so the Hudson "barely enters into the lives of its nearby inhabitants." It became "a neglected gem of the national domain, defiled and polluted throughout most of its tidal length by human and industrial wastes, unfit for drinking, swimming or fishing; a great natural resource awaiting the deliberations of a more enlightened society."

The Hudson as neglected gem seems a familiar theme to us now. But when *Chronicles of the Hudson* was first published in 1971, only a relative handful of voices were sounding the warning. Those voices rang with a common chorus however—society had turned its back to the Hudson River and the long process of recovery would only begin when we returned to its shores and acknowledged what we had wrought. That a serious historian chose to add his voice in those pioneer days was a significant event. That his observation has survived the decades should sound as a fresh reveille. This special Twentieth Anniversary Edition will insure that it does.

Dr. Van Zandt's passion and purpose is revealed to us in this last section. He had reached his final opportunity to just spell it out for us; in doing so he helps us feel our own passion, our own yearning to participate in the "deliberations of a more enlightened society"—all in the context of the lesson of our own history, the history of the Hudson River.

Leona Van Zandt recollects a Fourth of July vacation she and her husband took on a friend's houseboat on the Hudson. "It was a journey of exploration and discovery. For a time, we were cut off from the twentieth century. The experience of the river and the landscape from the river crystallized for Roland the idea to do this book. For both of us it was a truly joyous and unqualified happy time."

She recalls fondly that it was Roland's lifelong pleasure to serve as a tour guide for friends on forays throughout the Hudson Valley during which he would eagerly share his knowledge and passion for Hudson River history.

Each generation born to the Hudson is entitled to its own journey of discovery. It is entitled to the joy and happiness it brings. Roland Van Zandt's legacy to us is as a friend and tour guide on that journey. It is his instruction to us that the river's future, like the river's past, is all of ours to keep.

John Cronin
Hudson Riverkeeper
1992

Preface

THIS IS A JOURNEY through time, a journey through life and history as seen and recorded by travelers in the Hudson River Valley over three hundred years. Throughout most of the formative periods of American history, from the earliest years of the seventeenth century to the closing decades of the nineteenth, the Hudson River played a role in the national stream of events that was almost in reverse ratio to its geographical dimensions. A modest 315 miles from source to mouth, ranking only seventy-first in length among all American rivers, restricted in navigation to 150 miles of tidewater between New York City and Troy, the Hudson yet managed to become one of the most significant factors in the development of the United States. As was said only a few years ago, "scenically, historically and humanistically, in its tangibles and intangibles, its cumulative interest is scarcely exceeded, if indeed, it is even matched, by any other of our rivers." * It is to be hoped that this anthology of three hundred years of travelers' accounts may verify that accolade, and also reveal some of the day-by-day excitement and grandeur that gives it substantive meaning.

A definitive anthology is a contradiction in terms, and the present work is no exception. The editor of this volume cannot pretend to have read all the extant texts of the Hudson. The literature of the Hudson is vast enough to support more than one anthology. Much of this material, however, is irrelevant to the present purpose. As an attempt to recapture the primal experience of the Hudson—the experience of travel—the present volume has restricted itself, with one or two minor exceptions, to authentic accounts of specific voyages or journeys on or along the Hudson at specific periods of time. Imaginative or fictional works have been excluded,

* Paul Wilstach, *Hudson River Landings* (Indianapolis: 1933), p. 17.

even though this exclusion entailed the sacrifice of such beguiling writers as Washington Irving ("Peter Stuyvesant's Voyage up the Hudson" in *Knickerbocker's History of New York*), Michel-Guillaume Jean De Crèvecoeur ("A Trip up the Hudson" in *Crèvecoeur's Eighteenth-Century Travels in Pennsylvania and New York*), and James Fenimore Cooper (an imaginary trip up the Hudson in Chapter VIII of *Home as Found,* and another—with Lafayette!—in *The Travelling Bachelor*). Historical authenticity, rather than literary flair or interest, has been the guiding principle. Thus Charles Fenno Hoffman's more readable and literary account of the discovery of the sources of the Hudson has been sacrificed for the more detailed, informative, and authentic account by William C. Redfield, the official historian of the geological expedition of 1836. Similarly, if Johannes De Laet's seventeenth-century description of the Hudson gains admission to this anthology, even though it is not a first-hand traveler's account, it is because the selection contains the only known excerpts from Henry Hudson's long-lost journal of the famous voyage of 1609.

Matters of length have also determined the selection of material for this anthology. Pursuing the principle, once again, of recapturing the experience of travel as it was actually known on the Hudson, the editor has favored lengthy narratives. Millions of people traveled on the Hudson during three hundred years of history. Of these millions, only a small minority kept some record of their experiences (diaries and journals, letters to friends, etc.), and fewer still wrote formal essays or books. Yet all these travelers, at least until modern technology introduced new modes of transport in the nineteenth century, took long and leisurely voyages, and the authentic experience could only be captured in the formal narrative or in the small minority of detailed diaries and journals. Such, in any event, are the true chronicles of the Hudson.

Brief accounts of a few paragraphs or a few pages—the incredibly rich literary effluvia in the history of the Hudson—have therefore been rigidly excluded from this anthology. This has meant the sacrifice of a good deal of the glamor and charisma that attaches to the names of whole legions of famous people who traveled the Hudson. A few letters that George Washington wrote, for instance, about a journey he made from Newburgh to Saratoga in the summer of 1783 in the company of Governor George Clinton and Alexander Hamilton have not warranted his inclusion in this anthology. Similarly, Robert Fulton's scanty letters about the first voyage of the *Clermont* (though parts of them are quoted in an Introduction) placed the ban on his acceptance. Sir Charles Lyell was also excluded, despite his love of the Hudson as expressed in three pages he wrote about a steamboat trip of 1841. Many writers have been excluded: Charles Dickens (two trips in 1842), Chateaubriand (a romantically distorted account of 1791), Washington Irving (stenographic notes and diaries about various trips), Frederick Marryat (ten lively pages about a steamboat trip of 1837), Charles Brockden Brown (a few wonderful but all too brief pages about a sloop trip of 1801), William M. Thackeray (two paragraphs about a train and steamboat trip of 1853). The list, however, could go on indefinitely, for until the present century at least, almost all the famous people of Europe and America seemed to have traveled on the Hudson at one time or another in their lives.

Brevity was not the sole reason for the exclusion of texts, for in a few notable cases the editor even deemed it advisable to sacrifice lengthy texts. One such significant omission was Captain Basil Hall's fifty-page account of a trip by steamboat in the spring of 1827—the substance of two chapters from his well-known *Travels in North America*. Lengthy digressions within this narrative, plus the availability of alternative texts for the same period, determined its exclusion. Another significant omission was the Duke de La Rochefoucauld's fascinating narrative of travel in the upper Hudson Valley in 1795. It was discarded because it covers some of the same ground as the Marquis De Chastellux's account of 1780, yet lacks the narrative flow of the earlier work. Another even more important French source that was excluded was Jacques Gérard Milbert's *Itinéraire pittoresque du fleuve Hudson et des parties latérales de l'Amerique du Nord*. This superlative work of travel—which, strangely, has never been translated into English—was simply too long to be included in this anthology (it contains over 100 pages on the Hudson alone); and it deserves to be published as a separate book.

The selection of texts has also been influenced by certain geographical anomalies in the history of the Hudson. The majority of texts have followed the main stream of history along the navigable reaches of the river between New York City and Troy. Several have also embraced the upper river between Troy and the Adirondack Mountains. Three other narratives, however, have extended beyond the strict geographical limits of the Hudson to include the Champlain and Mohawk valleys. They have been included because of the exigencies of history. The Champlain and Mohawk valleys are natural extensions of the Hudson River corridor northward into Canada and westward into the American interior, and they are therefore indissolubly associated with the history of travel on the Hudson. We might even say that the role of the Hudson in American history is incomprehensible without due consideration of the two great laterals up the Champlain and Mohawk valleys. Two texts—Peter Kalm's of 1749 and Charles Carroll's of 1776—have therefore been included to display the role of the Champlain Valley during the seventeenth and eighteenth centuries; and one text—William L. Stone's narrative of the opening of the Erie Canal in 1825—has been included to display the role of the Mohawk Valley during the nineteenth century.

To keep the integrity and impact of the experience of the past in this anthology, the editor has adhered to original texts whenever possible. The Robert Juet text, for instance, is the original *Journal* as it was written by the first mate of the *Half Moon;* modernizations of this journal are available in many other recent sources. Internal editing or deletion has been kept at a minimum, and the editor has modernized spelling and punctuation only when confronted with a clear question of intelligibility. Extensive footnotes have been used to supply deficiencies, to explain allusions, and to help bridge the gap between the modern reader and the archaic but compleat traveller.

Roland Van Zandt
New York City
May 1971

PART I *Seventeenth-Century Beginnings*

The Hudson Valley

Seventeenth-Century Beginnings, 1609–1680

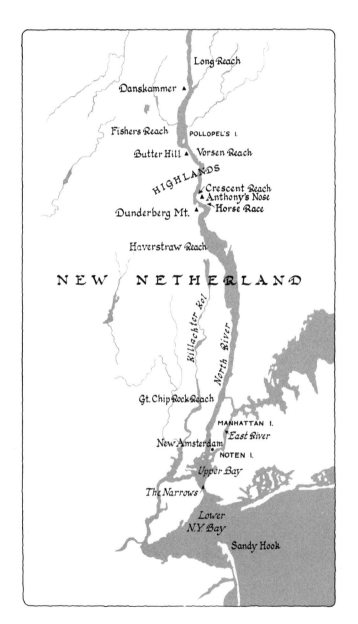

Long Reach

Danskammer ▲

Fishers Reach

POLLOPEL'S I.

Butter Hill ▲ · Vorsen Reach

HIGHLANDS

Crescent Reach
▲ Anthony's Nose
Dunderberg Mt. ▲ ↙ Horse Race

Haverstraw Reach

N E W   N E T H E R L A N D

Killachter Kol

North River

Gt. Chip Rock Reach

MANHATTAN I.
· East River
New Amsterdam
NOTEN I.
Upper Bay
The Narrows
Lower
N.Y. Bay
Sandy Hook

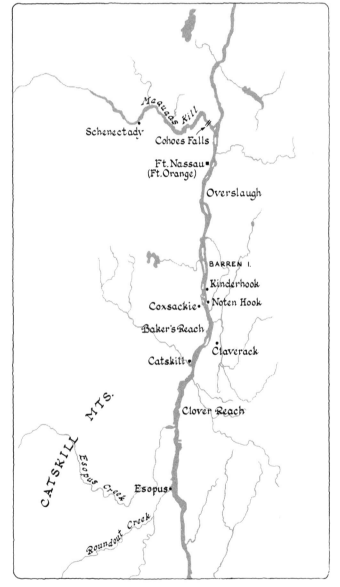

Schenectady ·

Maquaas Kill

Cohoes Falls

Ft. Nassau ■
(Ft. Orange)

Overslaugh

BARREN I.

· Kinderhook

Coxsackie · · Noten Hook

Baker's Reach

· Claverack

Catskill ·

Cloven Reach

C A T S K I L L   MTS.

Esopus Creek

Esopus ·

Roundout Creek

THE FIRST TWO HUNDRED years of history in the Hudson Valley are enveloped in paradox. The discovery and settlement of the Hudson Valley was the result of the westward thrust of the greatest commercial and military, financial and cultural power on earth in the first half of the seventeenth century. A little more than two hundred years later the valley finally fulfilled the golden promise of its beginnings by becoming the most populous and powerful commercial and cultural center in North America. Yet during all the intervening years it lagged far behind other regions of the Atlantic seaboard, and as late as 1790 the State of New York—still practically confined to the Hudson Valley and the cluster of islands around New York harbor—ranked next to Maryland in population or fifth among all the states of the Union. This protracted postponement of the destiny of the Empire State is one of the most singular facts in the colonial history of America.

The august concentration of power that initiated the history of New York may come as a surprise to students of American history reared on the Anglophile generalizations of the great historians of nineteenth-century New England. But the fact is that when the newly formed Republic of the United Netherlands sent forth Henry Hudson in 1609 to discover a northwest passage to the Orient—and incidentally stumble upon and explore the Hudson Valley—it was in the full tide of its successful rebellion against the Spanish Empire and was rapidly becoming the foremost power of Europe. The settlement of New Netherland coincided with the "Golden Age" of Dutch history. The year 1609 saw a truce in the war with Spain, but between the years 1621 and 1648, when the wars were resumed and independence finally achieved, the Dutch Republic forged an army and navy that were second to none in the world, Amsterdam became the commercial capital of Europe—

known in parts of the world that had never heard of London or Paris and setting standards of living that were the envy of the continent—and the United Provinces of the Free Netherlands had become the greatest trading nation in the world. That New Amsterdam under the guise of New York should become in the late nineteenth century "the commercial emporium of the world" seems an inevitable corollary of its origins in the seventeenth-century emporium of old Amsterdam.

Yet we still must contend with all those intervening years when that destiny was nowhere in evidence and New Netherland (and after 1664 New York) was overshadowed by the great English colonies to the north and south of it. The earliest statistics of the colonial period give dramatic proof of that harsh discrepancy. Although Plymouth, New Amsterdam, and Jamestown were all founded within a few years of each other with approximately the same number of people, Massachusetts had 16,000 by 1643, Virginia had 15,000 by 1649, but as late as 1653 New Netherland still had only 2,000 inhabitants. In 1664 when England acquired New Netherland by force of arms, Virginia had 40,000, New England had 50,000, and the conquered Dutch province had about 10,000. By 1698, the end of the seventeenth century, Virginia and Massachusetts each had 58 to 60,000, whereas New York still languished with less than 20,000. The same relative statistics, as we shall see in a later chapter, obtained throughout most of the eighteenth century.

Historians have offered many suggestions for the tardy development of the future Empire State of the Union. Much has been made, for instance, of the land policy of the Dutch West India Company, the patroonships, and the subsequent discouragement of farming and free settlement. Much has also been made of the relative absence of self-government and democratic political institutions in the Dutch as against the English colonies. John Fiske also offered the suggestion that life was just too good in Holland after the War of Independence to encourage emigration to New Netherland: "Had there been more poverty and discontent in the mother country, New Amsterdam would doubtless have grown more rapidly, and farmsteads would have sprung up on the banks of its noble river." All such suggestions, of course, have some truth to them; but they seriously err in concentrating the burden of responsibility on the Dutch phase of New York history. New York was still the stepchild of the seaboard colonies one hundred years after English rule. Historians must look deeper for more satisfying explanations.

The cardinal fact in the history of the Hudson is the river itself, or the fact that it is as much an arm of the sea, a fiord, as it is a river, and that it thereby provided the only navigable waterway of the Atlantic seaboard through the great Appalachian barrier. When the American Revolution and the War of 1812 finally resolved the problem of its ownership and stabilized its western and northern approaches, its supreme geographical advantage as the corridor to the vast interior of the American continent immediately precipitated the rise of New York as the foremost state in the Union. During the eighteenth century, however, this very advantage was the source of international rivalry and war, and retarded normal development. During the seventeenth century the same advantage retarded development for far different but perhaps even more significant reasons.

The Hudson River corridor permitted the Dutch to commit the same error as the French and Spanish in the New World and to lay claim to their part of the vast undeveloped American continent, not primarily for purposes of settlement and the planting of colonies, but for exploitation and trade. This is not to say that the English colonies were not originally settled by commercial companies or that they could ever subsist except on the basis of commercially viable relations with the homeland. But being late arrivals to these shores, the English could not outflank the great Appalachian barrier as the French and Spanish had done, and they were all but excluded from the rich fur trade of the French dominion in the north and the gold market of the southern Spanish empire. Confined to a narrow coastal region both in New England and Virginia, excluded from the two greatest sources of commercial wealth in the New World (at least until New Netherland was conquered in 1664), the English were forced to develop relatively compact and self-sufficient "plantations" based as much upon agriculture as trade, and the resulting density of population was to become the one sure foundation for the eventual expulsion of the Dutch, French, and Spanish and their extenuated posts and isolated settlements in North America.

The Hudson River corridor, as we have suggested, made intensive colonization an unlikely prospect in Dutch New Netherland. The confrontation of the greatest trading nation on earth with a deep tidal river that permitted ocean-going vessels to penetrate a hundred miles beyond the Appalachian barrier to the rich fur-bearing lands of the powerful Iroquois Confederation could have only one fateful conclusion: the continuation of an European obsession dating from the time of Columbus with the potentialities of quick profits through trade, rather than the questionable benefits of prolonged and hazardous colonization. Although the Dutch East India Company dropped all interest in the river that Henry Hudson had discovered as soon as he told the company it afforded no passage to the Orient, the very next year various Dutch merchants began to act on his suggestions of a lucrative fur trade and to outfit vessels for the voyage to the "great river of the mountains." The trade proved so profitable that four rude houses were built as a trading station on Manhattan in 1613, and the following year three of the merchants, Hendrick Christiansen, Cornelius May, and Adrian Block, acquired a right of monopoly from Holland and sailed three ships to the Hudson. Encouraged by the results, they petitioned for and were granted a charter in 1615 as "The United New Netherland Company" (the first appearance of the name New Netherland), established jurisdiction over all the land between the North (Hudson) and South (Delaware) Rivers, and in the next year or so restored an abandoned fort near present-day Albany that had been built by some French traders in 1540 and named it Fort Nassau. By 1620 there were a multitude of traders at Manhattan; and in 1621 the New Netherland Company was absorbed by the much larger Dutch West India Company, and the fate of New Netherland was placed in the hands of one of history's most powerful commercial monopolies. In 1623 the company was given the right of self-government through a Director General (Cornelius Jacobsen May) and the good ship *New Netherland*—the equivalent of New England's *Mayflower* —arrived with the first party of permanent settlers, most of whom were French-speaking refugees who had been driven into the southern Netherlands by the Spanish and were called Walloons. Of these first immigrants two families and six men went to the Connecticut River (which Holland also vaguely claimed), two families and eight men settled on the Delaware, eight men were left at Manhattan "to take possession," and the rest, some eighteen families, went on to establish Fort Orange (Fort Nassau having been abandoned) at present-day Albany. During the next five years, however, while New England underwent a great era of expansion, farming and immigration still languished in New Netherland.

In 1629 the Dutch West India Company tried to encourage colonization by establishing a system of patroonships, a semi-feudal device whereby any member of the Company could become the "patroon" of sixteen miles of land along the Hudson (eight miles if the grant embraced both sides of the river) provided he induced fifty grown people to accompany him as tenant farmers. The system failed to achieve its purpose: the patroons paid more attention to the fur trade than to farming and fresh settlers failed to arrive. The population of Manhattan actually declined during the period 1630–1635, while that of New England threatened to engulf the Dutch possessions, and New Netherland still looked more like a series of trading stations than a permanent colony. In 1638 the Dutch West India Company tried once again to rectify matters by abolishing all monopolies, both in agriculture and trade, and placing all nationalities on an equal footing, but the terrible Indian wars of the 1640s negated these efforts and almost wiped out New Netherland altogether. There was a change for the better after 1653; farmers began to arrive, rural settlements expanded on Long Island and Staten Island and on both sides of the Hudson, and the northern frontier advanced from Beverwyck (Albany) to Schenectady; the population of Manhattan doubled between 1653 and 1664 (800 to 1600), and the population of all New Netherland increased fivefold (2,000 to 10,000). Yet, when the English took over New Netherland in 1664, Virginia had a population more than three times greater and New England outranked the Dutch province five to one. After the conquest, trade and commerce continued to be the mainstay of the Hudson Valley (the fur trade had been one of the main inducements for the takeover), Dutch institutions were reconfirmed, and by 1700, when expansion was being stopped by wars with the French and Indians, the population of Virginia and Massachusetts was still six times greater than that of the province of New York. The destiny of the Hudson still lay in the future, when all the surrounding provinces would be unified under American control, and trade and commerce and migration would look to the trans-Appalachian West for the rising star of American civilization.

1.

Robert Juet 1609*

INTRODUCTION: The Dutch were not the first on the Hudson River nor the first to know of its presence. Actual discovery dates from the year 1524 when Giovanni da Verrazzano, an Italian navigator sailing under the flag of the King of France, entered what is today Lower New York Bay and discovered "a very agreeable site located within two small prominent hills [the Narrows], in the midst of which flowed to the sea a very big river, which was deep within the mouth." This is the first recorded statement by a European of the subject of this anthology. Verrazzano did not name or explore the great river he had discovered, for a sudden squall forced him to discontinue his exploration of Upper New York Bay and put out to sea again. But from that day onward the Hudson became of increasing importance to the cartography of the Western Hemisphere.

Other visitors, traders, and explorers followed Verrazzano during the remaining years of the sixteenth century: Estevan Gomez, a Portuguese mariner, was known to have visited the river during his voyage of 1525; various French traders probably came down from the north to traffic with the Indians along the Hudson, undoubtedly as early as 1540; a nebulous Englishman, one David Ingram, might have visited the Hudson during a reputed and fantastic overland journey from the Gulf of Mexico to Canada in 1567–1568; Dutch traders were well acquainted with the river by the end of the century. Such visitors and their all but unrecorded activities, however, are the usual precursors of formal history. The true narratives of the Hudson begin in the first decade of the seventeenth century, when an English navigator sailing under the Dutch flag systematically explored the

* Excerpts from Robert M. Lunny's edition of *Juet's Journal* published by The New Jersey Historical Society (Newark: 1959), pp. 27–37. Reprinted by permission of the publisher. Bracketed material is by Lunny.

river and finally dispelled a century-old myth regarding its possible passage to the great Sea of China. Henry Hudson's voyage of 1609 gave us our first known description of the river from its mouth to the head of navigation, and it provided the initial impetus for the first European colonization of the Hudson Valley. It is therefore appropriate that the river should bear his name, and that this anthology of three hundred years of travel on the Hudson should begin with the historic *Journal* of the 1609 voyage that was penned by "Robert Juet of Lime-house," a ship's officer on Hudson's *Half Moon*.

We do not know why Robert Juet kept this *Journal* of the third of Hudson's four voyages (Juet's second) in quest of a northwest passage to the Orient. But whether it was a ship's log, an official record kept for the Captain, or merely the personal diary of a rather literate man of the sea, the *Journal* is an historical treasure. Henry Hudson also wrote an account of the voyage, but except for a few extracts that have been preserved in Johannes De Laet's *New World* of 1625—our second narrative—the great navigator's own version of the 1609 voyage has been lost to history. Juet's *Journal* is therefore the authoritative and graphic account of one of the most momentous events in the early history of American exploration.

Hudson had contracted with the Dutch East India Company to sail a ship of 80 tons, manned by a crew of eighteen sailors, northward around the Arctic Island of Novaya Zemlya in Latitude 77°N. until he came to the Oriental Sea; then south to Latitude 60°N. where he was to make various observations confirming his discoveries, and then to return home. But there was a change of plans: when facing the rigors and hardships of the frozen north, Hudson's crew became mutinous, and he decided to avoid outright insurrection by turning south and exploring the warmer climes of the Amer-

1. *The "Half Moon,"* engraving by S. Hollyer from his "Old World Views"; courtesy of The New-York Historical Society.

"Then came one of the Savages that swamme away from us at our going up the River with many other, thinking to betray us. But wee perceived their intent, and suffered none of them to enter our ship."

A fanciful view of the *Half Moon* anchored off the Palisades, October 2, 1609, when Henry Hudson had another dramatic encounter with the Indians.

ican coast. The *Half Moon* sailed south as far as the latitude of Virginia and then turned north toward the end of August, hugging the coastline with the aid of a map given to the Captain by his friend, Captain John Smith. On August 26, according to Juet, the *Half Moon* entered Chesapeake Bay, but was shortly driven out by a sudden storm. Two days later, after dropping into Delaware Bay and finding it an unlikely passage to the Orient, Hudson set his course for the north again; and the morning of September 2 found him off the shore of New Jersey. The following extract begins at that point and follows the *Half Moon* during the ensuing four weeks of exploration along the banks of the Hudson.

September 2–October 4

Then the Sunne arose, and we steered away North againe, and saw the Land from the West by North, to the North-west by North, all like broken Ilands [*the coast between Atlantic City and Little Egg Inlet*], and our soundings were eleven and ten fathoms. Then wee looft in for the shoare, and faire by the shoare, we had seven fathoms. The course along the Land we found to be North-east by North. From the Land which we had first sight of, untill we came to a great Lake of water, as wee could judge it to bee, being drowned Land, which made it to rise like Ilands, which was in length ten leagues [*Barnegat Bay*]. The mouth of that Lake hath many shoalds, and the Sea breaketh on them as it is cast out of the mouth of it [*Barnegat Inlet*]. And from that Lake or Bay, the Land lyeth North by East, and wee had a great streame out of the Bay; and from thence our sounding was ten fathoms, two leagues from the Land. At five of the clocke we Anchored, being little winde,

and rode in eight fathoms water, the night was faire. This night I found the Land to hall the Compasse 8. degrees. For [*far*] to the Northward off us we saw high Hils [*Neversink Highlands, Staten Island Hills; or even Harbour Hill on Long Island*]. For the day before we found not above 2. degrees Variation. This is a very good Land to fall with, and a pleasant Land to see. [*Juet occasionally departed from his matter-of-fact account to express a personal opinion.*]

The third, the morning mystie untill ten of the clocke, then it cleered, and the winde came to the South Southeast, so wee weighed and stood to the Northward. The Land is very pleasant and high, and bold to fall withall [*the south coast of Staten Island or the Highlands*]. At three of the clocke in the afternoone, wee came to three great Rivers [*possibly Raritan Bay, the Narrows, and Rockaway Inlet*]. So we stood along to the Northermost [*the Narrows*], thinking to have gone into it, but we found it to have a very shoald barre before it, for we had but ten foot water. Then wee cast about to the Southward, and found two fathoms, three fathoms, and three and a quarter, till we came to the Souther side of them [*the shoals*], then we had five and six fathoms, and Anchored [*north of Sandy Hook*]. So wee sent in our Boate to sound, and they found no lesse water than foure, five, six, and seven fathoms, and returned in an houre and a halfe. So wee weighed and went in, and rode in five fathoms, Ozie ground, and saw many Salmons, and Mullets, and Rayes very great. The height is 40. degrees 30. minutes. [*Probably this was just inside the Hook.*]

The fourth, in the morning as soone as the day was light, wee saw that it was good riding farther up. So we sent our Boate to sound, and found that it was a very good Harbour; and foure and five fathoms, two Cables length from the shoare. Then we weighed and went in with our ship. Then our Boate went on Land [*generally considered to be Sandy Hook but also considered by some to be Coney Island]* with our Net to Fish, and caught ten great Mullets, of a foot and a halfe long a peece, and a Ray as great as foure men could hale into the ship. So wee trimmed our Boate and rode still all day. At night the wind blew hard at the North-west, and our Anchor came home, and wee drove on shoare, but tooke no hurt, thanked bee God, for the ground is soft sand and Oze. This day the people of the Countrey came aboord of us, seeming very glad of our coming, and brought greene Tobacco, and gave us of it for Knives and Beads. They goe in Deere skins loose, well dressed. They have yellow Copper. They desire Cloathes, and are very civill. They have great store of Maiz or Indian Wheate, whereof they make good Bread. The Countrey is full of great and tall Oakes.

The fifth, in the morning as soone as the day was light, the wind ceased and the Flood came. So we heaved off our ship againe into five fathoms water, and sent our Boate to sound the Bay, and we found that there was three fathoms hard by the Souther shoare. Our men went on Land there, and saw great store of Men, Women and Children, who gave them Tobacco at their comming on Land. So they went up into the Woods [*Neversink Highlands*], and saw great store of very goodly Oakes, and some Currants. For one of them came aboord and brought some dryed, and gave me some, which were sweet and good. This day many of the people came aboord, some in Mantles of Feathers, and some in Skinnes of divers sorts of good Furres. Some women also came to us with Hempe. They had red Copper Tobacco pipes, and other things of Copper they did weare about their neckes. At night they went on Land againe, so wee rode very quiet, but durst not trust them.

The sixth, in the morning was faire weather, and our Master sent John Colman [*who had sailed with Hudson in his first voyage of 1607 "for to discover a passage by the North Pole to Japan and China"*], with foure other men in our Boate over to the Northside, to sound the other River [*probably the Narrows*], being foure leagues from us. They found by the way shoald water two fathoms; but at the North of the River eighteen, and twentie fathoms, and very good riding for Ships; and a narrow River to the Westward betweene two Ilands [*most likely the Kill Van Kull*]. The Lands they told us were as pleasant with Grasse and Flowers, and goodly Trees, as ever they had seene, and very sweet smells came from them. So they went in two leagues and saw an open Sea [*Newark Bay*], and returned; and as they came backe, they were set upon by two Canoes, the one having twelve, the other fourteene men. The night came on, and it began to rayne, so that their Match went out; and they had one man slaine in the fight, which was an English-man, named John Colman, with an Arrow shot into his throat, and two more hurt. It grew so darke that they could not find the ship that night, but labored too and fro on their Oares. They had so great a streame, that their grapnell would not hold them.

The seventh, was faire, and by ten of the clocke they returned aboord the ship, and brought our dead man with them, whom we carryed on Land and buryed, and named the point after his name, Colmans Point [*Sandy Hook is generally agreed upon*]. Then we hoysed in our Boate, and raised her side with waste boords for defence of our men. So we rode still all night, having good regard to our Watch.

The eight, was very faire weather, wee rode still very quietly. The people came aboord us, and brought Tobacco and Indian wheate, to exchange for Knives and Beades, and offered us no violence. So we fitting up our Boate did marke them, to see if they would make any shew of the Death of our man; which they did not.

The ninth, faire weather. In the morning, two great Canoes came aboord full of men; the one with their Bowes and Arrowes, and the other in shew of buying of Knives, to betray us; but we perceived their intent. Wee tooke two of them to have kept them, and put red Coates on them, and would not suffer the other to come neere us. So they went on Land and two other came aboord in a Canoe: wee tooke the one and let the other goe; but hee which wee had taken, got up and leapt over-boord. Then we weighed and went off into the channell of the River [*near the Narrows*], and Anchored there all night.

The tenth, faire weather, we rode still till twelve of the clocke. Then we weighed and went over, and found it shoald all the middle of the River, for wee could finde but two fathoms and a halfe, and three fathomes for the space of a league; then wee came to three fathomes, and foure fathomes, and so to seven fathomes, and Anchored, and rode all night in soft Ozie ground. The banke is Sand.

The eleventh, was faire and very hot weather. At one of the clocke in the after-noone, wee weighed and went into the River [*the Narrows; less likely the Hudson*], the wind at South South-west, little winde. Our soundings were seven, sixe, five, seven, eight, nine, ten, twelve, thirteene, and fourteene fathomes. Then it shoalded againe, and came to five fathomes. Then wee Anchored, and saw that it was a very good Harbour for all windes, and rode all night [*in the Upper Bay*]. The people of the Countrey came aboord us, making shew of love, and gave us Tobacco and Indian Wheat, and departed for that night; but we durst not trust them.

The twelfth, very faire and hot. In the after-noone at two of the clocke wee weighed, the winde being variable, betweene the North and the North-west. So we turned into the River two leagues and Anchored [*at about the mouth of the Hudson off the Battery*]. This morning at our first rode in the River, there came eight and twentie Canoes full of men, women and children to betray us: but we saw their intent, and suffered none of them to come aboord of us. At twelve of the clocke they departed. They brought with them Oysters and Beanes, whereof wee bought some. They have great Tobacco pipes of yellow Copper, and Pots of Earth to dresse their meate in. It floweth South-east by South within.

The thirteenth, faire weather, the wind Northerly. At seven of the clocke in the morning, as the floud came we weighed, and turned foure miles into the River. The tide being done we anchored. Then there came foure Canoes aboord: but we suffered none of them to come into our ship. They brought great store of very good Oysters aboord, which we bought for trifles [*near Manhattanville*]. In the night I set the variation of the Compasse, and found it to be 13. degrees. In the after-noone we weighed, and turned in with the floud, two leagues and a halfe further, and anchored all night [*near Fort Lee*], and had five fathoms soft Ozie ground, and had an high point of Land, which shewed out to us, bearing North by East five leagues off us [*the highlands beyond Tarrytown*].

The fourteenth, in the morning being very faire weather, the wind South-east, we sayled up the River twelve leagues, and had five fathoms, and five fathoms and a quarter lesse; and came to a Streight betweene two Points [*Stony and Verplanck Points*], and had eight, nine, and ten fathoms: and it trended North-east by North, one league: and wee had twelve, thirteene and fourteene fathomes. The River is a mile broad: there is very high Land on both sides [*near Peekskill*]. Then wee went up North-west, a league and a halfe deepe water. Then North-east by North five miles; then North-west by North two leagues, and anchored [*about West Point*]. The Land grew very high and Mountainous. The River is full of fish.

The fifteenth, in the morning was misty untill the Sunne arose: then it cleered. So wee weighed with the wind at South, and ran up into the River twentie leagues, passing by high Mountains [*the Catskills*]. Wee had a very good depth, as sixe, seven, eight, nine, ten, twelve, and thirteen fathoms, and a great store of Salmons in the River. This morning our two Savages got out of a Port and swam away. After we were under sayle, they called to us in scorne. At night we came to other Mountaines, which lie from the Rivers side. There wee found very loving people, and very old men: where wee were well used. Our Boat went to fish, and caught great store of very good fish.

The sixteenth, faire and very hot weather. In the morning our Boate went againe to fishing, but could catch but few, by reason their Canoes had beene there all night. This morning the people came aboord, and brought us eares of Indian Corne, and Pompions, and Tobacco: which wee bought for trifles. Wee rode still all day, and filled fresh water; at night wee weighed and went two leagues higher, and we had shoald water: so we anchored till day.

The seventeenth, faire Sun-shining weather, and very hot. In the morning as soone as the Sun was up, we set sayle, and ran up sixe leagues higher, and found shoalds in the middle of the channell, and small Ilands, but seven fathoms water on both sides. Toward night we borrowed so neere the shoare, that we grounded: so we layed out our small anchor, and heaved off againe. Then we borrowed on the banke in the channell, and came aground againe; while the floud ran we heaved off againe, and anchored all night.

The eighteenth, in the morning was faire weather, and we rode still. In the after-noone our Masters Mate went on land with an old Savage, a Governour of the Countrey; who carried him to his house, and made him good cheere. [*The foregoing sentence is with little doubt a misprint. According to a fragment of his own account, it was Hudson himself, the master, who went ashore and later wrote of the kindness and hospitality of the Indians.*] The nineteenth, was faire and hot weather: at the floud being neere eleven of the clocke, wee weighed, and ran higher up two leagues above the Shoalds, and had no lesse water then five fathoms: wee anchored, and rode in eight fathomes. The people of the Countrie came flocking aboord, and brought us Grapes, and Pompions, which wee bought for trifles. And many brought us Bevers skinnes, and Otters skinnes, which wee bought for Beades, Knives, and Hatchets. So we rode there all night [*at the highest point reached by the* Half Moon, *near Albany*].

The twentieth, in the morning was faire weather. Our Masters Mate with foure men more went up with our Boat to sound the River, and found two leagues above us but two fathomes water, and the channell very narrow; and above that place seven or eight fathomes. Toward night they returned: and we rode still all night. The one and twentieth, was faire weather, and the wind all Southerly: we determined yet once more to goe farther up into the River, to trie what depth and breadth it did beare; but much people resorted aboord, so wee went not this day. Our Carpenter went on land, and made a Fore-yard. And our Master and his Mate determined to trie some of the chiefe men of the Countrey, whether they had any treacherie in them. So they tooke them downe into the Cabbin, and gave them so much Wine and Aqua vitae, that they were all merrie: and one of them had his wife with him, which sate so modestly, as any of our Countrey women would doe in a strange place. In the end one of them was drunke, which had been aboord of our ship all the time that we had beene there: and that was strange to them; for they could not tell how to take it. The Canoes and folke went all on shoare: but some of them came againe, and brought stropes of Beades: some had sixe, seven, eight, nine, ten; and gave him. So he slept all night quietly. [*This intoxication was long remembered in Indian tradition.*]

The two and twentieth, was faire weather: in the morning our Masters Mate and foure more of the companie went up with our Boat to sound the River higher up. The people of the Countrey came not aboord till noone: but when they came, and saw the Savages well, they were glad. So at three of the clocke in the afternoone they came aboord, and brought Tobacco, and more Beades, and gave them to our Master, and made an Oration, and shewed him all the Countrey round about. Then they sent one of their companie on land, who presently returned, and brought a great Platter full of Venison, dressed by themselves; and they caused him to eate with them: then they made him reverence, and departed all save the old man that lay aboord. This night at ten of the clocks wee weighed, and went downe two leagues to a sounding of the River; and found it to bee at an end for shipping to goe in. For they had beene up eight or nine leagues, and found but seven foot water, and unconstant soundings. [*This was the highest point reached by the ship's boat, perhaps near Waterford.*]

The three and twentieth, faire weather. At twelve of the clocke wee weighed, and went downe two leagues to a shoald that had two channels, one on the one side, and another on the other, and had little wind, whereby the tide layed us upon it. So, there wee sate on the ground the space of an houre till the floud came.[1] Then we had a little gale of wind at the West. So wee got our ship into deepe water, and rode all night very well.

The foure and twentieth was faire weather: the winde at the North-west, wee weighed, and went downe the River seven or eight leagues; and at halfe ebbe wee came on ground on a banke of Oze in the middle of the River, and sate there till the floud. Then wee went on Land, and gathered good store of Chest-nuts [*perhaps near Hudson*]. At ten of the clocke wee came off into deepe water, and anchored.

The five and twentieth was faire weather, and the wind at South a stiffe gale. We rode still, and went on Land to walke on the West side of the River, and found good ground for Corne, and other Garden herbs, with great store of goodly Oakes, and Wal-nut trees, and Chest-nut trees, Ewe trees, and trees of sweet wood in great abundance, and great store of Slate for houses, and other good stones.

The sixe and twentieth was faire weather, and the wind at South a stiffe gale, wee rode still. In the morning our Carpenter went on Land with our Masters Mate, and foure of our companie to cut wood. This morning, two Canoes, came up the River from the place where we first found loving people, and in one of them was the old man that had layen aboord of us at the other place. He brought another old man with him which brought more stropes of Beades, and gave them to our Master, and shewed him all the Countrey there about, as though it were at his command. So he made the two old men dine with him, and the old man's wife: for they brought two old women, and two young maidens of the age of sixteene or seventeene yeeres with them, who behaved themselves very modestly. Our Master gave one of the old men a Knife, and they gave him and us Tobacco. And at one of the clocke they departed downe the River, making signes that wee should come downe to them; for wee were within two leagues of the place where they dwelt.

The seven and twentieth, in the morning was faire weather, but much wind at the North, we weighed and set our fore top-sayle, and our ship would not flat, but ran on the Ozie banke at halfe ebbe. Wee layed out anchor to heave her off, but could not. So wee sate from halfe ebbe to halfe floud: then wee set our fore-sayle and mayne top-sayle, and got down six leagues. The old man came aboord, and would have had us anchor, and goe on Land to eate with him: but the wind being faire, we would not yeeld to his request; so hee left us, being very sorrowfull for our departure. At five of the clocke in the after-noone, the wind came to the South South-west. So wee made a boord or two, and anchored in fourteene fathomes water. Then our Boat went on shoare to fish against the ship. Our Masters Mate and Boat-swaine, and three more of the companie went on land to fish, but could not fine a good place. They tooke foure or five and twentie Mullets, Breames, Bases, and Barbils; and returned in an houre. We rode still all night.[2]

The eight and twentieth, being faire weather, as soone as the day was light, wee weighed at halfe ebbe, and turned downe two leagues belowe water; for, the streame doth runne the last quarter ebbe: then we anchored till high water. At three of the clocke in the after-noone we weighed, and turned down three leagues, untill it was darke: then wee anchored.

The nine and twentieth was drie close weather: the wind at South, and South and by West, we weighed early in the morning, and turned down three leagues by a lowe water, and anchored at the lower end of the long Reach; for it is six leagues long.[3] Then there came certain Indians in a Canoe to us, but would not come aboord. After dinner there came the Canoe with other men, wherof three came aboord us. They brought Indian Wheat, which wee bought for trifles. At three of the clocke in the afternoon wee weighed, as soone as the ebbe came, and turned downe to the edge of the Mountains, or the Northermost of the Mountaines, and an-

chored: because the high land hath many Points, and a narrow channell, and hath many eddie winds.[4] So we rode quietly all night in seven fathoms water.

The thirtieth was faire weather, and the wind at Southeast a stiffe gale betweene the Mountaynes. We rode still the afternoone. The people of the Countrey came aboord us, and brought some small skinnes with them, which we bought for Knives and Trifles. This is a very pleasant place to build a Towne on. The Road is very neere, and very good for all winds, save an East North-east wind. The Mountaynes looke as if some Metall or Minerall were in them. For the Trees that grow on them were all blasted, and some of them barren with few or no Trees on them. The people brought a stone aboord like to Emery (a stone used by Glasiers to cut Glasse) it would cut Iron or Steele: Yet being bruised small, and water put to it, it made a colour like blacke Lead glistering; It is also good for Painters Colours. At three of the clocke they departed, and we rode still all night.

The first of October, faire weather, the wind variable betweene the West and the North. In the morning we weighed at seven of the clocke with the ebbe, and got downe below the Mountaynes, which was seven leagues. Then it fell calme and the floud was come, and wee anchored at twelve of the clocke. The people of the Mountaynes came aboord us, wondring at our ship and weapons. We bought some small skinnes of them for Trifles. This afternoone, one Canoe kept hanging under our sterne with one man in it, which we could not keepe from thence, who got up by our Rudder to the Cabin window, and stole out my Pillow, and two Shirts and two Bandeleeres. Our Masters Mate shot at him, and strooke him on the brest, and killed him. Whereupon all the rest fled away, some in their Canoes, and so leapt out of them into the water. We manned our Boat, and got our things againe. Then one of them that swamme got hold of our Boat, thinking to overthrow it. But our Cooke tooke a Sword, and cut off one of his hands, and he was drowned.[5] By this time the ebbe was come, and we weighed and got downe two leagues, by that time it was darke. So we anchored in foure fathomes water, and rode well.

The second, faire weather. At breake of day wee weighed, the wind being at North-west, and got downe seven leagues; then the floud was come strong, so we anchored.[6] Then came one of the Savages that swamme away from us at our going up the River with many other, thinking to betray us. But wee perceived their intent, and suffered none of them to enter our ship. Whereupon two Canoes full of men, with their Bowes and Arrows shot at us after our sterne: in recompence whereof we discharged sixe Muskets, and killed two or three of them. Then above an hundred of them came to a point of Land to shoot at us. There I shot a Falcon [*a small cannon*] at them, and killed two of them: whereupon the rest fled into the Woods. Yet they manned off another Canoe with nine or ten men, which came to meet us. So I shot at it also a Falcon, and shot it through, and killed one of them. Then our men with their Muskets, killed three or foure more of them. So they went their way, within a while after, wee got downe two leagues beyond that place, and anchored in a Bay, cleere from all danger of them on the other side of the River, where we saw a very good piece of ground: and hard by it there was a Cliffe, that looked of the colour of a white greene, as though it were either Copper, or Silver Myne: and I thinke it to be one of them, by the Trees that grow upon it. For they be all burned, and the other places are greene as grasse, it is on that side of the River that is Mannahata [*either Manhattan or Hoboken; it is impossible to determine which side of the river was meant*]. There we saw no people to trouble us: and rode quietly all night, but had much wind and raine.[7]

The third, was very stormie; the wind at East Northeast. In the morning, in a gust of wind and raine our Anchor came home, and we drove on ground, but it was Ozie. Then as we were about to have out an Anchor, the wind came to the North North-west, and drove us off againe. Then we shot an Anchor, and let it fall in foure fathomes water, and weighed the other. Wee had much wind and raine, with thicke weather: so we rode still all night.

The fourth was faire weather, and the wind at North North-west, wee weighed and came out of the River [*the Hudson*], into which we had runne so farre. Within a while after, wee came out also of the great mouth of the great River [*the lower Bay to Raritan Bay inclusive*], that runneth up to the North-west, borrowing upon the Norther side of the same, thinking to have deepe water: for wee had sounded a great way with our Boat at our first going in, and found seven, six, and five fathomes. So we came out that way, but we were deceived, for we had but eight foot and a halfe water: and so to three, five, three, and two fathomes and a halfe. And then three, foure, five, sixe, seven, eight, nine and ten fathomes. And by twelve of the clocke we were cleere of all the Inlet. Then we tooke in our Boat, and set our mayne-sayle and sprit-sayle, and our top-sayles, and steered away East South-east, and South-east by East off into the mayne sea. . . .

2.
Johannes De Laet 1625*

INTRODUCTION: Fifteen years after Henry Hudson left New York Bay and sailed "off into the mayne sea," Johannes De Laet (1582–1649), a Belgian Protestant who lived most of his life in Holland and was a director of the Dutch West India Company, wrote a large descriptive work about the New World that contains the only known extracts from Hudson's lost *Journal* of the famous voyage of 1609. De Laet apparently had access to the *Journal* through the files of the Dutch East India Company. In any event, the original *Journal* has never been seen since, and the following extracts are all that we have today of the great explorer's own account of the discovery of the Hudson.

The following pages from De Laet's *New World, or Description of West-India* are also memorable because they contain matter culled from the notes of the Dutch traders who immediately followed Hudson to New Netherland—Adrian Block, Hendrick Christiansen, and Cornelius May. It is this that warrants their inclusion here, even though they are not, strictly speaking, travelers' accounts. The tenuousness of life in early New Netherland is reflected in the paucity of first-hand narratives, and it is not until 1680 that we encounter once again a truly marvelous account of a voyage up the Hudson River.

THE GREAT NORTH RIVER of New-Netherland is called by some the Manhattes River, from the people who dwell near its mouth; by others, also, Rio de Montaigne; but by our countrymen it is generally called the Great River.[1] There is a large bay at its entrance, which has now for

* Excerpts from J. Franklin Jameson's *The Narratives of New Netherland* (New York: 1909), pp. 45–50.

some time been named by our captains Port May,[2] and has at its mouth a sandy point;[3] and off the eastern point of the river extends a reef, that is very bold, since while we have twelve fathoms water at one cast, there will be only five or six at the next, and again but one and a half, at the bottom. About a league and a half within the hook of the river, near the eastern shore, lies an island not more than half a league in extent, to which our people give the name of Noten Island, because excellent nut trees grow there.[4] On the east side, upon the main land, dwell the Manhattans, a bad race of savages, who have always been very obstinate and unfriendly towards our countrymen.[5] On the west side are the Sanhikans, who are the deadly enemies of the Manathans, and a much better people; they dwell within the sandy hook, and along the bay, as well as in the interior of the country.

The entrance to this river lies in latitude 40°28' or 30'. Over against Noten Island, close by the western shore, there are four other small islands.[6] The river is fourteen or fifteen fathoms deep at its mouth, and continues at that depth in a straight channel; it is for the most part a musket shot wide, but varies somewhat in its width. Its course is between northeast and northwest, according as the reaches extend.[7] Within the first reach, on the western bank of the river, where the land is low, there dwells a nation of savages, named Tappaans. The river here is quite shallow in the middle, but deep on both sides. The stream flows north and south out of the northern channel, and a southeast and northwest moon causes the highest tides. About a league inland there is a bay sheltered from all winds, about six leagues and a half in circuit;[8] there flows here a strong flood and ebb, but the ebb is not more than four feet, on account of the great quantity of water that comes from above, overflowing the low lands in the spring.

The second reach of the river extends upward to a

narrow part, named by our people Haverstroo; then comes the Sailmaker's Reach, as our people call it; and next a curved reach, in the form of a crescent, called by our people the Cook's Reach. Next is High Reach, and then follows Foxes' Reach, which extends to Klinckersberch; this is succeeded by Fisher's reach, where, on the east bank of the river, dwells a nation of savages called Pachami. This reach extends to another narrow pass, where, on the west side of the river, there is a sharp point of land that juts out, with some shoals, and opposite a bend in the river, on which another nation of savages, the Waoranecks, have their abode, at a place called Esopus.[9] A little beyond on the west side, where there is a creek, and the river becomes more shallow, the Waranawankougs reside; here are several small islands.[10] Next comes another reach called Kleverack [Clover Reach], where the water is deeper on the west side, while on the eastern side are shoals. Then follow Baker's Reach, Jan Playsier's Reach, and Vasterack, as far as Hinnenhoeck. All these reaches are dotted with sands and shallow, both on the east side, and in the middle of the river.

Finally, the Hart's Reach succeeds as far as the Kinderhoeck; at this place and beyond, the river at its greatest depth has but five fathoms of water, and generally only two or three. Beyond the Kinderhoeck there are several small islands in the river, one of which is called Beeren Island.[11] After this we come to a sheltered retreat named Ouwe Ree,[12] and farther on are Sturgeon's Hook and Fisher's Hook, over against which, on the east side of the river, dwell the Mohicans. On the east lies a long broken island, through which several creeks find a passage, forming several islands, extending nearly to the island on which the fort was erected, in latitude 43°.[13] The tide flows to this place, and the river is navigable for ships. Higher up it becomes so shallow that small skiffs can with difficulty sail there; and one sees in the distance a high range of mountains, from which most of the water in the river flows.[14] Judging from appearances, this river extends to the great river of St. Lawrence, or Canada, since our skippers assure us that the natives come to the fort from that river, and from Quebecq and Tadoussac.[15]

The fort was built here in the year 1614, upon an island on the west side of the river, where a nation of savages dwells called the Mackaes,[16] the enemies of the Mohicans. Almost all those who live on the west side, are enemies of those on the east, and cultivate more intercourse and friendship with our countrymen than the latter. The fort was built in the form of a redoubt, surrounded by a moat eighteen feet wide; it was mounted with two pieces of cannon and eleven pedereros, and the garrison consisted of ten or twelve men. Henderick Christiaensz first commanded here, and in his absence Jaques Elckens, on behalf of the company which in 1614 received authority from their High Mightinesses, the States General.[17] This fort was constantly occupied for three years, after which it partly went to decay. On this river there is a great traffick in the skins of beavers, otters, foxes, bears, minks, wild cats, and the like. The land is excellent and agreeable, full of noble forest trees and grape vines, and nothing is wanting but the labor and industry of man to render it one of the finest and most fruitful lands in that part of the world; for the savages who inhabit there are indolent, and some of them are evil thieves and wicked people.

Hendrick Hudson, who first discovered this river, and all that have since visited it, express their admiration of the noble trees growing there. He himself describes to us the manners and appearance of the people that he found dwelling immediately within this bay, in the following terms:

When I came on shore, the swarthy natives all stood and sang in their fashion. Their clothing consists of the skins of foxes and other animals, which they dress and make the garments from skins of various sorts. Their food is Turkish wheat,[18] which they cook by baking, and it is excellent eating. They soon came on board, one after another, in their canoes, which are made of a single piece of wood. Their weapons are bows and arrows, pointed with sharp stones, which they fashion with hard resin. They had no houses, but slept under the blue heavens, some on mats of bulrushes interwoven, and some on the leaves of trees. They always carry with them all their goods, as well as their food and green tobacco, which is strong and good for use. They appear to be a friendlier people, but are much inclined to steal, and are adroit in carrying away whatever they take a fancy to.

In latitude 40°48′, where the savages brought very fine oysters to his ship,[19] the aforesaid Hudson describes the country in the following manner:

It is as pleasant a land as one can tread upon, very abundant in all kinds of timber suitable for ship-building, and for making large casks. The people had copper tobacco pipes, from which I inferred that copper must exist there; and iron likewise according to the testimony of the natives, who, however, do not understand preparing it for use.

He also states that they caught in the river all kinds of fresh-water fish with seines, and young salmon and sturgeon. In latitude 42°18′ the said Hudson landed.[20] He says:

I sailed to the shore in one of their canoes, with an old man, who was the chief of a tribe, consisting of forty men and seventeen women; these I saw there in a house well constructed of oak bark, and circular in shape, with the appearance of having a vaulted ceiling. It contained a great quantity of maize, and beans of the last year's growth, and there lay near the house for the purpose of drying enough to load three ships, besides what was growing in the fields. On our coming near the house, two mats were spread out to sit upon, and immediately some food was served in well made red wooden bowls; two men were also despatched at once with bows and arrows in quest of game, who soon after brought in a pair of pigeons which they had just shot. They likewise killed at once a fat dog, and skinned it in great haste, with shells which they get out of the water. They supposed that I would remain with them for the night, but I returned after a short time on board the ship. The land is the finest for cultivation that I ever in my life set foot upon, and it also abounds in trees of every description. The natives are a very good people; for when they saw that I would not remain, they supposed that I was afraid of their bows, and taking the arrows, they broke them in pieces, and threw them into the fire, etc.

They found there also vines and grapes, pumpkins, and other fruits. From all these things there is sufficient reason to conclude that it is a pleasant and fruitful country, and that the natives are well disposed, if they are only well treated; although they are very changeable, and of the same general character as all the savages in the north. They have no religion whatever, nor any divine worship, [but serve the Devil; yet not with such ceremonies as the Africans. They call him Menutto; and every thing that is wonderful and strange or that surpasses human understanding, that they also call Menutto].[21] Much less have they any political government, except that they have their chiefs, whom they call Sackmos, or Sagimos. On different occasions some of our people have been surprised by them and slain; for they are revengeful and very suspicious, and because often engaged in wars among themselves, they are very fearful and timid. But with mild and proper treatment, and especially by intercourse with Christians, this people might be civilized and brought under better regulation; particularly if a sober and discreet population were brought over and good order preserved. They are, besides, very serviceable, and allow themselves to be employed in many things for a small compensation; even to performing a long day's journey, in which they discover greater fidelity than could be expected of such people.

As to the climate and seasons of the year, they nearly agree with ours, for it is a good deal colder there than it ought to be according to the latitude; it freezes and snows severely in winter, so that often there is a strong drift of ice in the river. But this occurs some years more than others, as with us. There is also the same variety of winds in that country, and in summer thunder and lightning with violent showers. In short, it is a country well adapted for our people to inhabit, on account of the similarity of the climate and the weather to our own; especially since it seems to lack nothing that is needful for the subsistence of man, except domestic cattle, which it would be easy to carry there; and besides producing many things of which our country is destitute. . . .

3.
Jasper Dankers 1680*

INTRODUCTION: In September of 1679 two Labadist ministers, Jasper Dankers and Peter Shuyter, arrived in New York on a secret mission of discovery. Members of a new religious sect based upon the mystical teachings of Jean de Labadie, they had come to the New World to find a suitable site for a colony. Traveling under assumed names because they had been persecuted throughout France and Germany, they spent nine months touring the Atlantic seaboard from Boston to Delaware. The site they eventually chose was a large tract of wilderness in Bohemia Manor, Maryland. But between April 19 and May 7, 1680, they were on the Hudson and exploring the environs of Albany and Schenectady, and the account that Jasper Dankers has left us of that part of the journey is a priceless record of the tenuous hold that civilization still had in the Hudson Valley seventy years after the voyage of the *Half Moon*.

The greatest change that had occurred was the political transference of power from the Dutch to the British Crown. In 1664, after barely half a century of Dutch rule, four British men-of-war overwhelmed the defences of New Amsterdam without firing a shot, and seized New Netherland in the name of Charles II. Henceforth, except for one brief period in 1673 when the Dutch in turn overwhelmed the English, New Amsterdam was known as New York, Fort Orange (or Beverwyck) became Fort Albany, Esopus (or Wiltwyck) became Kingston, and the North River vacillated between its original Dutch designation and the English preference for the Hudson. When Jasper Dankers and his companion arrived in 1679 Sir Edmund Andros had been governor of New York for five years. The restrictive English policies

* From Bartlett Burleigh James and J. Franklin Jameson, eds., *Journal of Jasper Danckaerts, 1679–1680* (New York: 1913), pp. 185–228.

(established under the aegis of the Navigation Laws) that were to end a century later in revolution were already in evidence as the two ministers strove to get a "passport" to make the 145-mile voyage to Albany.

MARCH 31st, Sunday. We determined to make a journey to Albany at the first opportunity, but this could not be done without the special permission of the governor. Though a regulation exists that no one shall go up there unless he has been three years in the country, that means for the purpose of carrying on trade; for a young man who came over with us from Holland [1] proceeded at once to Albany, and continues to reside there. We went accordingly to request permission of the governor.[2] After we had waited two or three hours, his Excellency came in and received us kindly. We made our request, which he neither refused nor granted, but said he would take it into consideration. Meanwhile we inquired after vessels, of which there were plenty going up at this time of year.

APRIL 3rd, Wednesday. We went again to the lord governor for permission, who received us after he had dined. He inquired for what purpose we wished to go above; to which we answered, we had come here to see the country, its nature and fertility; and that we had heard there were fine lands above, such as Schoonechten, Rentselaerswick, and the Hysopus.[3] "Those are all small places," he said, "and are all taken possession of; but I am ashamed I did not think of this." He then requested us to come some morning and dine with him, when he would talk with us. We thanked him, and took our leave, reflecting whether it would be advisable to trouble his Excellency any more about the matter, as it was not of such great importance to us, and he, per-

2. *View of New Amsterdam*, engraving (so-called Schenk view), 1673; courtesy of the Eno Collection, Prints Division, New York Public Library.

"We went in search of a boat to go to Albany."

The still very Dutch town of New York as it looked about the time Jasper Dankers visited it and waited for weeks to get permission from the royal governor to visit Albany.

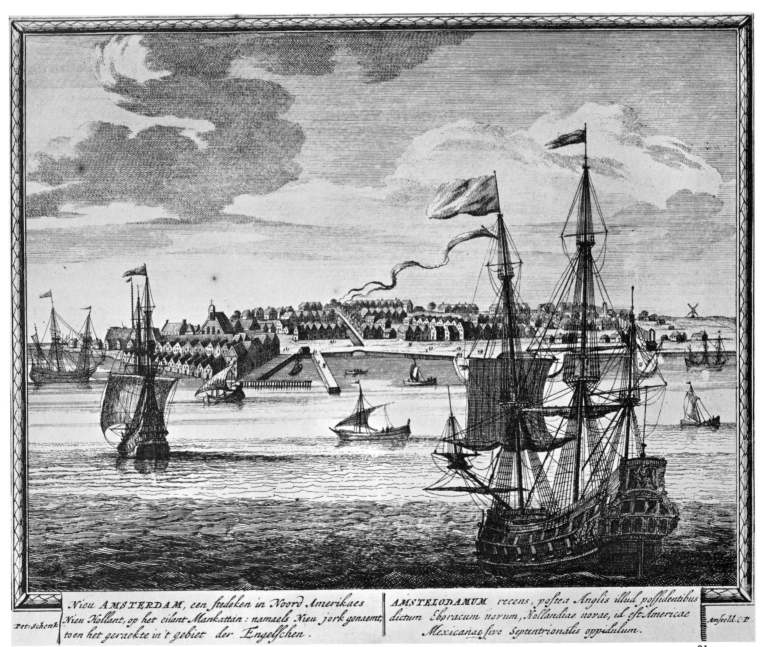

Nieu AMSTERDAM, een stedeken in Noord Amerikaes Nieu Hollant, op het eilant Mankattan : namaels Nieu jork genaemt, toen het geraekte in 't gebiet der Engelschen.

Pet: Schenk

AMSTELODAMUM recens, postea Anglis illud possidentibus dictum Eboracum novum, Hollandiae novae, id est Americae Mexicanae sive Septentrionalis oppidulum.

Amsteld. C.P.

haps, considered it of more moment than we did. We then felt inclined to leave the country the very first opportunity, as we had nothing more to do here, and it was the very best time of year to make a voyage. . . .

10th, Wednesday. . . . Two vessels sailed for Boston, where we much desired to go, but we were not prepared. . . .

13th, Saturday. We called upon the governor, and requested permission to leave. He spoke to us kindly, and asked us to come the next day after preaching, thus preventing our request.

14th, Sunday. About five o'clock in the afternoon, we went to the governor, who was still engaged, at our arrival, in the Common Prayer; but as soon as it was finished, he came and spoke to us, even before we had spoken to him, and said of a person who was with him, "This is Captain Deyer,[4] to whom I have given directions to write a permit or passport for you to go to Albany." He again asked us where we came from, and where we lived, which we told him. He also inquired something about the prince of Friesland, and the princess, and also about the differences of the people of Friesland and His Royal Highness and Their High Mightinesses, which we told him. We then thanked him for his favor, and said the object of our visit was not only to ask permission to go up the river, but also to leave the country. He thereupon stated that there would be no boat going to Boston for two or three weeks, but he intended to send one himself soon to Pennequicq,[5] which was at our service, and we could easily get to Boston from there by a fishing boat or some other vessel. We thanked him for the honor and kindness he had shown us, and further inquired of him whether it would be necessary to have a passport at our departure. He replied no. We inquired also whether it would be necessary to post our names, as there is an established regu-

lation that it should be done six weeks before leaving. To this he replied, if we were merchants, and owed anybody, it would be proper to do so, and then asked if such was the case with either of us. We answered no; then, he continued, it is not necessary. For all which we thanked his Excellency, and took our leave.

Reflecting upon this matter, we thought whether it would not be more respectful to make the voyage to Albany, than to leave, since we had several times requested permission to do so, and he had now granted it. Should we not go, it would perhaps not be well received by him, the more so as there would not be any vessel going to Boston for some weeks. Nevertheless, it was not bad that we had shown his Excellency it was not so important to us that we could not let it pass.

15th, Monday. We went in search of a boat to go to Albany, and found one ready to leave immediately. The name of the skipper was Meus Hooghbloom, to whom we agreed to pay, for the passage up and down, one beaver, that is, twenty-five guilders in *zeewant*, for each of us, and find ourselves. We gave him our names, to have ther inserted in the passport. . . .

19th, Friday. We had been several times for our passport, which we supposed would be a special one granted by his Excellency to us, but in that we were mistaken. Our names were merely added to the common passport to go up and down the river, as the names of all the passengers were written on it. We left New York about three o'clock in the afternoon with a southerly wind, in company with about twenty passengers of all kinds, young and old, who made great noise and bustle in a boat not so large as a common ferryboat in Holland; and as these people live in the interior of the country somewhat nearer the Indians, they are more wild and untamed, reckless, unrestrained, haughty, and more addicted to misusing the blessed name of God and to cursing and swearing. However there was no help for it; you have to go with those with whom you are shipped. We were scarcely in the North River when we saw a ship coming through the Narrows, but as it was so far off we could not discern what vessel it was. Each passenger had his own opinion on the subject. After we had sailed along for half an hour we heard five or six guns fired from the fort and otherwise, which was a proof that she was from sea. As we were sailing along a boat came up to us but lost her mast in boarding us. She was to the leeward and we were sailing before the wind with a good headway. She came too near our yard-arm, which carried away her mast, and it was lucky she was not upset. They put on board some tons of oysters, which are not to be found at Fort Albany or away from salt water. . . . We made rapid progress, but with the night the wind slackened, and we were compelled to come to anchor in order to stem the tide.

20th, Saturday. When the day broke we saw how far we had advanced. We were at the entrance of the Highlands,[6] which are high and rocky, and lie on both sides of the river. While waiting there for the tide and wind another boat came alongside of us. They had a very fine fish, a striped bass, as large as a codfish. The skipper was a son-in-law of D. Schaets, the minister at Albany, a drunken, worthless person who could not keep house with his wife, who was not much better than he, nor was his father-in-law. He had been away from his wife five or six years, and was now going after her.[7] The wind coming out of the south about nine o'clock we weighed anchor, and got under sail. It gradually increased until we had drifted through the Highlands, which is regarded as no small advantage whenever they wish to sail up or down the river; because, if they do not have a fresh breeze aft, they cannot have much favorable wind, as in blowing crosswise over the Highlands it blows above

the vessel, and sometimes comes down in whirlwinds which are dangerous. In the evening we sailed before the Hysopus,[8] where some of the passengers desired to be put ashore, but it blew too hard and we had too much headway. It did not seem to be very important. In consequence of the river above the Hysopus being difficult to navigate, and beset with shoals and passages, and of the weather being rainy with no moon, we could not proceed without continual danger of running aground, and so came to anchor.

21st, Easter Sunday. The wind was against us and calm, but we advanced as far as the Noorman's Kill,[9] where we were compelled to come to anchor, on account of the strong current running down the river. We went ashore here to walk about a little. There are two high falls on this kill, where the beautiful green water comes falling over incessantly, in a manner wonderful to behold, when you consider the power, wisdom, and directions of God. The water was the greenest I had observed, not only on the South River,[10] but in all New Netherland. Leaving the cause of it for further inquiry, I mention it merely in passing. At the falls on this river stands a fine saw-mill which has wood enough to saw. The man who lives there, although not the mildest, treated us nevertheless reasonably well. He set before us shad which had been caught the day before, and was very good, better, we thought, than the same fish in Fatherland. I observed along the shore, trees which they call in Holland the trees of life, such as we have in our garden,[11] but they grow here beautiful and large, like firs. I picked up a small stone in which there was some crystal, and you could see how the crystal was formed in the stone.

A breeze springing up from the south caused us to hurry on board the yacht, which we saw was making sail. We reached her after a good time of hard rowing, and were quite tired before we did so. The breeze did not continue a long time, and we came to anchor again. After several stoppages we proceeded to-day as far as Kinderhook.

22d, Monday. We had again this morning a southerly breeze, which carried us slowly along until noon, when we came to anchor before the *Fuyck,* and Fort Albany or Orange.[12] Every one stepped ashore at once, but we did not know where to go. We first thought of taking lodgings with our skipper, but we had been warned that his house was unregulated and poorly kept. M. van Cleif, wishing to do us a kindness, had given us a letter of recommendation to Mr. Robert Sanders,[13] and M. de la Grange [14] had also presented us to the same friend. We went ashore just as preaching was over, to deliver our letter. This person, as soon as he saw us at his house, was pleased and received us with every attention, and so did all his family, giving us a chamber for our accommodation. We did not remain his debtors in heartily serving him in what was necessary, whether by instruction, admonition or reproof, which he always received kindly, as it seemed, promising himself as well as all his family to reform, which was quite necessary.

23d, Tuesday. Mr. Sanders having provided us with horses, we rode out about nine o'clock to visit the Cahoos, which is the falls of the great Maquass Kill,[15] which are the greatest falls, not only in New Netherland, but in North America, and perhaps, as far as is known, in the whole New World.[16] We rode for two hours over beautiful, level, tillable land along the river, when we obtained a guide who was better acquainted with the road through the woods. He rode before us on horseback. In approaching the Cahoos from this direction, the roads are hilly, and in the course of half an hour you have steep hills, deep valleys, and narrow paths, which run round the precipices, which you must ride with care, in order to avoid the danger of falling over them, as sometimes happens. As you come near the falls, you can hear the roaring which makes everything tremble, but on reaching them and looking at them you see something wonderful, a great manifestation of God's power and sovereignty, of His wisdom and glory. We arrived there about noon. They are on one of the two branches into which the North River is divided up above, of almost equal size. This one turns to the west out of the high land, and coming here finds a blue rock which has a steep side, as long as the river is broad, which according to my calculation is two hundred paces or more, and rather more than less, and about one hundred feet high. The river has more water at one time than another; and was now about six or eight feet deep. All this volume of water coming on this side fell headlong upon a stony bottom, this distance of an hundred feet. Any one may judge whether that was not a spectacle, and whether it would not make a noise. There is a continual spray thrown up by the dashing of the water, and when the sun shines the figure of a rainbow may be seen through it. Sometimes there are two or three of them to be seen, one above the other, according to the brightness of the sun and its parallax. There was now more water than usual in consequence of its having rained hard for several days, and the snow water having begun to run down from the high land.

On our return we stopped at the house of our guide, whom we had taken on the way up, where there were some families of Indians living. Seeing us, they said to each other, "Look, these are certainly real Dutchmen, actual Hollanders." Robert Sanders asked them how they knew it. We see it, they said, in their faces and in their dress. "Yes," said one, "they have the clothes of real Hollanders; they look like brothers." They brought us some ground-nuts, but although the Dutch call them

3. *A North West View of the Cohoes or Great Cataract of the Mohawk River in the Province of New York in North America,* engraving by Mazell after the painting by Thomas Davies (active in America, 1759–1778); courtesy of the Albany Institute of History and Art.

"We rode out about nine o'clock to visit the Cahoos. . . . There is a continual spray thrown up by the dashing waters, and when the sun shines the figure of a rainbow may be seen through it."

A mecca of travelers and tourists well into the 19th century. The falls were long considered some of the most impressive in all North America.

A North West View of the Cohoes, or Great Cataract of the Mohawk River, in the Province of New York in North America.

The Perpendicular Height of the Fall 75 Feet.— Drawn on the Spot by Thos. Davis Capt Lieut. of the Royal Regt of Artillery

Mazell sculpsit

so, they are in fact potatoes, for of ground-nuts, or *mice with tails*,[17] there are also plenty. They cooked them, and gave us some to eat, which we did. There was a canoe made of the bark of trees, and the Indians have many of them for the purpose of making their journeys. It was fifteen or sixteen feet or more in length. It was so light that two men could easily carry it, as the Indians do in going from one stream or lake to another. They come in such canoes from Canada, and from places so distant we know not where. Four or five of them stepped into this one and rowed lustily through the water with great speed, and when they came back with the current they seemed to fly. They did this to amuse us at the request of Mr. Sanders. Leaving there for home, we came again to the house of one Frederick Pieters, where we had stopped in riding out. He is one of the principal men of Albany, and this was his farm; he possesses good information and judgment.[18] My comrade had some conversation with him. He expected us, and now entertained us well. My comrade was in pain from eating the ground-nuts. On arriving home in the evening, the house was full of people, attracted there out of curiosity, as is usually the case in small towns, where everyone in particular knows what happens in the whole place.

24th, Wednesday. My comrade's pain continued through the night, although he had taken his usual medicine, and he thought he would become better by riding on horseback. The horses were got ready, and we left about eight o'clock for Schoonechtendeel,[19] a place lying about twenty-four miles west or north-west of Albany towards the country of the Mohawks. We rode over a fine, sandy cart road through woods of nothing but beautiful evergreens or fir trees, but a light and barren soil. My companion grew worse instead of better. It was noon when we reached there, and arrived at the house of a good friend of Robert Sanders. As soon as we entered my comrade had to go and lie down. He had a high fever, and was covered up warm. I went with Sanders to one Adam,[20] and to examine the flats which are exceedingly rich land. I spoke to several persons of the Christian life, each one according to his state and as it was fit.

25th, Thursday. We had thought of riding a little further on, and so back to Albany; but my comrade was too sick, and had the chills and fever again. The weather, too, was windy and rainy. We concluded therefore to postpone it till the following day; and in the meantime I accompanied Sanders to the before mentioned Adam's. . . .

26th, Friday. . . . My comrade finding himself better, but still weak, we determined to leave, two of us on horseback and he in a wagon belonging at Albany, which we had the good fortune of meeting at Schoonechten, and in which he could ride over a very comfortable road. It had frozen quite hard during the night, but when the sun rose a little, it became warm enough, especially in the woods, where the wind, which was northwest, could not blow through. I went to take my leave of several persons with whom I had conversed. . . . Having mounted our horses and entered the wagon, we rode from there about ten o'clock, over a smooth sandy road, and arrived at half-past three at Albany, or Fort Orange, where Sanders' wife was glad to see us, and where we were well received by his whole family.

This Schoonechtendeel is situated, as we have said, twenty-four miles west of Fort Albany, toward the country of the Mohawks, upon a good flat, high enough to be free from the overflowing of the water of the river, which sometimes overflows their cultivated lands which lie much lower. Their cultivated lands are not what they call in that country *valleyen*, but large flats between the hills, on the margin or along the side of the rivers, brooks or creeks, very flat and level, without a single tree or bush upon them, of a black sandy soil which is four and sometimes five or six feet deep, but sometimes less, which can hardly be exhausted. They cultivate it year after year, without manure, for many years. It yields large crops of wheat, but not so good as that raised in the woodland around the city of [New] York and elsewhere, nor so productively; the latter on the other hand produce a smaller quantity, but a whiter flour. The wheat which comes from this place, the Hysopus, and some other places is a little bluer. Much of the plant called dragon's blood grows about here, and also yearly a kind of small lemon or citron, of which a single one grows upon a bush. This bush grows about five feet high, and the fruit cannot be distinguished from any other citron in form, color, taste or quality. It grows wild about the city of New York, but not well. I have not heard of its growing in any other places.

The village proper of Schoon echten [Schenectady], is a square, set off by palisades. There may be about thirty houses, and it is situated on the side of the Maquas Kill [Mohawk River], a stream however they cannot use for carrying goods up or down in yachts or boats. There are no fish in it except trout, sunfish, and other kinds peculiar to rivers, because the Cohoes stops the ascent of others, which is a great inconvenience for the *menage* and for bringing down the produce.

As soon as we arrived in Albany we went to our skipper Meus Hoogboom, to inquire when he was going to the city. He said tomorrow, but he said he would come and notify us of the time. We saw it would run on a much longer time, as it usually does in these parts.

27th, Saturday. We went to call upon a certain Madam Rentselaer, widow of the Heer Rentselaer, son of the Heer Rentselaer of the colony named the colony of Rentselaerswyck, comprising twelve miles square from Fort Orange, that is, twenty-four miles square in all. She is still in possession of the place, and still administers it as *patroonesse,* until one Richard van Rentselaer, residing at Amsterdam, shall arrive in the country, whom she expected in the summer, when he would assume the management of it himself. This lady was polite, quite well informed, and of good life and disposition.[21] She had experienced several proofs of the Lord. The breaking up of the ice had once carried away her entire mansion, and every thing connected with it, of which place she had made too much account. Also, in some visitations of her husband, death, and others before. In her last child-bed, she became lame or weak in both of her sides, so that she had to walk with two canes or crutches. In all these trials, she had borne herself well, and God left not Himself without witness in her. She treated us kindly, and we ate here exceedingly good pike, perch, and other fish, which now began to come and be caught in great numbers. We had several conversations with her about the truth, and practical religion, mutually satisfactory. We went to look at several of her mills at work, which she had there on an ever-running stream, grist-mills, saw-mills, and others. One of the grist-mills can grind 120 schepels[22] of meal in twenty-four hours, that is, five an hour. Returning to the house, we politely took our leave. Her residence is about a quarter of an hour from Albany up the river. This day we went to visit still other farms and milling establishments on the other side of the river, where there was a water-fall but not large, sufficient to keep about three mills going. This is indeed, I think, the highest that I have seen.

28th, Sunday. We went to church in the morning, and heard Dominie Schaets preach, who, although he is a poor, old, ignorant person, and besides is not of good life, yet had to give utterance to his passion, having taken his text largely upon us, at which many of his auditors, who knew us better, were not well pleased, and blamed, condemned, and derided him for it, which we corrected.[23]

In the afternoon, we took a walk to an island upon the end of which there is a fort built, they say, by the Spaniards. That a fort has been there is evident enough from the earth thrown up and strewn around, but it is not to be supposed that the Spaniards came so far inland to build forts, when there are no monuments of them to be seen elsewhere and down on the sea coasts, where, however, they have been according to the traditions of the Indians. This spot is a short hour's distance below Albany, on the west side of the river.[24]

29th, Monday. We should have left to-day, but it was not yet to happen, for our skipper, so he said, could not obtain his passport. We called upon several persons, and among others, upon the woman who had brought up Illetie, the Indian woman, and had first taken her from the Indians. . . .[25] This woman, although not of openly godless life, is more wise than devout, although her knowledge is not very extensive, and does not surpass that of the women of New Netherland. She is truly a worldly woman, proud and conceited, and sharp in trading with *wild* people,[26] as well as *tame* ones, or what shall I call them, not to give them the name of Christians, or if I do, it is only to distinguish them from the others. This trading is not carried on without fraud, and she is not free from it, as I have observed. She has a husband, which is her second one, and he I believe is a Papist. He remains at home quietly, while she travels over the country to carry on the trading. In fine she is one of the Dutch female traders, who understand their business so well. If these be the persons who are to make Christians of the heathen, what will the latter be?

But God employs such means as pleases Him to accomplish His purposes. He had given Illetie more grace than to her, we are very certain.

We were also invited to the fort by the Heer commandant, who wished to see us, but left it to our convenience. We went there with Robert Sanders, who interpreted for us. This gentleman received us politely. He said he was pleased to receive us, and to learn how we liked the lands up above, and made a few such common observations. He seemed to be not unreasonable, and a reliable person. If he was not a Scotchman, he seemed nevertheless to be a good Englishman, and, as we thought, a Presbyterian. We soon took a friendly leave, and returned home.

We spoke seriously to Robert Sanders about his pride, arrogance, temper, and passion, although according to the world's reputation he is not a bad character. His wife is more simple and a better person; we spoke to her also, as well as to their children, especially to the oldest, named Elizabeth, who was tender-hearted and affectionate. He and all of them promised to improve and reform themselves somewhat, and we saw with consolation that they in some things commenced to do so.

30th, Tuesday. We were ready to leave early, but it ran well on towards noon, when with a head wind, but a strong current down, we tacked over to Kinderhoeck, lying on the east shore sixteen miles below Albany.

Before we quit Albany, we must say a word about the place. It was formerly named the Fuyck by the Hollanders, who first settled there, on account of two rows of houses standing there, opposite to each other, which being wide enough apart in the beginning, finally ran quite together like a *fuyck*, and, therefore, they gave it this name, especially the Dutch and Indians living there. It is nearly square, and lies against the hill, with several good streets, on which there may be about eighty or ninety houses. Fort Orange, constructed by the Dutch, lies below on the bank of the river, and is set off with palisades, filled in with earth on the inside. It is now abandoned by the English, who have built a similar one behind the town, high up on the declivity of the hill, from whence it can command the place. From the other side of this fort the inhabitants have brought a spring or fountain of water, under the fort, and under ground into the town, where they now have in several places always fountains of clear, fresh, cool water. The town is surrounded by palisades, and has several gates corresponding with the streets. It has a Dutch Reformed and a Lutheran church. The Lutheran minister lives up here in the winter, and down in New York in the summer.[27] There is no English church or place of meeting, to my knowledge. As this is the principal trading-post with the Indians, and as also they alone have the privilege of trading, which is only granted to certain merchants there, as a special benefit, who know what each one must pay therefor, there are houses or lodges erected on both sides of the town, where the Indians, who come from the far interior to trade, live during the time they are there. This time of trading with the Indians is at its height in the months of June and July, and also in August, when it falls off; because it is then the best time for them to make their journeys there and back, as well as because the Hollanders then have more time outside their farm duties.

We came to anchor at Kinderhook,[28] in order to take in some grain, which the female trader before mentioned had there to be carried down the river.

MAY 1st, Wednesday. We began early to load, but as it had to come from some distance in the country, and we had to wait, we stepped ashore to amuse ourselves. We came to a creek where, near the river, lives the man whom they usually call the Child of Luxury,[29] because he formerly had been such an one, but who now was not far from being the Child of Poverty, for he was situated poorly enough. He had a saw-mill on the creek, on a water-fall, which is a singular one, for it is true that all falls have something special, and so had this one, which was not less rare and pleasant than others. The water fell quite steep, in one body, but it came down in steps, with a broad rest sometimes between them. These steps were sixty feet or more high, and were formed out of a single rock, which is unusual. I reached this spot alone through the woods, and while I was sitting on the mill, my comrade came up with the Child of Luxury, who, after he had shown us the mill and falls, took us down a little to the right of the mill, under a rock, on the margin of the creek, where we could behold how wonderful God is even in the most hidden parts of the earth; for we saw crystal lying in layers between the rocks, and when we rolled away a piece of the rock, there was, at least on two sides of it, a crust or bark, about as thick as the breadth of a straw, or a sparkling or glassy substance, which looked like alabaster, and this crust was full of points of gems, which were truly gems of crystal, or like substance. They sparkled brightly, and were as clear as water, and so close together that you could obtain hundreds of them from one piece of the crust. We broke some pieces off, and brought them away with us as curiosities. It is justly to be supposed that other precious stones rest in the crevices of the rocks and mines as these do. I have seen this sort of crystal as large and pointed as the joint of a finger. I saw one, indeed, at the house of Robert Sanders as large as your fist, though it was not clear, but white, like glassy alabaster. It had what they call a table point. Robert Sanders has much of this mountain crystal at his farm, about four miles from Albany, towards the Cahoos, on the east side of the river, but we have not been there.

On returning to the boat, we saw that the woman-trader had sent a quantity of bluish wheat on board, which the skipper would not receive, or rather mix with the other wheat; but when she came she had it done, in which her dishonesty appeared, for when the skipper arrived at New York he could not deliver the wheat which was under hers. We set sail in the evening, and came to Claver Rack,[30] sixteen miles further down, where we also took in some grain in the evening.

2d, Thursday. We were here laden full of grain, which had to be brought in four miles from the country. The boors who brought it in wagons asked us to ride out with them to their places, which we did. We rode along a high ridge of blue rock on the right hand, the top of which was grown over. This stone is suitable for burning lime, as the people of the Hysopus, from the same kind, burn the best.[31] Large, clear fountains flow out of these cliffs or hills, the first real fountains and only ones which we have met with in this country. We arrived at the places which consist of fine farms; the tillable land is like that of Schoonechtendeel, low, flat, and on the side of a creek, very delightful and pleasant to look upon, especially at the present time, when they were all green with the wheat coming up. The woodland also is very good for tillable land, and it was one of the locations which pleased me most, with its agreeable fountains. Coming back to the shore, I made a sketch, as well as I could, of the Catskill mountains, which now showed themselves nakedly, which they did not do to us when we went up the river. They lie on the west side of the river, deep in the country, and I stood on the east side of it.[32] In the evening we obtained a still more distinct view of them.

3d, Friday. We took on board early the rest of our lading. Our tradress [*sic*] left us here in order to go back to Albany, and we received two other passengers in her stead, a young man of this place, named Dirck, to whom we made mention of our crystal. He said they had at his place a rock, in which there was a yellow, glittering substance like gold, as they firmly believed it was; he did not know we were there, otherwise he would have presented us with a specimen. We spoke to him, as he was a good hearted youth, several times of God and Christ, and of the Christian life, and each time he was much concerned. Truly we discover gradually more and more there is here a hunger and thirst after God, and no one to help them. They go everywhere wandering without a shepherd, and know not where they shall turn. We also spoke to the skipper's daughter, a worldly child, who was not affected by what we said. The Lord will, in His own time, gather together those who are of His elect.

We sailed from there about nine o'clock, but after going eight or twelve miles got aground in consequence of our heavy lading, where we were compelled to remain until four o'clock in the afternon, waiting for high water. But what was unfortunate, we missed a fine, fair wind, which sprang up about eleven o'clock. Meanwhile the passengers went ashore. I walked a small distance into the country, and came to a fall of water, the basin of which was full of fish, two of which I caught with my hands. They were young shad. I went immediately after the other passengers for assistance to catch more, but when they came, they made such an agitation of the water, that the fish all shot to the bottom, and remained there under the rocks. We therefore could obtain no more; but if we had had a small casting net, we could have caught them in great numbers, or if I had remained there quiet alone. But as it was, we had to abandon it. These fish come at high water from the North River into these little streams, where they find clear, fresh water, and weeds and herbs.[33] They remain there eating and sporting, and in the meantime at low water they are left in these holes or basins, and they are thus caught in great numbers in many of the streams by the Indians.

The water having risen, and the wind being favorable, we went on board, and as soon as we were afloat, got under sail. We proceeded rapidly ahead, and at sundown came to anchor before the Hysopus, where we landed some passengers who lived there.

4th, Saturday. We went ashore early, and further inland to the village. We found Gerrit the glass-maker there,[34] with his sister. He it was who desired to come up here in company with us, and he was now happy to see us. He was engaged putting the glass in their new church,[35] but left his work to go with us through the country, where he was better acquainted than we were. We found here exceedingly large flats, which are more than three hours' ride in length, very level, with a black soil which yields grain abundantly.[36] They lie like those at Schoonecte and Claver Rach, between the hills and along the creek, which sometimes overflows all the land, and drowns and washes out much of the wheat. The place [Hysopus or Kingston] is square, set off with palisades, through which they are several gates; it consists of about fifty houses within the stockade. They were engaged in a severe war with the Indians during the administration of the Heer Stuyvesant, which is therefore still called the Hysopus war, partly because it was occasioned on account of the people of Hysopus, and because they have had to bear there the largest burden of it.[37] In returning to the village we observed a very large, clear fountain bubbling up from under a rock. When we arrived there, we went to the house of the person who was the head of the village, where some people had assembled, who, having no minister, and hearing that my comrade was a theologian, requested him to preach for them the next day. But our skipper having finished what he had to do, we left there. Here and in Albany they brew the heaviest beer we have tasted in all New Netherland, and from wheat alone, because it is so abundant. The glass-maker informed us that Willem, the son of our old people,[38] was going to follow the sea, and had left for Barbadoes; that Evert Duyckert, our late mate on our voyage out, who had gone as captain of a ketch to Barbadoes and Jamaica, had arrived; that it was his ship we had seen coming in, when we were leaving the city, and that perhaps he would go with her to Holland. This place [Kingston] is about three-quarters of an hour inland. At the mouth of the creek,[39] on the shore of the river, there are some houses and a redoubt, together with a general storehouse, where the farmers bring their grain, in order that it may be conveniently shipped when the boats come up here, and wherein their goods are discharged from the boats, as otherwise there would be too much delay in going back and forth. The woodland around the Hysopus is not of much value, and is nothing but sand and rock. We had hardly reached the river, when a man came running up to us as hard as he could, requesting to speak to us. We inquired of him what he desired, when he complained of being sorely afflicted with an internal disease, and said he had heard we well understood medicine, and knew what to prescribe for him. We told him we were no doctors, and had only brought a few medicines with us for our own use, and most of them we had given away. My comrade told him what he thought of his disease, and that we could not help him: whereupon this poor wretched man went sorrowfully back again, for he had spent much to be cured. We told him, however, we would send him a brackish powder which had done good in several cases, and which, if it pleased God to bless it, would perhaps help him. We went on board the boat, and immediately got under sail, with a favorable but light wind, and by evening arrived at the entrance of the Highlands.⁴⁰

5th, Sunday. The wind was ahead, but it was calm. When the tide began to fall, we tacked, or rather drifted along, but with little progress. We passed through the Highlands however, and came to anchor by the time the ebb was spent. The weather was very rainy.

6th, Monday. The wind was still contrary, and blew hard, therefore we tacked, but in consequence of our being very heavily laden we advanced but little. We anchored again when we went ashore at a place on the east side of the river, where there was a meadow on fire. We saw there a beautiful hard stone, as white and as clean as I have ever seen either here or in Europe, very fine for building; and also many cedar trees of beautiful color and strong perfume. Some Indians came alongside of us in their canoes, whom we called on board, and bought from them a very large striped bass, as large as a cod-fish in the Fatherland, for a loaf of stale bread worth about three stivers, Holland money, and some other fish for a little old salt meat.

7th, Tuesday. At daylight the tide served, but the wind was still ahead, though steady. We continued tacking with considerable progress, and at ten o'clock arrived before the city of New York, where we struck upon a rock. The water was falling, and we therefore immediately carried out an anchor, and wore the yacht off. A slight breeze soon afterward sprang up, and took us to the city. The Lord be praised and glorified for His grace. . . .

8th, Wednesday. . . . The North River is the most navigated and frequented river in these parts, because the country about it is the most inhabited. Its larger population as compared with other places is owing, for the most part, first to the fact that the capital was originally established here, and has even since remained here, under whatever government has prevailed, although the South River [Delaware] was first discovered; secondly, because it is the most convenient place for the purposes of navigation, I mean the capital, and is the middle and centre of the whole of New Netherland; and thirdly, because this place, and indeed the river, possess the most healthy and temperate climate. We will hereafter speak of New York, and confine ourselves now to the North River; which was so called for two reasons, and justly so: the first of which is because, as regards the South River, it lies in a more northerly latitude, the South River lying in 39°, and the North River in 40°25′, and being also thus distinguishable from the East River, which although it is more easterly, as its name denotes, nevertheless lies in the same parallel. The other reason is because it runs up generally in a northerly direction, or between north by east and north-northeast. It begins at the sea in a bay; for the sea coast, between the North and South Rivers, stretches northeast by north and northwest, and southwest and southwest by south; and from the North River along Long Island for the most part east and west. Besides this name, which is the most common and the best, it bears several others; such as Maurits River, because it was discovered and taken possession of in the time of Prince Maurice; Montagne River because one De la Montagne was one of the first and principal settlers, and lastly, Manhattans River, from the Manhattans Island, or the Manhattan Indians, who lived hereabouts and on the island of Manhattans, now the city of New York.⁴¹ To be more exact, its beginning, it seems to us, ought to be regarded as at the city of New York, where the East River as well as Kill achter Kol separate from the North River.⁴² The waters below the city are not commonly called the river, but the bay; for although the

4. *West Shore of Manhattan Island,* lithograph by **J.** Carson Breevort, 1679; redraft of the original drawing by Jasper Dankers; courtesy of The New-York Historical Society.

"We continued tacking with considerable progress, and at ten o'clock arrived before the city of New York."

This picture by Dankers is the only extant view of the western side of Manhattan dating from the 17th century. It shows the city looking south from present-day Duane Street. The lane on the left is the present-day Broadway. The two windmills were built about 1664 and 1674 respectively, and were located south of Fresh Water Pond.

river discharges itself into the sea at Sandy Hook, or Rentselaer's Hook, this discharge is not peculiarly its own, but also that of the East River, Achter Kol, Slangenbergh Bay, Hackingsack Creek, Northwest Creek, Elizabeth Creek, Woodbridge Creek, Milstone River, Raritan River, and Nevesinck Creek all of which deserve the name of rivers, and have nothing in common with the North River, but with Long Island on one side and Staten Island on the other. The water below the Narrows to Sandy Hook is usually called the Great Bay; and that of the Narrows and them as far as the city, and up to and beyond Sapocanikke,[43] the Little Bay. Although the Great Bay is so called, it is not by any means as large as that of the South River. Above Sapocanikke the river is about two miles wide, and is very uniformly of the same width as far up as the Hysopus and higher, except in the Highlands, where there are here and there a narrow strait and greater depth. Above the Hysopus, which is 90 to 96 miles from the city, it still maintains a fair width, but with numerous islands, shoals, and shallows, up to Fort Albany, where it is narrower. It is easily navigable to the Hysopus with large vessels, and thence to Fort Albany with smaller ones, although ketches and such craft can go up there and load. It carries the ordinary flood tide into the Highlands, but with much of a down flow of water, only up to them; though with an extraordinary flow down and a dead neap-tide, the water becomes brakish near the city. With a slight flow of water down and a spring tide, accompanied by a southeast storm, the flood tide is carried quite through the Highlands, and they said they had had a change in the water even as far up as the Hysopus.[44] The land on both sides of the river is high and rocky, but higher in some places than others, as at the Highlands, eminently so called because they are higher than the others. In passing by the Hysopus you see the Kat-skil Mountains, a little inland, which are the highest in this region, and extend from there, in the form of a crescent, into the country of the Maquaas. Although these mountains are from 112 to 120 miles distant from the sea, there are skippers who in clear weather have seen them while sailing along the coast. All the reaches, creeks, headlands, and islands, bear the names which were accidentally given them in the first instance: as Antonis Neus (Anthony's Nose) a headland and high hill in the Highlands, because it has a sharp edge running up and down in the form of a man's nose; Donderbergh (Thunder Hill), because it thundered there frightfully at the time the first explorers of the river passed it; Swadel Rack (Swath Reach), a short strait between high hills, where in sailing through they encounter whirlwinds and squalls, and meet sometimes with accidents, which they usually call *swadelen* (swaths or mowing sweeps); Danskamer (Dancing Chamber),[45] a spot where a party of men and women arrived in a yacht in early times, and being stopped by the tide went ashore. Gay, and perhaps intoxicated, they began to jump and dance, when the Indians who had observed them fell upon them in the height of their merriment and drove them away. In remembrance of this circumstance the place has since been called the Dancing Chamber. It is on the west side of the river, just through the Highlands. Boterberg (Butter Hill),[46] and Hoyberg (Hay Hill), the one because it is like the rolls of butter which the farmers in Holland take to market, and the other because it is like a haystack in Holland; 't Claver Rach (Clover Reach), from three bare places which appear on the land; [47] and Kinder Hoeck (Children's Point), Noten Hoeck (Nut Point), Potlepels Eylant (Potladle Island), Kock Achie [Coxsackie], etc.

Above Fort Albany there are occasionally good flats on both sides of the river, at the foot of the hills, and also some fine islands up to the Cahoos; which is where the colony of Rentselaerwyck is planted. The river begins above Fort Albany to divide itself, first by islands, and then by the main land, into two arms or branches, one of which turns somewhat towards the west and afterwards entirely west through Schoonechten, towards the country of the Maquaas, and this branch, on which the Cahoos lies, is called the Maquaas Kill [Mohawk]. The other preserves the course of the main river for the most part, or a little more easterly, and retains also the name of the North River. It runs far up into the country, and has it source in a lake 120 to 160 miles in length,[48] out of which a stream probably empties into the St. Lawrence, a river of Canada; for not only the Indians, but the French also, pass over here in canoes from Canada. We ourselves have conversed with persons who have thus come over, some by water, and others by land and on foot. Of the Cahoos we have already spoken, in relating our journey there. Those falls are a great and wonderful work of God; but although they have so much water that the wind causes the spray and moisture to rise continually in the air, so that spectators who stand two hundred feet or so higher are made wet, especially when there are any gusts of wind driving from one side, as happened to us, yet we regard the falls on the Northwest Kill [the Passaic] as more curious, though smaller, and having less water. Even on the North River, there are several small creeks and falls more rare to see than the Cahoos. Beyond the Cahoos the land is not so high above the water; and no fish pass from below into the river above, in consequence of the interruption caused by the falls, nor can any boats be carried over the falls, up or down, which is a great inconvenience for those who live above the Cahoos, at Schenectady and other places, although when the country shall become more inhabited, and they shall have more occasion, they will take means to remedy this difficulty.[49] Through the whole of that extensive country they have no fish, except some small kinds peculiar to the streams, such as trout, sunfish, roach, pike, etc.; and this is the case in all the creeks where there are falls.

The North River abounds with fish of all kinds, throughout from the sea to the falls, and in the branch which runs up to the lake. To relate a single instance: some persons near Albany caught in a single haul of a common seine between five and six hundred shad, bass, perch, and other fish, and there were, I believe, over five hundred of one kind. It is not necessary for those who live in the city [of New York], and other places near the sea, to go to the sea to fish, but they can fish in the river and waters inside; or even to the Great Bay, except such as live upon it, and they can by means of *fuycks* or seines not only obtain fish enough for their daily consumption, but also to salt, dry, and smoke, for commerce, and to export by shiploads if they wish, all kinds of them, as the people of Boston do; but the people here have better land than they have there, where they therefore resort more for a living to the water.

PART II *Frontier and Battleground*

The Hudson Valley
Frontier and Battleground, 1749–1780

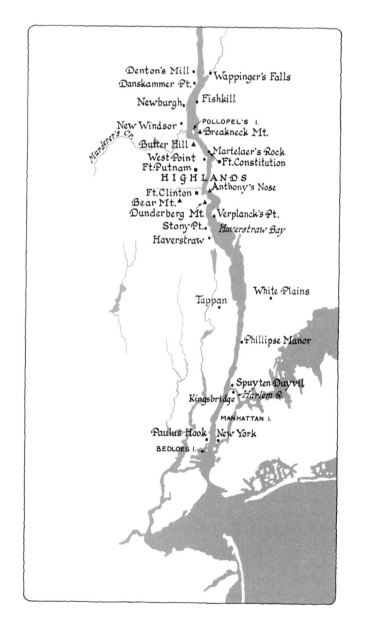

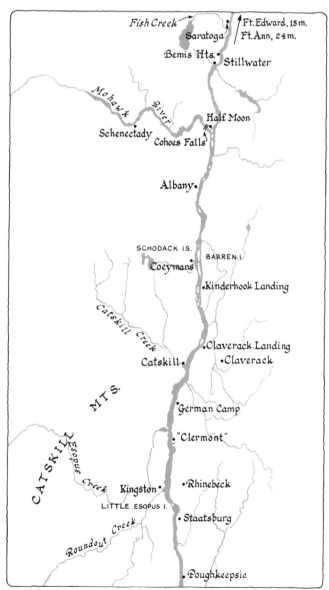

IF THE LAND POLICY and the narrow mercantile policies of the Dutch and English retarded the development of the Hudson Valley during the seventeenth century, wars and revolution exerted an even more regressive force throughout the course of the eighteenth century. Three preliminary wars over the control of the North American continent were fought between England and France in the years 1689–1748; the years 1754–1763 saw the devastating French and Indian Wars; and the American Revolution ravaged the years 1776–1783. Throughout most of this reign of Mars, and especially during the French and Indian War and the American Revolution, the Hudson River-Lake Champlain corridor was a major source of contention, the key to an empire.

The French who had a trading post at Albany as early as 1540 were the first to see the strategic importance of the Hudson, and at one time the French authorities in Canada urged the government in France to purchase the Hudson Valley, since its possession would make "His Majesty master of all North America." By the middle of the eighteenth century the English also saw the importance of the Hudson, and, during the French and Indian War, as noted by Otto L. Schreiber, the Hudson "became the strategical center of the English position in America, and the province [of New York] developed into the pivotal point or axis in the whole wide region between the Spanish territories in the south and the Frenchmen in the north" [*The River of Renown* (New York: 1959), p. 31]. The defeat of the French forces in the Hudson-Champlain corridor in 1759–60 opened the way to Montreal and the loss of all North America by the French.

The Hudson Valley was also crucial to the loss of the American colonies by the British during the War of Independence. As soon as the English saw that the rebellion was a full-fledged revolution involving the united colonies, the scene of action shifted from New England to New York, and the British seized Manhattan and held it as their administrative center throughout the war. The whole British strategy for winning the war hinged upon winning the Hudson, cleaving the colonies in two, and conquering each section in detail. This grand design for victory was frustrated at Bemis Heights just above the junction of the Mohawk and Hudson Rivers. The Battle of Saratoga in late 1777 was the single most important engagement between Lexington and Yorktown, and is considered by many historians one of the decisive battles of world history: it steeled the American determination to see the war through to a successful conclusion; it changed the complexion of the war from a disorganized rebellion to an organized revolution; and it brought the armed might of France to the American cause, thus securing final victory. Though the last battle of the war was fought at Yorktown, Washington immediately brought his army back to the banks of the Hudson to keep close watch on the British in New York City and to protect the life-line of the future Republic in case of a resumption of hostilities during the uneasy truce of 1781–1783. And it was the evacuation of the Island of Manhattan by the British in late 1783 that signalized the official end of the war and permitted Washington to take leave of his troops.

Statistically, the State of New York had borne a disproportionate share of the burdens and suffering of the war. Though it ranked only seventh in population, one-third of the total battles and engagements of the Revolution (an estimated 92 out of 308) had been fought on or near the banks of the Hudson. "No other equal area in any of the other thirteen original states," Paul Wilstach has well said, "saw so much of the Revolutionary Army and its great commander or of the British forces and their commanders" [*Hudson River Landings* (Indianapolis: 1933), p. 107]. Westchester County was a ravaged "no man's land" of both contending armies and their guerilla forces throughout the war. The northern frontier (forty miles north of Albany along the Hudson and eighty miles west of Albany along the Mohawk) was inflamed with border warfare from 1777 until the coming of peace. More than 12,000 farms had been abandoned, more than two-thirds of the population along the frontier had died or fled. No other state had known such protracted fury and destruction. At the end of the war, with a third of New York City in ruins and the population of the state as a whole still huddled, as a century past, on the islands around New York Bay or among the thin settlements of the Hudson Valley and the ravaged frontier communities of the Mohawk Valley, the State of New York gave little promise of the sudden resurgence of life and enterprise that would project it into the forefront of American commonwealths within a single generation.

4.
Peter Kalm 1749*

INTRODUCTION: Peter Kalm (1716–1779), an eighteenth-century Swedish naturalist, came to America in 1748 at the suggestion of the great botanist, Carolus Linneaus, to obtain seed specimens of North American herbs and trees for the Swedish Academy of Sciences. The scientific motive was joined with the broad humanistic interests of a cultured eighteenth-century gentleman, and the book that Peter Kalm subsequently published about his American experiences is at once a pioneer scientific report of American fauna and flora and an unprejudiced portrait of life and manners in the New World during the time of the French and Indian Wars.

Kalm was in America for almost two and a half years (September 1748–February 1751). After arriving at Philadelphia where he stayed at the home of Benjamin Franklin, he went after a time to New York City and boarded a sloop for the first lap of his journey to the French capital of Montreal. The following extract from his voluminous *Travels in North America* covers a three-week period in June and July of 1749 when he ascended the Hudson as far as Fort Nicholson (later Fort Edward) and then traveled through the wilderness to the French bastion of Fort Frédéric on Lake Champlain.

A remarkable change comes over Peter Kalm's narrative once he reaches the frontier north of Albany. There were still relatively few settlements along the tidal reaches of the lower Hudson, and Kalm could sail along for hours at a time, and often for the better part of a day, without seeing a break in the forest; still the scattered settlements below Albany lived in apparent peace and security. North of Albany, however, it was another matter. In 1749 there were still no permanent settlements between the mouth of the Mohawk and the St. Lawrence River, and the vast wilderness and its natural waterways —Lake Champlain and Lake George, the Sorel or Richelieu River and the Woodcreek—which connected the French and English possessions in America had become a major prize of the Colonial Wars. Kalm passed through this hostile wilderness during a temporary cessation of hostilities, one year after the conclusion of King George's War (1744–1748) and five years before the outbreak of the French and Indian Wars (1754–1760). In 1748 Schenectady had been ravaged by marauding forces of French and Indians; the year before that the fort at Saratoga had been destroyed for the second time. In 1749 the wilderness could still erupt into undeclared hostilities; signs of devastation were everywhere; settlers had just begun to return to their homes; and on at least one occasion Kalm feared for his life. North of Albany this sophisticated naturalist from Sweden is no longer the detached observer of the botanical curiosities of the lower Hudson Valley; he is a transplanted European facing for the first time the hardships, and indeed, the terrors, of a wide-open frontier.

* From Adolph B. Benson, ed., *The America of 1750; Peter Kalm's Travels in North America; the English Version of 1770, revised from the Original Swedish,* 2 vols. (New York: 1937), I, pp. 326–379. The reader is advised that the dates used in this narrative by Kalm are based on the Julian Calendar which was not abolished until 1752. To convert Kalm's dates into the Gregorian Calendar of today, add eleven days. Kalm's departure from New York was June 10 O.S. and June 21 N.S.

June the 10th, 1749

The Hudson River. At noon we left New York, and sailed with a gentle wind up the Hudson River, in a boat bound for Albany. All afternoon we kept seeing a whole fleet of little boats returning from New York, whither they had brought provisions and other goods for sale, which on account of the extensive commerce of this town

5. *A View in Hudson's River of the Entrance of what is called the Topan Sea*, engraving by Peter Benazech from the painting by Paul Sandby, 1768; courtesy of the Eno Collection, Prints Division, New York Public Library.

"These high and steep mountains continued for a few English miles on the western shore; but on the eastern side the land was diversified with hills and valleys."

One of the most beautiful prints of the early Hudson Valley, showing the northern terminus of the Palisades and the beginning of the Tappan Sea.

A View in Hudson's River of the Entrance of what is called the Topan Sea.

Vue sur la Rivière d'Hudson, de l'entrée connue sous le nom de Mer de Topan.

Sketch'd on the Spot by his Excellency Governor Pownal. Painted by Paul Sandby. Engraved by Peter Benazech.

and the great number of its inhabitants find a good market.[1] The Hudson River runs north and south here, except for some high pieces of land which sometimes project far into it, and alter its direction. Some porpoises played and tumbled in the river. The eastern shore, or the New York side, is at first very steep and high, but the western very sloping and covered with woods. There appeared farmhouses on both sides surrounded with plowed land. The soil of the steep shores is of a pale brick color and some little rocks of gray sandstone are seen here and there. About ten or twelve miles from New York, the western shore appears quite different from what it is further south; it consists of steep mountains with perpendicular sides towards the river, and they are exactly like the steep sides of the mountains of Hall and Hunnebärg in Västergötland, Sweden. Sometimes a rock projects out like the pointed angle of a bastion. The tops of these mountains are covered with oaks and other trees. A number of stones of all sizes lie along the shore, having rolled down from the mountains.

These high and steep mountains continued for a few English miles on the western shore; but on the eastern side the land was diversified with hills and valleys, which were commonly covered with hardwood trees, amongst which there appeared a farm now and then in a glade. The hills are covered with stones in some places. About twelve miles from New York we saw sturgeons (*Acipenser sturio*) leaping out of the water, and on the whole passage we met porpoises in the river. As we proceeded we found the eastern banks of the river very much cultivated, and a number of pretty farms surrounded with orchards, and fine plowed fields presented themselves to our view. About twenty-two miles from New York, the high mountains which I have before mentioned left us, and made as it were a high ridge here from east to west across the country. This altered the face of the land on the western shore: from mountainous it became interspersed with little valleys and round hillocks, which were scarcely inhabited at all; but the eastern shore continued to afford us a delightful prospect. After sailing a little while in the night, we cast our anchor and lay here till the morning,[2] especially as the tide was ebbing with great force.

June the 11th

This morning we continued our voyage up the river, with the tide and a faint breeze. We now passed the Highland mountains, which were to the east of us. They consisted of gray sandstone, were very high, quite steep, and covered with deciduous trees, firs and red cedars. The western shore was rocky, which however did not come up to the height of the mountains on the opposite shore. The tops of these eastern mountains were cut off from our sight by a thick fog which surrounded them. The country was unfit for cultivation, being so full of rocks, and accordingly we saw no farms. The distance from these mountains to New York is computed at thirty-six English miles.

Ascending the Hudson. A thick fog now rose from the high mountains like the thick smoke of a charcoal kiln. For the space of a few English miles we had hills and rocks on the western banks of the river, and a variation of lesser and greater mountains and valleys covered with young firs, red cedars and oaks, on the eastern side. The hills close to the riverside were usually low, but their height increased as they were further from the River. Afterwards we saw for some miles nothing but high rolling mountains and valleys, both covered with woods; the valleys were in reality nothing but low rocks, and stood perpendicular towards the river in many places. The breadth of the river was sometimes two or three musket shots, but commonly not over one. Every now and then we saw several kinds of fish leaping out of the water. The wind vanished after about ten o'clock in the morning, and forced us to go forwards with our oars, the tide being almost spent. In one place on the western shore we saw a wooden house painted red, and we were told that there was a sawmill further up. But besides this we did not see a farm or any cultivated grounds all forenoon.

The water in the river has here no longer a brakish taste; yet I was told the tide, especially when the wind is south, sometimes carries the salt water further north with it. The color of the water is likewise altered, for it appears darker here than before.—To account for the original course of rivers is very difficult, if not wholly impossible.[3] Some rivers may have come from a great reservoir of water, which being considerably increased by heavy rains or other circumstances overflows old bounds down to the lower countries through the places where it meets with least resistance. This is perhaps the reason why some rivers have such a winding course through the fields of soft earth, and where mountains, rocks and stones divert their passage. However, it seems that some rivers derive their origin from the Creation itself, and that Providence then pointed out their course; for their existence can, in all probability, not be owing to the accidental eruption of water alone. Among these rivers we may rank the Hudson. I was surprised on seeing its course and the varied character of its shores. It rises a long way north of Albany, and descends to New York, in a direct line from north to south, which is a distance of about a hundred and sixty English miles, and perhaps more, for the little windings which it makes are of no signification.[4] In many places between New York and Albany, are ridges of high mountains running east and west. But it is remarkable that they go on undisturbed till they come to the Hudson, which cuts directly across

them, and frequently their sides stand perpendicular towards the river. There is an opening left in the chain of mountains, as broad as the river, for it to pass through, and the mountains go on as before, on the other side, in the same direction. It is likewise remarkable, that the river in such places where it passes through the mountains is as deep, and often deeper, than in the other places.[5] The perpendicular rocks on the sides of the river are surprising, and it appears that if no passages had been opened by Providence for the river to pass through, the mountains in the upper part of the country would have been inundated, since these mountains, like so many dikes, would have hindered the water from going on. Query, why does this river go on in a direct line for so considerable a distance? Why do the many passages, through which the river flows across the mountains, lie along the same meridian? Why are there no rapids at some of these openings, or at least shallow water with a rocky bed?

We now perceived excessively high and steep mountains on both sides of the river, which echoed back each sound we uttered. Yet notwithstanding they were so high and steep, they were covered with small trees. The Blue Mountains,[6] which reared their towering summits above all the other mountains, were now seen before us towards the north, but at a great distance. The skipper told us that often on one of the mountains on the west side of the river one can see a light at night which people claim is a carbuncle. The country began here to look more cultivated and less mountainous. The last of the high western mountains was called Butterhill;[7] beyond it the country between the mountains grew more level. The farms became more numerous, and we had a view of many grain fields between the hills. Before we passed the latter we had the wind in our face, and we could only get forward by tacking, which took much time, as the river was hardly a musket shot in breadth. Afterwards we cast anchor, because we had both wind and tide against us. While we waited for the return of the tide and the change of wind we went on shore.

Sassafras trees and chestnut trees grow here in great abundance. I found a tulip tree in some parts of the wood, and also the *Kalmia latifolia*,[8] which was now in full blossom, though the flowers were already fading.

Some time after noon a fair wind arose from the southwest, so we weighed anchor and continued our voyage. The place where we lay at anchor was just at the end of those steep and amazingly high mountains.[9] They consisted of gray rock, and close to them, on the shore, lay a vast number of little stones. As soon as we had passed these mountains, the country became more level and higher. The river likewise increased in breadth, so as to be nearly an English mile broad.[10] After sailing for some time we found no more mountains along the river; but to the eastward was a high chain of mountains [of the Berkshire system] whose sides were covered with woods up to more than half of their height. The summits however were quite barren; for I suppose that nothing would grow there on account of the great degree of heat, dryness, and the violence of the wind, to which that part was exposed. The eastern side of the river was much more cultivated than the western, where we seldom saw a house. The land was covered with woods though it was in general very level. About fifty-six English miles from New York the country is not very high; yet it is everywhere covered with woods, except for some pioneer farms which were scattered here and there. The high mountains which we left in the afternoon, now appeared above the woods and the countryside. These mountains, which were called the Highlands, did not extend further north than the other on the opposite side, in the place where we anchored. Their sides (not those towards the river) were seldom perpendicular, but sloping, so that one could climb up to the top, though not without difficulty.

On some of the higher grounds near the river, the people burnt lime. The master of the boat told me that they quarry a fine bluish limestone in the highlands along both sides of the river, for the space of several English miles, and burn lime out of it. But for several miles distance there is no more limestone and they find also none on the banks till they come to Albany.[11]

We passed a little neck of land which projected on the western side of the river and was called Dance.[12] The name of this place is said to derive its origin from a festival which the Dutch celebrated here in former times, and at which they danced and diverted themselves; but once there came a number of Indians who killed them all.

We cast anchor late at night, because the wind ceased and the tide was ebbing. The depth of the river is twelve fathoms here. The fireflies flew over the river in large numbers at night and often settled upon the rigging.

June the 12th

This morning we proceeded with the tide, but against the wind. The river was here a musketshot broad. The country in general was low on both sides, consisting of low rocks and stony fields, which were however covered with woods. It is so rocky, stony, and poor that nobody can settle on it, or inhabit it, there being no spot of ground fit for cultivation. The country continued to have the same appearance for the space of a few miles, and we never perceived a single settlement. At eleven o'clock this morning we came to a little island, which lies in the middle of the river, and is said to be halfway between New York and Albany.[13] The shores were still

6. *A View in Hudson's River of Pokepsey & the Cattskill Mountains from Sopos Island, in Hudson's River,* engraving by Paul Sandby, 1761; courtesy of The New-York Historical Society.

"At eleven o'clock this morning we came to a little island, which . . . is said to be halfway between New York and Albany. The shores were still low, stony and rocky, as before. But at a greater distance we saw high mountains."

A Europeanized version of the Catskill Mountains seen from the vicinity of Esopus Island, eight miles below Kingston.

low, stony and rocky, as before. But at a greater distance we saw high mountains, covered with woods, chiefly on the western shore, raising their summits above the rest of the country; and still further off, the Blue Mountains rose up above them.[14] Towards noon it was quite calm, and we went on very slow. Here the land was well cultivated, especially on the eastern shore, and full of great plowed fields; yet the soil seemed sandy. Several villages lay on the eastern side, and one of them, called Strasburg, was inhabited by a number of Germans.[15] To the west we saw several cultivated places. The Blue Mountains could be seen very plainly here. They appeared through the clouds and towered above all other mountains. The river was fully an English mile broad opposite Strasburg.

They use a yellow *Agaricus,* or fungus, which grows on maple trees, for tinder. That which is found on the red-flowering maple (*Acer rubrum*) is reckoned the best, and next in goodness is that of the sugar maple (*Acer saccarinum*), which is sometimes reckoned as good as the former.

Rhinebeck is a place located a short distance from Strasburg, further from the river. It is inhabited by many Germans, who have a church here. Their clergyman at present was the Rev. Mr. Hartwig, who knew some Swedish, having been at Gothenburg for a time. This little town is not visible from the riverside.

At two in the afternoon it began to blow from the south, which enabled us to proceed. The country on the eastern side was high, and consisted of well cultivated soil. We had fine plowed fields, well-built farms and good orchards in view. The western shore was likewise somewhat high, but still covered with woods, and we now and then, though seldom, saw one or two little settlements. The river was more than an English mile broad in most places, and came in such a straight line from the north that the water vanished from view.

June the 13th

The wind favored our voyage during the whole night, so that I had no opportunity of observing the nature of the country. This morning at five o'clock we were but nine English miles from Albany. The country on both sides of the river was low and covered with woods, only here and there were a few scattered settlements. On the banks of the river were wet meadows, covered with sword grass (*Carex*), and they formed several little islands. We saw no mountains and hastened towards Albany. The land on both sides of the river was chiefly low, and more cultivated as we came nearer to Albany. Here we could see everywhere the type of haystacks with movable roofs which I have described before.[16] As to the houses which we saw, some were of wood, others of stone. The river was seldom above a musketshot broad, and in several parts of it were sandbars which required great skill in navigating the boats. At eight o'clock in the morning we arrived in Albany.

Arriving in Albany. All the boats which ply between Albany and New York belong to Albany. They go up and down the Hudson River as long as it is open and free from ice. They bring from Albany boards or planks, and all sorts of timber, flour, peas, and furs, which they get from the Indians, or which are smuggled from the French. They come home almost empty, and only bring a few kinds of merchandise with them, the chief of which is rum. This is absolutely necessary to the inhabitants of Albany. They cheat the Indians in the fur trade with it; for when the Indians are drunk they are practically blind and will leave it to the Albany whites to fix the price of furs. The boats are quite large, and have a good cabin, in which the passengers can be very commodiously lodged. They are usually built of red cedar or of white oak. Frequently the bottom consists of white oak, and the sides of red cedar, because the latter withstands decay much longer than the former. The red cedar is likewise apt to split when it hits against anything, and the Hudson is in many places full of sand and rocks, against which the keel of the boat sometimes strikes. Therefore people choose white oak for the bottom, as being the softer wood, and not splitting so easily. The bottom, being continually under water, is not so much exposed to weathering and holds out longer.

Canoes. The canoes which the boats always have along with them are made of a single piece of wood, hollowed out: they are sharp on both ends, frequently three or four fathoms long, and as broad as the thickness of the wood will allow. The people in it do not row sitting, but usually a fellow stands at each end, with a short oar in his hand, with which he controls and propels the canoe. Those which are made here at Albany are commonly of white pine. They can do service for eight or twelve years, especially if they be tarred and painted. At Albany they are made of pine since there is no other wood fit for them; at New York they are made of the tulip tree, and, in other parts of the country of red or white cedars: but both these trees are so small in the neighborhood of Albany that they are unfit for canoes. There are no seats in them, for if they had any, they would be more liable to upset, as one could not keep one's equilibrium so well. One has to sit in the bottom of these canoes.

Battoes [17] are another kind of boats which are much in use in Albany: they are made of boards of white pine; the bottom is flat, that they may row the better in shallow water. They are sharp at both ends, and somewhat higher towards the end than in the middle. They have seats in them, and are rowed as common boats. They are long, yet not all alike. Usually they are three and sometimes four fathoms long. The height from the bottom to the top of the board (for the sides stand almost perpendicular) is from twenty inches to two feet, and the breadth in the middle about a yard and six inches. They are chiefly made use of for carrying goods along the river to the Indians, that is, when those rivers are open enough for the battoes to pass through, and when they need not be carried by land a great way. The boats made of the bark of trees break easily by knocking against a stone, and the canoes cannot carry a great cargo, and are easily upset; the battoes are therefore preferable to them both. I saw no boats here like those in Sweden or other parts of Europe.

Temperature at Albany. Frequently the cold does a great deal of damage at Albany. There is hardly a month in summer during which a frost does not occur. [18] Spring comes very late, and in April and May are numerous cold nights which frequently kill the flowers of trees and kitchen herbs. It was feared last May that the blossoms of the apple trees had been so severely damaged by the frost that next autumn there would be but very few apples. Even the oak blossoms in the woods are very often killed by the cold. The autumn here is of long continuance, with warm days and nights. However, the cold nights commonly commence towards the end of September, and are frequent in October. The people are forced to keep their cattle in stables from the middle of November till March or April, and must find them hay during that time.

During summer, the wind blows mostly from the south and brings a great drought along with it. Sometimes it rains a little, and as soon as it has rained the wind veers to the northwest, blowing for several days from that point and then returning to the south. I have had frequent opportunities of seeing this condition of wind happen precisely, both this year and the following.

June the 15th

The fences were made of pine boards, of which there is an abundance in the extensive woods; and there are many saw mills to cut it into boards.

Fruit Trees. The several sorts of apple trees were said to grow very well here, and bear as fine fruit as in any other part of North America. Each farm has a large orchard. They have some apples here which are very large, and very palatable; they are sent to New York and other places as a rarity. People make excellent cider in the autumn in the country round Albany. . . . Pear trees do not succeed here. This was complained of in many other parts of North America. But I fear that they do not take sufficient care in the management and planting of them, for I have seen fine pears in several parts of Pennsylvania. Peach trees have often been planted here, and never succeed well. This was attributed to a worm which lives in the ground and eats through the root, so that the tree dies. Perhaps the severity of the winter contributes much to it. They plant no other fruit trees at Albany besides these I have mentioned.

Grains. They sow as much hemp and flax here as they want for home consumption. They sow corn in great abundance; a loose soil is reckoned the best for this purpose, for it will not thrive in clay. From half a bushel they reap a hundred bushels. They reckon corn a very suitable kind of crop, because the young plant recovers after being hurt by the frost. They have had instances here of the plants freezing off twice in the spring, close to the ground, and yet surviving and yielding an excellent crop. Corn has likewise the advantage of standing much longer against a drought than wheat. The larger sort of corn which is commonly sown here ripens in September.

Wheat is sown in the neighborhood of Albany to great advantage. From one bushel they get twelve sometimes; if the soil is good, they get twenty bushels. If their crop amounts only to a ten-fold yield, they think it a very mediocre one. The inhabitants of the country round Albany are Dutch and Germans. The Germans live in several great villages, and sow great quantities of wheat which is brought to Albany, whence they send many boats laden with flour to New York. The wheat flour from Albany is reckoned the best in all North America, except that from Sopus (Esopus) or King's Town (Kingston), a place between Albany and New York. All the bread in Albany is made of wheat. At New York they pay for the Albany flour with a few shillings more per hundred weight than for that from other places.

Rye is likewise sown here, but not so generally as wheat. They do not sow much barley, because they do not reckon the profits very great. Wheat is so plentiful that they make malt of that. In the neighborhood of New York, I saw great fields sown with barley. They do not sow more oats than are necessary for their horses.

Peas. The Dutch and Germans who live hereabouts sow peas in great abundance; they grow very well, and are annually carried to New York in great quantities. They were free from insects for a considerable time. But of late years the same pest which destroys the peas in Pennsylvania, New Jersey, and the lower parts of the province of New York, has likewise appeared destructive among the peas here. It is a real loss to this town, and to the other parts of North America, which used to get so many peas from here for their own consumption and that of their sailors. It had been found that if they procured good peas from Albany and sowed them near King's Town, or the lower part of the province of New York, they succeeded very well the first year, but were so full of worms the second and following years that nobody could or would eat them.—Some people put ashes into the pot, among the peas, when they will not boil or soften well; but whether this is wholesome and agreeable to the palate, I do not know.

Potatoes are planted by almost everyone. Some people preferred ashes to sand for keeping them in during winter. Some people in Ireland are said to have the custom in autumn of placing the potatoes in an oven and drying them a bit, when they are said to keep better over winter; but these potatoes cannot later be planted, only eaten. The Bermuda potatoes have likewise been planted here, and succeed pretty well. The greatest difficulty is to keep them during winter, for they generally rot in that season.

The humming bird comes to this place sometimes, but is rather a scarce bird.

The *shingles* with which the houses are covered are made of the white pine, which is reckoned as good and as durable and sometimes better than the white cedar. It is claimed that such a roof will last forty years. The white pine is found in abundance here, in such places where common pines grow in Sweden. I have never seen them in the lower parts of the province of New York, nor in New Jersey or Pennsylvania. A vast quantity of lumber from the white pine is prepared annually on this side of Albany, which is brought down to New York and exported.

Grapevines. The woods abound with grapevines, which likewise grow on the steep banks of the river in surprising quantities. They climb to the tops of trees on the bank and bend them by their weight. But where they find no trees they hang down along the steep shores and cover them entirely. The grapes are eaten after the frost has touched them, for they are too sour before. They are not much used in any other way.

Gnats. The vast woods and uninhabited grounds between Albany and Canada contain immense swarms of gnats which annoy the travellers. To be in some measure secured against these insects some besmear their face with butter or grease, for the gnats do not like to settle on greasy places. The great heat makes boots very uncomfortable; but to prevent the gnats from stinging the legs they wrap some paper round them, under the stockings. Some travellers wear caps which cover the whole face, and some have gauze over the eyes. At night they lie in tents, if they can carry any with them, and make a great fire at the entrance so that smoke will drive the pests away.

June the 16th

The porpoises seldom go higher up the Hudson River than the salt water goes; after that, the sturgeons fill their place. It has however sometimes happened that porpoises have gone clear up to Albany.

There is a report that a whale once came up the river to this town.

The fireflies (*Lampyris*), which are the same as those that we find in Pennsylvania during the summer, are seen here in abundance every night. They fly up and down in the streets of the town. They come into the houses if the doors and windows are open.

June the 19th

. . . . . .

An Island near Albany. This afternoon I went to see an island which lies in the middle of the river about a mile below the town.[19] This island is an English mile long, and not above a quarter of a mile broad. It is almost entirely turned into plowed fields, and is inhabited by a single planter, who besides possessing this island is the owner of three more. Here we saw no woods, except for a few trees which were left round the island on the shore and formed as it were a tall, large hedge. The red maple (*Acer rubrum*) grows in abundance in several places. Its leaves are white or silvery on the under sides, and, when agitated by the wind, they make the tree appear as if it were full of white flowers. The water beech (*Plantanus occidentalis*) grows to a great height and is one of the best shade trees here. The water poplar is the most common tree hereabouts, grows exceedingly well on the shores of the river, and is as tall as the tallest of our aspens. In summer it affords the best shade for men and cattle against the scorching heat. On the banks of rivers and lakes it is one of the most useful trees, because it holds the soil by its extensively branched roots, and prevents the water from washing it away. The water beech and elm tree (*Ulmus*) serve the same purpose. The wild plum trees are plentiful here and full of unripe fruit. Its wood is not made use of, but its fruit is eaten. Sumach (*Rhus glabra*) is plentiful here, as also the wild grapevines which climb up the trees and creep along the high shores of the river. I was told that the grapes ripen very late, though they are already pretty large. The American elm tree (*Ulmus Americana*) forms several high hedges. The soil of this island is a rich mould, mixed with sand, which is chiefly employed in corn plantations. There are likewise large fields of potatoes. The whole island was leased for one hundred pounds of New York currency. The person who had taken the lease again let some greater and smaller lots of ground to the inhabitants of Albany for kitchen gardens, and by that means reimbursed himself. Portulaca (*Portulaca oleracea*) grows spontaneously here in great abundance and looks very well.

June the 20th

The Hudson River at Albany. The tide in the Hudson goes about eight or ten English miles above Albany, and consequently runs one hundred and fifty-six miles from the sea. In spring when the snow melts there is hardly any high tide near this town, for the great quantity of water which comes from the mountains during that season occasions a continual ebbing. This likewise happens after heavy rains.

The cold is generally reckoned very severe here. The ice in the Hudson is commonly three or four feet thick. On the third of April some of the inhabitants crossed the river with six pairs of horses. The ice commonly dissolves about the end of March, or beginning of April. Great pieces of ice come down about that time, which sometimes carry with them the houses that stand close to the shore. The water is very high at that time because the ice stops sometimes and piles up in places where the river is narrow. The water often has been observed to rise three fathoms higher than it commonly is in summer. The ground is frozen here in winter to the depth of three, four or five feet. On the sixteenth of November the boats are put up, and about the beginning or middle of April they are in motion again. People here are unacquainted with stoves, and their chimneys are so wide that one could almost drive through them with a horse and sleigh.

Drinking Water. The water of several wells in this town was very cool about this time, but had a kind of acid taste, which was not very agreeable. On a nearer examination, I found an abundance of little insects in it, which were probably *monoculi*. . . .[20] Almost each house in Albany has its well, the water of which is applied to common use; but for tea, brewing, and washing, they commonly take the water of the Hudson, which flows close by the town. The water is generally quite muddy and very warm in summer; and, on that account, it is kept in cellars, in order that the sediment may settle to the bottom, and that the water may cool a little.

We lodged with a gunsmith, who told us that the best charcoal for the forge was made of black pine. The next best in his opinion was that made of beech. The best and most expensive stocks for his muskets were made of wild cherry, and next to these he valued most those of the red maple. They scarcely make use of any other wood for this purpose. The black walnut tree affords excellent wood for stocks, but it does not grow in the neighborhood of Albany.

June the 21st

Description of Albany. Next to New York Albany is the principal town, or at least the most wealthy, in the province of New York. It is situated on the slope of a hill, close to the western shore of the Hudson River, about one hundred and forty-six English miles from New York. The town extends along the river, which flows here from N.N.E. to S.S.W. The high mountains in the west, above the town, bound the view on that side.[21] There are two churches in Albany, one English and the other Dutch. The Dutch church stands a short distance from the river on the east side of the market. It is built of stone and in the middle it has a small steeple with a bell. It has but one minister who preaches twice every Sunday. The English church is situated on the hill at the west end of the market, directly under the fort. It is likewise built of stone but has no steeple. There is no service at the church at this time because they have no minister, but all the people understand Dutch, the garrison excepted. The minister of this church has a settled income of one hundred pounds sterling, which he gets from England. The town hall lies to the south of the Dutch church, close by the riverside. It is a fine building of stone, three stories high it has a small tower or steeple, with a bell, and a gilt ball and vane at the top of it.

The houses in this town are very neat, and partly built of stones covered with shingles of white pine. Some are slated with tile from Holland, because the clay of this neighborhood is not considered fit for tiles. Most of the houses are built in the old Frankish way, with the gable-end towards the street, except for a few, which were recently built in the modern style. A great number of houses are built like those of New Brunswick,[22] . . . the gable-end towards the street being of bricks and all the other walls of boards. The outside of the houses is never covered with lime or mortar, nor have I seen it practised in any North American towns which I have visited; and the walls do not seem to be damaged by the weather. The eaves on the roofs reach almost to the middle of the street. This preserves the walls from being damaged by the rain, but it is extremely disagreeable in rainy weather for the people in the streets, there being hardly any means of avoiding the water from the eaves. The front doors are generally in the middle of the houses, and on both sides are porches with seats, on which during fair weather the people spend almost the whole day, especially on those porches which are in the shade. The people seem to move with the sun and the shade, always keeping in the latter. When the sun is too hot the people disappear. In the evening the verandas are full of people of both sexes; but this is rather troublesome because a gentleman has to keep his hat in constant motion, for the people here are not Quakers whose hats are as though nailed to the head. It is considered very impolite not to lift your hat and greet everyone. The streets are broad, and some of them paved. In some parts they are lined with trees. The long streets are almost parallel to the river, and the others intersect them at right angles. The street which goes between the two churches is five times broader than the others and serves as a marketplace. The streets upon the whole are very dirty because the people leave their cattle in them during the summer nights. There are two marketplaces in town, to which the country people come twice a week. There are no city gates here but for the most part just open holes through which people pass in and out of the town.

The fort lies higher than any other building on a high steep hill on the west side of the town. It is a great building of stone surrounded with high and thick walls. Its location is bad, as it can serve only to keep off plundering parties without being able to sustain a siege. There are numerous high hills to the west of the fort, which command it, and from which one may see all that is done within it. There is commonly an officer and a number of soldiers quartered in it. They say the fort contains a spring of water.

Trade. The location of Albany is very advantageous in regard to trade. The Hudson River which flows close by it is from twelve to twenty feet deep. There is not yet any quay made for the better landing of the boats, because the people fear it will suffer greatly or be entirely carried away in spring by the ice which then comes down the river. The vessels which are in use here may come pretty near the shore in order to be loaded, and heavy goods are brought to them upon canoes tied together. Albany carries on a considerable commerce with New York, chiefly in furs, boards, wheat, flour, peas, several kinds of timber, etc. There is not a place in all the British colonies, the Hudson's Bay settlements excepted, where such quantities of furs and skins are bought of the Indians as at Albany. Most of the merchants in this town send a clerk or agent to Oswego, an English trading town on Lake Ontario, to which the Indians come with their furs. . . . The merchants from Albany spend the whole summer at Oswego, and trade with many tribes of Indians who come with their goods. Many people have assured me that the Indians are frequently cheated in disposing of their goods, especially when they are drunk, and that sometimes they do not get one half or even one tenth of the value of their goods. I have been a witness to several transactions of this kind. The merchants of Albany glory in these tricks, and are highly pleased when they have given a poor Indian a greater portion of brandy than he can stand, and when they can, after that, get all his goods for mere trifles. The Indians often find when they are sober again, that they have for once drunk as much as they are able of a liquor which they value beyond anything else in the whole world, and they are quite insensible to their loss if they again get a draught of this nectar. Besides this trade at Oswego, a number of Indians come to Albany from several places especially from Canada; but from this latter place, they hardly bring anything but beaver skins. There is a great penalty in Canada for carrying furs to the English, that trade belonging to the French West India Company. Notwithstanding that the French merchants in Canada carry on a considerable smuggling in trade. They send their furs by means of the Indians to their agent at Albany, who purchases them at the price which they have fixed upon with the French merchants. The Indians take in return several kinds of cloth, and other goods, which may be bought here at a lower rate than those which are sent to Canada from France.

The greater part of the merchants at Albany have extensive estates in the country and a large property in forests. If their estates have a little brook, they do not fail to erect a sawmill upon it for sawing boards and planks, which many boats take during the summer to New York, having scarcely any other cargo.

Many people at Albany make wampum for the Indians, which is their ornament and money, by grinding and finishing certain kinds of shells and mussels. This is of considerable profit to the inhabits. . . . The extensive trade which the inhabitants of Albany carry on, and their sparing manner of living, in the Dutch way, contribute to the considerable wealth which many of them have acquired.

The Dutch in Albany. The inhabitants of Albany and its environs are almost all Dutchman. They speak Dutch, have Dutch preachers, and the divine service is performed in that language. Their manners are likewise quite Dutch; their dress is however like that of the English. It is well known that the first Europeans who settled in the province of New York were Dutchmen. During the time that they were masters of this province, they seized New Sweden of which they were jealous. However, the pleasure of possessing this conquered land and their own was but of short duration, for towards the end of 1664 Sir Robert Carr,[23] by order of King Charles the second, went to New York, then New Amsterdam, and took it. Soon after Colonel Nicolls[24] went to Albany, which then bore the name of Fort Orange, and upon taking it, named it Albany, from the Duke of York's Scotch title. The Dutch inhabitants were allowed either to continue where they were, and under the protection of the English to enjoy all their former privileges, or to leave the country. The greater part of them chose to stay and from them the Dutchmen are descended who now live in the province of New York, and who possess the greatest and best estates in that province.

The avarice, selfishness and immeasurable love of money of the inhabitants of Albany are very well known throughout all North America, by the French and even by the Dutch, in the lower part of New York province. . . . I was here obliged to pay for everything twice, thrice and four times as much as in any part of North America which I have passed through. If I wanted their assistance, I was obliged to pay them very well for it, and when I wanted to purchase anything or be helped in some case or other, I could at once see what kind of blood ran in their veins, for they either fixed exorbitant prices for their services or were very reluctant to assist me. Such was this people in general. However, there are some among them who equalled any in North America or anywhere else, in politeness, equity, goodness, and readiness to serve and to oblige; but their number fell far short of that of the former. If I may be allowed to declare my conjectures, the origin of the inhabitants of Albany and its neighborhood seems to me to be as follows. While the Dutch possessed this country, and intended to people it, the government sent a pack of vagabonds of which they intended to clear their native country, and sent them along with a number of other settlers to this province. The vagabonds were sent far from the other colonists, upon the borders towards the Indians and other enemies, and a few honest families were persuaded to go with them, in order to keep them in bounds. I cannot in any other way account for the difference between the inhabitants of Albany and the other descendants of so respectable a nation as the Dutch, who are settled in the lower part of New York province. The latter are civil, obliging, just in prices, and sincere; and though they are not ceremonious, yet they are well meaning and honest and their promises may be relied on.[25]

The behavior of the inhabitants of Albany during the war between England and France, which ended with the peace of Aix la Chapelle, has, among several other causes, contributed to make them the object of hatred in all the British colonies, but more especially in New England. For at the beginning of that war when the Indians of both parties had received orders to commence hostilities, the French engaged theirs to attack the inhabitants of New England, which they faithfully executed, killing everybody they met with, and carrying off whatever they found. During this time the people of Albany remained neutral, and carried on a great trade with the very Indians who murdered the inhabitants of New England. Articles such as silver spoons, bowls, cups, etc. of which the Indians robbed the houses in New England, were carried to Albany, for sale. The people of that town bought up these silver vessels, though the names of the owners were engraved on many of them, and encouraged the Indians to get more of them, promising to pay them well, and whatever they would demand. This was afterwards interpreted by the inhabitants of New England to mean that the colonists of Albany encouraged the Indians to kill more of the New England people, who were in a manner their brothers, and who were subjects of the same crown. Upon the first news of this behavior, which the Indians themselves spread in New England, the inhabitants of the latter province were greatly incensed, and threatened that the first step they would take in another war would be to burn Albany and the adjacent parts.[26] In the present war [27] it will sufficiently appear how backward the other British provinces in America are in assisting Albany, and the neighboring places, in case of an attack from the French or Indians. The hatred which the English bear against the people at Albany is very great, but that of the Albanians against the English is carried to a ten times higher degree. This hatred has subsisted ever since the time when the English conquered this section, and is not yet extinguished, though they could never have gotten larger advantages under the Dutch government

than they have obtained under that of the English. For, in a manner, their privileges are greater than those of Englishmen themselves.

In their homes the inhabitants of Albany are much more sparing than the English and are stingier with their food. Generally what they serve is just enough for the meal and sometimes hardly that. The punch bowl is much more rarely seen than among the English. The women are perfectly well acquainted with economy; they rise early, go to sleep very late, and are almost superstitiously clean in regard to the floor, which is frequently scoured several times in the week. Inside the homes the women are neatly but not lavishly dressed. The children are taught both English and Dutch. The servants in the town are chiefly negroes. Some of the inhabitants wear their own hair very short, without a bag or queue, because these are looked upon as the characteristics of Frenchmen. As I wore my hair in a bag the first day I came here from Canada, I was surrounded with children, who called me a Frenchman, and some of the boldest offered to pull at my French head dress, so I was glad to get rid of it.

Their food and its preparation is very different from that of the English. Their breakfast is tea, commonly without milk. About thirty or forty years ago, tea was unknown to them, and they breakfasted either upon bread and butter, or bread and milk. They never put sugar into the cup, but take a small bit of it into their mouths while they drink. Along with the tea they eat bread and butter, with slices of dried beef. The host himself generally says grace aloud. Coffee is not usual here. They breakfast generally about seven. Their dinner is buttermilk and bread, to which they add sugar on special occasions, when it is a delicious dish for them, or fresh milk and bread, with boiled or roasted meat. They sometimes make use of buttermilk instead of fresh milk, in which to boil a kind of porridge that tastes very sour but not disagreeable in hot weather. With each dinner they have a large salad, prepared with an abundance of vinegar, and very little or no oil. They frequently drink buttermilk and eat bread and salad, one mouthful after another. Their supper consists generally of bread and butter, and milk with small pieces of bread in it. The butter is very salt. Sometimes too they have chocolate. They occasionally eat cheese at breakfast and at dinner; it is not in slices, but scraped or rasped, so as to resemble coarse flour, which they pretend adds to the good taste of the cheese. They commonly drink very weak beer, or pure water. . . . The Governor of New York often confers at Albany with the Indians of the Five Nations, or the Iroguois, (Mohawks, Senekas, Cayugaws, Onondagoes, and Oneidas), especially when they intend either to make war upon, or to continue a war against the French. . . .[28]

June the 21st (P.M.)

Leaving Albany. About five o'clock in the afternoon we left Albany, and proceeded towards Canada. We had two men with us, who were to accompany us to the first French place, which is Fort St. Frédéric, or as the English call it, Crown Point.[29] For this service each of them was to receive five pounds of New York currency, in addition to food and drink. This is the common price here, and he that does not choose to conform to it, is obliged to travel alone. We were forced to use a canoe, as we could get neither battoes, nor boats of bark; and as there was a good road along the west side of the Hudson, we left the men to follow in the canoe, and we went along the shore, that we might be able to examine it and its natural characteristic with greater accuracy. It is very inconvenient to row in these canoes; for one stands at each end and pushes the boat forwards. They commonly keep close to the shore, that they may be able to reach the ground easily. The rowers [or paddlers] are forced to stand upright while they row in a canoe.[30] We kept along the shore all evening. It consisted of large hills, and next to the water grew the trees, which I have mentioned above, and which likewise are to be seen on the shores of the isle, in the river, situated below Albany. The easterly shore of the river is uncultivated, woody, and hilly; but the western is flat, cultivated, and chiefly turned into plowed fields, which has no drains, though they need them in some places. It appears very plainly here that the river has formerly been broader, for there is a sloping bank on the grain fields, at about thirty yards distance from the river, which always runs parallel. From this it sufficiently appears that the rising ground formerly was the shore of the river, and the fields its bed. As a further proof, it may be added that the same shells which abound on the present shore of the river, and are not applied to any use by the inhabitants, lie plentifully scattered on these fields. I cannot say whether this change was occasioned by the diminishing of the water in the river, or by its washing some earth down the river and carrying it to its sides, or by the river's cutting deeper in on the sides.

Agriculture. All land was plowed very even, as is usual in the Swedish province of Uppland. Some fields were sown with yellow and others with white wheat. Now and then we saw great fields of flax, which was not beginning to flower. In some parts it grew very well, and in others it was poor. The excessive drought which had continued throughout this spring had parched all the grass and plants on hills and higher grounds, leaving no other green plant than the common mullein (*Verbascum thapsus* L.) which I saw in several places, on the driest and highest hills, growing in spite of the parching heat of the sun, and though the pastures and meadows were excessively poor and afforded scarcely any food at all; yet the cattle never touched the mullein. Now and then I found fields with peas, but the charlock (wild mustard) (*Sinapsis arvensis* L.) kept them quite under. The soil in most of these fields in a fine black mould, which goes down pretty deep.

The wild vines cover all the hills along the rivers, on which no other plants grow, and on those which are covered with trees they climb to the tops and wholly cover them, making them bend down with their weight. They had already large grapes; we saw them in abundance all day, and during all the time that we kept to the Hudson, on the hills, along the shores, and on some little islands in the river.

The white-beaked corn thieves (*blackbirds*) appeared now and then, flying amongst the bushes; their note is pleasant and they are not so large as the black corn thieves (*Oriolus Phaeniceus*). We saw them near New York, for the first time.

We found a water beech tree (*Platanus occidentalis*) cut down near the road, measuring about five feet in diameter.

This day and for some days afterwards we met islands in the river. The larger ones were cultivated and turned into grain fields and meadows. We walked about five English miles along the river today, and found the ground, during that time, very uniform and consisting of pure earth. I did not see a single stone on the fields. The red maple, the water beech, the water aspen, the wild plum tree, the sumach, the elm, the wild grapevines, and some species of willows were the trees which we found on the rising shores of the river, where some asparagus (*Asparagus officinalis*) grew wild.

North of Albany. We passed the night about six miles from Albany in a countryman's cottage. On the west side of the river we saw several houses, one after another, inhabited by the descendants of the first Dutch settlers, who lived by cultivating their grounds. About an English mile beyond our lodgings was a place where the tide stops in the Hudson, there being only small and shallow streams above it.[31] At that place they catch a good many kinds of fish in the river.

The barns were generally built in the Dutch way . . . for in the middle was the threshing floor, above it a place for the hay and straw, and on each side stables for horses, cows, and other animals. The barn itself was very large. Sometimes the buildings of a farm consisted only of a small cottage with a garret above it, together with a barn upon the above plan.

June the 22nd

This morning I followed one of our guides to the waterfall near Cohoes, in the Mohawk River, before it empties into the Hudson River. These falls are about three English miles from the place where I passed the night. The country as far as the falls is a plain, and is hilly only about the fall itself. The wood is cleared in most places, and the ground cultivated and interspersed with pretty farmhouses.

The Cohoes Falls are among the greatest in this locality. . . . Above and below the falls both sides and the bottom are of rock, and there is a cliff at the fall itself, running everywhere equally high, and crossing the river in a straight line with the side which forms the fall. It represents, as it were, a wall towards the lower side, which is not quite perpendicular, wanting about four yards. The height of this wall, over which the water rolls, appeared to me about twenty or twenty-four yards. I had noted this height in my diary, and afterwards found it agreed pretty well with the account which that ingenious engineer, Mr. Lewis Evans, gave me at Philadelphia.[32] He said that he had geometrically measured the breadth and height of the falls, and found it nine hundred English feet broad and seventy-five feet high. There was very little water in the river and it only ran over the falls in a few places. In some spots where the water had rolled down before, it had cut deep holes below into the rock, sometimes to the depth of two or three fathoms. The bed of the river, below the falls, was quite dry, there being only a channel in the middle fourteen feet broad, and a fathom or somewhat more deep, through which the water passed which came over the falls. We saw a number of holes in the rock below the falls, which bore a perfect resemblance to those in Sweden which we call giants' pots, or mountain kettles. They differed in size, there being large deep ones, and small shallow ones. We had clear uninterrupted sunshine, not a cloud above the horizon, and no wind at all. However, close to this fall, where the water was in such a quantity, there was a continual drizzling rain, occasioned by the vapors which rose from the water during its fall, and were carried about by the wind. Therefore, in coming within a musketshot of the falls, against the wind, our clothes became wet at once, as from rain. The whirlpools, which were in the water below the falls, contained several kinds of fish; and they were caught by some people, who amused themselves with angling. The rocks hereabouts consist of the same black stone which forms the hills about Albany. When exposed to the air, it is apt to split into horizontal flakes, as slate does.

I saw here a kind of fence which we had not seen before, but which was used all along the Hudson where there was a quantity of woods. It can be called a timber fence, for it consisted of long, thick logs, and was about four feet high. It was made by placing the long logs at right angles to and upon short ones and fitting them together by having suitable crescent-shaped hollows in the short logs [in the manner of building log cabins]. Such a fence is possible only where there is plenty of trees.

En route for Canada. At noon we continued our journey to Canada in the canoe, which was pretty long and made of white pine. Somewhat beyond the farm where we lay at night, the river became so shallow that the men could reach bottom everywhere with their oars, it being in some parts not above two feet, and sometimes but one foot deep. The shore and bed of the river consisted of sand and pebbles. The river was very rapid, and against us, so that our men found it hard work to propel themselves forward against the stream. The hills along the shore consisted merely of earth, and were very high and steep in places. The breadth of the river was generally near two musketshots.

Sturgeons abound in the Hudson River. We saw them all day long leaping high up into the air, especially in the evening. Our guides, and the people who lived hereabouts, asserted that they never see any sturgeons in winter time, because these fish go into the sea late in autumn, but come up again in spring and stay in the river all summer. They are said to prefer the shallowest places in the river, which agreed pretty well with our observations, for we never saw them leap out of the water except in shallow spots. Their food is said to be several kinds of *confervae*,[33] which grow plentifully in some places on the bottom of the river, for these weeds are found in their little bellies when they are opened. The Dutch who settled here, and the Indians, fish for the sturgeon, and every night of our voyage upon this river we observed several boats with people who speared them with harpoons. The torches which they employed were made of that kind of pine which they call the black pine here. The nights are exceedingly dark, though they were now the shortest, and though we were in a country so much to the south of Sweden. The shores of the river lay covered with dead sturgeons, which had been wounded with the harpoon, but escaped, and died afterwards; they occasioned an insupportable stench during the excessive heat of the day.

Indians. As we went further up the river we saw an Indian woman and her boy sitting in a boat of bark, and an Indian wading through the river, with a great cap of bark on his head. Near them was an island which was temporarily inhabited by a number of Indians who had gone there for sturgeon fishing. We went to their huts to learn if we could get one of them to accompany us to Ft. Anne [34] and help us make a bark canoe to get to Fort St. Frédéric. On our arrival we found that all the men had gone into the woods hunting this morning, and we persuaded their boys to go and look for them. They demanded bread for payment, and we gave them twenty little round loafs; for as they found that it was of great importance to us to speak with the Indians, they raised difficulties and would not go till we gave them what they wanted. The island belonged to the Dutch, who had cultivated it. But they had now leased it to the Indians who planted their corn and several kinds of melon on it. The latter built their huts or wigwams on this island, on a very simple plan. Four posts were put into the ground perpendicularly, over which they had placed poles, and made a roof of bark upon them. The huts had either no walls at all, or they consisted of branches with leaves, which were fixed to the poles. The beds consisted of deerskins which were spread on the ground. The utensils were a couple of small kettles, two ladles, and a bucket or two, of bark, made tight enough to hold water. The sturgeons were cut into long slices, and hung up in the sunshine to dry, to be ready to serve as food in winter. The Indian women were sitting at their work

on the hill, upon deer-skins.—They never use chairs, but sit on the ground. However, they do not sit crosslegged, as the Turks do, but between their feet, which though they be turned backwards, are not crossed, but bent outwards. The women wear no headdress, and have black hair. They have a short blue petticoat which reaches to their knees, the edge of which is bordered with red or other-colored ribbons. They wear their blouses over their petticoats. They have large ear-rings, and their hair is tied behind and wrapped in ribbons. Their wampum, or pearls, and their money, which is made of shells, are tied round the neck and hang down on the breast. This is their whole dress. They were now making several articles of skins, to which they sewed the quills of the American porcupine, having dyed them black or red or left them in their original color.

Towards evening we went from there to a farm close to the river where we found only one man looking after the corn and the fields, the inhabitants not having yet returned from [King George's] war.

The little brooks here contain crawfish, which are exactly the same as ours, with this difference only that they are somewhat smaller; however, the Dutch settlers will not eat them.

June the 23rd

Bargaining with Indians. We waited a good while for the Indians, who had promised to come home in order to show us the way to Fort St. Anne, and to assist us in making a boat of bark to continue our voyage. About eight o'clock three of the men arrived. Their hair was black, and cut short; they wore light gray pieces of woolen cloth over their shoulders, shirts which covered their thighs, and pieces of cloth or skins which they wrapped round the legs and parts of the thighs in place of stockings. They had neither hats, caps nor breeches. Two of them had painted the upper part of their foreheads and their cheeks with vermilion. Round their necks were ribbons from which bags hung down to the breast, containing a knife. They promised to accompany us for thirty shillings, but soon after changed their minds and went with an Englishman who gave them more. Thus we were obliged to make this journey quite alone. The Indians, however, were honest enough to return us fifteen shillings, which we had paid them beforehand.

Our last night's lodging was about ten English miles from Albany. During the war which had just ended, the inhabitants had all retreated from thence to Albany, because the French Indians had taken or killed all the people they met with, set the houses on fire, and cut down the trees. Therefore, when the inhabitants returned, things looked wretched; they found no houses, and were forced to lie under a few boards which they propped up against each other.

The river was almost a musketshot broad, and the ground on both sides cultivated. The hills near the river were steep, and the earth a pale color. The American elder (*Sambucus occidentalis*) grows in incredible quantities on those hills, which appear white from the abundance of flowers on the tree.

All day long we had one group of rapids after another, full of rocks, which were great obstacles to our getting ahead. The water in the river was very clear, and generally shallow, being only from two to four feet deep, running very violently against us in most places. The shore was covered with pebbles and a gray sand. The hills consisted of earth, and were high and abrupt. The river was near two musketshots broad. On both sides the land was sometimes cultivated, and sometimes it was covered with floods.

The hills near the river abound with red and white clover. We found both these kinds plentiful in the woods. It is therefore difficult to determine whether they were brought over by the Europeans, as some people think, or whether they were originally in America, which the Indians deny.

We found purslane (*Portulaca oleracea*) growing plentifully in a dry sandy soil. In gardens it was one of the worst weeds.

We found people returning everywhere to their habitations, which they had been forced to leave during the war.

The farms were commonly built close to the river, on the hills. Each house had a little kitchen garden and a still lesser orchard. Some farms, however, had large gardens. The kitchen gardens yielded several kinds of pumpkins, watermelon and kidney beans. This year the trees had few or no apples on account of the frosty nights which had come in May and the drought which had continued throughout the summer.

Houses north of Albany. The houses hereabouts are generally built of beams and of unburnt bricks dried by the sun and the air. The beams are first erected, and upon them a gable with two walls, and the spars. The wall on the gable is made of nothing but boards. The roof is covered with shingles of fir. They make the walls of unburnt bricks, between the beams, to keep the rooms warmer; and that they might not easily be destroyed by rain and air they are covered with boards on the outside. There is generally a cellar beneath the house. The fireplaces among the Dutch were always built in, so that nothing projected out, and it looked as though they made a fire against the wall itself.

The farms are either built close to the riverside or on the high grounds, and around them are large fields of corn.

Muskrats. We saw great numbers of muskrats (*Castor zibethicus* L.) on the shores of the river, where they had many holes, some on a level with the surface of the water. These holes were large enough to admit a kitten. Before and in the entrance to the holes, lay a quantity of empty shells, the animals of which had been eaten by the muskrats. They are caught in traps placed along the waterside and baited with corn or apples.

Sassafras trees abound here but never grow to any considerable height. Chestnut trees appear now and then. The cockspur hawthorne (*Crataegus crus galli* L.) grows in the poorest soil, and has very long spines, which shows that it may be very advantageously planted in hedges, especially in a poor soil.

This night we lodged with a farmer, who had returned to his farm after the war was over. All his buildings except the big barn had been burnt.

June the 24th

The farm where we passed the night was the last in the province of New York, towards Canada, which had been left standing and which was now inhabited.[35] Further on we met other inhabitants, but they had no houses and lived in huts of boards, the houses having been destroyed during the war.

As we continued our journey we observed the country on both sides of the river was generally flat, but sometimes hilly, and large tracts of it covered with fir trees. Now and then we found some parts turned into plowed fields and meadows; however, the greater part was covered with woods. From Albany almost halfway to Saratoga the river ran very rapidly, and it was difficult to make headway northward. But afterwards it became very deep for the space of several miles and the water moved very slowly. The shores were very steep, though they were not very high. The river was two musketshots broad. In the afternoon it changed its direction, for hitherto it had been from north to south, but now it came from N.N.E. to S.S.W. and sometimes N.E. to S.W.[36]

Anthills are very scarce in America and I do not remember seeing a single one before I came to the Cohoes Falls. We observed a few in the woods today. The ants were the same species as our common red ones (*Formica rufa* L.). The anthills consisted chiefly of the slate-like crumbled stone which abounds here, there being no other material for them.

The Flora of Northern New York. Chestnut trees grew scattered in the woods. We were told that mulberry trees (*Morus rubra* L.) likewise grew wild here, but were rather scarce. This is the most northerly place where they grow in America; at least, they have not been observed further north. We met with wild parsnips every day but usually where the land was or had been cultivated. Hemp grew wild in great abundance near old plantations. The woods abounded with woodlice, which were extremely troublesome to us. The *Thuya occidentalis* L.[37] appeared along the shores of the river. I had not seen it there before. The trees which grew along the shores and on the adjacent hills, within our sight to-day were elms, birches, white firs, alders, dogwood trees, lime trees, red willows and chestnut trees. The American elder (*Sambucus Canadensis* L.) and the wild grapevines appeared only in places where the ground had been somewhat cultivated, as if they were desirous of being the companions of men. The lime trees and white walnut trees were the most numerous. The horn beams, with inflated cones (*Carpinus ostrya* L.), appeared now and then; but the water beech and water poplar never came within sight any more.

A little distance from Saratoga, we met two Indians in

their boats of bark, which could scarce contain more than one person.

Near Saratoga the river became shallow and rapid again. The ground had here been turned into grain fields and meadows, but on account of the war it lay waste.

Saratoga [38] was a fort built of wood by the English to stop the attacks of the French Indians upon the English inhabitants in these parts, and to serve as a rampart to Albany. It was situated on a hill, on the west side of the Hudson River, and was built of thick posts driven into the ground, close to each other, in the manner of palisades, forming a square, the length of whose sides was within reach of a musketshot. At each corner were the houses of the officers, and within the palisades the barracks, all of timber. This fort had been kept in order and was garrisoned till the last war, when the English themselves in 1747 set fire to it, not being able to defend themselves in it against the attacks of the French and their Indians; for as soon as a party of them went out of the fort, some of these enemies lay concealed and either took them all prisoners or shot them. [39]

I shall only mention one out of many artful tricks which were played here, and which both the English and French who were present here at that time told me repeatedly: a party of French with their Indians, concealed themselves one night in a thicket near the fort. In the morning some of their Indians, as they had previously resolved, went to have a nearer view of the fort. The English fired upon them as soon as they saw them at a distance. The Indians pretended to be wounded, fell down, got up again, ran a little way, and dropped again. Above half the garrison rushed out to take them prisoners, but as soon as they had come up with them, the French and the remaining Indians came out of the bushes between the fortress and the English, surrounded them and took them prisoners. Those who remained in the fort had

hardly time to shut the gates, nor could they fire upon the enemy, because they equally exposed their countrymen to danger, and they were vexed to see their enemies take and carry them off in their sight and under their cannon. Such French artifices as these made the English weary of their ill-planned fort. We saw some of the palisades still on the ground. There is an island in the river, near Saratoga, much better suited for a fortification. [40] The country is flat on both sides of the river near Saratoga and its soil fertile. The wood round about was generally cut down. The shores of the river were high, steep and consisted of mould. We saw some hills in the north beyond the distant forests. The inhabitants are of Dutch extraction, and bear an inveterate hatred to all Englishmen.

We lay over night in a little hut of boards erected by the people who had come to live here.

June the 25th

Several sawmills had been built here before the war, which were very profitable to the inhabitants on account of the abundance of wood which grows here. The boards were easily brought to Albany and thence to New York in rafts every spring with the high water; but all the mills were burnt at present.

This morning we proceeded up the river, but after we had advanced about an English mile, we encountered a waterfall which cost us a deal of pains before we could get our canoe over it. [41] The water was very deep just below the rapids, owing to its hollowing the rock out by the fall. In every place where we met with rocks in the river we found the water very deep, from two to four fathoms and upwards; because by finding a resistance it had worked a deeper channel into the ground. Above the falls the river was very deep again, the water sliding along silently, and increasing its speed suddenly near the shores. On both sides up to Fort Nicholson [42] the shore was covered with tall trees. After rowing several miles we passed another waterfall, which was longer and more dangerous than the preceding one. [43]

Giants' pots, which I have described in the *Memoirs* of the Royal Swedish Academy of Sciences, are abundant near the fall of the rock which extends across the river. The rock was almost dry at present because the river contains very little water at this season of the year. Some of the giants' pots were round, but in general they were oblong. At the bottom of most of them lay either stones or grit in abundance. Some were fifteen inches in diameter, but some were less. Their depth was likewise different and some that I observed were above two feet deep. It is plain that thy owed their origin to the whirling of the water round a pebble, which by that means was put in motion, together with the sand.

Through the Wilderness on Foot. We had intended to proceed close up to Fort Nicholson in the canoe, which would have been a great convenience to us; but we found it impossible to get over the upper falls, the canoe being heavy, and there being scarcely any water in the river except in one place where it flowed over the rock, and where it was impossible to get up on account of the steepness and the violence of the fall. We were accordingly obliged to leave our canoe here, and to carry our baggage through unfrequented woods to Fort Anne, on the river Woodcreek, which is a space from forty-three to fifty English miles, during which we were quite exhausted through the excess of heat. [44] Sometimes we had no other way of crossing deep rivers than by cutting down tall trees, which stood on their banks, and throwing them across the water. All the land we passed over this afternoon was rather level, without hills or stones, and entirely covered with a tall and thick forest in which we continually met trees which had fallen down, because no one made the least use of the woods. We passed the next night in the midst of the forest, plagued with mosquitoes, gnats and woodlice, and in fear of all kinds of snakes.

June the 26th

Early this morning we continued our journey through the woods, along the Hudson. There was an old path leading to Fort Nicholson, but it was so overgrown with grass that we discovered it only with great difficulty. In some places we found plenty of raspberries, some of which were already ripe.

Fort Nicholson is the place on the eastern shore of the Hudson where a wooden fortification formerly stood. We arrived there some time before noon and rested a while. Colonel Lydius [45] resided here till the beginning of the last war, chiefly with a view of carrying on a greater trade with the French Indians; but during the war, they burnt his house and took his son prisoner. The fort was situated on a plain, but at present the place is overgrown with a thicket. It was built in the year 1709, during the war which Queen Anne carried on against the French, and it was named after the brave English general Nicholson. [46] It was not so much a fort as a storehouse to Fort Anne. In the year 1711, when the English naval attempt upon Canada miscarried, the English themselves set fire to this place. The soil hereabout seems to be pretty fertile. The river Hudson passed close by here.

Some time in the afternoon we continued our journey. We had hitherto followed the eastern shore of the Hudson and gone almost due north; but now we left it, and went E.N.E. or N.E. across the woods, in order to come to the upper end of the river Woodcreek, which flows to Fort St. Frédéric, where we might go in a boat from the former place. The ground we passed over this afternoon was generally flat and somewhat low. Now and then we passed rivulets, which were generally dried up during this season. Sometimes we saw a little hill, but neither mountains nor stones, and the country was everywhere covered with tall and thick forests. The trees stood close and afforded a fine shade, but the pleasure which we enjoyed from it was lessened by the incredible quantity of gnats which fill the woods. . . .

We lodged this night near a brook, in order to be sufficiently supplied with water, which was not everywhere at hand during this season. The mosquitoes, punchins or gnats and the woodlice were very troublesome. Our fear of snakes and especially of the Indians made the night's rest very uncertain and insecure.

Punchins,[47] as the Dutch call them, are the little gnats (*Culex pulicaris* L.) which abound here. They are very minute, and their wings grey, with black spots. They are often ten times worse than the larger ones (*Culex pipiens* L.) or mosquitoes, for their size renders them next to imperceptible; they are everywhere careless of their lives, suck their fill of blood and cause a burning pain.

We heard several great trees fall of themselves in the night, though it was so calm that not a leaf stirred. They made a dreadful cracking noise.

June the 27th

We continued our journey in the morning. We found the country like that which we passed over yesterday, except for a few hills. Early this morning we plainly heard a waterfall or some rushing rapids in the Hudson River.[48] In every part of the forest we found trees thrown down either through storms or age; but none were cut down, there being no inhabitants. And though the wood was very fine, nobody made use of it. We found it very

difficult to get over such trees, because they had blocked all the paths, and close to them was the chief retreat of rattlesnakes during the intense heat of the day.

Arrival at Fort Anne. About two o'clock this afternoon we arrived at Fort Anne. It lies on the Woodcreek River, which is here at its source no bigger than a little brook. We stayed here all day, and the next, in order to make a new boat of bark, because there was no possibility to go down the river to Fort St. Frédéric without one. We arrived in time, for one of our guides fell ill that morning and could not have gone any further with his load. If he had been worse, we should have been obliged to stop on his account, which would have put us under great difficulties, as our provisions would soon have been exhausted, and from the wilderness where we were we could not have arrived at any inhabited place in less than three or four days. Happily we reached the wished-for place, and the sick man had time to rest and recover.

Around Fort Anne we found a number of common mice. They were probably the offspring of those which were brought to the fort in the soldiers' provisions, at the time when it was kept in a state of defense.—We saw some apple and plum trees, which were certainly planted when the fort was in a good condition.

June the 28th

The American elm grew in abundance in the forest hereabouts. There were two kinds of it. One was called white elm, on account of the inside of the tree being white. It was more plentiful than the other species, which was called the red elm, because the color of the wood was reddish. The boats here were commonly made of the white bark. With the bark of hickory, which was employed as bast, they sewed the elmbark together, and with the bark of the red elm they joined the ends of the boat so close as to keep the water out. They beat the bark between two stones or, for want of them, between two pieces of wood.

The Making of a Bark Boat. The making of the boat took up half our time yesterday and all to-day. . . . The building of these boats is not always quick; for sometimes it happens that after peeling the bark off an elm, and carefully examining it, it is found pierced with holes and splits, or it is too thin to venture one's life in. In such a case another elm must be found; and it sometimes happens that several elms must be stripped of their bark, before one is found fit for a boat. The boat which we made was big enough to carry four persons, with our baggage, which weighed somewhat more than a man.

All possible precautions must be taken in rowing on the rivers and lakes of these parts with a bark boat. For as the rivers, and even the lakes, contain a number of fallen trees, which are commonly hidden under the water, the boat may easily run against a sharp branch which will tear half the boat away, if one is rowing energetically, exposing the people in it to great danger, where the water is very deep, and especially if such a branch also holds the boat fast.

The boarding of such a frail vessel must be done with great care, and for the greater safety without shoes. For with the shoes on, and still more with a sudden leap into the boat, the heels may easily pierce the bottom of it, which might sometimes result in dire consequences, especially when the boat is near a rock or close to deep water; and such places are common in the lakes and rivers here.

I never saw the *mosquitoes* more plentiful in any part of America than they are here. They were so eager for our blood that we could not rest all night, though we had surrounded ourselves with fire.

Woodlice (Acarus Americanus L.) abound here, and were more plentiful than on any part of the journey. Scarcely had a person sat down before a whole swarm of them crept upon his clothes. They caused us as much inconvenience as the gnats had the previous night, and continued to do so during the whole, short time we stayed here. Their bite is very disagreeable and they would prove very dangerous if any of them should creep into a man's ear, from whence it is difficult to extract them. There are examples of people whose ears were swelled to the size of a fist on account of one of these insects creeping into them and biting. More is said about them in the description which I have given to the Royal Swedish Academy of Sciences.

The whipperiwill, or whippoorwill, cried all night on every side. Fireflies flew in large numbers through the woods at night.

A Colonial "Pork-Barrell"! Fort Anne, where we now encamped, derives its name from Queen Anne; for in her time it served as a fortification against the French. It lies on the western side of the river Woodcreek, which is here as small as a brook, of a fathom's breadth, and may be waded through in any part during this season. The fort is built in the same manner as the forts Saratoga and Nicholson, that is to say, of palisades, within which were blockhouses providing lodgings for the officers. The whole consisted of wood, because it was erected only with a view for protection against wandering marauders. It is built on a little rising ground which runs obliquely to the river. The country round about it is partly flat, partly hilly, and partly marshy, but it consists merely of earth, and not a stone could be found there even if you would pay for it. General Nicholson built this fort in the year 1709; but at the conclusion of the war against the French it shared the fate of Saratoga and Fort Nicholson, being in 1711 burnt by the English themselves.[49] The facts were these: in 1711 the English resolved to attack Canada, by land and by sea, at the same time. A powerful English fleet sailed up the St. Lawrence to besiege Quebec, and General Nicholson, who was the greatest promoter of this expedition, led a large army to this place by land, to attack Montreal simultaneously; but a great part of the English fleet was shipwrecked in the St. Lawrence, and obliged to return to New England. The news of this misfortune was immediately communicated to General Nicholson, who was advised to retreat. Captain [Walter] Butler, who commanded Fort Mohawk during my stay in America, told me that he had been at Fort Anne in 1711 and that General Nicholson was about to leave it and go down the river Woodcreek in boats ready for that purpose, when he received the accounts of the disaster which had befallen the fleet. He was so enraged that he endeavored to tear his wig, but it being too strong for him he flung it to the ground and trampled on it, crying out, "Roguery, treachery!" He then set fire to the fort and returned. We saw the remains of the burnt palisades in the ground, and I asked my guides why the English had gone to such great expense in erecting the fort, and why they had afterwards burnt it without any previous consideration? They replied that it was done to have another opportunity to extract money from the government; for the latter would appropriate a large sum for the rebuilding of the fort, the biggest proportion of which would perhaps reach the pockets of a few of the promoting authorities, who would then again erect only a wretched fort. They further told me that some of the richest people in Albany had promoted their poor relations to the places for supplying the army with bread, etc., with a view to patch up their broken fortunes, and that they had acquired such wealth as rendered them equal to the richest inhabitants of Albany.

Excessive Heat. The heat was excessive to-day, especially in the afternoon when it was quite calm. We were on the very spot where Fort Anne formerly stood; it was a little place free from trees, but surrounded with them on every side, where the sun had full liberty to heat the air. After noon it grew as warm as in a hot bath, and I never felt a greater heat. I found it difficult to breathe and it seemed to me as if my lungs could not draw in a sufficient quantity of air. I was more eased when I went down into the valleys, and especially along the Woodcreek. I tried to fan the air to me with my hat, but it only increased the difficulty of breathing and I received the greatest relief when I went to the water, and in a shady place frequently sprinkled some water in the air before me. My companions also suffered a great deal, but they did not find such difficulty in breathing as I had experienced. However, towards evening the air became somewhat cooler.

June the 29th

Having completed our boat, after a great deal of labor and trouble, we continued our journey this Sunday morning. Our provisions, which were much diminished, urged us to make great haste, for being obliged to carry everything on our backs through this wilderness to Fort Anne, we had not been able to take a great quantity of provisions with us, having been compelled to include in our baggage several other very necessary things; nevertheless we always ate very heartily. As there was very little water in the river, and several trees had fallen across it, which frequently stopped the boat, I left the men in it and walked along the shore with Jungström. The ground on both sides of the river was so low that it must be under water in spring and autumn. The shores were covered with several sorts of trees which stood at moderate distances from each other, and a great deal of grass grew between them. The trees afforded the fine shade which is so necessary and agreeable in this hot season: but the pleasure it gave was considerably lessened by the number of gnats which we encountered. The soil was extremely rich.

Beaver Dams. As we came lower down the river, the dams, which the beavers had made in it, produced new difficulties. These laborious animals had carried together all sorts of boughs and branches and placed them across the river, putting mud and clay in betwixt them, to stop the water. They had bit off the ends of the branches as neatly as if they had been chopped off with a hatchet. The grass about these places was trod down by them, and in the neighborhood of the dams we sometimes came upon paths in the grass, where the beavers probably had dragged trees along. We found a row of dams before us, which stopped us a considerable while, as we could not get forwards with the boat till we had cut through them.

A Discovery. As soon as the river was more open we got into the boat again, and continued our journey in it. The breadth of the river, however, did not exceed eight or nine yards, and frequently it was not above three or four yards broad, and generally so shallow that our boat got on with difficulty. Sometimes it acquired such a sudden depth that we could not reach the ground with sticks of seven feet in length. The stream was very rapid in some places and very slow in others. The shores were low at first, but afterwards remarkably high and steep, and now and then a rock projected into the water which always caused a great depth in such places. The rocks consisted here of a gray quartz, mixed with gray limestone, lying in strata. The water in the river was very clear and transparent, and we saw several little paths leading to it from the woods, said to be made by beavers and other animals, which came here to drink. After

going a little more than three British miles we came to a place where a fire was yet burning and we could see from the trodden grass that people had been lying there the night before,[50] and then we little thought that we had narrowly escaped death the night before, as we heard this evening. Now and then we ran into trees lying across the river, and some beaver dams, which obstructed our way.

How Kalm Escaped Death. Towards night we met a French sergeant, and five French soldiers, who had been sent by the commander of Fort St. Frédéric, to accompany three Englishmen to Saratoga, and to defend them in case of necessity against six French Indians who had gone to be revenged on the English for killing the brother of one of them in the last war. The peace had already been concluded at that time, but as it had not yet been proclaimed in Canada the Indians thought they could take this step; therefore they silently got away, contrary to the order of the Governor of Montreal, and proceeded towards the English plantations. We here had occasion to perceive the care of Providence for us, in escaping these savage barbarians. We had found the grass trod down all the day long, but had had no thoughts of danger, as we believed that everything was quiet and peaceable. We were afterwards informed, that these Indians had trod the grass down, and passed the last night in the place where we found the burning brands in the morning. The usual route which they were to have taken was by Fort Anne, but to shorten their journey they had gone an unfrequented path. If they had gone on towards Fort Anne, they would have met us without doubt, and looking upon us all as Englishmen, for whose blood they were thirsting, they could easily have surprised and shot us all, and by that means have been rid of the trouble of going any further to satisfy their cruelty. We were not a little agitated when the Frenchmen told us how near death we had been to-day. We passed the night here, and though the French repeatedly advised and desired me not to venture any further with my English company, but to follow them to the first English settlement, and then back to Fort St. Frédéric, yet I resolved, with the protection of the Almighty, to continue my journey the next day.

Wild Pigeons. We saw immense numbers of the wild pigeons . . . flying in the woods, and which sometimes come in incredible flocks to the southern English colonies, without the inhabitants there knowing where they come from.[51] They have their nests in trees here, and almost all night make a rustling, whirring noise and cooing in the trees where they roost. The French shot a great number of them, and gave us some, in which we found a great quantity of the seeds of the elm, which evidently demonstrated the care of Providence in supplying them with food; for in May the seeds of the red maple, which abounds here, are ripe, and drop from the trees and are eaten by the pigeons during that time: afterwards, the seeds of the elm ripen, which then become their food, till other seeds mature for them. Their flesh is the most palatable of any bird's flesh I have ever tasted.

Falling Trees. Almost every night we heard some trees crack and fall while we lay here in the wood, though the air was so calm that not a leaf stirred. The reason for this breaking I am totally unacquainted with. Perhaps the dew or something else loosens the roots of trees more at night; or perhaps something falls too heavily on the branches on one side of the tree. It may be that the above-mentioned wild pigeons settle in such quantities on one tree as to weigh it down; or perhaps the tree begins to bend more and more to one side from its center of gravity, making the weight continuously greater for the roots to support till it comes to the point when it can no longer keep upright, which may as well happen in the midst of a calm night as at any other time. When the wind blows hard it is reckoned very dangerous to sleep or walk in the woods on account of the many trees which fall in them; and even when it is very calm there is some danger in passing under very large and old trees. I was told, in several parts of America that the storms or hurricanes sometimes pass over only a small part of the woods and tear down the trees in it; and I have had opportunities of confirming the truth of this observation by finding places in the forests where almost all the trees had crashed down, and lay in one direction.

Tea, which is brought in great quantities from China, is differently esteemed by different people, and I think we would be as well, and our purses much better, if we were without both tea and coffee. However, I must be impartial, and mention in praise of tea that if it be useful it must certainly be so in summer on such journeys as mine through a vast wilderness, where one cannot carry wine or other liquors and where water is generally unfit for use, being full of insects. In such cases it is very refreshing when boiled and made into tea, and I cannot sufficiently describe the fine taste it has under such circumstances. It relieves a weary traveller more than can be imagined, as I myself have experienced, and as have also a great many others who have travelled through the primeval forests of America. On such journeys tea is found to be almost as necessary as food.

June the 30th

This morning we left our boat to the Frenchmen, who used it to carry their provisions; for we could not make any further use of it on account of the number of trees which the French had thrown across the river during the last war to prevent the attacks of the English upon Canada.[52] The Frenchmen gave us leave to make use of one of their birch canoes, which they had left behind them, about six miles from the place where we passed the last night. Thus we continued our journey on foot, along the river, and found the country flat, with some little vales here and there. It was everywhere covered with tall deciduous trees, among which the beech, the elm, the American lime tree, and the sugar maple were the most numerous. The trees stood some distance from each other, and the soil in which they grew was extremely rich.

Description of the Country. After we had walked about a Swedish mile, or six English miles, we came to the place where the six Frenchmen had left their bark boats, of which we took one, and rowed down the river, which was now between nineteen and twenty yards broad.[53] The banks on both sides were very smooth and not very high. . . . As we went further on we saw high steep hills on the riverside, partly covered with trees; but in other parts the banks consisted of a swampy turf ground, which gave way when it was walked upon and had some similarity to the sides of our marshes which my country-men are now about to drain. In those parts where the ground was low and flat we did not see any stones either on the ground or on the softer shore, and both sides of the river, when they are not hilly, were covered with tall elms, American lime trees, sugar maples, beeches, hickory trees, some water beeches and white walnut trees.

On our left we saw an old fortification of stones laid above one another; but nobody could tell me whether the Indians or the Europeans had built it.

Kalm's Party Goes Astray. We had rowed very fast all afternoon in order to make a good distance, and we thought that we were upon the right road, but found ourselves greatly mistaken; for towards night we observed that the reeds in the river bent towards us; whereas, if we had been on the right body of water it should have run in the direction we were going. We likewise observed from the trees which lay across the river, that nobody had lately passed that way, though we should have seen the tracks of the Frenchmen in the grass along the shore, when they brought their boat over these trees. At last we plainly saw that the river flowed against us, and we were convinced that we had gone twelve English miles and upwards upon a wrong river, which obliged us to return, and to row till very late at night. We sometimes thought, through fear, that the Indians, who had gone to murder some English, would unavoidably meet us. Though we rowed very fast, we were not able to-day to get halfway back to the place where we first left the right river.[54]

The most odoriferous effluvia sometimes came from the banks of the river at nightfall, but we could not determine what flowers diffused them. However, we supposed they chiefly arose from the *Asclepias syriaca,* and the *Apocynum androsaemifolium.*

The muskrats could likewise be smelled at night. They had many holes in the shores even with the surface of the water.

We passed the night on an island, where we could not sleep on account of the gnats. We did not venture to make a fire, for fear the Indians should find us out and kill us. We heard several of their dogs barking in the woods, at a great distance from us, which added to our uneasiness in this wilderness.

July the 1st

At daybreak we got up, and rowed a good while before we got to the place where we left the true course. The country which we passed was the poorest and most disagreeable imaginable. We saw nothing but a row of amazingly high mountains covered with woods,[55] steep and rough on their sides, so that we found it difficult to get to an open place in order to land and boil our dinner. In many places the ground, which was very smooth, was under water, and looked like the sections of our Swedish morasses which are being drained; for this reason the Dutch in Albany call these parts the "Drowned Lands." Some of the mountains run from S.S.W. to N.N.E., and along the river they form perpendicular shores, and are full of rocks of different sizes. The river flows for several miles from south to north.

The wind blew from the north all day, and made it very hard work for us to travel on, though we all rowed as hard as we could, for what little we had left of our provisions was eaten to-day at breakfast. The river was frequently an English mile and more broad, then it became narrow again, and so on alternately; but upon the whole it kept a good breadth, and was surrounded on both sides by high mountains.

Approaching Fort St. Frédéric. About six o'clock in the evening we arrived at a point of land about twelve English miles from Fort St. Frédéric. Behind this point the river is converted into a spacious bay,[56] and as the wind still kept blowing pretty strong from the north, it was impossible for us to proceed, since we were extremely tired. We were therefore obliged to pass the night here, in spite of the remonstrances of our hungry stomachs.

It is to be attributed to the peculiar grace of God towards us that we met the above-mentioned Frenchmen on our journey, and that they gave us leave to take one of their bark boats. It hardly happens once in three years that the French take this route to Albany; for they commonly pass over Lake St. Sacrement, or, as the English call it, Lake George, which is the nearer and better way, and everybody wondered why they took this troublesome one. If we had not gotten their large, strong boat, and

had been obliged to keep the one we had made, we would in all probability have been very ill off; for to venture upon the great bay during the least wind with so wretched a vessel, would have been a great piece of temerity, and we should have been in danger of starving if we had waited for a calm. For being without fire-arms, and these wildernesses having but few quadrupeds,[57] we would have been obliged to subsist upon frogs and snakes, which (especially the latter) abound in these parts. I can never think of this journey, without reverently acknowledging the peculiar care and providence of the merciful Creator.

July the 2nd

At Crown Point. Early this morning we set out on our journey again, it being moonlight and calm, and we feared lest the wind should change and become unfavorable to us if we stopped any longer. We all rowed as hard as possible, and happily arrived about eight in the morning at Fort St. Frédéric, which the English call Crown Point.[58] Monsieur Lusignan, the governor, received us very politely. . . .[59]

July the 5th

Indian Revenge. While we were at dinner we heard several times a repeated, disagreeable, bloodcurdling outcry, some distance from the fort, in the river Woodcreek: Mr. Lusignan, the commander, told us this cry was ominous, because he could conclude from it that the Indians, whom we escaped near Fort Anne, had completed their design of avenging the death of one of their brethren upon the English, and that their shouts showed that they had killed an Englishman. As soon as I came to the window, I saw their boat, with a long pole at the front, at the extremity of which they had put a bloody human scalp. As soon as they had landed, we heard that they, being six in number, had continued their journey (from the place where we saw marks of their passing the night) till they had gotten within the English boundaries, where they found a man and his son employed in harvesting. They crept on towards this man and shot him dead. This happened near the very village where the English, two years before, killed the brother of one of these Indians, who had gone out to attack them. According to their custom they cut off the scalp of the dead man and took it with them, together with his clothes and his son, who was about nine years old. As soon as they came within a mile of Fort St. Frédéric, they put the scalp on a pole in the fore part of the boat, and shouted as a sign of their success. They were dressed in shirts, as usual, but some of them had put on the dead man's clothes; one his coat, the other his breeches, another his hat, etc. Their faces were painted with vermilion, with which their shirts were marked across the shoulders. Most of them had great rings in their ears, which seemed to be a great inconvenience to them, as they were obliged to hold them when they leaped or did anything which required a violent motion. Some of them had girdles of the skins of rattlesnakes, with the rattles on them; the son of the murdered man had noth-ing but his shirt, breeches, and cap, and the Indians had marked his shoulders with red. When they got on shore they took hold of the pole on which the scalp was put, and danced and sung at the same time. Their object of taking the boy was to carry him to their tent, to bring him up instead of their dead brother, and afterwards to marry him to one of their relations so that he might become one of them. Notwithstanding they had perpetrated this act of violence in time of peace, contrary to the command of the governor of Montreal, and to the advice of the governor of St. Frédéric, the latter could not at present deny them provisions and whatever they wanted for their journey, because he did not think it advisable to exasperate them; but when they came to Montreal, the governor called them to account for his action, and took the boy from them, whom he afterwards sent to his relations. Mr. Lusignan asked them what they would have done to me and my companions, if they had met us in the wilderness. They replied that as it was their chief intention to take their revenge on the Englishmen in the village where his brother had been killed, they would have left us alone. But it would have depended on the humor they were in when we first came in sight. However, the commander and all the Frenchmen said that what had happened to me was infinitely safer and better.

5.
Richard Smith 1769*

INTRODUCTION: Twenty years after Peter Kalm traveled through the frontier regions of the upper Hudson Valley, the province of New York was still one of the smallest in population and resources of all the thirteen colonies. In 1769 it contained less than 150,000 people, ranked seventh in population, and had less than half of the population of Virginia and was even inferior to the small province of Maryland.

The pioneer stage was therefore still very much in evidence when Richard Smith (1735–1803), a New Jersey lawyer, diarist and later member of the Continental Congress, journeyed up the Hudson in the spring of 1769. Unlike the Dutch missionary, Jasper Dankers, who came in quest of religious asylum, or the Swedish naturalist, Peter Kalm, who came in quest of scientific knowledge, Richard Smith's mission could not have been more thoroughly American, and the account of his voyage on the Hudson affords a striking contrast to the European narratives of his two predecessors. A native-born American, Smith traveled in quest of economic opportunity. When the French and Indian Wars came to a close and the Treaty of Fort Stanwix (1768) released a large area of central New York to white settlement, Smith became one of several proprietors who received a grant of land under the "Otego Patent" and immediately set out with several surveyors to inspect his new lands. The grant comprised 4,000 acres of a 69,000-acre tract that lay in the present Otsego County close by the headwaters of the Susquehanna River. An inveterate diarist, Smith kept a detailed journal of the circuitous route he followed up the Hudson and Mohawk and down the Susquehanna and Delaware Rivers. The excerpt that follows is restricted to the interval between May 5th and May 11th when he took a sloop from New York to Albany. The account is a diary in the strict sense of the term: Smith had no intention of converting his on-the-spot observations into a formal treatise or travel book à la Peter Kalm's *Travels in North America*. We may therefore miss Kalm's long sedate sentences or reflective cast of mind; but we gain a businessman's scrupulous regard for facts and a wealth of topical detail that can often compress more living history in a single paragraph than can pages of descriptive analysis.

The journey that Smith took in the spring of 1769 was not without its practical results. He helped to promote settlement in the "Otego Patent"; built "Smith Hall" in what is now the town of Laurens; moved from Burlington, New Jersey, to his frontier home in 1790; and lived to see his son become the first sheriff of the new Otsego County. He was an American pioneer.

* Excerpts from Francis W. Halsey's edition of Richard Smith's *A Tour of Four Great Rivers, the Hudson, Mohawk, Susquehanna and Delaware in 1769* (New York: 1906), pp. 3–18.

WITH A VIEW to survey a large tract of Land then lately purchased from the Indians I departed from Burlington for Otego May 3ᵈ 1769 in company with Richᵈ Wells, now of Philadelphia and the Surveyors Joseph Biddle Junʳ and William Ridgway as also John Hicks. . . .

May 5ᵗʰ In the Mornᵍ we arrived at Paulus Hook [1] Ferry, went over and dined at Burns's Tavern [2] in New York and this we deemed an indifferent House; here we saw the Govʳ Sir Henry Moore [3] and other noted men. In the afternoon we took Passage in a sloop, Richᵈ Scoonhoven, Skipper, for Albany; had fine weather and found it extremely agreeable Sailing with the country seats of the Citizens on the Right Hand, and the high lands of Bergen [4] on the left and the Narrows abaft. We sailed about 13 or 14 miles and then came to Anchor for the

Night; the great Rains just before we set out had caused the Water of the North River to tast almost fresh at this place. The Bergen Shore is high and Rocky and the Eastern Side diversified with Hill and Gully.

6th These Albany Sloops contain very convenient Cabins. We eat from a regular Table accommodated with Plates, Knives and Forks and enjoyed our Tea in the Afternoon. We had laid in some Provision at N. York and the Capt some more, so that we lived very well. Our Commander is very jocose and good company. About 7 oCloc we passed Spite the Devil (why so called I know not),5 or Harlem River, which divides the Manhattan Island from the Connecticut.6 The Entrance here appears to be narrow, bounded on each side with high Land; Kings Bridge said to be about a Mile from this Entrance but not in sight.7 The Bergen Coast continues to be lined with lofty Rocks, thinly overspread with Cedars, Spruce and Shrubs.

Nearly opposite to Tappan we took a Turn on Shore to a Part of Col. Philips's Manor,8 from the Hills of which are beautiful Prospects. All the Country on both sides of the River from the City is hilly. The Manor of Philipsburg according to our Information, extends about —Miles on the River and about 6 Miles back and is joined about by the Manor of Cortland.9 This Morng the Sloop passed by Col. Philips's Mansion House and Gardens situate in a pleasant Valley between Highlands. The country hereabouts excels ours by far in fine prospects and the Trees and Vegetables appear to be as forward almost as those at Burlington when we left; but I conceive that our countrymen excel the People here in cultivation. Hardly any Houses appear on the Bergen Side from Paulus Hook to the Line of Orange County.

The Tenant for Life here tells me he pays to Col. Philips only £7, per Annum for about 200 acres of Land and thinks it an extravagant Rent because, on his demise or Sale, his Son or Vendee is obliged to pay to the Landlord one Third of the Value of the Farm for a Renewal of the Lease. The Skipper have here 5 coppers for a Quart of Milk and Mr Wells bought Ten small Rock Fish for 12 coppers. The Freight of a Bushel of Wheat from Albany to N York according to our Skipper is Four Pence, of a Barrel of Flour one shilling and of a Hogshead of Flour 7/6 and he thinks they have the same Rates from Kaatskill. In the Night we ran ground among the Highlands about 50 Miles for N.York between Orange and Duchess Counties. The Highlands here are not so lofty as I expected and the River at this place appears to be Half a Mile wide.

7th Our Company went on Shore up the Rocks to a miserable Farm and House in Orange and left with the Farmer a Direction for Otego 10 as he and a few of his Neighbors seemed desirous to seek new Habitations. He pays Seven Pounds a Year Rent for about 100 acres including Rocks and Mountains. Hudson's River is straight to the Highlands, but thro them very crooked, many strawberries are to be seen about the Banks and Stony Felds. Martiler's Rock 11 stands in a part of the River which is exceedingly deep with a bold shore encircled on either Hand by aspiring Mountains and thro them there is a View of a fine Country above. Here it is chiefly that the sudden Flaws sometimes take the River Vessels for which Reason they have upright Masts for the more expeditious lowering of the Sails on any sudden Occasion. Beyond the above Rock lies Pollaple's Island.12

But a few Wheat and Rye Fields appear along the East Side of the River from N York hither and a very few Fields are ploughed as if intended for Indian Corn. The Lands seem proper for Sheep or perhaps (if the Severity of our Winters will admit) for Vineyards. On the West Side among the Highlands are only a few Houses seated in the small Vallies between the Moun-

7. *A View of Phillipps's Manner and the Rocks on the Hudson or North River, North America,* anonymous engraving, 1784; courtesy of Sleepy Hollow Restorations, Tarrytown, N.Y.

"This Morn⁣ᵍ the Sloop passed by Col. Philips's Mansion House and Gardens situate in a pleasant Valley between Highlands."

Though depicting the manor fifteen years after Richard Smith saw it, the scene is substantially the same. When Charles Carroll sailed up the river in 1776 with Benjamin Franklin, he called it a "pretty situation near the river." The major changes occurred in the 19th century, when factories arose on the stream in the foreground and the manor house became the city hall of the surrounding city of Yonkers.

A VIEW OF PHILLIPPS'S MANNER
(NOW YONKERS)
AND THE ROCKS ON THE HUDSON OR NORTH RIVER, NORTH AMERICA
June 18th 1784   DR fecit

74

tains. From the Streights between Butter Hill and Broken Neck Hill [13] and below them there is a distant Prospect of the Kaatskill Mount^s to the N.W. Murderers Creek [14] which runs by the Butter Hill, divides the Counties of Orange and Ulster, there are a few Houses at the Mouth of the Creek. The soil in these Parts is broken, stony and few places proper for the Plow. What grain we saw growing was but indifferent.

About one oCloc we passed by the Town of New Windsor on the Left, seeming at a Distance to consist of about 50 Houses Stores and Out houses placed without any regular Order. Here end the Highlands. This town has some Trade and probably hereafter may be a place of Consequence as the fine Country of Goshen is said to lie back about 12 or more Miles. On the East Side of the River a little above Windsor is the Fish Kill and Landing whence the Sloops carry the Produce of that Side for Market. The North River is here thought to be near Two Miles wide and the general range of the Highlands by the Compass as taken on the N. Side by our Surveyors is W.S.W. and E.N.E.

We took a Turn on Shore at Denton's Mill [15] called 60 Miles from N. York and walked above Two Miles down the River to Newbury a small scattered village and to Denton's Ferry. We found excellent Cyder at both. The New England men cross here and hereabouts almost daily for Susquehannah; their Rout is from hence to the Minisink's accounted only 40 Miles distant,[16] and we are told that 700 of their Men are to be in that Country by the First of June next. A sensible Woman informed Us that Two Men of her Neighborhood have been several Times across to those Parts of Susquehanna which lie in York Government and here the people say our Rout by the Albany is above 100 Miles out of the Way. This is since found to be true, yet that Rout is used because it is the only Waggon Road to Lake Otsego.

The Lands near Hudsons River now appear less Hilly tho not level and few Settlements are visible here and there; the Houses and Improvements not extraordinary. Denton's Mill above mentioned has a remarkable large Fall of Water forming a beautiful Cascade. We saw several other Cascades and Rills; divers Limekills and much Lime Stone on each Shore hereaway and some Appearance of Meadow Land of which we have hitherto seen very little. Lime Stone, it is said, may be found on either side of the River from the Highlands to Sopus. We have the pleasure of seeing sundry Sloops and Shallops passing back and forwards with the Produce of the Country and Returns. In the Evening we sailed thro' a remarkable Undulation of the Water for a Mile or Two which tossed the Sloop about much and made several passengers sick, the more observable as the Passage before and after was quite smooth and little Wind stirring at the Time. We anchored between Two high Shores bespread with spruce, Chestnut Oaks and other Trees, very like the towering Banks of Bergen.

8th There is a high road from New York to Albany on both sides of the River, but that on the East side is most frequented; both Roads have a View now and then of the River. Poughkeepsing the County Town of Duchess stands above the Fishkill a little beyond the rough Water already noted. We passed the Town in the Night. Slate Stone Rocks are on the West Shore at and below Little Sopus [17] from whence N York has of late been supplied. They reckon Little Sopus Island to be Half Way between N York and Albany. The Weather yesterday and to day very warm but the Mornings and Evenings are cool. Our Skipper says there are at Albany 31 Sloops all larger than this, which carry from 400 to 500 Barrels of Flour each, trading constantly from thence to York and that they make Eleven or 12 Trips a year each. The general Course of Hudson's River as taken by compass is N and by E. and S. and by W. in some Places North and South. Between the Highlands and Kaatskill both these Mountains are in view at the same time.

At Two ocloc we arrived off the Walkill, there are 2 or 3 Houses at the Mouth of the Creek and a Trade carried on in Six or Seven Sloops. Kingston [18] the County Town of Ulster stands about Two Miles distant but not visible from the Water. The Kaatskill Mountains to the N.W. appear to be very near tho they are at a considerable Distance. The Country on both Sides continues still hilly and rugged and what Wheat is growing, looks much thrown out and gullied—more Houses and Improvements shew themselves along the Sopus Shore and Opposite being an old settled Country.

Our Vessel came to anchor a little above the Walkill about 60 Miles from Albany. We went on shore to Two stone Farm Houses on Beekman Manor [19] in the County of Duchess. The Men were absent and the Women and children could speak no other Language than Low Dutch. Our Skipper was interpreter. One of these Tenants for Life or a very long Term or for Lives (uncertain which) pays 20 Bushels of Wheat in Kind for 97 Acres of cleared Land and Liberty to get Wood for necessary uses any where in the Manor. Twelve eggs sold here for six pence, Butter 14ᵈ per pound and 2 shad cost 6ᵈ One woman was very neat and the Iron Hoops of her Pails scowered bright. The Houses are mean; we saw one Piece of Good Meadow which is scarce here away. The Wheat was very much thrown out, the Aspect of the Farms rough and hilly like all the rest and the soil a stiff clay. One Woman had Twelve good countenanced Boys and Girls all clad in Homespun both Linen and Woolen. Here was a Two wheeled Plow drawn by 3 horses abreast, and a Scythe with a Short crooked Handle and a Kind of Hook both used to cut down Grain for the

Sickle is not much known in Albany County or in this Part of Duchess.

9ᵗʰ We arose in the Mornᵍ opposite to a large Brick House on the East Side belonging to Mᵣ Livingston's Father, Robᵗ R. Livingston the Judge,[20] in the Lower Manor of Livingston. Albany County is now on either Hand, and sloping Hills here and there covered with Grain like all the rest we have seen, much thrown out by the Frost of last Winter.

Landing on the West Shore we found a Number of People fishing with a Sein; they caught plenty of Shad and Herring and use Canoes altogether having long, neat and strong Ropes made by the People themselves of Elm Bark. Here we saw the first Indian a Mohicon named Hans clad in no other Garment than a shattered Blanket; he lives near the Kaatskill and had a Scunk Skin for his Tobacco Pouch. The Tavern of this Place is most wretched. Trees are out in Leaf. Cattle and Sheep, nothing different from ours, are now feeding on the Grass which seems to be nearly as forward as with us when we left Burlington, the Trees quite as forward and the White Pine is common. One Shad taken with the rest had a Lamprey Eel about 7 inches long fastened to his Back.

I was informed here by a person concerned in measuring it that the Distance from Kaatskill Landing to Schoharie is 32½ Miles reckoned to Capᵗ Eckerson's House, a good Waggon Road and Produce broᵗ down daily; from thence to Cherry Valley [21] half a Day's Journey; that People are now laying out a New Road from Sopus Kill to Schoharie which is suppoed to be about 32½ Miles. Sopus Creek is about 11 Miles below Kaatskill Creek [22] and a Mile below where we landed. They say that 7 or 8 Sloops belong to Sopus.[23] The Fish are the same in Hudsons River above the Salt Water as in the Delaware. The Skipper bought a Parcel of Fish here cheap. These Fishermen draw their Nets oftner than ours not stopping between the Draughts.

At 3 o'Cloc we passed by the German Camp [24] a small Village so called having Two Churches, situated on the East side of the River, upon a rising Ground which shews the Place to Advantage. Some distance further on the same Side of the River we sailed by the Upper Manor House of Livingston. [25] A Quantity of low cripple Land may be seen on the opposite Side and this reaches 4 miles to the Kaatskill called 36 miles from Albany. Off the mouth of this Creek we have a View of the large House built by John Dyer the Person who made the Road from hence to Schoharie at the expense of £400, if common Report may be credited. [26]

Two Sloops belong to Kaatskill, a little beyond the Mouth whereof lies the large Island of Vastric. [27] There is a House on the North Side of the Creek and another with several Saw Mills on the South Side but no town as we expected. [28] Sloops go no further than Dyer House about Half a Mile up the Creek. The Lands on both Sides of Kaatskill belong to Vanberger, Van Vechté, Salisbury, Dubois and a Man in York. Their Lands, as our Skipper says, extend up the Creek 12 Miles to Barker the English Gentleman his Settlement. The Creek runs thro the Kaatskill Mount.s said hereabouts to be at the Distance of 12 or 14 Miles from the North River but there are Falls above which obstruct the Navigation.

We landed in the Evening on the Kaatskill Shore 4 Miles above the Creek [29] but could gain no satisfactory Intelligence only that the [Dowager] Dutchess of Gordon and her Husband Col. Staats Long Morris [30] were just gone from Dyer's House for Cherry Valley and Susqueh.h with Two Waggons; they went by the Way of Freehold at the Foot of the Mountains on this Side and so over them to Schoharie guessed to be about 32½ Miles as was said before. [31]

10.th We passed by Sunday Islands whereof Scutters Island affords a good low Bottom fit for Meadow and some of it improved. Bear's Island is said to be the Beginning of the Manor of Renslaerwic which extends on both Sides of the River. The Lords of the Manors are called by the common People Patroons. Bearen Island or Bears Island just mentioned is reputed to be 12 Miles below Albany. [32] Cojemans Houses with Two Grist Mills and Two Saw Mills stand a little above on the West Side and opposite is an Island of about Two Acres covered with young Button wood Trees which Island, our Skipper says, has arisen there to his Knowledge within 16 years and since he has navigated the River.

More low, bottom Land is discovered as we pass up, generally covered with Trees; being cleared might be made good Meadow by Banking an Improvement to which the Inhabitants are altogether Strangers. The upper End of Scotoc's Island [33] is a fine cleared Bottom not in Grass but partly in Wheat and partly in Tilth. However there was one rich Meadow improved. We saw the first Batteaux a few Miles below Albany, [34] Canoes being the Common Craft. One Staat's House is prettily fixed on a rising Ground in a low Island, the City of Albany being 3 miles aHead. We discovered for the First Time a Spot of Meadow Ground, ploughed and sowed with Peas in the Broad Cast Way; the Uplands are now covered with Pitch Pine and are sandy and barren as the Desarts of N. Jersey.

As we approach the Town the Houses multiply on each Shore and we observe a person in the Act of sowing Peas upon a fruitful Meadow of an Island to the right. The Hudson near Albany seems to be about Half a Mile over. Henry Cuyler's Brick House on the East Side about a mile below the Town looks well and we descry the King's stables a long wooden Building on the left and on the same side Philip Schuyler's Grand House with whom at present resides Col. Bradstreet.[35] Col. John Van Renslaer has a good House on the East Side.

At Half after 10 oCloc we arrived at Albany estimated to be 164 Miles by Water from N.York and by Land 157. In the afternoon we viewed the Town which contains according to several Gentlemen residing there, about 500 Dwelling Houses besides Stores and Out Houses. The Streets are irregular and badly laid out, some paved others not, Two or Three are broad and the rest narrow and not straight. Most of the Buildings are pyramidically shaped like the old Dutch Houses of N York. We found cartwright's a good Tavern tho his charges were exorbitant and it is justly remarked by Kalm the Swedish Traveller in America that the Townsmen of Albany in general sustained the character of being close, mercenary and avaricious. They deem it 60 miles from Albany to Cherry Valley.

We did not note any extraordinary Edifices in the Town nor is there a single Building facing Albany on the other Side of the River. The Fort is in ruinous neglected Condition and nothing now to be seen of Fort Orange built by the Dutch but part of the Fossé or Ditch which surrounded it. The Barracks are built of Wood and of ordinary Workmanship; the same may be said of the King's Store Houses. The Court House is large and the Jail under it. One miserable Woman is now in it for cutting the Throat of her Child about 5 years old. There are 4 Houses of Worship for different Denominations and a Public Library which we did not visit. Most of the Houses are built of Brick or faced with Brick. The Inhabitants generally speak both Dutch and English and some do not understand the latter. The Shore and Wharves 3 in Number abounded in Lumber. Stephen Van Renslaer the Patron or Lord of the Manor of Renslaerwick [36] his House stands a little above the Town; he is a young man.

The Site of the Town is hilly and the soil clay but round the place it is mere Sand bearing pine Trees chiefly of the Pitch Pine. Some Lime or Linden Trees as well as other Trees are planted before the Doors as at N York and indeed Albany has in other Respects much the Aspect of that City. The Houses are for the most Part covered with Shingles made of White Pine, some few with red or black Tiles. In one of the Streets there is a Sign of the Jersey Shoe Warehouse being supplied in Part with Shoes by Henry Guest of N. Brunswick; there is a Town Cloc which strikes regularly. We saw some Indians here and found the Weather very warm and sultry.

6.

Charles Carroll of Carrollton 1776*

INTRODUCTION: In April 1776, three months before the Declaration of Independence, a momentous voyage occurred on the troubled waters of the Hudson River.

The month of April was one of frantic preparation in New York City. The British had been driven out of Boston by General Washington on March 17, and New York City was the next objective of a powerful British expeditionary force determined to suppress the American rebellion. Anticipating this move, Washington sent six regiments from Boston to New York on March 21, and by April 1 there were 8,000 men under arms on the Island of Manhattan. Washington himself arrived from Cambridge to take command on April 13.

Meanwhile the way to Canada by way of the Hudson and Champlain Valleys had been cleared by the capture of Ticonderoga and Crown Point, and an American army under General Benedict Arnold was laying siege to Quebec. At this juncture of affairs the Continental Congress decided to supplement military action with political pressure and appointed a commission of four representatives to go to Canada to spread revolutionary propaganda and attempt to get the Canadian people to join the American cause. The Commission was composed of Samuel Chase of Maryland, Charles Carroll of Carrollton, his brother John Carroll (a Catholic priest with a knowledge of French), and Dr. Benjamin Franklin. It was a well-chosen delegation, but as the seventy-year-old Franklin knew, the mission was foredoomed to failure.

The commissioners left New York by sloop on April 2 and arrived in Albany five days later. After resting for a couple of days in General Philip Schuyler's home and being briefed on the declining fortune of the American

army in Canada, the party left Albany on April 9 for Saratoga accompanied by General and Mrs. Schuyler and their two daughters. A week was then spent in Schuyler's Saratoga home while Franklin tried to regain his strength (he was ill throughout the journey). April 19 saw the party embarking upon the ice-laden waters of Lake George after a difficult two-and-a-half-day wagon transit from Saratoga. There was then a delay of four days as the party prepared their bateau to be drawn on wheels by six yoke of oxen across the four-mile stretch of land separating Lake George and Lake Champlain. After four frigid days on Lake Champlain the party arrived at St. Johns, and there was another day of excruciating travel by means of calashes before reaching Montreal. There on April 29 General Arnold gave the commissioners a royal welcome. But they were also treated to the bad news that the war was already lost in Canada: a British fleet had appeared in the St. Lawrence, and on May 5 the American army had to abandon Quebec and begin a long and costly retreat to Lake Champlain. On May 11 the ailing Franklin decided the cause was lost and left Montreal accompanied by John Carroll, reaching New York City on May 26 after traveling the distance from Albany in a chariot loaned by General Schuyler. Meanwhile Samuel Chase and Charles Carroll tarried in Canada with the retreating American army and did not leave St. Johns for the return journey until June 2.

The *Journal* of this tortuous and abortive mission was written by Charles Carroll of Carrollton (1737–1832), the distinguished revolutionary leader, signer of the Declaration of Independence, and United States Senator from the State of Maryland. Neither the ailing Franklin, nor Samuel Chase (1741–1811), a later Justice of the United States Supreme Court, nor John Carroll (1735–1815), the first Roman Catholic bishop in the United States (1790),

* Extract from Brantz Mayer's edition of *Journal of Charles Carroll of Carrollton, During His Visit to Canada in 1776. As One of the Commissioners from Congress; With a Memoir and Notes* (Baltimore: 1876), pp. 47–88.

8. *The "Phoenix" and the "Rose" Engaged by the Enemy's Fire Ships and Galleys on the 16 Aug. 1776*, engraving from the original picture by D. Serres, from a sketch by Sir James Wallace; courtesy of the I. N. Phelps Stokes Collection, New York Public Library.

This action occurred off the Palisades four months after Charles Carroll and Benjamin Franklin sailed up the river.

The PHŒNIX and the ROSE Engaged by the ENEMY'S FIRE SHIPS and GALLEYS on the 16 Aug.ˢᵗ 1776.

Engrav'd from the Original Picture by D. Serres from a sketch of Sir James Wallace's.

Published according to Act of Parliament April 2 1778 by J.F.W. Des Barres Esq.ʳ

kept a diary or record of the ill-fated journey. But the following account is ample recompense and sufficient unto itself: it is a telling document of the vicissitudes of a month-long journey that only a hundred years later could be accomplished with ease in a couple of days; and it is a southerner's novel impressions of the Hudson-Champlain corridor under the initial impact of the American Revolution.

The following extract begins with the departure from New York on April 2 and terminates on April 27 when Carroll and his party reached the American-held fort of St. Johns, twenty-five miles north of the present Canadian-American border on the Richelieu River.

April 2d, 1776. Left New York at 5 o'clock, P.M.; sailed up North river, or Hudson's, that afternoon, about thirteen miles.[1] About one o'clock in the night were awaked by the firing of cannon: heard three great guns distinctly from the *Asia;* [2] soon saw a great fire, which we presumed to be a house on Bedloe's islands,[3] set on fire by a detachment of our troops. Intelligence had been received that the enemy were throwing up intrenchments on that island, and it had been determined by our generals to drive them off. Dr. Franklin went upon deck, and saw waving flashes of light appearing suddenly and disappearing, which he conjectured to be the fire of musquetry, although he could not hear the report.

3d. A bad, rainy day; wind north-east; quite ahead. A.M., eleven o'clock, opposite to Colonel Phillip's (a tory);[4] pretty situation near the river; garden sloping down to it; house has a pretty appearance; a church [5] at a little distance on the south side, surrounded by cedar trees. The banks of the river, on the western side exceedingly steep and rocky; pine trees growing amidst the rocks. On the eastern, or New York side, the banks are not near so steep, they decline pretty gradually to the water's edge. The river is straight hitherto. About five o'clock wind breezed up from the south; got under way, and ran with a pretty easy gale as far as the highlands, forty miles from New York. The river here is very contracted,[6] and the lands on each side very lofty. When we got into this strait the wind increased, and blew in violent flaws; in doubling one of these steep craggy points we were in danger of running on the rocks; endeavored to double the cape called St. Anthony's nose,[7] but all our efforts proved ineffectual; obliged to return some way back in the straits to seek shelter; in doing this our mainsail was split to pieces by a sudden and most violent blast of wind off the mountains. Came to anchor: blew a perfect storm all night and all day the fourth. Remained all day (the fourth) in Thunder Hill bay, about half a mile below Cape. St. Anthony's nose, and a quarter of a mile from Thunder Hill.[8] Our crew were employed all this day in repairing the mainsail. The country round about this bay has a wild and romantic appearance; the hills are almost perpendicularly steep, and covered with rocks, and trees of a small size. The hill called St. Anthony's nose is said to be full of sulphur. I make no doubt this place has experienced some violent convulsion from subterraneous fire: the steepness of the hills, their correspondence, the narrowness of the river, and its depth, all confirm me in this opinion.

5th. Wind at north-east, mainsail not yet repaired. Sailed about twelve o'clock from Thunder Hill bay; just before we doubled Cape St. Anthony's nose, Mr. Chase and I landed to examine a beautiful fall of water.[9] Mr. Chase, very apprehensive of the leg of mutton being boiled too much, impatient to get on board; wind breezing up, we had near a mile to row to overtake the vessel. As soon as we doubled Cape St. Anthony's nose a beautiful prospect opened on us. The river, from this place to Constitution fort, built on Marbler's rock,[10] forms a fine canal, surrounded with high hills of various shapes; one, in particular, resembles a sugar loaf, and is so called. About three miles from Cape St. Anthony's nose is another beautiful cascade, called "the Buttermilk." [11] This is formed by a rivulet which flows from a lake on the top of a neighboring mountain; this lake, we are told, abounds with trout and perch. Arrived about five o'clock at Constitution fort; Mr. Chase went with me on shore to visit the fort; it is built on a rock called Marbler's rock: the river at this place makes a sudden bend to the west; the battery (for it does not deserve the name of a fort, being quite open on the north-east side) has two flanks, one fronting the south, and the other the west;—on the south flank were planted thirteen six and one nine pounder; but there were no cannoneers in the fort, and only one hundred and two men fit to do duty; —they intend to erect another battery on an eminence called Gravel Hill, which will command vessels coming up the river as soon as they double Cape St. Anthony's nose.[12] A little above this cape a battery is projected to annoy the enemy's vessels, to be called Fort Montgomery; they intend another battery lower down the river, and a little below Cape St. Anthony's nose. In the highlands are many convenient spots to construct batteries on; but, in order to make them answer the intended purpose, weighty metal should be placed on these batteries, and skillful gunners should be engaged to serve the artillery. About nine o'clock at night, the tide making, we weighed anchor, and came to again about two o'clock in the morning, the sixth instant. The river is remarkably deep all the way through the highlands, and the tide rapid. When we came to an anchor off Constitution fort we found the depth of water above thirty fathoms. These highlands present a number of romantic views, the steep hills over-

shadow the water, and in some places the rocks, should they be rolled down, would fall into the river several feet from the banks on which they stood. This river seems intended by nature to open a communication between Canada and the province of New York by water, and, by some great convulsion, a passage has been opened to the waters of Hudson river through the Highlands. These are certainly a spur of the Endless mountains.[13]

6th. Weighed anchor about seven o'clock in the morning: had a fine breeze; the country more cultivated above the highlands; passed several mills, all of them overshot; [14] saw two frigates on the stocks at Pokeepsay, building for the service of the United Colonies; [15] saw a great many limekilns in our run this morning, on both sides of the river, the banks of which begin to slope more gradually to the water's edge. We wrote to General Heath,[16] from off Constitution fort, and sent the letter to the commanding officer of the fort, with orders to forward it by express immediately to the general at New York. The purport of the letter was to inform the general of the very defenceless condition of the fort, that measures might be immediately taken to put it in a better posture of defence. If Howe was a man of enterprise, and knew of the weak state of the fort, he might take it in its present situation with sixty men, and without cannon. He might land his party a little below the fort on the east side, march over a marsh, and attack it on the back part. It was proposed to erect a battery of some cannon to sweep the marsh; but this, and also the battery above mentioned, on Gravel Hill, have been strangely neglected, and nothing as yet has been done towards constructing either of these batteries, more than levelling the top of Gravel Hill.

Six o'clock, P.M., came to anchor four miles from Albany; had a most glorious run this day, and a most pleasant sail; including our run in the night, we ran this day ninety-six miles—Constitution fort being one hundred miles from Albany, and sixty from New York. We passed several country houses pleasantly situated on the banks, or, rather, eminences commanding the banks of the river; the grounds we could discover from the vessel did not appear to be highly improved. We had a distant view of the Katskill mountains. These are said to be some of the highest in North America; they had a pleasing appearance; the weather being somewhat hazy, they appeared like bluish clouds at a great distance; when we were nearest to them, they were distant about ten miles. Vast tracts of land on each side of Hudson's river are held by the proprietaries, or, as they are here styled, the *Patrones* of manors.[17] One of the Rensalaers has a grant of twenty miles on each side of the river.[18] Mr. Robert R. Livingston informed me that he held three hundred thousand acres.[19] I am told there are but ten original patentees between Albany and the highlands.[20] The descendants of the first proprietaries of these immense tracts still keep them in possession; necessity has not as yet forced any of them to sell any part.[21]

7th. Weighed anchor this morning about six o'clock. Wind fair: having passed over the overslaw,[22] had a distinct view of Albany, distant about two miles:—landed at Albany at half past seven o'clock; received, at landing, by GENERAL SCHUYLER,[23] who, understanding we were coming up, came from his house, about a mile out of town, to receive us and invite us to dine with him; he behaved with great civility; lives in pretty style; has two daughters (Betsy and Peggy), lively, agreeable, black eyed girls.[24] Albany is situated partly on a level, and partly on the slope of a hill, or rising ground, on the west side of the river. Vessels drawing eight and nine feet water may come to Albany, and five miles even beyond it, at this season of the year, when the waters are out. The fort is in a ruinous condition, and not a single gun mounted

on it. There are more houses in this town than in Annapolis, and I believe it to be much more populous.[25] The citizens chiefly speak Dutch, being mostly the descendents of Dutchmen; but the English language and manners are getting ground apace.

9th. Left Albany early this morning, and travelled in a wagon in company with Mrs. Schuyler,[26] her two daughters, and Generals Schuyler and Thomas.[27] At six miles from Albany I quitted the wagon and got on horseback to accompany the generals to view the falls on the Mohawk's river, called the Cohooes. The perpendicular fall is seventy-four feet, and the breadth of the river at this place, as measured by General Schuyler, is one thousand feet. The fall is considerably above one hundred feet, taken from the first ripple or still water above the perpendicular fall. The river was swollen with the melting of the snows and rains, and rolled over the frightful precipice an impetuous torrent. The foam, the irregularities in the fall broken by projecting rocks, and the deafening noise, presented a sublime but terrifying spectacle. At fifty yards from the place the water dropped from the trees, as it does after a plentiful shower, they being as wet with the ascending vapor as they commonly are after a smart rain of some continuance. The bottoms adjoining the river Hudson are fine lands, and appeared to be well cultivated; most of them that we passed through were in wheat, which, though commonly overflowed in the spring, we were informed by our driver, suffered no hurt, but were rather improved by the innundation. We arrived in the evening, a little before sunset, at Saratoga, the seat of General Schuyler,[28] distant from Albany thirty-two miles. We spent the whole day in the journey, occasioned by the badness of the roads, and the delay the wagons met with in crossing two ferries. The roads at this season of the year are generally bad, but now worse than ever, owing to the great number of wagons employed in carrying the baggage of the regiments marching into Canada, and supplies to the army in that country. General Schuyler informed me that an uninterrupted water-carriage between New York and Quebec might be perfected at fifty thousand pounds sterling expense, by means of locks, and a small canal cut from a branch that runs into Wood creek, and the head of a branch which falls into Hudson's river; the distance is not more than three miles. The river Richelieu or Sorel is navigable for batteaux from Lake Champlain into the St. Lawrence. The rapids, below St. John's [29] are not so considerable as to obstruct the navigation of such vessels.

The lands about Saratoga are very good, particularly the bottom lands. Hudson's river runs within a quarter of a mile of the house, and you have a pleasing view of it for two or three miles above and below. A stream called Fishkill, which rises out of Lake Saratoga, about six miles from the general's house, runs close by it, and turns several mills; one, a grist mill, two saw mills, (one of them carrying fourteen saws,) and a hemp and flax mill. This mill is a new construction, and answers equally well in breaking hemp or flax. I requested the general to get a model made for me by the person who built it. Descriptions of machines are seldom accurately made, and when done with exactness are seldom understood. I was informed by the general that it is customary for the great proprietaries of lands to lease them out for three lives, sometimes on fee-farm-rents, reserving, by way of rent, a fourth, or, more commonly, a tenth of all the produce; but the proprietaries content themselves with a tenth of the wheat. On every transmutation of property from one tenant to another, a quarter part of what the land sells for is sometimes paid to the original proprietary or lord of the manor. The general observed to me that this was much the most advantageous way of leas-

ing lands;—that in the course of a few years, from the frequent transmutations of tenants, the alienation fines would exceed the purchase of the fee-simple, though sold at a high valuation. General Schuyler is a man of good understanding improved by reflection and study; he is of a very active turn, and fond of husbandry, and when the present distractions are composed, if his infirm state of health will permit him, will make Saratoga a most beautiful and most valuable estate. He saws up great quantities of plank at his mills, which, before this war, was disposed of in the neighborhod, but the greater part of it sent to Albany.

11th. Generals Thomas and Schuyler set off this morning for Lake George; the former to be in readiness to cross the lake on the first breaking up of the ice, the latter to forward the embarkation and transportation of military stores and supplies.

12th. It snowed all this morning until eleven o'clock; the snow above six inches deep on the ground: it was not off the neighboring hills when we left Saratoga.

16th. This morning we set off from Saratoga; [30] I parted with regret from the amiable family of General Schuyler; the ease and affability with which we were treated, and the lively behavior of the young ladies, made Saratoga a most pleasant *séjour,* the remembrance of which will long remain with me. We rode from Saratoga to McNeill's ferry, [distance two miles and a half,] [31] crossed Hudson's river at this place, and rode on to one mile above Fort Miller, [32] which is distant from McNeill's two miles. A Mr. Dover has a country-seat near Fort Miller; you see his house from the road. [33] There is a very considerable fall in the river at Fort Miller. Just above it our baggage was put into another boat; it had been brought up in a wagon from Saratoga to McNeill's, carried over the ferry in a wagon, and then put on board a boat, in which it was conveyed to the foot of Fort Mil-

9. *Schuylersville, New York,* anonymous colored lithograph, 1834; courtesy of The New-York Historical Society.

"A stream called Fishkill, which rises out of Lake Saratoga, about six miles from the general's [Schuyler's] house, runs close by it, and turns several mills."

View of the mills on the Fishkill at Schuylersville (formerly Saratoga) more than fifty years after Charles Carroll and Benjamin Franklin passed by.

10. *View near Fort Miller,* aquatint engraved by J. Hill from the painting by W. J. Wall, 1821–1822; courtesy of The New-York Historical Society.

"A Mr. Dover has a country-seat near Fort Miller; you see his house from the road."

The scene near Fort Miller forty-five years after Charles Carroll and Benjamin Franklin passed by.

ler falls; [34] then carried over land a quarter of a mile and put into a second boat. At a mile from Fort Miller we got into a boat and went up the Hudson river to Fort Edward. Although this fort is but seven miles distant from the place where we took boat, we were above four hours rowing up. The current is exceedingly rapid, and rapidity was increased by a freshet. In many places the current was so strong that the batteau men were obliged to set up with poles, and drag the boat by the painter. Although these fellows were active and expert at their business, it was with the greatest difficulty they could stem the current in particular places. The congress keeps in pay three companies of batteau men on Hudson's river, consisting each of thirty-three men with a captain;—the pay of the men is £4.10 per month. The lands bordering on Hudson's river, as you approach Fort Edward, become more sandy, and the principal wood that grows on them is pine. There are several saw mills both above and below Fort Miller. The planks sawed at the mills above Fort Miller are made up into small rafts and left without guides to the current of the river; each one is marked, so that the raft-men that remain just below Fort Miller falls, watching for them coming down, may easily know their own rafts. When they come over the falls they go out in canoes and boats and tow their rafts ashore, and then take them to pieces and make them again into larger rafts. The smaller rafts are called *cribs*. The ruins only of Fort Edward remains; [35] there is a good large inn, where we found quartered Colonel Sinclair's regiment. Mr. Allen, son of old Mr. Allen, is lieutenant-colonel; he received us very politely and accommodated us with beds. The officers of this regiment are in general fine sized men, and seemed to be on a friendly footing;—the soldiers also are stout fellows.

17th. Having breakfasted with Colonel Allen, we set off from Fort Edward on our way to Fort George. We had not got a mile from the fort when a messenger from General Schuyler met us. He was sent with a letter by the general to inform us that Lake George was not open, and to desire us to remain at an inn kept by one Wing at seven miles distance from Fort Edward and as many from Fort George. The country between Wing's tavern and Fort Edward is very sandy and somewhat hilly. The principal wood is pine. At Fort Edward the river Hudson makes a sudden turn to the westward; it soon again resumes its former north course, for, at a small distance, we found it on our left and parallel with the road which we travelled, and which, from Fort Edward to Fort George, lies nearly north and south. At three miles, or thereabouts, from Fort Edward, is a remarkable fall in the river. We could see it from the road, but not so as to form any judgment of its height. We were informed that it was upwards of thirty feet, and is called the Kingsbury falls. [36] We could distinctly see the spray arising like a vapor or fog from the violence of the fall. The banks of the river, above and below these falls for a mile or two, are remarkably steep and high, and appear to be formed or faced, with a kind of stone very much resembling slate. The banks of the Mohawk's river at the Cohooes are faced with the same sort of stone;—it is said to be an indication of sea-coal. Mr. Wing's tavern is in the township of Queensbury, and Charlotte county; [37] Hudson's river is not above a quarter of a mile from his house. There is a most beautiful fall in the river at this place. From still water, to the foot of the fall, I imagine the fall cannot be less than sixty feet, but the fall is not perpendicular; it may be about a hundred and twenty or a hundred and fifty feet long, and in this length, it is broken into three distinct falls, one of which may be twenty-five feet nearly perpendicular. I saw Mr. Wing's patent,—the reserved quit-rent is two shillings and six-pence sterling per hundred acres; but he informs me it has never been yet collected.

18th. We set off from Wing's tavern about twelve o'clock this day, and reached Fort George [38] about two o'clock; the distance is eight miles and a half;—you can not discover the lake [George] until you come to the heights surrounding it,—the descent from which to the lake is nearly a mile long;—from these heights you have a beautiful view of the lake for fifteen miles down it. Its greatest breadth during these fifteen miles does not exceed a mile and a quarter, to judge by the eye, which, however, is a very fallacious way of estimating distances. Several rocky islands appear in the lake, covered with a species of cedar called here *hemlock*. Fort George is in as ruinous a condition as Fort Edward, it is a small bastion faced with stone, and built on an eminence commanding the head of the lake. There are some barracks in it, in which the troops were quartered, or rather *one* barrack, which occupied almost the whole space between the walls. At a little distance from this fort, and to the westward of it, is the spot where the Baron Dieskau was defeated by Sir William Johnson. About a quarter of a mile further to the westward the small remains of Fort William Henry are to be seen across a little rivulet which forms a swamp, and is the morass mentioned by Sir William Johnson in his account of the action with Dieskau.[39] Fort William Henry was taken last war by Montcalm and destroyed;—the garrison, consisting of four hundred men, and sixteen hundred others that were intrenched without the fort, capitulated;—a considerable part of these men were murdered by the Indians, on their march to Fort Edward, after they had delivered up their arms, according to the terms of capitulation. The bay in which Montcalm landed is seen from Fort George; he left a guard of five hundred men only to protect his boats and artillery, and marched over the heights to come to the southward of Fort William Henry. When on these heights, he discovered the intrenched body within the fort, and seeing the great indiscretion he had been guilty of in leaving so small a force to guard his baggage and boats, he rashly marched back to secure them. Had our troops attacked Montcalm's five hundred men, they would probably have defeated them, taken his cannon and boats, and forced him to surrender with his whole army. There was nothing to impede the attack but want of enterprise and conduct in the commanding officer.[40] The neighborhood of Fort George abounds with limestone, and so indeed does all the country surrounding the lake, and all the islands in it.[41] Their rocky coast and bottom contribute, no doubt, to the clearness of the lake water. Never did I see water more transparent, and to its transparency, no doubt, must be ascribed the excellency of the fish in this lake, which much exceed the fish in Lake Champlain. Lake George abounds with perch, trout, rock, and eels.

19th. We embarked at Fort George this evening, about one o'clock, in company with General Schuyler, and landed in Montcalm's bay about four miles from Fort George. After drinking tea on shore, and arranging matters in our boats, we again embarked, and went about three or four miles further, then landed, (the sun being set,) and kindled fires on shore. The longest of the boats, made for the transportation of the troops over lakes George and Champlain, are thirty-six feet in length and eight feet wide; they draw about a foot water when loaded, and carry between thirty and forty men, and are rowed by the soldiers. They have a mast fixed in them, to which a square sail, or a blanket is fastened, but these sails are of no use unless with the wind abaft or nearly so. After we left Montcalm bay we were delayed considerably in getting through the ice; but, with the help of tentpoles, we opened ourselves a passage through it into free water. The boats fitted up to carry us across had awnings over them, under which we made up our beds, and my fellow travellers slept very comfortably; but this was not my case, for I was indisposed the whole night, with a violent sickness at my stomach and vomiting, occasioned by an indigestion. We left the place where we passed the night very early on the 20th.

20th. We had gone some miles before I rose; soon after I got out of bed we found ourselves entangled in the ice. We attempted, but in vain, to break through it in one place, but were obliged to desist and force our passage through another, which we effected without much difficulty. At eight o'clock we landed to breakfast. After breakfast the general looked to his small boat; being desirous to reach the landing at the north end of Lake George, we set off together; but the general's boat and the other boat, with part of the baggage, soon got before us a considerable way. After separating, we luckily fell in with the boat bringing the Montreal and Canada mail, by which we were informed that the west shore of the lake, at a place called Sabatay point,[42] was much encumbered with ice, but that there was a free passage on the east side; accordingly, we kept along the east shore, and found it free from ice, by which means we got before the general and the other boat; for the general, who was foremost, had been delayed above an hour in breaking through the ice, and, in one place, was obliged to haul his boat over a piece or neck of land thirty feet broad. Dr. Franklin found in the Canada mail, which he opened, a letter for General Schuyler. When we had weathered Sabatay point, we stood over for the western shore of the lake, and a mile or two below the point [43] we were overtaken by the general, from whom we learned the cause of his delay. Mr. Chase and myself went on board the general's boat, and reached the landing place at the south end [44] of Lake George near two hours before the other boats. Lake George lies nearly north

and south, or rather, as I think, somewhat to the eastward of a due north course. Its shores are remarkably steep, high, and rocky (particularly the east shore), and are covered with pine and cedar, or what is here termed hemlock; the country is wild, and appears utterly incapable of cultivation; it is a fine deer country, and likely to remain so, for I think it never will be inhabited.[45] I speak of the shores, and I am told the inland country resembles these. The lake, in its greatest width, does not exceed, I think, two miles; the widest part is nearest the north end, immediately before you enter the last narrows, which are not, in their greatest width, above half a mile. There are two places where the lake is considerably contracted, one about the middle of it, the other, as I have said, at the north end; [46] this last gradually contracts itself in breadth to the size of an inconsiderable river, and suddenly, in depth, to that of a very shallow one. The landing place of Lake George is a few yards to the southward of the first fall or ripple in this river, through which the waters of Lake George drain into Lake Champlain. We passed through this ripple, and though our boat did not draw seven or eight inches, her bottom raked the rocks; the water ran through this passage about as swift as it does through your tail race. From the landing place to Ticonderoga is three miles and a half. The boats, in coming through Lake George, pass through the passage just described, and unload at a quarter of a mile below the usual landing place. Their contents are then put into wagons, and carried over to Ticonderoga. General Schuyler has erected a machine for raising the boats when emptied, and then letting them gently down on a carriage constructed for the purpose, on which they are drawn over land to Ticonderoga, on Lake Champlain, to carry the troops over the last mentioned lake, and down the Sorel [or Richelieu] into the river St. Lawrence. These carriages consist of four wheels, united by a long sapling, at the extremities of which the wheels are placed; over the axletrees is fixed a piece of wood, on which each end of the boat is supported and made fast by a rope secured round a bolt at the undermost part, and in the centre of the axletree. This bolt is made of iron, and passes through the aforesaid pieces of wood and the axletree. These carriages are drawn by six oxen, and this morning (21st instant) I saw three or four boats carried over upon them. Lake George, from the south end of it to the landing place at the north extremity, is thirty-six miles long. Its average width does not, I think, exceed a mile, and this breadth is interspersed and broken by innumerable little rocky islands formed of limestone; the shores of which are commonly so steep that you may step from the rocks into ten or twelve feet water. The season was not sufficiently advanced to admit of catching fish, a circumstance we had reason to regret, as they are so highly praised by the connoisseurs in good eating, and as one of our company is so excellent a judge in this science. There are no considerable rivers that empty themselves into Lake George. We saw some brooks or rivulets, which, I presume, after the melting of the snows, are almost dry. The lake must be fed, principally, with springs, the melting of snows, and the torrents that must pour into it, from its high and steep shores, after rains. As there is no considerable river that flows into it, so is the vent of its waters into Lake Champlain very inconsiderable. In summer you may step, dry-footed, from rock to rock, in the place which I have called the first ripple, and which I said we passed, coming out of Lake George. The water suddenly shallows from a great depth to nine or ten feet or less. This change is immediately discoverable by the great change in the color of the water. The lake water is of a dark bluish cast, and the water of the river of a whitish color, owing not only to the differences of

the depth, but the difference of the bottoms and shores, which, adjoining the river, are of white clay.

21st. I took a walk this evening to the saw-mill which is built on the principal fall of the river flowing from Lake George into Lake Champlain.[47] At the foot of this fall, which is about thirteen feet high, the river is navigable for batteaux into Lake Champlain. From the saw-mill to the place where the batteaux are put on carriages to be carried over land, the distance is one mile and a half. I saw them unload a boat from the carriage, and launch it, at the same time, into the river; this was performed by thirty-five or forty men. To-day they carried over this portage fifty batteaux. I saw the forty-eighth put on the carriage. A little to the north-westward of the saw-mill, on the west side of the river, I visited the spot where Lord Howe was killed.[48] At a small expense a continued navigation for batteaux might be made between the lakes George and Champlain, by means of a few locks.[49] General Schuyler informed me that locks, sufficient and adequate to the above purpose, might be constructed for fifteen hundred pounds sterling. There are but four or five falls in this river, the greatest of which is not above fourteen or fifteen feet. But the general informs me a much more advantageous water carriage may be opened through Wood creek, and the most convenient branch which heads near it and falls into Hudson's river. If this water communication between Lake Champlain and the province of New York should be perfected, there is little danger of the enemy's gaining the mastery of Lake Champlain, or of their ever having it in their power to invade these colonies from Canada with any prospect of success, besides the security which will be obtained for the colonies in time of war by making this navigation.[50] Trade, during peace, will be greatly benefited by it, as there will then be a continued water communication between New York and

Canada, without the inconvenience and expense attending the portages over land.

22d. I this morning took a ride with General Schuyler across the portage, or from the landing place at the bottom of Lake George, to Ticonderoga. . . . From the foot of the saw-mill falls there is still water into Lake Champlain. It is at the foot of these falls that the batteaux, brought over land [from Lake George], are launched into the water, and the artillery and the apparatus belonging to it are embarked in them; the stores, such as provisions, ball, powder, etc., are embarked from Ticonderoga. At sixty or seventy yards below the saw-mill there is a bridge built over the river:—the bridge was built by the king during the last [or French and Indian] war; the road from the landing place to Ticonderoga passes over it, and you then have the river on the right; when you have passed the bridge you immediately ascend a pretty high hill, and keep ascending till you reach the famous lines made by the French in the last war, which Abercrombie was so infatuated as to attack with musquetry only;—his cannon was lying at the bridge, about a mile or something better from these lines. The event of the day is too well known to be mentioned; we lost [killed and wounded] near one thousand six hundred men; had the cannon been brought up, the French would not have waited to be attacked;—it was morally impossible to succeed against these lines with small arms only, particularly in the manner they were attacked;—our army passing before them, and receiving a fire from the whole extent;—whereas, had it marched lower down, or to the northwest of these lines, it would have flanked them:—they were constructed of large trunks of trees, felled on each other, with earth thrown up against them.[51] On the side next the French troops, they had, besides felling trees, lopped and sharpened their branches, and turned them towards the enemy; the trunks of the trees remain to this day piled up as described, but are fast going to decay. As soon as you enter these lines you have a full view of Lake Champlain and Ticonderoga fort, distant about a quarter of a mile. The land from thence gradually declines to the spot on which the fort is built. Lake Champlain empties itself opposite the fort, and runs south twenty-eight miles to Skeenesborough [Whitehall]. Crown Point is fifteen miles down the lake from Ticonderoga. The lake is no where broad in sight of the last mentioned place, but the prospect from it is very pleasing; its shores are not as steep as those of Lake George. They rise gradually from the water, and are covered more thickly with woods, which grow in good soils, or at least in soils much better than can be seen on Lake George. There is but one settlement on the latter, at Sabatay point;[52] I understood there were about sixty acres of good land at that point. Ticonderoga fort is in a ruinous condition; it was once a tolerable fortification.[53] The ramparts are faced with stone. I saw a few pieces of cannon mounted on one bastion, more for show, I apprehend, than service.[54] In the present state of affairs this fort is of no other use than as an *entrepôt* or magazine for stores, as from this place all supplies for our army in Canada are shipped to go down Lake Champlain. I saw four vessels, viz: three schooners and one sloop; these are to be armed, to keep the mastery of the lake in case we should lose St. John's and be driven out of Canada;[55] in the meantime they will be employed in carrying supplies to our troops in that country. Of these three schooners, two were taken from the enemy on the surrender of St. John's, one of them is called the *Royal Savage,* and is pierced for twelve guns; she had, when taken, twelve brass pieces—I think four and six pounders; these were sent to Boston. She is really a fine vessel, and built on purpose for fighting; however, some repairs are wanted; a new mainmast must be put in, her old one being shattered with one of our cannon balls. When these vessels are completely rigged, armed and manned, we may defy the enemy on Lake Champlain for this summer and fall at least, even should we unfortunately be driven out of Canada. When our small army last summer, or rather fall, [in number about one thousand seven hundred,] came to *Isle aux Noix*,[56] this vessel was almost ready to put to sea, she wanted only as much to be done to her as could easily have been finished in three days, had the enemy exerted themselves. Had she ventured out our expedition to Canada must have failed, and probably our whole army must have surrendered, for she was greatly an overmatch for all the naval strength we then had on the lake. Had Preston, who commanded at St. John's, ventured out with his garrison, consisting of six hundred men, and attacked our people at their first landing, he would, in all probability, have defeated them, as they were a mere undisciplined rabble, made up chiefly of the offings and outcasts of New York.[57]

23d. We continued this day at the landing place, our boats not being yet ready and fitted to carry us through Lake Champlain. General Schuyler and the troops were busily engaged in carting over land, to the saw-mill, the batteaux, cannon, artillery stores, provisions, etc., there to be embarked on the navigable waters of Lake Champlain, and transported over that lake to St. John's.

24th. We this day left the landing place at Lake George and took boat at the saw-mill. From the saw-mill to Ticonderoga, the distance, by water, is about a mile; the water is shallow, but sufficiently deep for batteau navigation. A little below the bridge before mentioned, the French, during the last war, drove pickets into the river, to prevent our boats getting round from the saw-mill to Ticonderoga with the artillery; some of the pickets still remain, for both our boats struck them. Ticonderoga fort is beautifully situated, but, as I said before, it is in a ruinous condition;—neither is the place, in my opinion, judiciously chosen for the construction of a fort; a fort constructed at the saw-mill would much better secure the passage or pass into the province of New York by way of Lake George. Having waited at Ticonderoga an hour or two, to take in provisions for the crews of both boats, consisting entirely of soldiers, we embarked at eleven o'clock, and reached Crown Point a little after three, with the help of our oars only. Crown Point is distant from Ticonderoga only fifteen miles. The lake, all the way, from one part to another, is narrow, scarce exceeding a mile on an average. Crown Point is situated on a neck or isthmus of land, on the west side of the lake; it is in ruins; it was once a considerable fortress, and the English must have expended a large sum in constructing the fort and erecting the barracks, which are also in ruins.[58] A great part of the ditch is cut out of the solid limestone rock.[59] This ditch was made by blowing the rocks, as the holes bored for the gunpowder are plainly to be seen in the fragments. By some accident the fort took fire, the flames communicated to the powder magazine, containing at that time ninety-six barrels. The shock was so great as to throw down the barracks—at least the upper stories. The explosion was distinctly heard ten miles off, and the earth shook at that distance as if there had been an earthquake. This intelligence I received from one Faris, who lives ten miles down the lake, and at whose house we lay this night. The wood-work of the barracks is entirely consumed by fire, but the stone work of the first stories might be converted into a fine manufactory.[60] The erecting of these barracks and the fort must have cost the government not less, I dare say, than one hundred thousand pounds sterling. The lake is narrow opposite the fort,[61] and makes a bend, by which the vessels passing on the lake were much exposed to the artillery of the fort; and this advantageous situation first induced the French, and then the English, to erect a fort here. The French fort was inconsiderable, and close to the water; the English fort is a much more extensive fortification, and farther from the lake, but so as to command it.

25th. We set off from Faris's [62] at five o'clock in the morning. If Faris's information may be relied on, his land and the neighboring lands are exceedingly fine;—he told us he had reaped thirty bushels of wheat from the acre; the soil appears to be good; but, to judge of it from its appearance, I should not think it so fertile. Three miles north of Faris's the lake begins to contract itself, and this contraction continues for six miles, and is called the narrows.[63] At Faris's the lake is about two miles wide. We breakfasted in a small cove at a little distance to the southward of the Split rock.[64] The Split rock is nine miles from Faris's house. At the Split rock [65] the lake grows immediately wider as you go down it; its width, in this place, can not be much short of seven miles. When we had got four or five miles from the rock, the wind headed us, and blew a fresh gale, which occasioned a considerable swell on the lake, the wind being northeast, and having a reach of twenty miles. We were constrained to put in at one McCaully's, where we dined on cold provisions.[66] The wind abating about four o'clock, we put off again and rowed seven miles down the lake to a point of land a mile or two to the southward of four islands called the Four Brothers; [67] these islands lie nearly in the middle of the lake, which is very wide in this place, and continues as far as you can see down it. Mr. Chase and I slept this night on shore under a tent made of bushes.

26th. We set off this morning at four o'clock from the last mentioned point, which I called "Commission-

ers' point." Wind fair; a pretty breeze. At five o'clock reached Schuyler's island; [68] it contains eight hundred acres, and belongs to Montreson, distant seven miles from the Four Brothers. Schuyler's island lies near the western shore. The lake continues wide; at ten o'clock got to Cumberland head, fourteen miles from Schuyler's island. Cumberland head is the south point of Cumberland bay.[69] The bay forms a deep recess on the western side of the lake; its length, from Schuyler's island, at the point of land opposite to it, to Cumberland headland, is fourteen miles, and its depth not less than nine or ten miles. The wind luckily favored us until we reached Cumberland head; it then ceased;—it grew cloudy, and soon began to rain, and the wind shifted to the north-east. We breakfasted at Cumberland head on tea and good biscuit, our usual breakfast, having provided ourselves with the necessary furniture for such a breakfast. As soon as it cleared up we rowed across a bay, about four miles wide, to *Point aux Roches,*[70] so called from the rocks of which it is formed. Indeed it is one entire stone wall, fifteen feet high, but gradually inclining to the northeast. At that extremity it is little above the water. Having made a short stay at this place to refresh our men, we rowed round the point, hugged the western shore, and got into a cove which forms a very safe harbor.[71] But the ground being low and swampy, and no cedar or hemlock trees, of the branches of which our men formed their tents at night, we thought proper to cross over to *Isle la Motte,* bearing from us about north-east, and distant three miles.[72] The island is nine miles long and one broad. The south-west side of it is high land, and the water is deep close in shore, which is rocky and steep. We lay under this shore all night in a critical situation, for had the wind blown hard in the night, from the west, our boats would probably have been stove against the rocks.[73] We passed the night on board the boats, under the awning which had been fitted up for us. This awning could effectually secure us from the wind and rain, and there was space enough under it to make up four beds. The beds we were provident enough to take with us from Philadelphia. We found them not only convenient and comfortable, but necessary; for, without this precaution, persons travelling from the colonies into Canada at this season of the year, or indeed at any other, will find themselves obliged either to sit up all night, or to lie on the bare ground or planks. Several of the islands in Lake Champlain have different claimants, as patents have been granted by the French government and the government of New York. According to the present division, most of them, indeed all, except *Isle aux Noix,*[74] are in the colony of New York.

27th. A fine morning. We left our nation's station at four o'clock, and rowed ten miles to *Point au Fer,*[75] so called from some iron mines at no great distance from it; the land here, and all the adjacent country, is very flat and low. Colonel Christie has built a house at this point, which is intended for a tavern; the place is judiciously chosen. A small current begins here, and the raftsmen are not obliged to row; after they bring their rafts to *Point au Fer,* the current will carry them in a day to St. John's, which is distant from this point thirty measured miles. Windmill point is three miles below *Point au Fer;* and, a mile or two below the former, runs the line which divides the province of Quebec from New York.[76] At Windmill point the lake begins to contract itself to the size of a river, but of a large and deep one. Opposite to this point the width can not be much short of two miles; [77] six miles below Windmill point you meet with a small island called *Isle aux Têtes:* [78] from a number of heads that were stuck upon poles by the Indians after a great battle that was fought between them on this island, or near it. At this island the current is not only perceptible, but strong. We went close by the island, and in shallow water, which gave us a better opportunity of observing the swiftness of the current. A mile or two below this island, we breakfasted at a tavern kept by one Stodd. At *Isle aux Têtes,* the river *Richelieu,* or St. John's, or Sorel (for it goes by all these names), may be properly said to begin.[79] It is in this place above a mile wide, deep, and the current considerable;—its banks are almost level with the water,—indeed, the water appears to be rather above the banks; the country is one continued swamp, overflowed by the river at this season; as you approach St. John's the current grows stronger. *Isle aux Noix* is half way between St. John's and *Point au Fer,* and consequently fifteen miles from each. . . . Having passed the *Isle aux Noix,* the wind sprang up in our favor;—assisted by the wind and current, we reached St. John's at three o'clock. . . . It may not be improper to make some remarks on the navigation of Lake Champlain, the adjacent country, and its appearance. The navigation appears to be very secure, as there are many inlets, coves, and harbors, in which such vessels as will be used on the lake may at all times find shelter; the water is deep, at least wherever we touched, close in with land. There are several islands in the lake, the most considerable of which we saw; the principal is *Grand isle,*—it deserves the appellation, being, as we were informed, twenty-seven miles long, and three or four miles wide. *Isle la Motte* is the next largest, and *Isle de Belle Cour* ranks after that. *Isle la Motte* we touched at; the others we could plainly distinguish. We saw several of the islands on the eastern shore of the lake, some of which appear as large as Poplar's island; but having no person on board our boats acquainted with the lake, we could not learn their names. The lake, on an average, may be six miles broad; in some places it is above fifteen miles wide, particularly about Cumberland bay and Schuyler's island; but in others it is not three miles, and in the narrows not above a mile and a half, to judge by the eye. As you go down the lake, the mountains which hem it in on the east and west extend themselves wider, and leave a greater extent of fine level land between them and the lake on each shore.[80] Some of these mountains are remarkably high. In many places, on or near their tops, the snow still remains. They form several picturesque views, and contribute much, in my opinion, to the beauty of the lake. The snow not dissolving, in their latitude, at the end of April, is a proof of their height:—the distance at which some of these mountains are visible is still a stronger proof. Several of them may be distinctly seen from Montreal, which can not be at a less distance from the most remote than seventy or eighty miles, and, I am inclined to think, considerably further. If America should succeed, and establish liberty throughout this part of the continent, I have not the least doubt that the lands bordering on Lake Champlain will be very valuable in a short time, and that great trade will be carried on over Lake Champlain, between Canada and New York.

11. *Forcing the Hudson River Passage,* oil painting by D. Serres, the Elder, 1776; courtesy of the U.S. Naval Academy Museum.

This action occurred off Fort Lee, N.J., four years before Chastellux visited the Hudson.

7.
Marquis de Chastellux
1780*

INTRODUCTION: On February 6, 1778, less than four months after the Battle of Saratoga, the French signed an alliance with "these free and independent States" and on July 11, 1780, landed an expeditionary force of 6,000 men under the command of Count Rochambeau at Newport, Rhode Island. The third in command was Francois-Jean, Marquis de Chastellux (1734–1788), an Encyclopaedist and *Philosophe,* member of the French Academy, and future friend of Washington and Jefferson. Chastellux had already become somewhat well known in France as the friend of Voltaire and the author of an ambitious philosophical work called *An Essay on Public Happiness* (1772), but his chief claim to fame today is a work written while he was in the French service in America, entitled *Travels of the Marquis de Chastellux in North America in the Years 1780, 1781, and 1782.* Originally published in a limited edition by a press of the French fleet while the author was still in Newport, the work subsequently appeared in many French and English editions and became one of the classic sources of life in America during the period of the American Revolution.

Chastellux was with the French forces in America for two and a half years. The first year was spent mostly in Newport, where a blockade by the British fleet had forced the French army to go into winter quarters. In the summer of 1781 he accompanied the army to Yorktown, played a notable role in the concluding campaign of the Revolution, and remained with the army in Virginia until the summer of 1782, when he accompanied it back to New England and relinquished his command. The last few months of 1782 were spent in Philadelphia; and in January, 1783, he boarded a French frigate in Annapolis for the return voyage to France.

The *Travels* record several trips Chastellux made while he was not on duty with the army, mostly during the winter months when all armies were forced to suspend military operations and go into winter quarters. The excerpt that follows is part of a sightseeing tour he made in November–December of 1780 while the French army was still encamped in Newport. The object of the journey was to visit Lafayette and Washington (in winter quarters at Preakness, New Jersey), tour the sights of Philadelphia and its environs, then return to the Hudson, visit the battlefield of Saratoga, and rejoin the army at Newport. The following excerpt is restricted to the Hudson Valley phase of the journey and opens on November 20, 1780, nine days after Chastellux had left Newport by way of the main-traveled route through central Connecticut (forced by the English occupation of the coastal regions) to the American lines at Fishkill, New York.

Between Carroll's voyage of 1776 and Chastellux's visit of 1780 the Hudson Valley has seen its full share of the military operations of the Revolution. Though the British were not to evacuate New York City and Washington was to maintain his army at Newburgh until 1783, the Hudson has seen the last of the famous battles and episodes that give it a record second to none in the history of the war. The battles of Long Island, Manhattan, Harlem Heights, White Plains; the storming of Stony Point; General Vaughan's raid up the valley; the burning of Kingston; the skirmishes and battles at Bear Mountain; the crucial victory at Saratoga; Arnold's treason at West Point—all had passed into history by the time Chastellux visited the scene of the action in the winter of 1780. Yet the war is still on, the battles of the Hudson Valley are still fresh in the minds of those who fought

* Excerpt from George Greive's translation of the Marquis de Chastellux's *Travels in North-America, in the Years 1780–81–82. Translated from the French by an English Gentleman.* . . . (New York: 1827), pp. 42–57, 160–176, 182–198. An American reprint of a London edition of 1787. Minor changes have been made in the text, and all bracketed interpolations are the present editor's.

them. With the Marquis De Chastellux we return once again to this most glorious period in the history of the Hudson.

I

November 20–23: Fishkill, N.Y. to Preakness, N.J.

[*November 20.*] The country [on the east bank of the Hudson in southern Dutchess County] is well cultivated; affording the prospect of several pretty farms, with some mills; and notwithstanding the war, Hopel [Hopewell] township is building, inhabited chiefly by Dutch people, as well as the greatest part of the state of New-York, which formerly belonged to the republic of Holland, who exchanged it for Surinam. My intention was to sleep five miles on this side of Fishkill, at Colonel Griffin's tavern.[1] I found him cutting and preparing wood for fences; he assured me his house was full, which was easy to be believed, for it is very small. I continued my journey therefore, and reached Fishkill about four o'clock. This town, in which there are not more than fifty houses in the space of two miles, has been long the principal depot of the American army. It is there they have placed their magazines, their hospitals, their workshops, etc., but all these form a town of themselves, composed of handsome large barracks, built in the wood at the foot of the mountains; for the Americans, like the Romans in many respects, have hardly any other winter quarters, than wooden towns, or barricaded camps, which may be compared to the *hiemalia* of the Romans.

As for the position of Fishkill, that it was a post of great importance is evident from the campaign of 1777. It is clear that the plan of the English was to render themselves masters of the whole course of the North River, and thus to separate the Eastern and Western States. It was necessary therefore to secure a post on that river; West-Point was made choice of as the most important to fortify, and Fishkill as the place of provisions, ammunition, etc.: these two positions are connected together. I shall soon speak of West Point, but I shall remark here, that Fishkill has all the qualities necessary for a place of depot, for it is situated on the high road from Connecticut, and near the North River, and is protected at the same time by a chain of inaccessible mountains, which occupy a space of more than twenty miles between the Croton river and that of Fishkill.

The approach of winter quarters, and the movement of the troops occasioned by this circumstance, made lodgings very scarce: it was with difficulty I found any, but I got at last into a middling inn, kept by an old Mrs. Egremont. The house was not so clean as they usually are in America; but the most disagreeable circumstance was the want of several panes of glass. In fact, in all repairs, that of windows is the most difficult, in a country where, from the scattered situation and distance of the houses from each other, it is sometimes necessary to send twenty miles for a glazier. We made use of everything that came to hand to patch up the windows in the best way we could, and we made an excellent fire. Soon after, the doctor of the hospital, who had seen me pass, and knew me to be a French General-Officer, came with great politeness to see if I wanted any thing, and to offer me every service in his power. I made use of the English word doctor, because the distinction of surgeon and physician is as little known in the army of Washington, as in that of Agamemnon. We read in Homer, that the physician Macaon himself dressed the wounds; but our physicians, who are no Greeks, will not follow that example. The Americans conform to the ancient custom, and it answers very well; they are well pleased with their doctors, whom they hold in the highest consideration.

Doctor Craig, whom I knew at Newport, is the intimate friend of General Washington; and the Marquis de la Fayette had very lately an aide-de-camp, Colonel Mac-Henry, who the year before performed the functions of doctor in the same army.

[*November 21.*] The 21st, at nine in the morning, the Quarter-Master of Fishkill, who had come the night before with the utmost politeness to offer me his services, and to place two sentinels at the door, an honour I refused in spite of every thing he could say, called upon me; and after drinking tea according to custom, he conducted me to see the barracks, the magazines, and work-houses of the different workmen employed in the service of the army. These barracks are wooden houses, well built, and well covered, having garrets, and even cellars, so that we should form a false idea, were we to judge of them by what we see in our armies, when our troops are *barraqués.* The Americans sometimes make them like ours, but this is merely to cover the soldiers when they are more within reach of the enemy. They call these *huts,* and they are very expert in constructing one and the other. They require only three days to build the former, reckoning from the moment they begin to cut down the trees; the others are finished in four and twenty hours. They consist of little walls made of stones heaped up, the intervals of which are filled with earth kneaded with water, or simply with mud; a few planks form the roof, but what renders them very warm is that the chimney occupies the outerside, and that you can only enter by a small door, at the side of the chimney. The army has passed whole winters under such huts, without suffering, and without sickness. As for the barracks, or rather the little military town of Fishkill, such ample provision is made for everything which the service and discipline of the army may require, that a prévôté and a prison are built there, surrounded by palisades.

One gate only affords access to the enclosure of the prévôté; and before it is placed a guard-house. Through the windowbars of the prison, I distinguished some prisoners, with the English uniform; they were about thirty soldiers, or regimented tories. These wretches had accompanied the savages in the incursion they had made by Lake Ontario and the Mohawk river. They had burnt upwards of two hundred houses, killed the horses and cows, and destroyed above one hundred thousand bushels of corn. The gallows should have been the reward of these exploits, but the enemy having also made some prisoners, reprisals were dreaded, and these robbers were only confined in rigorous and close imprisonment.

After passing some time in visiting these different settlements, I got on horseback, and under the conduct of a guard which the Quarter-Master gave me, I entered the wood and followed the road to West-Point, where I wished to arrive for dinner. Four or five miles from Fishkill, I saw some felled trees, and an opening in the wood, which on coming nearer I discovered to be a camp, or rather huts inhabited by some hundred invalid soldiers. These invalids were all in very good health; but it is necessary to observe, that in the American armies, every soldier is called an invalid, who is unfit for service; now these had been sent here because their clothes were truly invalids. These honest fellows, for I will not say creatures, (they know too well how to suffer, and are suffering in too noble a cause) were not covered, even with rags; but their steady countenances, and their good arms in good order, seemed to supply the defect of clothes, and to display nothing but their courage and their patience. Near this camp I met with Major Liman, aide-de-camp to General Heath, with whom I was particularly intimate at Newport, and Mr. de Villefranche, a French officer, serving as an Engineer at West-Point. General Heath [2] had been informed of my arrival by an express, sent without my knowledge, by the Quarter-Master of Fishkill, and he had despatched these two officers to meet me. I continued my journey in the woods, in a road hemmed in on both sides by very steep hills, which seemed admirably adapted for the dwelling of bears, and where in fact they often make their appearance in winter. We availed ourselves at length of a less difficult part of these mountains to turn to the westward and approach the river, but which is still invisible. Descending them slowly, at the turning of the road, my eyes were struck with the most magnificent picture I had ever beheld. It was a view of the North River, running in a deep channel formed by the mountains, through which in former ages it had forced its passage. The fort of West-Point and the formidable batteries which defend it fix the attention on the western bank, but on lifting your eyes you behold on every side lofty summits, thick set with redoubts and batteries.[3] I leaped off my horse, and viewed them a long time with my spying glass, the only method of acquiring a knowledge of the whole of the fortifications with which this important post is surrounded. Two lofty heights, on each of which a large redoubt is constructed, protect the eastern bank. These two works have no other name than the northern, and the southern redoubts; but from the fort of West-Point properly so-called, which is on the edge of the river, to the very top of the mountain at the foot of which it stands, are six different forts, all in the form of an amphitheatre, and protecting each other. They compelled me to leave this place, where I should willingly have spent the whole day, but I had not travelled a mile before I saw the reason of their hurrying me. I perceived a corps of infantry of about two thousand five hundred men, ranged in a line of battle on the bank of the river. They had just passed it to proceed by Kingsbridge, and cover a grand foraging party which it was proposed to send towards the White-Plains, and to the gates of New York. General Stark, who beat the English at Bennington, had the command of these troops, and General Heath was at their head; he was desirous of letting me see them before they marched.[4] I passed before the ranks, being saluted with the espontoon by all the officers, and the drums beating a march, an honour paid in America to Major-Generals, who are the first in rank, though it only corresponds with our *Marechal de Camp*. The troops were ill clothed, but made a good appearance; as for the officers they were every thing that could be wished, as well for their countenance, as for their manner of marching, and giving the command. After passing the front of the line, they broke it, filed off before me, and continued their route. General Heath conducted me to the river, where his barge was waiting to carry me to the other side. A new scene now opened to my view, not less sublime than the former. We descended with our faces towards the north: on that side is an island covered with rocks, which seem to close the channel of the river, but you soon perceive, through a sort of embrasure formed by its bed in separating immense mountains, that it comes obliquely from the westward, and that it has made a sudden turn round West-Point to open itself a passage, and to endeavor to gain the sea, without making hereafter the smallest bend. The eye carrying itself towards the North Bay and Constitution-Island, (the isle I have been speaking of) again perceives the river, distinguishes New-Windsor on its left bank, and is then attracted by different amphitheatres formed by the Apalachian Mountains, the nearest summits of which, that terminate the scene, are distant upwards of thirty miles. We embarked in the barge, and passed the river, which is about a mile wide. As we approached the opposite shore, the fort of West-Point, which, seen from the eastern bank, seemed humbly situated at the foot of the mountains, elevated itself to our view, and appeared like the summit of a steep rock; this rock however was only the bank of the river. Had I not remarked that the chinks on it, in several places, were embrasures for cannon, and formidable batteries, I should soon have been apprised of it by thirteen twenty-four pounders, which were fired successively. This was a military salute, with which General Heath was pleased to honour me in the name of the Thirteen States. Never was an honour more commanding, nor more majestic; every gun was, after a long interval, echoed back from the opposite bank, with a noise nearly equal to that of the discharge itself. When we recollected that two years ago West-Point was a desert, almost inaccessible, that this desert has been covered with fortresses and artillery, by a people, who six years before had scarcely ever seen cannon; when we reflect that the fate of the United States depended in great measure on this important post; and that a horse dealer,[5] transformed into a general, or rather become a hero, always intrepid, always victorious, but always purchasing victory at the price of his blood; that this extraordinary man, at once the honour, and the opprobrium of his country, actually sold, and expected to deliver this *Palladium* of American liberty to the English; when so many extraordinary circumstances are brought together in the physical and moral order of things, it may easily be imagined that I had sufficient exercise for reflection, and that I did not tire on the road.

On landing, or rather on climbing the rocks on the banks of the river, we were received by Colonel Lamb, and Major Bowman, both officers of artillery; by Major Fish, a handsome young man, witty and well formed; and Major Franks, formerly aide-de-camp to Arnold.[6] The latter had been tried and honourably acquitted by a council of war, demanded by himself after the escape and treason of his General. He speaks good French, as well as Colonel Lamb, which they both learnt in Canada, where they were settled. The latter received a musket shot in his jaw at the attack of Quebec, fighting by the side of Arnold, and having early penetrated into the upper town. Pressed by dinner time we went immediately to General Heath's barrack. The fort, which was begun on much too extensive a plan, has been since curtailed by Mr. du Portail, so that this barrack is no longer within its precincts. Around it are some magazines, and farther to the north-west, barracks for three or four battalions; they are built of wood, and similar to those of Fishkill. Whilst dinner was preparing, General Heath took me into a little closet, which served him as a bed chamber, and showed me the instructions he had given General Stark for the grand foraging party he commanded. This expedition required a movement of troops in a space of more than fifty miles; and I can affirm, that they were as well conceived as any instructions of that kind I have ever seen, either in print, or manuscript. He showed me also a letter in which General Washington only ordered him to send this detachment, and pointed out its object, without communicating to him, however, another operation connected with it, which was to take place on the right bank of the North river. From various intelligence, by indirect ways, General Heath was persuaded, that in case the enemy collected his force to interrupt the forage, Mr. de la Fayette would attack Staten-Island, and he was not deceived; but Mr. Washington contented himself with announcing generally some movements on his side, adding, that he waited for a more safe method of communicating the nature of them to General Heath. Secrecy is strictly observed in the American army; very few persons are in the confidence of the Commander, and in general there is less said of the operations of war, of what we call news, than in the French army. . . . It was with real satisfaction he [General Heath] received me at West-Point; he gave me a plain but very good dinner. It is true there was not a drop of wine; but I find that with excellent cider, and toddy, one may very well dispense with it. As soon as we rose from the table, we hurried to avail ourselves of the remaining daylight to examine the fortifications. The first fort we met with above West-Point, on the declivity of the mountain, is called Fort Putnam, from the General of that name.[7] It is placed on a rock very steep on every side; the ramparts were at first constructed with trunks of trees; they are rebuilt with stone, and are not quite finished. There is a powder magazine bomb-proof, a large cistern, and souterrains for the garrison. Above this fort, and when we reach the loftiest summit, there are three strong redoubts lined with cannon, at three different eminences, each of which would require a formal siege. The day being nearly spent, I contented myself with judging by the eye of the very intelligent manner in which they are calculated for mutual protection. Fort Wallis, whither General Heath conducted me, was near and more accessible. Though it be placed lower than fort Putnam, it still commands the river to the south. It is a large pentagonal redoubt, built of huge trunks of trees; it is picketed, and lined with artillery. Under the fire of this redoubt, and lower down, is a battery of cannon, to range more obliquely the course of the river. This battery is not closed at the gorge, so that the enemy may take, but never keep it; which leads me to remark that this is the best method in all field fortifications. . . . A battery yet lower, and nearer to the river, completes the security of the southern part.

In returning to West-Point, we saw a redoubt that is suffered to go to ruin, as being useless, which in fact it is. It was night when we got home, but what I had to observe did not require daylight. It is a vast souterrain, formed within the fort of West-Point, where not only the powder and ammunition necessary for this post are kept in reserve, but the deposite of the whole army. These magazines completely filled, the numerous artillery one sees in these different fortresses, the prodigious labour necessary to transport, and pile up on steep rocks, huge trunks of trees, and enormous hewn stones, impress the mind with an idea of the Americans very different from that which the English ministry have laboured to give to Parliament. A Frenchman would be surprised that a nation, just rising into notice, should have expended into two years upwards of twelve millions (half a million sterling) in this desert. He would be still more so on learning that these fortifications cost nothing to the state, being built by the soldiers, who received not the smallest gratification, and who did not even receive their stated pay; but he would doubtless feel some satisfaction, in hearing that these beautiful and well contrived works, were planned and executed by two French Engineers, Mr. du Portail, and Mr. du Gouvion, who received no more pay than their workmen.

But in this wild and warlike abode, where one seems transported to the bottom of Thrace and the dominions of the god Mars, we found, on our return in the evening, some pretty women, and an excellent dish of tea. Mrs. Boman, wife of the Major of that name, and a young sister who had accompanied her to West-Point, were waiting us. They lodged in a little barrack neatly arranged. The room they received us in, was hung with handsome paper, furnished with mahogany tables, and even ornamented with several prints. After staying a little time, it was necessary to return to General Heath's quarters, and to dispose matters for passing the night, which was an easy affair; for the company were much increased in the course of the evening, by the arrival of the Vicomte de Noailles, the Comte de Damas, and the Chevalier Duplessis-Mauduit [who] had reached West-

Point, which post they had intended to examine minutely;[8] but the motions of the American army determined them to set out with me, in order to join Mr. de la Fayette, the next evening, or early the following morning. Though General Heath had a great deal of company to provide for, his *Marechal de Logis,* had much to do: there were only three rooms in the barracks; the General's chamber, that of his aide-de-camp, who resigned it to me; and the dining-room, in which some blankets were spread before a large fire, where the other gentlemen passed as comfortable a night as could be expected.

[*November 22.*] The morning gun soon summoned them from their beds; the blankets were removed, and the dining-room, resuming its rights, was quickly furnished with a large table covered with beef-steaks, which we ate with a very good appetite, swilling down from time to time a cup of tea. Europeans would not find this food and drink, taken together, to their taste; but I can assure you that it made a very comfortable breakfast. There now fell a very heavy rain, which had begun in the night, and still continued, with a dreadful wind, which rendered the passage of the ferry very dangerous for our horses, and prevented us from making use of the sail, in the barge General Heath had given us, to carry us to King's Ferry.[9] In spite of these obstacles we embarked under the firing of thirteen guns, notwithstanding our representations to the contrary. Another circumstance, however, gave additional value to these honours, for the pieces they discharged had belonged to Burgoyne's army. Thus did the artillery sent from Woolwich to Canada in 1777, now serve to defend America, and do homage to her allies, until it was to be employed in the siege of New-York.

General Heath, who was detained by business at West-Point, sent Major Liman [Lyman] to accompany me to Verplank's Point, where we did not arrive till between twelve and one, after a continued journey amidst the immense hills which cover this country, and leave no other interval than the bed of the river. The highest of them is called Antony's Nose; it projects into the river, and compels it to make a little change in its course. Before we arrive at this point, we see the ruins of fort Clinton: this fort, which was named after the governor of the state of New-York, was attacked and taken in 1777 by the English General Clinton, as he was remounting the river to Albany to join hands with Burgoyne.[10] It was then the principal fort on the river, and built on a rock, at the foot of a mountain, thought to be inaccessible, and was farther defended by a little creek which falls into the main river. Sir Henry Clinton scaled the top of the mountain, himself carrying the British colours, which he always held aloft, until his troops descended the steep rock, passed the creek, and carried the post. The garrison, consisting of 700 men, were almost all taken. Since the defeat of Burgoyne and the alliance with France has changed the face of affairs in America, General Washington has not thought proper to repair fort Clinton; he preferred placing his communication and concentrating his forces at West-Point, because the Hudson there makes a circuit which prevents vessels from remounting with the wind abaft, or with the tide; and Constitution-Isle, which is precisely at the turn of the river, in a direction north and south, is perfectly well situated to protect the chain which closes the passage for ships of war.[11]

The English, however, had preserved a very important post at King's Ferry, where they were sufficiently well fortified; so that by the aid of their ships, they were masters of the course of the river for the space of more than fifty miles, and were thus able to repel to the northward the very important communication between the Jerseys and Connecticut. Such was the state of things, when, in the month of June, 1779, General Wayne, who commanded in the Clove [12] a corps of 1,500 men, formed the project of surprising Stony-Point. This fort was in an entrenchment, surrounded with abattis, which crowned a steep rock, and formed a well picketed redoubt. General Wayne marched, in the night, in three columns, the principal of which was led on by Monsieur de Fleury, who, without firing a musket, forced the abattis, and entrenchments, and entered the redoubt with the fugitives. The attack was so brisk on the part of the Americans, and such the terror of the English, that Mr. de Fleury, who was the first that entered, found himself in an instant loaded with eleven swords which were delivered to him by those who asked for quarter. It must be added to the honour of our allies, that from that moment not a drop of blood was spilt. The Americans, once masters of one of the banks of the river, lost no time in getting possession of the other.[13] Mr. de Gouvion constructed a redoubt at Verplank's-Point, (nearly opposite,) where we landed, and where, by a lucky accident, we found our horses, arrived as soon as us. This redoubt is a peculiar form, hardly ever used but in America: the ditch is within the parapet, which is made steep on both sides, and picketed at the height of the cordon; lodgings for the soldiers are formed below. The middle of the work is a space constructed with wood, and in the form of a square tower. There are battlements every where, and it commands the rampart. An abattis formed of the tops of trees interwoven, surrounds the whole, and is a substitute for a covered way. We may easily perceive that such a work cannot be surprised, nor taken without cannon. Now as this is backed by the mountains, of which the Americans are always masters, it is almost impossible that the English should besiege it. A creek which falls into Hudson river, and runs to the southward of this redoubt, renders its position still more advantageous.

Colonel Livingston,[14] who commands at King's Ferry, has established himself there in preference to Stony-Point, to be nearer White-Plains, where the English frequently made incursions. This is a very amiable and well informed young man. Previous to the war he married in Canada, where he has acquired the French language: in 1775, he was one of the first who took arms; he fought under the orders of Montgomery, and took fort Chambly, whilst the former was besieging St. John's. He received us in his little citadel with great politeness; but to leave it with the honours of war, the American laws required that we should breakfast. It was the second we had taken that day, and consisted of beef-steaks, and tea, accompanied with a few bowls of grog; for the commander's cellar was no better stored than the soldier's wardrobe. The latter had been sent into this garrison as being the worst clothed of the whole American army, so that one may form some idea of their dress.

About two o'clock we crossed the river, and stopped to examine the fortifications of Stony-Point. The Americans finding them too extensive, had reduced them to a redoubt, nearly similar to that of Verplank's but not quite so good. There I took leave of Mr. Livingston, who gave me a guide to conduct me to the army, and I set off, preceded by Messieurs de Noailles, de Damas, and de Mauduit, who wished to join Mr. de la Fayette that night, though they had thirty miles to go, through very bad roads. This impatience was well suited to their age; but the intelligence I collected proving to me that the army could not move before the next day, I determined to stop on the road, content to profit by the little daylight that remained to travel ten or twelve miles. On leaving the river, I frequently turned round to enjoy the magnificent spectacle it presents in this place, where its bed becomes so large, that in viewing it to the southward, it has the appearance of an immense lake, whilst the northern aspect is that of a majestic river.[15] I was advised to observe a sort of promontory, from whence Colonel Livingston had formed the project of taking the *Vulture* sloop of war, which brought André, and was waiting for [Benedict] Arnold.[16] This vessel having come too near the shore, grounded at low water; the colonel acquainted Arnold with it, and asked him for two pieces of heavy cannon, assuring him that he would place them so as to sink her. Arnold eluded the proposal on frivolous pretences, so that the colonel could only bring one four pounder, which was at Verplank's to bear on her. This piece raked the vessel fore and aft, and did her so much damage, that if she had not got off with the flood, she must have struck. The next day Colonel Livingston being on the shore, saw Arnold pass in his barge, as he was going down the river to get on board the frigate. He declares that he had such a suspicion of him, that had his guard boats been near, he would have gone after him instantly, and asked him where he was going. This question probably would have embarrassed the traitor, and Colonel Livingston's suspicions thence being confirmed, he would have arrested him.

My thoughts were occupied with Arnold and his treason, when my road brought me to *Smith's* famous house, where he had his interview with André, and formed his horrid plot.[17] It was in this house they passed the night together, and where André changed his clothes. It was there that the liberty of America was bargained for and sold; and it was there that chance, which is always the arbiter of great events, disconcerted this horrible project, and that satisfied with sacrificing the imprudent André, she prevented the crime, only by the escape of the criminal. André was repassing the river quietly, to gain New-York by the White-Plains, had not the cannon fired at the frigate, made him apprehend the falling in with the American troops. He imagined, that favoured

by his disguise, he should be safer on the right bank: a few miles from thence he was stopped, and a few miles farther he found the gibbet.[18]

Smith, who was more than suspected, but not convicted of being a party in the plot, is still in prison, where the law protects him against justice. But his house seems to have experienced the only chastisement of which it was susceptible; it is punished by solitude; and is in fact so deserted, that there is not a single person to take care of it, although it is the mansion of a large farm. I pursued my route, but without being able to give so much attention as to recollect it; I only remember that it was as gloomy as my reflections; it brought me into a deep vale, covered with cypresses; a torrent rolled over the rocks, which I passed, and soon after night came on. I had still some miles to an inn, where I got tolerably well accommodated. It is situated in Haverstraw, and is kept by another *Smith,* but who in no way resembles the former; he assured me he was a good whig, and as he gave me a good supper, I readily believed him.

[*November 23.*] The 23d I set out at eight o'clock, with the intention of arriving in good time at the Marquis de la Fayette's camp; for I had learnt that the army was not to move that day, and I was desirous of being presented by him to General Washington. The shortest road was by Paramus; but my guide insisted on my turning to the northward, assuring me that the other road was not safe, that it was infested with tories, and that he always avoided it, when he had letters to carry. I took the road to the right therefore, and followed for some time the rivulet of Romopog [Ramapo River]; I then turned to the left, and soon got into the township of Pompton [N.J.], and into the Totohaw [Totowa] road; but being informed that it led me straight to the main body of the army, without passing by the van commanded by M. de la Fayette, I inquired for some cross road to his quarters, and one was pointed out to me, by which, passing near a sort of lake which forms a very agreeable point of view, and then crossing some very beautiful woods, I arrived at a stream which falls into Second river [Passaic River], exactly at the spot where M. de la Fayette was encamped.[19]

II

December 20–31: New Windsor to Saratoga

[After spending four days with Lafayette and Washington at Preakness, N.J., Chastellux went on to Philadelphia to spend three weeks touring the nearby sights and battlefields of Pennsylvania. On December 16, 1780, he left Philadelphia for his return journey to the Hudson, his object being to pay a brief visit to Washington, now in winter quarters at New Windsor, and then ascend the Hudson Valley to tour the battlefield of Saratoga. On the 19th he retraced his steps through "the Clove" north of Suffern and spent the night at Hern's tavern, about ten miles west of West Point.]

[*December 20.*] I left it the 20th, as early as possible; having still twelve miles to New-Windsor, and intending to stay only one night, I was anxious to pass at least the greatest part of the day with General Washington. I met him two miles from New-Windsor; he was in his carriage with Mrs. Washington, going on a visit to Mrs. Knox, whose quarters were a mile farther on, near the artillery barracks.[20] They wished to return with me, but I begged them to continue their way. The general gave me one of his aid-de-camps, (Colonel Humphreys) to conduct me to his house, assured me that he should not be long in joining me, and he returned accordingly in half an hour. I saw him again with the same pleasure, but with a different sentiment from what he had inspired me with at our first interview. I felt that internal satisfaction, in which self-love has some share, but which we always experience in finding ourselves in an intimacy already formed, in real society with a man we have long admired without being able to approach him. It then seems as if this great man more peculiarly belongs to us than to the rest of mankind; heretofore we desired to see him; henceforth, so to speak, we exhibit him; we knew him, we are better acquainted with him than others, have the same advantage over them, that a man having read a book through, has in conversation over him who is only at the beginning.

The General insisted on my lodging with him, though his house was much less than that he had at Prakness [*sic*]. Several officers, whom I had not seen at the army, came to dine with us. The principal of whom were Colonel Malcomb, a native of Scotland, but settled in America, where he has served with distinction in the continental army; he has since retired to his estate, and is now only a militia Colonel; Colonel Smith, an officer highly spoken of, and who commanded a battalion of light infantry under M. de la Fayette;[21] Colonel Humphreys, the General's aid-de-camp,[22] and several others, whose names I have forgot, but who had all the best *ton*, and the easiest deportment. The dinner was excellent; tea succeeded dinner, and conversation succeeded tea, and lasted till supper. The war was frequently the subject: on asking the General which of our professional books he read with the most pleasure, he told me the King of Prussia's Instructions to His Generals, and the Tactics of M. de Guibert; from whence I concluded that he knew as well how to select his authors as to profit by them.

[*December 21.*] I should have been very happy to accept of his pressing invitation to pass a few days with him, had I not made a solemn promise, at Philadelphia, to the Vicomte de Noailles, and his travelling companions, to arrive four and twenty hours after them if they stopped there, or at Albany, if they went straight on.

We were desirous of seeing Stillwater and Saratoga, and it would have been no easy matter for us to have acquired a just knowledge of that country had we not been together, because we reckoned upon General Schuyler, who could not be expected to make two journeys to gratify our curiosity.[28] I was thus faithful to my engagement, for I arrived at New-Windsor the same day that they left West Point; I hoped to overtake them at Albany, and General Washington finding that he could not retain me, was pleased himself to conduct me in his barge to the other side of the river. We got on shore at Fishkill Landing Place, to gain the eastern road, preferred by travellers to the western. I now quitted the General, but he insisted that Colonel Smith should accompany me as far as Poughkeepsie. The road to this town passes fairly close to Fishkill, which we leave on the right, from thence we travel on the heights, where there is a beautiful and extensive prospect, and traversing a township, called Middlebrook, arrive at the creek, and at Wapping Fall [Wappingers Falls]. There I halted a few minutes to consider, under different points of view, the charming landscape formed by this river, as well as from its cascade, which is roaring and picturesque, as from the groups of trees and rocks, which combined with a number of saw mills and furnaces, compose the most capricious and romantic prospect.

It was only half past three when I got to Poughkeepsie, where I intended sleeping; but finding that the "Sessions" were then holding and that all the taverns were full, I took advantage of the little remaining day to reach a tavern I was told of at three miles distance. Colonel Smith who had business at Poughkeepsie remained there, and I was very happy to find myself in the evening with nobody but my two aids-de-camp. It was, in fact, a new enjoyment for us to be left to ourselves, at perfect liberty to give mutual accounts of the impression left on our minds by so many different objects. I only regretted not having seen Governor Clinton, for whom I had letters of recommendation. He is a man who governs with the utmost vigour and firmness, and is inexorable to the tories, whom he makes tremble, though they are very numerous: he has been able to control this great province, one extremity of which borders on Canada, the other on the city of New-York. He was then at Poughkeepsie, but taken up with the business of the Sessions: besides, Saratoga, and Burgoyne's different fields of battle, being henceforth the sole object of my journey, I was wishing to get forward for fear of being hindered by the snow, and of the roads becoming impassable. On my arrival at Pride's tavern, I asked a number of questions of my landlord respecting the appearance he thought there was of a continuance or a change of weather, and perceiving that he was a good farmer, I interrogated him on the subject of agriculture, and drew the following details from him. The land is very fertile in Duchess County, of which Poughkeepsie is the capital, as well as in the state of New-York, but it is commonly left fallow one year out of two or three, less from necessity than from their being more land than they can cultivate. A bushel of wheat at most is sown upon an acre, which renders twenty, and five and twenty for one. Some farmers sow oats on the land that has borne wheat the preceding year, but this grain in general is reserved for lands newly turned up: flax is also a considerable object of cultivation: the land is ploughed with horses, two or three to a plough; sometimes even a greater number when on new land, or that which has long lain fallow. Mr. Pride, while he was giving me these details, always flattered me with the hopes of fine weather the next day. I went to rest, highly satisfied with him and his prognostics.

[*December 22.*] In the morning, however, when I awakened, I saw the ground already entirely white, and snow, which continued to fall in abundance, mixed with hail and ice. There was nothing to be done under the circumstances, but to continue my journey, as if it were fine weather, only taking a little better breakfast than I should otherwise have done. But I regretted most that the snow, or rather small hail that drove against my eyes, prevented me from seeing the country; which, as far as I could judge, is beautiful and well cultivated. After travelling about ten miles, I traversed the township of Strasbourg, called by the inhabitants of the country, Strattsborough [Staatsburg]. This township is five or six miles long, yet the houses are not far from each other. As I was noticing one which was rather handsome, the owner came to the door, doubtless from curiosity, and asked me, in French, if I would alight, and step in and dine with him. Nothing can be more seducing in bad weather, than such a proposal; but on the other hand, nothing is more cruel, when one has once got under shelter, than to quit the fire-side, a second time to expose oneself to frost and snow.

I refused therefore the dinner offered me by this gallant man, but not the questions he put to me. I asked him, in my turn, whether he had not seen some French officers pass, meaning the Vicomte de Noailles, the Comte de Damas, and the Chevalier de Mauduit, who, as they had three or four servants, and six or seven horses, might have been noticed on the road. My Dutchman, for I have since learnt that his name is Le Roy, a Dutch merchant, born in Europe, and acquainted with France, where he lived some time; my Dutchman, replied like a man who knew France, and who speaks French: "Sir, it is very true that the Prince de Conti passed by here yesterday evening, with two officers, on their way to Albany." I could not discover whether it was to the Vicomte de Noailles, or to the Comte de Damas, that I ought to do homage for his principality; but as they are both my relations, I answered with strict truth, that my cousin having gone on before, I was very glad to know at what hour they passed, and when I should be able to join them; so that if Mr. Le Roy, as no doubt he did, consulted his almanack, he will have set me down for the Duke of Orleans, or the Duke of Chartres; which was the more probable as I had nine horses with me, whilst the French de Conti, being farther removed from the crown, had only seven.

You scarcely get out of Strasborough, before you enter the township of Rhinebeck. It is unnecessary to observe, that all these names reveal a German origin. At Rhinebeck nobody came out to ask me to dinner. But this snow mixed with hail was so cold, and I was so fatigued with keeping my horse from slipping, that I should have stopped here even without being invited by the handsome appearance of the inn called Thomas' Inn.[24] It was no more, however, than half past two; but as I had already come three and twenty miles, the house was good, the fire well lighted, my host a tall good looking man, a sportsman, a horse dealer, and disposed to chat, I determined, according to the English phrase, to spend the rest of my day there. The following is all I got interesting from Mr. Thomas. In time of peace, he carried on a great trade of horses, which he purchased in Canada, and sent to New-York, there to be shipped to the West-Indies. It is incredible with what facility this trade is carried on in winter; he assured me that he once went to Montreal, and brought back with him, in a fortnight seventy-five horses which he bought there. This is effected by travelling in a straight line, traversing Lake George upon ice and the snow, the desert between that lake and Montreal. The Canadian horses easily travel eighteen or twenty hours a day, and three or four men, mounted, are sufficient to drive one hundred before them. "It was I," added Mr. Thomas, "who made, or rather repaired, the fortune of that rogue, [Benedict] Arnold. He had failed in the little trade he carried on at New-Haven. I persuaded him to purchase horses in Canada, and to go himself and sell them at Jamaica. This speculation alone was sufficient to pay his debts, and set him once more afloat." [25] After talking of trade, we got to agriculture. He told me that in the neighborhood of Rhinebeck that land was uncommonly fruitful, and that for a bushel of sown wheat, he reaped from thirty to forty. The corn is so abundant that they do not take the trouble of cutting it with a sickle, but mow it like hay. Some dogs of a beautiful kind moving about the house, awakened my passion for the chase. On asking Mr. Thomas what use he made of them, he told me that they were only for fox hunting; that deer, stags, and bears were pretty common in the country, but they seldom killed them except in winter, either by tracing on the snow, or by tracking them in woods. All American conversation must finish with politics. Those of Mr. Thomas appeared to me rather equivocal; he was too rich, and complained too much of the flour he furnished for the army to let me think him a good whig. He gave himself out for such notwithstanding, but I observed that he was greatly attached to an opinion which I found generally diffused throughout the state of New-York; that there is no expedition more useful, nor more easy than the conquest of Canada. It is impossible to conceive the ardour the inhabitants of the north still have to recommence that enterprise. The reason is, that their country is so fertile, and so happily situated for commerce, that they are sure to become very wealthy as soon as they have nothing to fear from the savages; and indeed the savages are only formidable when they are supported and animated by the English.

[December 23.] I left Thomas' Inn the 23d, at 8 in the morning, and travelled three hours without leaving Livingston Manor. The road was good, and the country rich and well cultivated. We pass several sizable villages, the houses of which are handsome and neat, and every object here bespeaks prosperity. On leaving this district we enter that of Claverack, then descend from the hills, and approach the Hudson River. We soon after come to a creek, which is also called by the name of Claverack, and which falls not far from this place into the Hudson River.[26] As soon as you pass this creek, an immense rock which cuts across the path of the road, obliges you to turn to the right to reach Claverack meeting-house, and to pursue the road to Albany. This rock, or rather chain of rocks, merits all the attention of naturalists. It is about three miles in length. . . .

Claverack is a pretty considerable township, and extends very far. On quitting it you traverse several woods before arriving at the first houses of Kinderhook. I found in these woods new improvements, and log cabins. But on approaching one of them I perceived, with regret, that the family who inhabited it had been long settled there, without thinking of building a better house, an uncommon circumstance in America, and which is almost unexampled, except in the Dutch settlements, for the latter people are more economical than industrious, and are more desirous of amassing wealth than of adding to their comfort. When you arrive at the first hamlet of Kinderhook, you must make a long circuit to reach the meeting-house, which is in the center of what may be properly called the town of Kinderhook. There you pass a pretty large stream, and have the choice of three or four inns; but the best is that of Mr. Van Burragh.[27] The preference given to this, however, does no honour to the others; it is a very small house, kept by two young people of a Dutch family; they are civil and attentive, and you are not badly off with them, provided you are not difficult to please. It would have ill become me now to have been so, for I had nothing but snow, hail, and frost during the whole day, and my fireside was an agreeable asylum for me.

[*December 24.*] It was a difficult question to know where I should the next day pass the North river, for I was told that it was neither sufficiently frozen to cross it on the ice, nor free enough from floes to venture it in a boat. Apprized of these obstacles, I set out early on the 24th, that I might have time to discover the easiest passage. I was only twenty miles from Albany; so that after a continuous journey through a forest of fir trees, I arrived at one o'clock on the banks of the Hudson. The valley in which this river runs, and the town of Albany, which is built in the form of an amphitheatre on its western bank, must have afforded a very agreeable coup d'oeil, had it not been disfigured by the snow. A handsome house half way up the bank opposite the ferry seems to attract the eye and to invite strangers to stop at General Schuyler's, who is the owner as well as architect. I had recommendations to him from all quarters, but particularly from General Washington and Mrs. Carter.[28] I had besides made arrangements to meet Colonel [Alexander] Hamilton, who had just married another of his daughters,[29] and furthermore was preceded there by the Vicomte de Noailles and the Comte de Damas, who I knew had arrived the night before. The sole difficulty therefore consisted in crossing the river. Whilst the boat was making its way with difficulty through the floes of ice, which we were obliged to break as we advanced, Mr. Lynch, who is not indifferent to a good dinner, contemplating General Schuyler's house, mournfully says to me, "I am sure the Vicomte and Damas are now at table, where they have good cheer and good company, whilst we are kicking our heels here,

merely in hopes of getting this evening to some wretched alehouse." I partook a little of his anxiety, but diverted myself by assuring him they saw us from the windows, that I even distinguished the Vicomte de Noailles who was looking at us through a telescope, and that he was going to send somebody to conduct us on our landing to that excellent house, where we should find dinner ready to be served; I even pretended that a sleigh I had seen descending towards the river was destined for us. As chance would have it, never was conjecture more just. The first person we saw on shore was the Chevalier de Mauduit, who was waiting for us with the general's sleigh, and into which we quickly stepped and were immediately conveyed to a handsome drawing room, near a good fire, with Mr. Schuyler, his wife and daughters. Whilst we were warming ourselves, dinner was served, to which every one did honour, as well as to the Madeira which was excellent and made us completely forget the rigour of the season and the fatigue of the journey.

General Schuyler's family was composed of Mrs. Hamilton, his second daughter, who has a mild agreeable countenance; of Miss Peggy Schuyler, whose features are animated and striking; of another charming girl, only eight years old, and of three boys, the eldest of whom is fifteen, and are the handsomest children you can see.[30] He is himself about fifty, but already gouty and infirm. His fortune is very considerable, and it will become still more so, for he possesses an immense extent of territory, but derives more credit from his talents and knowledge than from his wealth. He served with General Amherst in the Canadian war as Quarter-Master-General. From that period he made himself known and became distinguished; he was very useful to the English, and was sent to London after the peace to settle the accounts of everything furnished by the Americans. His marriage with Miss Renssalaer, the rich heiress of a family which has given its name to a district, or rather a whole province, still added to his credit and influence; so that it was not surprising he should be raised to the rank of Major-General at the beginning of the war, and have the command of the troops on the frontiers of Canada. It was in this capacity that he was commissioned in 1777 to oppose the progress of General Burgoyne, but having received orders from Congress, directly contrary to his opinion, without being provided with any means for carrying them into execution, he found himself obliged to evacuate Ticonderoga and fall back on the Hudson. These measures, undoubtedly prudent in themselves, being unfavorably construed in a moment of ill humour and anxiety, he was tried by court martial, as well as General St. Clair, his second in command, and both of them were soon after honourably acquitted. St. Clair resumed his station in the army, but General Schuyler, justly offended, demanded more satisfactory reparation, and reclaimed his rank which, since this event, was contested with him by two or three generals of the same standing. This affair not being settled, he did not rejoin the army, but continued his services to his country. Elected a member of Congress the following year, he was almost chosen president in opposition to Mr. Laurens. Since that time he has always enjoyed the confidence of the government, and of General Washington, who are at present paying court to him and pressing him to accept the office of Secretary of War.

Whilst we were in this excellent asylum the weather continued doubtful, fluctuating between freezing and thawing. There was a little snow on the ground, and there probably would soon be more. The council of travellers assembled, and it appeared wise to them not to delay their departure for Saratoga. General Schuyler offered us a house which he has upon his own estate; but he could not serve as guide because of an indisposi-

tion and his fear of a fit of the gout. He proposed giving us an intelligent officer to conduct us to the different fields of battle, whilst his son should go in advance to prepare lodgings for us. We could still travel on horseback, and were supplied with horses of the country to replace ours which were fatigued, and a few of whom still remained on the other side of the river. All these arrangements being accepted, we were conveyed to Albany in a sleigh. On our arrival we waited on Brigadier-General [James] Clinton, to whom I delivered my letters of recommendation. He is an honest man, but of no distinguished talents, and is only employed out of respect to his brother the governor. He immediately ordered the horses for our journey, and Major Popham, his aid-de-camp, an amiable and intelligent officer, was ordered to conduct us. He was to take with him Major Graham, who knows the ground perfectly, and served in the army under General [Horatio] Gates.

All our measures being well coordinated, we each retired to our quarters; the Vicomte de Noailles and his two companions to an inn, kept by a Frenchman called Louis, and I to that of an American by the name of Blennissnes.

[*December 25.*] At daybreak tea was ready, and the whole caravan assembled at my quarters; but wet snow was falling, promising a disagreeable ride. We were in hopes, however, that it was a real thaw, and set out upon our journey. But the snow fell thicker and thicker and was six inches deep when we arrived at the junction of the Mohawk and Hudson rivers. Here is a choice of two roads to Saratoga: one obliges you to cross the Hudson, to keep some time along the left bank, then cross it a second time at Half-Moon; [31] the other goes up the Mohawk river till you get above the falls where you cross that river and go through the woods to Stillwater. Even had there been no difficulty in crossing the North river on account of the ice, I should have preferred the other road in order to see the falls of Cohoes which is one of the wonders of America. Before we left the Hudson I noticed an island in the middle of its channel which offers a very advantageous position for erecting batteries to control shipping.[32] The two majors to whom I communicated this observation, told me that this point of defence was neglected because there was a better one, a little higher up, at the tip of one of the three branches into which the Mohawk river divides itself, in falling into the Hudson. They added that this position had merely been given a cursory inspection; the other one higher up, having begun to be fortified, was sufficient to stop the enemy. Thus the more you examine the country, the more you are convinced that the expedition of Burgoyne was extravagant, and must sooner or later have miscarried, independent of the engagements which decided the event.

The junction of the two rivers is six miles north of Albany, and after travelling two more in the woods, we began to hear a murmuring noise, which increased till we came in sight of Cohoes Falls. This cataract is the whole breadth of the river, that is to say, nearly two hundred *toises,* or about 1,200 English feet wide. It is a vast sheet of water, which falls 76 English feet.[33] The river in this place is contracted between two steep banks formed by the declivity of the mountains; these precipices are covered by an earth as black as iron ore, and on which nothing grows but firs and cypresses. The course of the river is straight, both before and after its fall, and the rocks forming this cascade are nearly on a level, but their irregular shape breaks the water whilst it is falling and forms a variety of whimsical and picturesque appearances. This picture was rendered still more awesome by the snow which covered the firs, the brilliancy of which gave a black colour to the water,

gliding gently along, and a yellow tinge to that which was passing over the cataract.

After feasting our eyes on this sublime spectacle, we travelled a mile higher up to the ferry where we hoped to pass the river. But on our arrival we found the boat so entangled in the ice and snow that it was impossible to make use of it. We were assured that some people had crossed via a ferry two miles higher that very morning, so we immediately went there, determined to pursue our journey, though the snow was falling much harder and we were benumbed with wet and cold. The boatman of this ferry made many objections because of the bad weather and the smallness of the boat, which could only transport three horses at a time; but this difficulty did not stop us, and we agreed to make several trips. The first attempt was made to pass over my *valet de chambre,* with three horses. I was waiting by the fireside for my turn when they came to tell me that the boat was coming back to shore with some difficulty, and that the current had almost driven it towards the cataract. We were obliged therefore to submit to our destiny, which was not yet disposed to let us fulfill the object of our journey. On this occasion I displayed a magnanimity which placed me high in the esteem of the whole company: whilst others were fuming and growing impatient, uncertain of the measures to be taken, I serenely gave the signal for a retreat, and thought no more of anything but supper, for which I made the most prudent dispositions on the spot. The innkeeper of M. de Noailles being a Frenchman and consequently a better cook, or at least more active than mine, it was decided that he should provide our supper. The best mounted cavalier of the troop was despatched to give the necessary orders, whom we followed in half an hour. We arrived as night was coming on, and presently sat down to table. Thus passed the day's work of the 25th, which was not very agreeable till the hour of supper, but terminated very happily; for what consolation does one not derive under disappointment, from a good fire, a good supper, and good company?

[*December 26.*] The 26th, the rivers not being frozen yet, nor the roads hard enough to make a long journey in a sleigh, I determined to remain in Albany. My morning was employed in adjusting my notes, which occupation was only interrupted by a visit from Colonel Hamilton. He told us that Mrs. Schuyler was a little indisposed, but that the General would be equally glad to receive us. Accordingly, he sent us his sleighs in the early evening. We found him in his drawing room with Mr. and Mrs. Hamilton. A conversation soon took place between the General, the Vicomte de Noailles and me. We had already talked, when we were last with him, of some important faults relative to the northern campaigns, of which we had asked some explanations. Mr. Schuyler appeared no less desirous of giving them. He is pretty communicative, and is well entitled to be so; his conversation is very easy and agreeable; he knows well what he says, and expresses himself well on everything he knows. To give the best answer to our questions, he proposed to us to read his political and military correspondence with General Washington, which we accepted with great pleasure. Leaving the rest of the company with Mr. and Mrs. Hamilton, we retired into another room. . . .

I did not finish my reading before ten o'clock; and I continued in conversation with General Schuyler whilst the company was at supper. . . . We then separated well pleased with each other, and I returned home to await the decision of the weather respecting the next day's journey.

[*December 27.*] The 27th in the morning, understanding that the rivers were not yet frozen, and the weather being fine but very cold, I wished to take advantage of it to go to Schenectady. This is a town situated 14 miles from Albany, on the Mohawk river. It excites some curiosity, from being built in the very country of the savages; from its being picketed, that is to say, surrounded with lofty palisades, like their villages; and from their still retaining some habitations there, which form a sort of suburb, to the east of the town. . . . I did not arrive [back in Albany] at the apartments of Vicomte de Noailles till near eight o'clock, where supper, tea, and conversation detained me till midnight. Still nothing was decided respecting our journey, and the news we had received by no means satisfactory.

[*December 28.*] The next morning I received a letter from General Schuyler, who informed me that having sent word the evening before, he was told that I was gone to Schenectady, and from thence to Saratoga; but that he was glad to know I was detained at Albany, for that finding himself much better of his gout, he intended accompanying me the next day. He requested me to come and pass the evening with him, to settle our route and time of departure. I answered this letter by accepting all his propositions, and employed part of the morning in walking about Albany, not without taking many precautions, for the streets were covered with ice. My first visit was to the artillery park, or rather to the trophies of the Americans; for there is no other artillery in this place than eight handsome mortars and twenty ammunition wagons, which made part of Burgoyne's artillery. I entered a large workshop where they were employed in making muskets for the army. The barrels of these muskets, and the bayonets, are forged a few miles from Albany, and polished and finished here. I inquired the price of them, and found that the complete weapon costs about five dollars. The armourers are enlisted, and receive besides their rations, very considerable salaries, if they were paid at all. From thence I went to another barracks situated towards the west of the town, which serves as a military hospital. The sick are served by women. Each of them has a separate bed, and they appear in general to be well taken care of, and kept very clean. At dinner all the company who were to be of the Saratoga party collected at my lodgings, and we went afterwards to General Schuyler's to settle matters for our journey.

[*December 29.*] Accordingly, we set out the next day at sunrise in five different sleighs. General Schuyler took me in his own. We passed the Mohawk river on the ice, a mile above the cataract. It was almost the first attempt and succeeded with all but Major Popham, whose two horses broke through the ice and sank into the river. This event will appear fatal to Europeans; but let them not be alarmed. It is a very common accident, and is remedied in two ways: one by dragging the horses onto the ice by force, and, if possible, by the help of a lever or plank to raise them up; the other by strangling them with their own halters or reins: as soon as they have lost their respiration and motion, they float on the water, and are then lifted up by their forefeet onto the ice; the stricture is loosened, they are bled, and in a quarter of an hour are reinstated in the harness. As there were a great many of us, the first method which is the surest, was employed. All this may be easily conceived, but it will be asked what becomes of the sleigh, and how do we dare approach the hole created by the horses? The answer is, that these animals being much heavier than the sleigh, and supported by four slender bases, they break the ice under their hoofs without causing the sleigh to sink, which is light of itself, and its weight supported by long pieces of wood which serve as shafts. The travellers are not less safe, the ice being always thicker than is necessary to bear them.

As for the horses, they easily kept themselves up on the surface of the water by means of their four legs, and by resting their heads upon the ice.

The accident which happened to Major Popham's sleigh did not detain us above seven or eight minutes; but we went a little astray in the woods we had to pass to reach the high road. We came into it between Half Moon and Stillwater. A mile from thence I saw, on the left, an opening in the wood, and a pretty extensive plain, below which runs a creek. I told General Schuyler that there must be a good [military] position there. He told me I was not mistaken, and that it had been reconnoitered for that purpose in case of need. The creek is called Anthony's Kill; the word *kill* among the Dutch, having the same meaning as *creek* with the Americans. Three miles farther on we traversed a hamlet called Stillwater Landing, for it is here that boats coming down from Saratoga are obliged to stop to avoid the rapids.[34] From hence there is a portage of eight or ten miles to the place where the river is navigable. I imagine the name of *Stillwater* is derived from its tranquillity here previous to the commencement of the rapids. General Schuyler showed me some redoubts he had constructed to defend the park where his boats and provisions were collected, after the evacuation of Fort Anne and Fort Edward.[35] We stopped there to refresh our horses. The General had made an appointment with a militia officer, called Swang, who lives in this neighborhood and who served in the army of General Gates. He put me into his hands, and continued his [Schuyler's] way to Saratoga to prepare for our reception. I presently got into a sleigh with my guide, and at the end of three miles we saw two houses on the bank of the river; it was here that General Gates had his right [flank] and his bridge of boats defended by a redoubt on each bank. We alighted to examine this interesting position which blasted Burgoyne's hopes and prepared his ruin. I shall attempt to give some idea of it, which however incomplete, may throw some light on the accounts given by General Burgoyne, and may even serve to rectify his errors.

The eminences, called *Braem's Heights* [Bemis Heights], from whence this famous camp is named, are only a part of those high grounds which extend along the right [west] bank of the Hudson from the Mohawk river to that at Saratoga.[36] At the spot chosen by General Gates for his position, they form, on the side of the river, two different slopes or terraces. In mounting the first slope you see three redoubts placed parallel to each other. In front of the last, on the north side, is a little hollow beyond which the ground rises again, on which are three more redoubts, placed nearly in the same pattern as the former. In front of them is a deep ravine which runs from the west, in which is a small creek. This ravine takes its rise in the woods, and all the ground on the right of it is extremely thick set with woods. If you will now retrace your steps, place yourself near the first redoubts we mentioned, and climb the second slope toward the west, you will find, on the highest point, a large entrenchment which is parallel with the river, and then turns northwest where it terminates in some fairly steep hills which were also fortified with redoubts. To the left of these heights, and at a place where the slope becomes more gentle, begins another entrenchment which turns toward the west, and makes two or three angles, always following the tops of the heights to the southwest. You come out of the lines towards the northwest, then descend the slope to another plain; this position is most favorably situated, for it commands the surrounding woods and blocks any possible movement against the left flank of the army. It is here that Arnold was encamped with the advanced guard.

If you descend again from this height and proceed towards the north, you are presently in the midst of the woods near Freeman's Farm where the actions of the 19th of September and the 7th of October occurred. I avoid the term *field of battle;* for these two engagements were in the woods, and the ground over which they were fought is so intersected and covered, that it is impossible either to conceive or detect the smallest resemblance between it and the account that was published by General Burgoyne. But what appears to be very clear to me is that this general who was encamped about four miles from the camp on Bream's [Bemis] Heights, wishing to approach and reconnoitre the avenues to it, marched through the woods in four columns; and having several ravines to pass, he made General Frazer, with the advance guard, turn them at their origin; that two other columns crossed the ravines and woods as well as they could without either communicating with each other or waiting for each other; that the left columns, chiefly composed of artillery, followed the course of the river where the ground is more level, and built bridges over the ravines and rivulets, which are deeper on that side, as they all terminate in the river; that the engagement first began with the *riflemen* and American militia, who were supported as necessity required, without any prior disposition; that the advance guard and the right column were the first engaged, and that the combat lasted until the columns on the left arrived, that is to say, till sunset; that the Americans then retired to their camp, where they had taken care to carry their wounded; that the English advance guard and the right column greatly suffered, both of them having fought for a long time in the woods without any support.

General Burgoyne purchased dearly the frivolous honour sleeping on the field of battle: he now encamped at Freeman's Farm so near the American camp that it

12. *View of the West Bank of the Hudson's River 3 Miles above Still Water, upon which the Army under the command of L. General Burgoyne took post on the 20th Sept. 1777,* anonymous engraving; courtesy of The New-York Historical Society.

"General Burgoyne . . . now encamped at Freeman's Farm so near the American camp that it was impossible for him to maneuver."

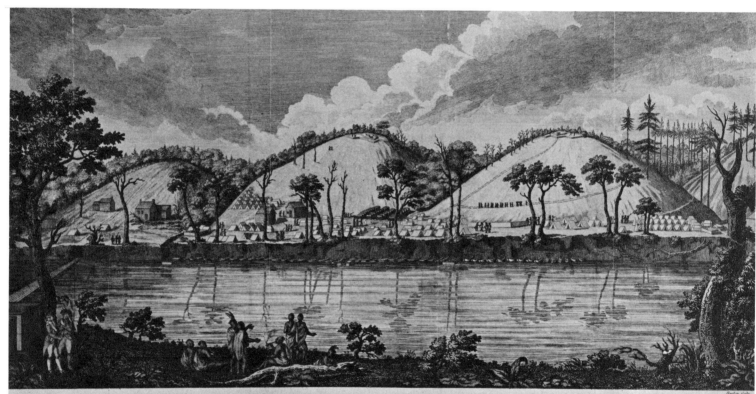

View of the West Bank of the Hudson's River 3 Miles above Still Water, upon which the Army under the command of L. General Burgoyne, took post on the 20th Sep. 1777.
(Shewing General Frazer's Funeral.)
Published as the Act directs, Jan. 1, 1789, by William Lane, Leadenhall Street, London.

was impossible for him to maneuver, so that he found himself in the position of a chess player who has permitted himself to be stalemated. He remained in this position until the 7th of October when, seeing his provisions depleted, hearing nothing of Clinton, and being too near the enemy to retreat without danger, he tried a second attack, and again made an attempt to turn their left flank with his advance guard. The Americans, with whom the woods were filled, penetrated his design, themselves turned the left flank of the corps which threatened theirs, put them to rout, and pursued them so far as to find themselves, without knowing it, opposite the camp of the Germans. This camp was situated *en potence* and a little in the rear of the line. Arnold and [Benjamin] Lincoln, animated with success, attacked and carried the entrenchments: both of them bought victory at the price of their own blood; each of them had a leg broke by musket shots. I saw the spot where Arnold, uniting the boldness of a *jockey* [37] with that of a soldier, leaped his horse over the entrenchment of the enemy. Like all such entrenchments in this country, it is a sort of parapet formed by the trunks of trees piled on top of each other. This action was very brisk, to which the fir trees, which are torn by musket and cannon shot, will long bear testimony; for the term of their existence seems as remote, as does the period of their origin. [38]

I continued reconnoitering there till night, sometimes walking in the snow, where I sank to my knees, and sometimes moving about with even less success in a sleigh —my guide having taken care to tip me over, most gently, in a big pile of snow. After finally finishing my inspection of Burgoyne's lines, I got down to the high road, passing through a field where he had established his hospital. We then travelled more easily, and I got to Saratoga at seven in the evening, after a thirty-seven miles journey. We found good rooms well warmed, an excellent supper, and had a gay and agreeable conversation; for General Schuyler, like many European husbands, is still more amiable when he is absent from his wife. He gave us instructions for our next day's expedition to both Fort Edward and the great cataract of the Hudson river, [39] eight miles above the fort and ten from Lake George.

[*December 30*.] Pursuing these plans, we set out the next morning at eight o'clock with Majors Graham and Popham, whom he had requested to accompany us. We ascended the right bank of the Hudson for almost three miles before we found a safe place to cross the river in our sleighs. Our choice of a crossing exposed us to no danger, the ice being as thick as we could wish it; but on approaching the opposite side the banks appeared to be so high and steep that I could not see how we could get up them. As it is my principle to form no judgment of anything I do not understand, and always, whether travelling by land or sea, to put my trust in the people who know the route, I was sitting quietly in my sleigh, waiting the event, when my guide, a farmer of the country, *called* his horses with a ferocious cry, something like that of the savages; and instantly, without a stroke of the whip, they set off with the sleigh, and in three bounds were at the top of a precipice, twenty feet high and nearly perpendicular.

The road to Fort Edward is almost always parallel to the river, but you frequently lose sight of it in passing through the forests of fir. From time to time you notice modestly handsome houses on the two banks. That of the unfortunate *Miss MacRea* [Jane McCrea], who was killed by the savages, was pointed out to me. If the Whigs were superstitious, they would attribute this event to divine vengeance. The parents of Miss McCrea were Whigs, nor did she belie the sentiments with which they had inspired her, until she became acquainted with an English officer in New-York who triumphed at once over her virtue and her patriotism. From that moment she espoused the cause of England, and waited for the day when she could marry her lover. The war, which soon extended to New-York as well as Boston, obliged her father to retire to his country house, which he immediately abandoned on the approach of Burgoyne's army. But Miss McCrea's lover was in this army; she wished to see him again as a conqueror, to marry him, and then to share his toils and successes. Unfortunately the Indians composed the vanguard of this army; these savages are not used to distinguishing friend from foe; they pillaged the home of Miss McCrea and carried her off. When they had conducted her to their camp, it was a matter of dispute to whom she belonged; they could not agree, and to terminate the quarrel, some of them killed her with a tomahawk. The recital of this sad catastrophe, whilst it made me deplore the miseries of war, concentrated all my interest in the person of the English officer, to whom it was allowable to listen at once to his passion and his duty. I know that a death so cruel and unforeseen, would furnish a subject full of pathos for a drama or an elegy; [40] but nothing short of the charms of eloquence and poetry is capable of moving the heart for such a destiny, by exhibiting only the effect, and throwing the cause into the shade; for such is the true character of love, that all the noble and generous affections seem to be its natural attendants; and if it be that it can sometimes ally itself with blameable circumstances, everything at least which tends to humiliate or degrade it, either annihilates or disguises its genuine features.

As you approach Fort Edward the houses become more rare. This fort is built sixteen miles from Saratoga in a little valley near the river, on the only spot which is not covered with wood, and where you can have a prospect to the distance of a musket-shot around you. Formerly it consisted of a square, fortified by two bastions on the east side, and by two demi-bastions on the side facing the river; but this old fortification is abandoned, because it was too easily commanded from the heights; and a large redoubt with a simple parapet and a wretched palisade, is built on a more elevated spot; within are a small barracks for about two hundred soldiers.[41] Such is Fort Edward, so much spoken of in Europe, although it could in no time have been able to resist five hundred men with four pieces of cannon. I stopped there an hour to refresh my horses, and about noon set off to proceed as far as the cataract, which is eight miles beyond it. On leaving the valley and pursuing the road to Lake George I found a tolerable military position which was occupied during the last war: it is a sort of entrenched camp, adapted to abbatis, guarding the passage from the woods, and commanding the valley.

I had scarcely lost sight of Fort Edward before the spectacle of devastation presented itself to my eyes, and continued to distress them as far as the place I stopped at. Peace and industry had brought cultivators into these ancient forests, men happy and content before the period of the war. Those who were in Burgoyne's path alone experienced the horrors of his expedition; but on the last invasion of the savages, the desolation spread from Fort Schuyler (or Fort Stanwix) [42] as far as Fort Edward. I beheld nothing around me but the remains of conflagrations; a few bricks, proof against the fire, were the only indications of ruined houses; whilst the fences that were still standing, and the cleared lands, announced that these deplorable habitations had once been the abode of riches and of happiness. When we reached the cataract it was necessary to quit our sleighs and walk half a mile to the bank of the river. The snow was fifteen inches deep, which made walking difficult and

13. *Fort Edward,* engraving by John Hill, 1820; courtesy of
The New-York Historical Society.

"As you approach Fort Edward the houses become more rare."

forced us to proced in Indian file in order to make a path. Each of us put ourselves alternately at the head of this little column, as the wild geese take turns leading the point of the triangle they form while in flight. But even if our march had been doubly difficult, the sight of the cataract would have been ample reward. It does not form a sheet of water as at Cohoes and Totowa: here the river is confined and interrupted in its course by different rocks, through the midst of which it glides and precipitates itself obliquely over several cascades. The falls of Cohoes is more majestic; this one is more awesome: the Mohawk river seems to fall from its own dead weight; that of the Hudson frets, and becomes enraged; it foams and forms whirlpools, and flies like a serpent making its escape, still continuing its threats with horrible hissings.

It was almost two o'clock when we regained our sleighs, having twenty-two miles to go to Saratoga, so that we trod back over our steps as fast as possible. However, we still had to halt at Fort Edward to refresh our horses. We employed this time, as we had done in the morning, in warming ourselves by the fire kept by the officers who command the garrison. They are five in number, and command about one hundred and fifty soldiers. They are stationed in this wilderness for the whole winter, and I leave the reader to imagine whether this garrison be much gayer than those of Gravelines or Briancon.[43] We set off again in an hour, and night soon overtook us. Before it was dark, however, I had the satisfaction of seeing the first game I had met with in my journey: it was a covey of quails, by some called partridges, though they look more like quails. They were perched, seven in a row, on a fence. I left my sleigh to get a closer view of them; they permitted me to approach within four paces, and to make them rise I was obliged to throw my cane at them. They all went off together, in a flight similar to that of partridges. They are also like partridges in being sedentary.[44]

Our return was quick and fortunate: we had no accident to fear with the exception of the second crossing of the river and the descent of the precipice we had ascended. I waited for this fresh trial with as much confidence as the former; but a sleigh, which preceded mine, containing the Vicomte de Noailles and the Comte de Damas, stopped at that place; and since the darkness of the night prevented me from distinguishing anything, I imagined the company was going to alight. I was myself no sooner alighted when I saw this sleigh set out with all its load and slide down the precipice with such swiftness that it could not be stopped thirty yards beyond the bottom. They make no more fuss about descending these hills than mounting them: the horses are accustomed to these maneuvers and hurl themselves forward as soon as they set the sleigh in motion; the sleigh thus slides down like the Ramasse of Mount Cenis, and cannot touch their hind legs and make them fall.

At half past six we reached General Schuyler's where we spent our evening as agreeably as the former.

[*December 31.*] The 31st we got on horseback at eight o'clock, and Mr. Schuyler conducted us himself to the camp occupied by the English when General Burgoyne capitulated. We could not have had a better guide, and he was absolutely necessary to us in every respect: for other than the fact that this event happened before his very eyes and he was therefore able to give us a better account than anyone else, he was also the proprietor of the land; and although the fences and entrenchments were buried beneath a foot of snow, he was able to conduct us safely through the woods.

In glancing at a map, you will see that Saratoga is situated on the bank of a small river that issues from a lake of the same name and falls into the Hudson. On the right bank of the Fishkill, the name of that little river, stood formerly a handsome country house belonging to General Schuyler; a large farm belonging to it, two or three saw-mills, a meetinghouse, and three or four middling houses, composed all the habitations of this celebrated place, the name of which will be handed down to the last posterity. After the affair of the 7th of October [1777], General Burgoyne began his retreat: he marched the whole night of October 8th, but did not cross the creek until the 13th due to the difficulty he had in dragging his artillery, which he persisted in preserving, though the greatest part of his horses were killed, or dead with hunger. It took him four days therefore to retire eight miles; this gave the Americans time to follow him on the right bank of the Hudson, and to get in front of him on the left bank, where they occupied in force all the crossings. General Burgoyne had scarcely reached the other side of the creek before he set fire to General Schuyler's house, rather from malice than for the safety of his army, for this house, situated in a low area, could afford no advantage to the Americans; and he left the farm standing, which is at present the only asylum for the owner. It is here that Mr. Schuyler lodged us in some temporary apartments he fitted up, until happier times should allow him to build another house.[45] The creek runs between two steep banks, the tops of which are about the same height; it then descends by several rapids which turn the mills; at that place the ground is more open, and continues so to the North River, that is to say, for half a mile. As for General Burgoyne's position, it is difficult to describe it, because the ground is so irregular, and the General finding himself surrounded, was obliged to divide his troops into three camps on three different fronts: one facing the creek, another the Hudson, and the third the mountains to the west. General Burgoyne's [published] map gives a reasonably accurate idea of this

position which was not ill taken and was only weak on the German front where the ground forms an incline, the slope of which was against them. All that is necessary to observe is that the woods continually rise towards the west; so that the General might very well occupy some advantageous eminences, but never the summits. Accordingly, General Gates who arrived at Saratoga almost as soon as the English, passed two thousand men over the creek with orders to erect a battery for two cannons. This battery was ordered to begin firing on the 14th, and considerably incommoded the English. General Schuyler criticizes this position; he assumes that this corps was so advanced as to be in danger, while it was not strong enough to oppose the retreat of the enemy. But when we consider that these two thousand men were posted in very thick woods; that they were protected by abbatis; that they had a safe line of retreat through the immense forest in their rear; and that they only had to harass a fleeing enemy whose courage was broken; then every military man will agree with me that this was rather the criticism of a stern rival rather than of a well informed and methodical tactician. Be this as it may, it is very certain that Burgoyne had no other alternative but to let his troops be slaughtered or capitulate. His army had only five days' provision, and it was impossible for him to retain his position. It was proposed to him to restore an old bridge of boats which had been constructed in the very front of his camp; but a corps of two thousand men was already posted on the heights on the opposite side of the river where they had raised a battery of two pieces of cannon. Had he undertaken to go back up the right bank [of the Hudson] to reach the fords which are near Fort Edward, he would have had ravines to pass and bridges to repair; besides, these defiles were already occupied by the militia, and the vanguard alone must have been engaged with them, whilst he had a whole army on his rear and on both flanks. He scarcely had time to deliberate when cannon shot began to shower into his camp; one shot fell in the house where the council of war was being held, and obliged them to quit it to take refuge in the woods.

Let us now compare the situation of General Burgoyne, collecting his trophies and publishing his insolent manifesto at Ticonderoga,[46] with that in which he now stood when vanquished and surrounded by a troop of peasants; not even a place was left him where he could discuss the terms of supplication. I confess that when I was conducted to the spot where the English laid down their arms, and to that where they filed off before Gates' army,[47] I could not but partake of the triumph of the Americans, and at the same time admire their magnanimity; for the soldiers and officers watched their presumptuous and sanguinary enemies pass by without offering the slightest insult, without suffering an insulting smile or gesture to escape them. This majestic silence offered a very striking refutation of the vain declarations of the English general, and seemed to confirm all the rights of our allies to the victory. Chance alone gave rise to a remark with which General Burgoyne was very sensibly affected. It is the custom in England, and in America, on approaching any person for the first time, to say, "I am very happy to see you." General Gates chanced to make use of this expression in accosting General Burgoyne. "I believe you are," replied the general. "The fortunes of war are entirely yours." General Gates pretended to give no attention to this answer, and conducted Burgoyne to his quarters where he gave him, as well as most of the English officers, a good dinner. Everyone ate and drank heartily and seemed mutually to forget their misfortunes or their successes.

Before dinner, and at the moment when the Americans were vying to see who should entertain the British officers, somebody came to ask where Madame Riedesel, the wife of the Brunswick General, was to be conducted. Mr. Schuyler, who had followed the army as a volunteer after having quitted his command, ordered her to be shown to his tent, where he went soon after, and found her trembling and speechless, expecting to find in every American a savage, like those who had followed the English army. She had with her two charming little girls, about six or seven years old. General Schuyler caressed them greatly; the sight of this touched Madame de Riedesel and removed her apprehension in an instant. "You are tender and sensible," she said. "You must then be generous, and I am happy to have fallen into your hands."

In consequence of the capitulation, the English army was conducted to Boston. During their march the troops encamped, but lodgings were to be procured for the generals, and there being some difficulty in procuring near Albany proper quarters for General Burgoyne and his suite, Mr. Schuyler offered him his handsome house. He was himself detained by business at Saratoga, where he remained to visit the ruins of his other house, which General Burgoyne had just destroyed. But he wrote to his wife to prepare everything for giving him the best reception, and his intentions were perfectly fulfilled. Burgoyne was extremely well received by Mrs. Schuyler and her little family; he was lodged in the best apartment in the house. An excellent supper was served him in the evening, the honours of which were done with so much grace, that he was affected even to tears; and he could not help saying, with a deep sigh, "Indeed, this is doing too much for the man who has ravaged their lands and burnt their [summer] retreat." The next morning, however, he was again reminded of his disgrace by an episode which would have appeared gay to anyone but him. He was afflicted by an ingenuous act. His bed was prepared in a large room; but as he had a numerous suite, or "family," several mattresses were spread upon the floor for some officers to sleep near him. Mr. Schuyler's second son, a little spoilt child of about seven years old, very forward and arch, as all the American children are, but very amiable, was running about the house all morning, according to custom. Opening the door of the bedroom, he burst out laughing when he saw all the congregated Englishmen, and shutting the door after him, cried: "Ye are all my prisoners." This innocent remark could not

have been more cruel, and rendered them more melancholy than the preceding evening.

I hope I shall be pardoned these little anecdotes, which only appeared interesting to myself, perhaps solely because I acquired them first-hand at their point of origin. Besides, a plain journal merits some indulgence, and when one does not write history, it is allowable to write little stories. Henceforth I have only to take leave of General Schuyler, detained by business at Saratoga, and to tread back my steps as fast as possible to Newport [R.I.].

PART III *Peacetime Travel by Sloop*

The Hudson Valley

Peacetime Travel by Sloop, 1800–1807

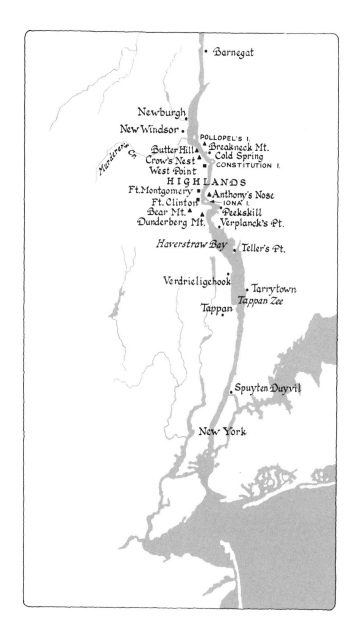

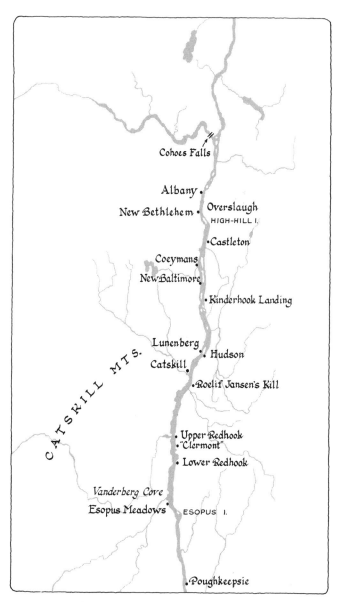

FROM THE END of the American Revolution in 1783 until the arrival of the steamboat in 1807 the Hudson enjoyed what might be termed a halcyon period of travel by sail and sloop. Peace had finally come after a century of conflict; the heavy shipping and frenetic travel coincident with the rise of the steamboat and the opening of the Erie Canal still lay in the future. The pace of life in the Hudson Valley at the turn of the century was measured by the quiet, leisurely pace of the slow, broad-bottomed Hudson River sloop and its picturesque but capricious and unpredictable course against tide and wind.

The rule of the sloop, to be sure, was by no means limited to the pre-steamboat era. Having all but dominated the shipping of the Hudson throughout the seventeenth and eighteenth centuries, it was to remain a main source of transportation right up until the age of the railroads. In 1810 there were about 206 sloops on the Hudson; by 1850, however, there were four to five hundred sloops plying the waters between New York and Albany. A turning point occurred in 1847–1851 when a major decline in the number of vessels first set in. By 1860 almost no new sloops were being built and the year 1900 saw only half the number of sloops that had existed in 1850. The last Hudson River sloop was reported to have been destroyed by a hurricane in 1938.* Though the sloop thus continued to be a ubiquitous feature of Hudson River traffic up until the middle of the nineteenth century and beyond, its golden era, as we have suggested, was in the period 1783–1807, when it alone dominated the traffic of the river and for two or three decades perfectly fulfilled the peacetime needs and aspirations of the pre-industrial towns and villages of the Hudson Valley.

* In May, 1969, the Hudson River Sloop Restoration, Inc., launched the *Clearwater*, a full-scale replica of a classic sloop, to sail between Albany and New York as a historical museum.

The sloop by this time had evolved into an ideal carrier for the unique navigational conditions of the Hudson River. The early sloops were keel boats with high sides, which drew as much as twelve feet of water. They also carried three jibs and were thus serviceable as ocean-going vessels. Structural innovations by the Dutch converted this cumbersome vessel into a flat-bottomed, shallow-draft vessel that could weather the tricky tides and winds of the Hudson and also stay clear of the innumerable shoals and sand bars of the upper river. The Dutch discarded the three jibs of the ocean-going vessels for one big jib that could swing across itself, thus simplifying the job of hauling over of headsails every time the sloop went about. But perhaps the main innovation in yacht design was the substitution of a centerboard for the older lee-board—an innovation that made the vessel much easier to handle in the capricious currents and breezes of the Hudson. As the typical Dutch sloop finally evolved, it was a very shallow, burdensome vessel, wide and low-sided, and carrying a great quantity of sail easily handled, and filled with an enormous amount of freight.

The average size of the Hudson River sloop was sixty tons, and it generally carried a crew of four—captain, pilot, sailor, and cabin boy or cook. One of the largest boats was the "Utica," built in Albany in 1833, which weighed 220 tons, was 96 feet long, and carried a crew of ten or twelve. Every town and village of the Hudson had its own fleet of sloops, running from five or six to fifty or sixty sail. During the height of sailing days a hundred sails could be seen at once of a summer's day on the Tappan Zee. A great variety of freight, mostly of an agricultural nature, was carried downriver to the cities, and manufactured goods of every conceivable type went upriver to fill the shelves and warehouses of the merchants of the inland as well as riverside communities.

What it meant to travel by sloop during the early years

of the nineteenth century has been beautifully evoked by the pen of Washington Irving. Reminiscing many years later about his first voyage up the Hudson in 1800, he declared:

My first voyage up the Hudson was made in early childhood, before steamboats and railroads had annihilated time and space. A voyage to Albany then was equal to a voyage to Europe at present, and took almost as much time. We enjoyed the beauties of the river in those days; the features of nature were not all jumbled together, nor the towns and villages huddled one into the other by railroad speed as they are now.

I was to make the voyage under the protection of a relative of mature age; one experienced in the river. His first care was to look out for a favorite sloop and captain, in which there was great choice.

The constant voyaging in the river craft by the best families of New York and Albany made the merits of captains and sloops matters of notoriety and discussion in both cities. The captains were mediums of communication between separated friends and families. On the arrival of one of them at either place he had messages to deliver and commissions to execute which took him from house to house. Some of the ladies of the family had, peradventure, made a voyage on board of his sloop, and experienced from him that protecting care which is always remembered with gratitude by female passengers. In this way the captains of Albany sloops were personages of more note in the community than captains of European packets or steamships at the present day. A sloop was at length chosen; but she had to complete her freight and secure a sufficient number of passengers. Days were consumed in "drumming up" a cargo. This was a tormenting delay to me who was about to make my first voyage, and who, boy-like had packed up my trunk on the first mention of the expedition. How often that trunk had to be unpacked and repacked before we sailed!

What a time of intense delight was that first sail through the Highlands! I sat on the deck as we slowly tided along at the foot of those stern mountains, and gazed with wonder and admiration at cliffs impending far above me, crowned with forests, with eagles sailing and screaming around them; or listened to the unseen stream dashing down precipices or beheld rock, and tree, and cloud, and sky reflected in the glassy stream of the river. And then how solemn and thrilling the scene as we anchored at night at the foot of these mountains, clothed with overhanging forests; and everything grew dark and mysterious; and I heard the plaintive note of the whippoorwill from the mountain-side, or was startled now and then by the sudden leap and heavy splash of the sturgeon.

But of all the scenery of the Hudson, the Kaatskill Mountains had the most witching effect on my boyish imagination. Never shall I forget the effect upon me of the first view of them predominating over a wide extent of country, part wild, woody, and rugged, part softened away into all the graces of cultivation. As we slowly floated along, I lay on the deck and watched them through a long summer's day; undergoing a thousand mutations under the magical effects of atmosphere, sometimes seeming to approach; at other times to recede; now almost melting into hazy distance, now burnished by the setting sun, until, in the evening, they printed themselves against the glowing sky in the deep purple of an Italian landscape.*

Irving, unfortunately, left no extended account of the innumerable voyages he made on the Hudson. Like his fellow writers, James Fenimore Cooper and Michel-Guillaume Crèvecoeur, who only wrote imaginary accounts of travel on the Hudson (Cooper in Chapter VII of *Home as Found* and Crèvecoeur in Chapter I of Percy G. Adams' edition of *Crèvecoeur's Eighteenth Century Travels in Pennsylvania and New York*), Irving compressed his extensive knowledge of the Hudson into the fanciful history of "Peter Stuyvesant's Voyage up the Hudson and the Wonders and Delights of that Renowned River" (Chapter III of *Knickerbocker's History of New York*). The few notes and diaries he kept of actual voyages—three pages of comment on a voyage of 1803 and about nine pages of stenographic notes on a trip made in 1833 with his friend Martin Van Buren—are too brief to warrant inclusion in this anthology.

* Wallace Bruce, *Along the Hudson with Washington Irving* (Poughkeepsie, N.Y.: 1913), 9–12.

For extended journals based on firsthand experience we turn to two English travelers of the early nineteenth century, John Maude and John Lambert. Both substantiate the charm and romance that Irving discovered in traveling by sloop in the relatively placid days before the advent of the steamboat.

8.
John Maude 1800*

INTRODUCTION: John Maude, an English commoner who traveled extensively in America between the years 1793 and 1803, must have been an ideal traveling companion. Affable and sociable, curious and yet entirely devoid of prejudice—and this at a time when the usual upper-class English traveler had come to taunt and ridicule—Maude was ever ready to join in the life around him and to turn a long and sometimes difficult voyage into as pleasant and rewarding an experience as possible. Reading his *Journal* we can well believe his confession that his years in America were "the happiest period" in his life.

The *Journal* was written from memoranda "penciled on the spot," as Maude said in his Preface, "and written down on the evening of each day." It is therefore free of literary pretension or the peculiar calcification that often results from more formal composition, and is an immediate and spontaneous evocation of everyday life aboard a Hudson River sloop more than a century and a half ago.

Maude's ultimate goal in this particular trip of 1800 was a visit to Niagara Falls. The following excerpts from his *Journal*, however, are restricted to the months of June and October when he ascended and descended the Hudson between New York and Albany on the first and last laps of his journey. We thus follow John Maude on that part of his journey which he considered "the most interesting Tour in all North America."

I. *New York to Albany*

Saturday, June 21st

5:30 P.M. Embarked on board the Sloop Sally, Captain Peter Donnelly, seventy tons, four hands, viz. the Captain, his brother Andrew, John, who was on board Admiral De Winter's Ship on the memorable 11th October, 1797,[1] and Nicholas, a free black acting as steward, cook, cabin-boy, etc. had purchased his own freedom and that of his wife, hoping soon to effect that of his children; performs well on the violin, and is *very smart*. Twenty-four passengers, not berths for more than half. Board and liquors, *as may happen*. Principal passengers, General Alleser, of New York, violent democrat; Caul, of Seratoga [*sic*], ditto; Mr. Mousley, warm aristocrat and federalist; Mr. Putnam, Mr. Williams, Lieutenant Kipp, all three federalists; the youth Octavius, son of Timothy Pickering, Esq. late Secretary of State,[2] under the care of Messrs. Williams and Putnam, both relations of Mr. Pickering; Jonas, of Montreal, Grocer: ——— of Michillimackinac; a drunken, Scotch Presbyterian Minister; Mr. Sanger, etc., etc. four raft-men, and a man and his wife from Staten Island.

7 P.M. Unmoored; fine S.E. breeze; ten knots.

8 P.M. Breeze slackened.

Midnight; cast anchor twenty-five miles from New York, entrance of Tappan Bay, not wind to stem the ebb. In the night, severe storm of thunder, lightning and rain. Not finding a berth unoccupied, or scarcely one that did not contain two persons, the Captain gave me his own state room.

Sunday, June 22d

5 A.M. Turned out, got under weigh: Tappan Bay, or Sea, five miles wide and ten long; extremities marked by two remarkable high bluffs;[3] scarcely a breath of air; fog

* Excerpt from John Maude's *Visit to the Falls of Niagara in 1800* (London: 1826), 3–20, 265–279. Bracketed interpolations are by the present editor.

on the high banks of the bay; heavy rain; fell calm when opposite to Tarry-Town.

10 A.M. Sun broke out and light airs from the north; beat slowly through the Tappan to Haverstraw-Bay, six miles wide, ten long. Stakes in the river for the convenience of taking Shad. Sturgeons constantly leaping out of the water. Shewn the field from whence the three youths first described Major André: and the large white-wood tree under which he was examined.

2 P.M. Cast anchor; took boat and landed at the ferry-house opposite to Mount Pleasant, thirty-six miles from New York; river here four miles wide. Climbed the mountains to visit a lake on its opposite side; large, considerably above the level of the Hudson; [4] pike, yellow bass, and sun-fish. Strawberries on its banks. Much chat with Betsy, who, born at the foot of the mountain and apparently secluded from the world, said she had been a great traveller, "*once* to the meeting and *twice* to the mill."

7 P.M. Got under weigh; light airs from the north; progress trifling. Came to anchor in the Horse-race, foot of St. Anthony's Nose; river half a mile wide, channel from forty to fifty fathoms wide three miles above Peekskill, and forty-eight from New York; turned in at 11 P.M. [5]

Monday, June 23d

Turned out at four A.M. Sketched a view [6] of **Fort Clinton**, **Fort Montgomery**, **St. Anthony's Nose**, the **Bear Mountain** and surrounding scenery; highly romantic and beautiful, being the entrance of the Highlands; to the south very extensive and pleasing prospect down the river through Haverstraw to Tappan Bay; dense fog on the lower part of Fort Clinton, Fort Montgomery and St. Anthony's; the site of Fort Clinton is now occupied by the handsome dwelling-house of Mr. Ducet, a french gentleman; dreary situation and without society. [7]

5 A.M. Took boat and landed on a small Island: [8] filled a cask with excellent water, picked up some drift wood, and got a pitcher of new milk for breakfast.

8 A.M. Returned and explored the Island; strange serpentine form: rocks and marsh; much scrub wood; four kinds of huckleberries; the swamp huckleberry, a tall shrub like the alder, an excellent fruit just beginning to ripen; the other still green; could only gather a few strawberries, the season being past. Laurel and Prickly Pear in blossom; the flower of the first, white with red spots, shaped like the convolvulus; that of the Prickly Pear, yellow and in appearance like the bloom of the melon and cucumber. Gathered the root of the Sarsaparilla and a branch of Spice wood, this latter is a great sweetener of the blood and a pleasant flavor; flushed a pair of partridges or pheasants; though these birds more resemble Grouse than Partridge or Pheasant, I may observe here that the animals of America differ materially from those of the Old Continent, yet for want of more appropriate designations, they frequently receive the names of such European animals as they most resemble; but these names are by no means settled; for instance, what are known as Partridges in one part of the Country are called Quails in another, and these birds will alight in Trees, or on Paling. The Hares have white flesh. I have been informed that some Sporting Gentlemen have imported the English Red Fox as affording better diversion than the native Grey; and that although the Red Fox is the smaller animal, it is the more ferocious, and is *eating-out* the Grey one. . . .

At the cottage observed a child about three years of age, whose foot having been much burnt had been bound up close to the leg, and now adhered to it; he walked on his heel.

9 A.M. Got under weigh; head wind.

1 P.M. L——— Mills, are superior to most in construction and situation, and very profitable; four pairs of stones; fifty-five miles from New York; the Miller takes down a cargo of flour and returns with wheat.

3 P.M. Landed at West-Point, the Gibraltar of America; center of the Highlands; fifty-eight miles from New York. Yet who would have ever heard of West-Point but for the defection of Arnold, and the melancholy death of Major André!

Lieutenant Kipp being personally acquainted with the Commandant Captain Stille, and Messrs. Williams and Putnam bearing letters to him, we were politely received, and permitted to range over this impregnable fortress. Though very sultry, we could not resist the temptation of climbing up to the ruins of Fort Putnam; where at a vast height above the Hudson, overlooked much of the Highlands, and still more of the majestic river, which here deviates from its usual direct course from north to south, and in no place more so than at West Point, washing two sides of the triangle, so that a wind fair for approaching it, is a-head when passing it, consequently no enemy's vessel could escape destruction, if hardy enough to attempt the passage. The view from our present situation was most sublime and magnificent. I do not recollect one that I enjoyed so much; it was *historic* ground—had been trodden by Washington, was his favorite post, and his own selection! The scenery is, I think, however, unequal to one of the views near Windermere.[9] I allude to the view looking towards Langdale Pikes, Hard Knot, and Wry Nose.

There were at present in garrison only one company of Artillery and Engineers. The Barracks are on a tolerably level plain of several acres, on which were feeding a few horses and about twenty cows.

While we were ranging over the garrison, the Captain had taken boat and gone upon a foraging expedition to the opposite shore, from whence he brought off a quarter of veal, a pitcher of milk, with some butter and cheese.

Lieutenant Kipp found here three or four of his company, who, when disbanded on the 15th Inst. entered into the service of the Artillery and Engineers. . . .

9 P.M. Got under weigh; having no wind, drifted with the tide, boat a-head towing.

10:30 P.M. Light southerly breeze; turned the Scotch Presbyterian Minister out of the cabin and put him into the hold. This man had given himself up to dram-drinking, which kept him in a continual state of intoxication, so that he never left his berth but for a few moments; his legs had running sores, which, being neglected, were offensive to such a degree, that the passengers had determined to pass the night on deck, unless he were put below.

11 P.M. Passed Butter-Hill, and the [Turk's] Face [or Breakneck] Mountain, the last of the Highlands.

11:30 P.M. Turned in; the cabin being by this time tolerably ventilated.

Tuesday, June 24th

4 A.M. Turned out opposite to Barnegat [Camelot] and its lime-kilns, twenty miles from West Point, and seventy-eight from New York; light southerly air; two knots.

6 A.M. Fell calm; went on shore and got a supply of milk and eggs; could not procure bread.

7 A.M. Light southerly air; got under weigh; hot sun.

8 A.M. Fine favorable breeze.

8:30 A.M. Pough-keepsie, seventy-nine miles, high wooded banks each side the river; came up with and passed four sloops. Esopus Island ninety-five miles from New York. Esopus Flats one hundred miles; these flats, or shoals, throw the channel of the river on the opposite shore, where it forms a large bay; [10] fine view here of the Katskill Mountains. Pass Judge Lewis's and Mr. Livingston's country seats. [11]

2 P.M. Redhook one hundred miles from New York, beautiful situation; opposite to the Katskill Mountains; two Islands decorate the river. [12] We were now carried along at the rate of ten miles an hour, having scarcely time to examine the beauty of the country, through which we were so rapidly passing.

3 P.M. The city of Hudson, one hundred and thirty miles; opposite to Hudson is Lunenberg, or Algiers; this latter name was given to it in consequence of the piratical practices of the inhabitants. In De Witt's map it is called Esperanza. [13] Above Hudson is a wind-mill; I do not know that there are four in the United States. There are two near Newport.

4:30 P.M. Kinderhook one hundred and forty miles; twenty houses; Mr. M'c Machin's is the principal one; fine view; Islands numerous in this part of the river. Heavy thundering; took in sail: cast anchor.

5:30 P.M. Got under weigh, in doing which, fished up an excellent and large anchor, a valuable prize for the Captain. The gust, as expected, killed the wind; in summer I never knew an instance to the contrary. Had the gust kept off, we should have been in Albany by seven o'clock.

9 P.M. The wind having entirely failed us, took the Sloop in tow, and at 7 P.M. had her moored alongside a Wharf in Baltimore, one hundred and forty-five miles. Went on shore; took with us Nicholas and his violin, the fiddle soon got the girls together; we kicked up a dance and kept it up till midnight. Treated with spruce-beer and gingerbread. Baltimore is a shabby place, every other house a tavern; in number about a dozen. [14]

Wednesday, June 25th

3 A.M. Not a breath of air; took Sloop in tow; not possible to see from stem to stern, yet passed a dangerous and difficult passage and a bar, which require, it is said, your having all your eyes about you.

6 A.M. Made land; the fog beginning to disperse; put the Presbyterian Minister on shore; he is engaged by a Mr. Nichols as a *tutor* to his children! Boat returned with milk for breakfast.

7:30 A.M. Dropped anchor; took Boat and landed on High-hill Island, four miles in length; two farms; got a few sour cherries; one hundred and fifty-four miles from New York. Crossed to the opposite or west shore, and landed at a farm house called Bethlehem, six miles from Albany; [15] numerous and handsome family.

9 A.M. Having hired a waggon, seven of our passengers took their departure. The day being remarkably sultry, I determined to stay by the Sloop. Returned on board with potatoes and sallad.

Noon. Got under weigh; light south air.

2 P.M. Passed safely the Overslough.

3 P.M. Albany, one hundred and sixty miles from New York. Took up my quarters at Lewis's Tavern, where I found Mr. Williams, Mr. Putnam, young Octavius and Lieutenant Kipp at dinner. Paid the Captain two dollars for passage-money, and four dollars and fifty cents, for board and liquors; the same sum of six dollars and fifty cents was charged for my servant, though neither his bed nor board were so good as mine. Our passage of four days may be considered a long one, at this season of the year, yet it was a pleasant one and no way tedious. The Hudson is one of the finest Rivers in America, and superior to them all in romantic and sublime scenery, more especially in its progress through the Highlands, a distance of sixteen miles. What further added to the pleas-

antness of this trip, were our frequent expeditions on shore. We landed seven times, and each time employed two or three hours in exploring the country. We saw, too, the whole of the River; as we progressed but very few miles during the time we occupied our berths. We usually retired at eleven, and rose at four or five o'clock. The shortest passage ever made on this River was by this same Sloop and Captain; he made it in sixteen hours and six minutes, from which should be deducted one hour for time occupied in landing passengers by the way. The passage often takes a fortnight to perform it, and sometimes twenty-five or thirty days. The passage is always shortest, the winds being equally favorable, *up* the river, as you carry the flood with you; in the other case you outrun the ebb. Captain Donnelly has taken 1,675 Dollars passage money in one year.

II. *Albany to New York*

[Maude spent the next three months traveling up the Mohawk to Niagara Falls. At the beginning of October, 1800, he was back in Albany; and on October 3rd he set out for the return voyage to New York.]

Friday, October 3d

I passed the morning in wandering about the environs of Albany.

4:30 P.M. Embarked. On stepping on board the Sloop Magdelene, Capt. Wendal, I recognized Mr. Cuyler, of Green-bush, from whom I had received civilities on my first visit to Albany in 1795, and father to Mr. Wm. Cuyler, of Bath, Steuben County, with whom I had formed a friendly intimacy during my residence in Captain Williamson's family.[16]

Mr. Cuyler introduced me to my fellow-passengers, Mrs. Bruce, a widow of New York; and Mrs. Le Roy, his daughter, the wife of Mr. Robert Le Roy, Merchant, of New York.[17] I was much pleased with the appearance of these Ladies, as to be happy in so respectable an introduction; while to them it was no little gratification to find that their future associate was no stranger, but one to whose protection Mr. Cuyler cheerfully confided them as his acquaintance and his son's friend.

Mrs. Le Roy had her two children with her; Jacob, about seven years of age, and Louisa, in her third year. Immediately after my introduction, Mr. Cuyler took his leave, and we set sail with a smart fair wind at N.W.

5 P.M. Grounded on the Upper Overslaugh, three miles.

7 P.M. Grounded on the Lower Overslaugh, eight miles. As there was no prospect of our getting over this shoal till the tide had attained its highest point, we took in all our sail and carried out an anchor into deep water. This Lower Overslaugh had seldom more than eight feet water upon it even in Spring tides, and our Sloop drew seven feet, though a great part of her lading was on board a Lighter, and not to be shipped till we had passed these shoals, which are a severe interruption to the navigation between New York and Albany, and which might otherwise be carried on in vessels of larger burthen than are now employed in this trade. There are a variety of channels among those beds of sand called the Overslaughs, and the main channel shifts almost every year. The remedy is easy: block up all the channels except one, and the water will accumulate there and keep it ever free.[18]

Having made all snug on deck, we sat down to an excellent supper, which had been sent on board by Mr. Cuyler. I found the two Ladies precisely what I wished Ladies in a ship's cabin to be;—not so *free* and *easy,* as to forget the manners of the drawing-room; nor so starch and full of self-importance, as to raise contempt and disgust.

Hitherto I had *voyaged* with Ladies too free, or too consequential. Having at this time nothing to fear from coarse manners, or mistaken pride, I had only to guard against, and prevent, another source of much uneasiness and constraint, which, among those the best disposed for harmonious intercourse, inevitably arises from the want of that proper understanding which delicacy, seemingly, forbids. I thus opened the subject:—"You will observe, Ladies, that we all sleep in the same cabin; that a slight curtain only separates us. I know from experience that a system, understood by both parties, should be adopted for our mutual convenience; for where false delicacy has prevented explanation,—constraint, inquietude, and real indelicacy, has been the consequence. My plan is simply this:—that we sup at eight, breakfast at eight, and dine, as wind, weather, and circumstances permit;—that we chat and talk an hour or two after supper, when I will keep the watch on deck for an hour,—time sufficient, surely, for you to put on your night-caps! One hour before, and two hours after dinner, I will leave you in full possession of the cabin; but at no time do I wish to have exclusive possession of it myself, as I shall always make my toilet before breakfast. I am an early riser, and will walk the deck till you announce breakfast."

The Ladies very kindly thanked me for yielding so much to their accommodation, assuring me, at the same time, that I had removed their only objection to the sloops, so superior in other respects to the journey by land.—Pleasant weather and fair wind, N.W.; very bright moonlight night.

Saturday, October 4th

We went early on deck; the dawn brought on a heavy fog.

7 A.M. Being high water, we endeavoured to warp off the shoal; we succeeded only in part, and were obliged to wait another tide. It is always high water at Albany at the rising and setting of the moon.

8 A.M. The fog having dispersed, I took the boat and rowed to Castleton, on the E. shore, and having procured milk and eggs, I hastened back to breakfast. On the W. shore I noticed Colonel Nicol's house, where we landed the *accomplished* tutor of his children on my voyage up. An Island, which lay a short distance above us, I recognized to be Overberg or High-hill Island, which in June last afforded me nothing better than sour cherries; I determined, therefore, to try my fortune after breakfast on a smaller Island that lay nearer to the Sloop, and was about two miles in length. I took two hands in the boat with me, and finding the Island uninhabited, we took formal possession of it. The province of discovery was left to me, while my companions undertook to procure a mess of fish.

There was great plenty of good Timber on the Island, and so much Underwood, that I found it very difficult to make the tour of it. I collected the small black frost-grape, and the large tough fox-grape. I was informed that on some of the Islands in this part of the Hudson, there were not only other species of the fox-grape, but also a red grape, and a very fine white grape, both unknown in other parts of the United States.

On re-joining the two sailors at our rendezvous, I found that they had caught a dish-full of Yellow Perch.

On my return on board, I was sorry to observe that we had received two additional passengers, a Mr. Thurman, and his niece, Miss Brazier.

6 P.M. Being high water we succeeded in warping off the Overslaugh. We now took on board our full lading from the Lighter, our cargo consisting of four hundred

barrels of potash, of four cwt. each, value £3 per cwt. or £4,800 New York Currency, being thirty dollars per barrel.[19]

Falling calm we out sweeps, and rowed three miles, eleven miles from Albany, when we came to an anchor.— Very fine day and night.

Sunday, October 5th

As the moon set the fog rose.

9:30 A.M. Fog cleared off with a light air from the North.

10 A.M. Light head-wind from the South.

Noon; Drifted to leeward of an Island opposite Coeyeman's, twelve miles. Here was another detention, but fully compensated to the *original* party, by the beauty of the surrounding scenery, and the harmony of our society. Mr. Thurman was a sensible person, of a quiet and serious cast. His niece was apparently of an unsociable disposition, which every effort of ours to amend proved unavailing. She seemed best pleased when left to her own meditations; and these, judging from her countenance, were not very profound.

As for Jacob [Le Roy], he was too wild for his mother, and was put entirely under my care. Louisa was my little darling. In the evening I took Jacob with me, (a great favour) and made a trip to the Village of Coeyeman's, consisting of about thirty houses on the W. shore, and at the mouth of Coeyeman's-kill [Coeyman's Creek]. Visited General Mc Kay's.—Calm morning; rain in the night.

Monday, October 6th

During the whole of this morning we had a severe storm of wind and rain, thunder and lightning from the South. Our situation is leeward of Coeyeman's Island, which we yesterday considered as a piece of bad fortune, now turned out to be the most secure situation we could have chosen.

3 P.M. The storm having spent its fury, and the wind having got into the W. and being moderate, we got under weigh.

3:30 P.M. Abreast of [New] Baltimore, fourteen miles. This is a shabby Village on the W. shore, and contains about twenty-five houses.

5 P.M. Abreast of Mr. Mc. Machin's house, near Kinderhook Landing [Stuyvesant], on E. side, twenty miles. Moderate as was our present rate of sailing, we made still less progress in the night, the wind having less influence than the tide.

Tuesday, October 7th

1 A.M. Came to an anchor off Lunenburg [Athens], thirty-four miles.

6 A.M. As I did not care to trust myself among the *Algerines* [sic],[20] I took the boat, and allowing my young friend to accompany me, we crossed over to the E. side of the River, and landed at the City of Hudson, thirty-four miles, where we procured milk, bread, and beef, but no porter could be had. Jacob was quite delighted with the frequent trips I made on shore, when I never failed to take him with me, if circumstances would admit of it. It had two beneficial effects: it put him on his good behaviour, and tranquilized his mother, who never thought him safe but when I had charge of him; for, like a true *"Pickle,"* his delight was to alarm her by running into danger: the more danger, the more fun. Louisa saw her interest in these expeditions;—she never was forgotten in our trafficking with the *natives;* she took care

to be the first to rummage the basket, and generally found something for her own store-room.

8 A.M. Weighed anchor. The wind being S. we had to beat down the River.

10 A.M. Abreast of the Village at the mouth of the Katskill, forty miles. It is a pretty situation in Jay's Valley. We had a fine prospect, including the Katskill Mountains. On the opposite or E. side of the River was Oakhill, the seat of John Livingston, Esq., of New York; [21] forty miles.—Up top-sail.

11 A.M. The Old Manor-House of the Livingstons, on E. side, forty-two miles.[22]

2:30 P.M. Chancellor Livingston and his mother's house, a fine situation, fifty miles.[23] Wind increased.—Down top-sail.

3:30 P.M. Abreast of the pretty and well-built Village of Redhook [Tivoli], E. side, fifty-two miles. The Katskill Mountains now appeared to their greatest advantage.

4:30 P.M. A stately house, built by John Livingston, which, with two hundred acres of land, cost fifty thousand dollars, E. side, fifty-six miles.[24] When we were abreast of the Esopus Meadows, (sixty miles) we thought it time to fill our water-casks, but to our vexation this work had been deferred too long, for the water was already brackish, at this distance of one hundred miles from New York. The Captain, in justification, assured us, that he had never known the water brackish so high up the River; that the water is generally fresh in the Highlands, and sometimes even in Haverstraw-bay, sixty miles below our present situation.

10 P.M. Abreast of Poughkeepsie, E. side, half way between Albany and New York, eighty miles. The wind had been very variable the whole day, and our rate of sailing about three knots an hour.—Fine clear weather.

Wednesday, October 8th

1 A.M. Came to an anchor.

6 A.M. Weighed anchor with wind S.W.

8 A.M. Took the boat and landed at Newburgh, on the W. shore, ninety-eight miles. This is a large and neat town, and a considerable part of it appeared to be recently built. If I may judge from a Newspaper printed here once a week, the great body of inhabitants are high-flying Democrats. The title of the Paper is, *"The Rights of Man,"* and sold for one dollar and a half, or six shillings and ninepence sterling per annum. Breakfast waited my return. I brought on board a supply of bread, milk, butter, tea, and porter; for the porter I paid three shillings and six-pence per bottle, or two shillings sterling.

10 A.M. Passed the small Village of New Windsor, on the W. side, one hundred miles. The Southerly wind died gradually away. On its falling calm we came to an anchor; instantly Jacob and I jumped into the boat, and landed at a solitary house called Marlborough, near the mouth of Murderer's Creek, on the W. side, one hundred and one miles. Wild chestnuts were all that this place afforded us.

We here received a forecastle passenger on board,—a black wench, who surprised me much by addressing me by name. She had been servant to my Landlady at New York, Mrs. Ford, a buxom widow, who married Belvidere, a miserable Frenchman, who not being able to pay for his board and lodging, was happy to surrender his person.

5 P.M. Weighed anchor; the wind being from the S. we were obliged to beat down the River. At this place the River forms a large Bay, contracting at Polleple [Palopel], or Porpoise Island, being the entrance into the Highlands.

14. *Newburgh,* aquatint engraved by J. Hill from the painting by W. G. Wall, 1821–1822; courtesy of The New-York Historical Society.

"Took the boat and landed at Newburgh. . . . This is a large and neat town."

15. *View on the Hudson,* engraving by John Stockdale from the drawing by Isaac Weld, 1799; courtesy of The New-York Historical Society.

"Polleple's Island appears to have been the foreground of Weld's 'View on the Hudson.'"

This impression of the scenery around Storm King Mountain came from the pen of Isaac Weld, an Irish topographer who traveled up the Hudson in 1796.

Polleple's Island appears to have been the foreground of [Isaac] Weld's "View on the Hudson." [25] the Mountain on the right being the Butter Mountain [Storm King], and that on the left the [Turk's] Face [or Breakneck] Mountain; though it has more the appearance of a fancy piece, so little is it characteristic of the sublime and romantic scenery of the Highlands. The profile of the Face Mountain so strongly resembles the profile of the human face, that I had for some time my doubts whether art had not assisted in improving the likeness. I have seen other *blockheads* which did not possess so sensible a countenance.

8 P.M. Abreast West-point, one hundred and five miles.

10 P.M. St. Anthony's Nose, Fort Clinton, and Fort Montgomery,[26] one hundred and nine miles.

11 P.M. Pass Peekskill, on E. side, and Dunderberg, or Thunder Mountain, on W. side, one hundred and twelve miles.

Midnight. Pass Verplank-point, on E. side, and Stoney-point, on W. side, and enter Haverstraw Bay.

Thursday, October 9th

6 A.M. Pass Teller's-point, on the E. side, and Verdrieligehook,[27] on the W. side, one hundred and twenty-five miles, and enter the Tapan-bay.

10 A.M. Abreast of Tarry-town, one hundred and thirty miles. The wind being still S. we continued to beat down the River.

Noon. Came to an anchor during the flood-tide; took the boat and went on shore; got a supply of bread, milk, hay, and apples. We were here informed that a sloop on her voyage up from New York was lost in the Bay during the severe gale of the 6th.

This event most strongly impressed upon us the folly of repining at what we called "bad luck," when if we did not "see through a glass darkly," if we did not "see in part," and therefore only "know in part," we should often know these apparently untoward events to be the merciful interferences of the Almighty.

Had we not run aground on the Overslaugh, we should most probably have been in these open and exposed parts of the River during the gale of Monday, and might have shared the fate of the vessel which was overtaken by the storm and perished.

5 P.M. Got under weigh, and, with a strong ebb tide under us, beat down the River till midnight, when we cast anchor off the Spiking Devil [Spuyten Duyvil] Creek, north end of [New] York Island, one hundred and forty-five miles.

Friday, October 10th

5 A.M. Weighed anchor, and at

8 A.M. Landed in New York, one hundred and sixty miles. Mrs. Le Roy was only a few paces from her own door; I saw Mrs. Bruce to her house in Broadway, and took breakfast with her.

I have now brought to a conclusion my narrative of the events and reflections which occurred during this my third Voyage between New York and Albany. The first was made in two days and eighteen hours; the second in three days and twenty-one hours and a half; and the third (an extraordinary coincidence!) was *exactly* the length of the two preceding ones, being six days and fifteen hours and a half;—a very long passage when it is considered the run has been made in less than seventeen hours.

Contrary to general experience, my passages up and down this majestic River have been pleasant in proportion to their length: my expedition last Summer was productive of more agreeable incidents than that in the Summer of 1795, and inferior to this last in those circumstances that give so much character and interest to scenes viewed in unison with congenial minds.

My former expeditions were made in crowded society, discordant in mind and manners: where civility could not overcome rudeness, nor good-breeding grossness; and where noisy ignorance gloried in putting modest merit to silence. How much superior, then, was my friendly intercourse with Ladies elegant in their manners, of cheerful dispositions, cultivated minds, and possessing that knowledge of the world which one of them had perfected in the troubles and persecutions of civil discord, which wrecked its vengeance on the wife, for the political sin of loyalty in the husband; Mrs. Bruce having been imprisoned because her husband (a physician) was a loyalist.

With my arrival at New York I shall conclude the Journal of this Tour. . . . The view I have given of the manners and hospitality of our Transatlantic brethren is faithfully depicted without either partiality or prejudice; and therefore, from motives of gratitude for a continued series of friendly attentions to a stranger, as I was, I sincerely hope that it will tend, in some degree, to dissipate those unfavorable impressions which former travellers have seemed anxious to encourage.

9.
John Lambert 1807*

INTRODUCTION: The following account of a voyage by sloop from the city of Hudson to New York in late November 1807 was written by an obscure young Englishman who had been sent to Canada in 1806 under the sanction of the board of trade to foster the cultivation of hemp in the English province. Failing in that mission, the young Lambert decided to prolong his visit and see the sights of North America. He returned to England in 1809 and the following year published a three-volume work of his travels which immediately went through three editions. Nothing further is known of his life save that he was born about 1775 and in 1811 published an English edition of the works of Washington Irving.

Judging from the narrative of his travels, however, we may say that the young Englishman was a congenial and observant traveler, singularly free from bias. Lambert left Montreal on November 10, 1807, on the start of his journey through America and arrived in Albany after a week of difficult travel by way of Lake Champlain, Skenesborough, and the Wood Creek. At Albany he discovered that the river was already frozen for several miles below the city and that the steamboat which he had intended to take to New York was laid up for the winter. Sorely disappointed—for the steamboat in question was none other than Robert Fulton's "Clermont" which had just finished its first season as a commercial packet—Lambert had to travel overland to the city of Hudson and there board a sloop for the voyage to New York. Though disappointed because he could not take the "celebrated vessel" that traveled at the astonishing rate of "five miles an hour against wind and tide," Lambert soon found ample recompense in traveling upon

* Excerpt from John Lambert's *Travels through Canada and the United States of North America in the Years 1806, 1807, and 1808* (London: 1814), 2 Vols., 2nd Edition, Vol. II, pp. 41–50.

"the largest and best" sloop that then plied the waters of the Hudson. The account of his voyage thus brings to a happy conclusion the history of sloop travel at the very moment it was first challenged by the new age of the steamboat.

THE NEXT MORNING, Sunday 22d November, we embarked on board the Experiment, a fine new sloop of 130 tons, built expressly for carrying passengers between Hudson and New York.[1] The whole vessel was handsomely fitted up. It had two private cabins abaft, containing several bed-places for ladies. In the midship was a large general room upwards of sixty feet long, and twenty feet wide, containing a double tier of bed-places on each side for gentlemen, with printed cotton curtains drawn before them. At the head of this cabin or room there was a bar, like that of a coffee-house, where the company were supplied with wine, bottled porter, ale, segars, and such articles as were not included in the passage-money. Between the bar and the forecastle was a very complete kitchen fitted up with a good fire-place, copper boilers, and every convenience for cooking. The forecastle was appropriated to the use of the sailors. The passage-money was five dollars, for which the passengers were provided during the voyage with three meals a-day, including spirits; all other liquors were to be separately paid for.

About nine o'clock in the morning we left the wharf, which was crowded with people to see the vessel depart; for it was the largest and best of the kind, except for the steam-boat, that sailed on the river as a packet. It had not been established above six months. The mainmast, boom, and mainsail were of an immense size for a sloop, but we had ten or a dozen fine young fellows

16. *Hudson, N.Y.*, aquatint engraved by J. Hill after the painting by W. G. Wall, 1821–1822; courtesy of The New-York Historical Society.

The City of Hudson fourteen years after Lambert departed from it on the sloop "Experiment." The parade ground on the bluff to the left of the town was no doubt filled with people, for it had been used as a place of promenade since 1795. Spectators again flocked to this vantage point to greet the arrival of Lafayette in 1824.

to work the vessel; and having a smart breeze, we soon left the town of Hudson far behind us. Mr. Elihu Bunker, who commanded the vessel, was part owner as well as captain, and seemed to be a plain religious sort of man. He had more the look of a parson than a sailor; and had posted up a long list of regulations at the cabin door, which, if properly enforced, were well calculated to keep his passengers in good order. In truth, something of the kind was necessary; for we had upwards of fifty persons on board, nearly all men. Among the forbidden articles were playing at cards and smoking in the cabin.

The morning was remarkably fine; the wind favoured us, and we had every prospect of an agreeable voyage. The month of November was but ill adapted to view the country to advantage; for the gay verdure of the fields and forests was now supplanted by the brown and gloomy hue of winter. Yet the scenes that presented themselves along the shores of the Hudson were in some places of that grand and romantic description, and in others so beautifully picturesque, that they could not fail to interest the spectator at any season of the year. This river affords some of the noblest landscapes and scenery that are to be found in any part of North America. Nature and art have both contributed to render its shores at once sublime and beautiful.

The river in many places is intersected with numerous islands. In others it is diversified with handsome windings. Sometimes its waters are contracted between stupendous rocks that frown aloft in sullen majesty. At other times they are expanded to a great extent between a fine open country containing well cultivated settlements. The rocks which line the shore in numerous parts of the river are steep and rugged; and rise to such a height above the water's edge, that the largest trees which grow upon their summits are dwindled in appearance to the smallest shrubs. Behind these rocks are ranges of enormous mountains which extend far into the country, and are covered with trackless forests.

> ——"Gigantic vast,
> O'ershadowing mountains soar, invested thick
> Their shaggy waists, and to their summits far
> A Wilderness unbounded to the eye,
> Profuse, and pathless, unsubdued by toil.
> Diminutive beneath, the Hudson, deep
> Coerced by rocks, and silent penetrates
> The solitudinous and woodland scene;
> ——struggling for a passage."

In other places the shores rise from the water's edge into small hills, and descending on the opposite side form beautiful valleys; beyond them arise other acclivities, which at length terminate at the base of lofty mountains. The country thus gently undulated is covered with rich farms, plantations, orchards, and gardens, and studded with neat and handsome dwelling-houses. The cultivated parts are intersected with small woods, copices, and clumps of trees, which add much to the diversity of the scenery, and form a pleasing contrast to lawns, meadows, and corn-fields. In several places along shore are elegant mansions and country seats belonging to the principal persons in the State of New York. Some were pointed out to us, and the names of their owners mentioned; but I only recollect those of Mr. Livingston and Mrs. Montgomery, the widow of the general who fell at Quebec.[2] The river is also ornamented with several little towns and villages near the water-side; and except in the neighbourhood of the rocks and mountains the country appeared to be well inhabited. The fineness of the weather contributed much to heighten the beauty of the scenes which every where opened upon our view as the vessel glided with the stream. In short, words are inadequate to do justice to the variety and splendour of the objects that presented themselves at every turn and winding of this beautiful river. The pencil of a Claude can alone delineate them as they deserve, and portray their beauties with fidelity and truth.

We had not more than half a dozen ladies on board, the rest of our numerous company were *gentlemen* of all descriptions. Most of them appeared to be methodists, baptists, and other dissenters, who are very numerous in the States; and it being Sunday, several of them got together and sung hymns. They had good voices, and sung in different keys; but there was a melancholy monotony in the tunes which I did not much admire. We had two singing groups; one on deck, and the other in the cabin. Beside which, there was a third group assembled around a methodist parson, who harangued for a considerable time with much self-satisfaction, until he happened unfortunately to broach some curious doctrines, when he was cut short by a gentleman, who, from the opinions he advanced in opposition to the parson, seemed to doubt the authenticity of revealed religion. I really believe, however, that he was not in earnest, and only started difficulties to puzzle the other, who now quitted his preaching to enter the lists with the sceptic as he called him. For upwards of two hours they combated each other with great ardour, affording the rest of the company high entertainment. The gentleman pointed out all the incongruities in the Old and New Testament, seeming to doubt every thing which had been accomplished by miracles, and challenged the other to prove their authenticity. The parson proceeded in the commonplace way to satisfy the doubts of his antagonist. In some instances he succeeded tolerably well; but in others he was completely confounded, and was obliged to digress from the subject to something which he thought unanswerable by his opponent. The latter, however, endeavoured to keep him always to the point;

and the parson was at times so much perplexed, that he became the butt of the company. He however bore their jokes with great good humour and patience; but finding that he could not satisfy the gentleman's scruples, he began upon politics. We soon discovered that he was a Jeffersonian; and there happening to be a large majority of Federalists on board, among whom were the editor and printer of the Albany Balance, a strong anti-democratic paper, the poor parson got most roughly handled; and I perceived that it was a more difficult task for him to keep his temper upon politics than upon religion.[3]

In this manner the morning was passed, and we were glad to find our party of disputants and politicians sit down to dinner with great cordiality, and in the pleasures of the table forget the fretfulness of an empty stomach. Our dinner consisted of every thing in season, and was admirably served up: indeed, it would not have disgraced a tavern in London. At seven o'clock we had tea and coffee together with the cold turkeys and ham left at dinner. This was our last meal. At ten o'clock some few of the passengers turned into their births: others, not inclined to go to bed so soon, called for wine, and began to sing some patriotic songs, such as Hail Columbia, etc. One of them sung several English songs, which not exactly suiting the democratic principles of two or three persons on board, the captain came into the cabin, and said that he was desired by some of the passengers to request, that as it was Sunday night the gentlemen would not sing: it also prevented those who had lain down from going to sleep. The poor methodist parson was immediately suspected, and charged with endeavouring to interrupt the conviviality of the company. He however came forward and assured them he was innocent of the charge. The jovial party declared that it was very hard they were not permitted to amuse themselves with a few innocent songs, when they had so quietly listened all the morning to the dismal psalm-singing and political disputes of other gentlemen: but as it was near twelve o'clock they acquiesced in the wishes of the captain. They were, however, determined to have another bottle or two of wine; and sat up a considerable time longer, cracking their jokes upon the parson, and on those who had expressed their disapprobation of singing songs on Sunday.

We sailed all night; but as the wind shifted to an opposite quarter, we made but little progress. The next morning it became more favourable; and the weather being fine, we had an agreeable passage. The prospects that presented themselves were equally beautiful and varied as yesterday; but the country was more rocky and mountainous. This day we passed the fort at West Point, where Arnold betrayed the cause of his country, and brought upon the gallant Major André an ignominious death.

> ———"Far within the lofty desert we beheld
> The fort, and thundering cannon on its brow,
> Raised on the western rocks, where travellers long
> The base and vain design that had betray'd
> Columbia, shall relate."

About ten o'clock at night we arrived at New York; it was very dark, and as we sailed by the town, lighted lamps and windows sparkled everywhere, amidst the houses, in the streets, and along the water-side. The wharfs were crowded with shipping, whose tall masts mingled with the buildings, and together with the spires and cupolas of the churches, gave the city an appearance of magnificence, which the gloomy obscurity of the night served to increase.

When the vessel was made fast to one of the wharfs, I went ashore with Mr. Mackenzie, Mr. Lyman, and the rest of our party to find a boarding house. Mrs. Loring's house in the Broadway, where we intended to have lodged, was full; so that, after rambling about the streets for an hour, we were obliged to return on board again for the night. After so long an absence from London, I could not help experiencing a degree of satisfaction at once more treading the pavement of a large and populous city. Neither Montreal nor Quebec had the least resemblance to that which I had left: but New York seemed to present an exact epitome of it; and at the distance of 3,000 miles, I now pleased myself with the idea of finding the manners, customs, and institutions of my own country reflected on this portion of the new world.

PART IV *The Age of the Steamboat*

The Hudson Valley

The Age of the Steamboat, 1824–1838

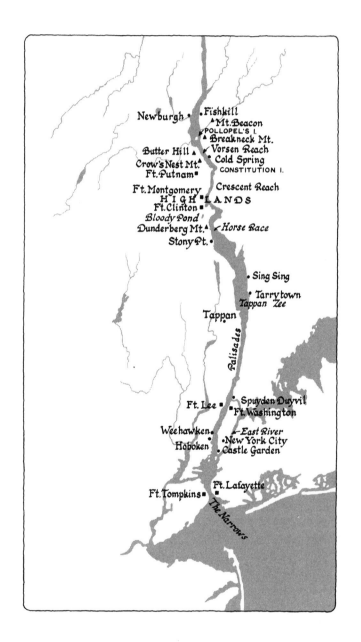

Newburgh • • Fishkill
▲ Mt. Beacon
POLLOPEL'S I. ◢
▲ Breakneck Mt.
✓ Vorsen Reach
Butter Hill ▲ Cold Spring
Crow's Nest Mt. ▲ CONSTITUTION I.
Ft. Putnam ■
Ft. Montgomery ■ Crescent Reach
H I G H L A N D S
Ft. Clinton ■
Bloody Pond ▪
Dunderberg Mt. ▲ ✓ Horse Race
Stony Pt. ▪

• Sing Sing

• Tarrytown
Tappan Zee
Tappan

Palisades

Ft. Lee ■ • Spuyden Duyvil
▪ Ft. Washington
Weehawken • ✓ East River
• New York City
Hoboken • • Castle Garden

▪ Ft. Lafayette
Ft. Tompkins • The Narrows

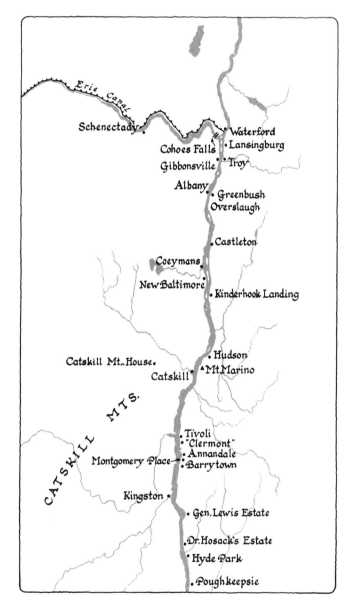

Erie Canal

Schenectady • • Waterford
Cohoes Falls • • Lansingburg
Gibbonsville • • Troy
Albany •
• Greenbush
Overslaugh

• Castleton

Coeymans •
New Baltimore •
• Kinderhook Landing

Catskill Mt. House. • • Hudson
Catskill • ▲ Mt. Marino

C A T S K I L L   M T S.

• Tivoli
• "Clermont"
Montgomery Place → • Annandale
• Barrytown

Kingston •

• Gen. Lewis Estate

• Dr. Hosack's Estate
• Hyde Park
• Poughkeepsie

150

A NEW ERA OF TRAVEL began on the Hudson and subsequently on every navigable river in America—and finally throughout the world—on the afternoon of August 17, 1807. At one o'clock on that momentous afternoon in New York City Robert Fulton launched the first successful steamboat in the world, "The North River Steamboat of Clermont." As an Irish scientific writer of the mid-nineteenth century asserted, "Whatever may be the dispute maintained among the historians of art as to the conflicting claims for the invention of steam navigation,[1] it is an incontestable fact that the first steamboat practically exhibited for any useful purpose, was placed on the Hudson, to ply between New York and Albany, in the beginning of the year 1808.[2] From that time to the present, this river has been the theatre of the most remarkable series of experiments on locomotion on water ever recorded in the history of man." [3]

The revolutionary event had a very inauspicious beginning. Writing shortly after the occasion, Fulton confessed:

To me it was a most trying and interesting occasion. I wanted my friends to go on board, and witness the first successful trip. Many of them did me the favor to attend, as a matter of personal respect, but it was manifest that they did it with reluctance, fearing to be partners of my mortification and not of my triumph. I was well aware that in my case there were many reasons to doubt of my success. The machinery was new and ill-made; and many parts of it were constructed by mechanics unacquainted with such work; and unexpected difficulties might reasonably be presumed to present themselves from other causes. The moment arrived in which the word was to be given for the boat to move. My friends were in groups on the deck. There was anxiety mixed with fear among them. They were silent, sad and weary. I read in their looks nothing but disaster, and almost repented of my efforts. The signal was given and the boat moved on a short distance and then stopped and became immovable. To the silence of the preceding moment, now succeeded murmurs of discontent, and agitations,

and whispers and shrugs. I could hear distinctly repeated—"I told you it was so; it is a foolish scheme: I wish we were well out of it."

I elevated myself upon a platform and addressed the assembly. I stated that I knew not what was the matter, but if they would be quiet and indulge me for half an hour, I would either go on or abandon the voyage for that time. This short respite was conceded without objection. I went below and examined the machinery, and discovered that the cause was a slight maladjustment of some of the work. In a short time it was obviated. The boat was again put in motion. She continued to move on.[4]

As the boat continued on her way without further mishap, incredulity soon yielded to surprised elation. "When the guests realized the safety and success of the invention," a relative of Fulton has said, "they were moved to merriment and broke into song. In the stern sat a throng of gaily dressed gentlemen and ladies, and as the boat moved through the glorious scenery of the Highlands some one struck up 'Ye Banks and Braes o' Bonny Doon,' said to be Fulton's favorite song, appropriate enough from the lips of the members of the Scottish Fulton and Livingston families upon America's most bonny river." [5]

The response of the people on shore who happened to see the vessel steam up-river on that sunny afternoon was somewhat different. The *Clermont* seemed to have been designed to strike terror in those who had never seen a sailless vessel before. A snub-nosed little boat spouting smoke and sparks from its ungainly smokestack, it had two uncovered paddle-wheels that splashed water on the unprotected passengers, and was described as looking like a "back-woods saw-mill mounted on a scow and set on fire." The single Watt steam-engine stood exposed to view on the forward part of the boat, and the only cover was two small cabins located on the bow and stern. The surprise and bewilderment of those on shore or among the crews of passing sloops and schooners can well be imagined. It has been said that "the terrific spectacle, particularly after dark, appalled the crews of other vessels, who saw it rapidly approaching in spite of adverse wind and tide; many of them fell upon their knees in humble prayer for protection, while others disappeared beneath their decks or escaped to the shore." [6]

But history had been made. As Fulton wrote with commendable understatement to his friend Joel Barlow after returning to New York: "My steamboat voyage to Albany and back has turned out rather more favorably than I had calculated. The distance from New York to Albany is one hundred and fifty miles. I ran it up in thirty-two hours, and down in thirty. I had a slight breeze against me the whole way, both going and coming, and the voyage has been performed wholly by the power of the steam engine. I overtook many sloops and schooners, beating to the windward, and parted with them as if they had been at anchor. The power of propelling boats by steam is now fully proved." [7]

The success of the *Clermont* soon aroused the imagination of the general public. By the time Fulton was ready to put it into regular packet service on September 4, 1807, half of New York was on hand to cheer its departure. An eyewitness testified that "the wharves, piers, housetops, and every spot from which a sight could be obtained, were filled with spectators," and when the boat turned up the river and was fairly underway "there arose such a huzza as ten thousand throats never gave before." [8] The enthusiastic reception continued throughout the voyage up-river:

As we passed West Point the whole garrison was out and cheered us. At Newburgh it seemed as if all Orange County had collected there; the whole side-hill city seemed animated with life. Every sailboat and water craft was out; the ferry-boat from Fishkill was filled with ladies. Fulton was engaged in

seeing a passenger landed, and did not observe the boat until she bore up alongside. The flapping of the sail arrested his attention, and as he turned, the waving of so many handkerchiefs and the smiles of bright and happy faces, struck him with surprise. He raised his hat and exclaimed, "That is the finest sight we have seen yet." [9]

The following season Fulton and Livingston added two more steamboats to the New York-Albany run, and by 1811, when they put the first steamboat—the "New Orleans"—on the Mississippi, they had built a total of eight vessels to run at various times between New York and Albany. The significance of this achievement may be seen in the fact that there wasn't a steamboat on the River Clyde in Scotland until 1813, and no boat plied between Liverpool and Glasgow until the year 1815. In 1819, when twelve steamboats were in regular service in New York, the Missouri River acquired its first steamboat. None appeared on the Tennessee River until 1821; none on the upper Mississippi until 1823.

After 1824 when the Supreme Court broke the Fulton-Livingston monopoly and Chief Justice Marshall in *Gibbons v. Ogden* opened steamboating to general competition, the growth in the number and quality of the steamboats on the Hudson was phenomenal. By 1840 there were approximately one hundred "floating palaces" plying the river; ten years later there were at least 140. In 1851 at least a million passengers traveled on steamers between New York and Albany. The size of the boats had increased from the 133-foot *Clermont* to the 352-foot *New World* (1848), with a carrying capacity of several thousand passengers. Speed increased with each passing year: a trip which required thirty to thirty-six hours in 1807 could be done in ten by the 1830s (in seven by the 1860s). A voyage to Albany which once required two days to a week by sloop, could now be done between the hours of sunset and sunrise of a single day.

17. *Steamboat "Clermont" on North River,*
watercolor by Varick de Witt, 1861; courtesy of
The New-York Historical Society.

"A back-woods saw-mill mounted on a scow and set on fire."

The "North River Steamboat of Clermont" showing the
alterations made to fit her out for her first commercial run.
A wheel for more effective steering has been put amidships,
replacing the man at the tiller; the paddle wheels have
been covered to keep the passengers from getting drenched.

Though many other rivers in America witnessed a similar development, the Hudson was without peer in the number and variety of steamboats it presented per square mile of river. Even after the turn of the century we still hear that there is not in all America "a watercourse of equal length which has so frequent and such luxurious steamer-boat service as the tidal Hudson." [10]

Fulton had foreseen the tremendous impact the steamboat would have on the development of American society and civilization, but as the following narratives reveal, that impact was nowhere more in evidence than in his own native state of New York, where the steamboat had its first practical application and its highest development. The Hudson River during this period became the main artery of trade and travel in the nation, the State of New York the largest in wealth and population. The role of the steamboat in that remarkable evolution is amply demonstrated in the following chronicles of the 1820s and 1830s. Reading them we share the opinion of a modern historian that "no one had seen America until he had seen the Hudson River, and no one had seen the Hudson River properly unless he had done so from the deck of a Day Line steamer." [11]

10.
Lafayette 1824*

BY FREDERICK BUTLER

INTRODUCTION: At one o'clock in the morning on Wednesday, September 15, 1824, the *James Kent,* a celebrated steamship owned by the company established by Fulton and Livingston, pulled up to Castle Garden on the tip of Manhattan and waited for its passengers. The famous thick-walled building, originally built as a fortress to protect New York harbor during the War of 1812 and now used as a place of public celebration, was aglow with festivity. At 2 A.M. "a great number of ladies and citizens" came out of the huge hall and boarded the waiting steamboat. In a few minutes, "and notwithstanding the darkness of the night, which had succeeded the light of the moon"—as one member of the party later described the event—the ship weighed anchor. "We speedily lost sight of Castle Garden; and in place of the joyful sounds of music, we heard only the monotonous and regular noise of our steam engine, labouring against the rapid tide of the Hudson." [1] It was the beginning of one of the most colorful events in the history of steamboating in the Hudson Valley, the triumphant five-day tour of the Marquis de Lafayette from New York City to Albany. The popular hero of the American Revolution had been induced to come to America at the personal invitation of President James Monroe, who even offered to send an American frigate to fetch the general across the Atlantic. Flattered by such royal attention, Lafayette accepted the invitation but modestly declined the use of

* Excerpt from *A Complete History of the Marquis de Lafayette, Major General in the Army of the United States of America, in the War of the Revolution; Embracing an Account of His Late Tour through the United States to the Time of His Departure, September, 1825,* by an Officer in the Late Army (New York: 1826), pp. 420–442. The "Tour" was written by Frederick Butler and first appeared in Butler's *Memoirs of the Marquis de Lafayette.* Bracketed material is by the present editor.

the frigate, and arrived at New York City aboard the packet ship *Cadmus* with his son and secretary on August 15, 1824. His arrival immediately precipitated "an epochal tour which Charles Sumner said 'belongs to the poetry of history.' " [2]

Writing a half century after the event, Thurlow Weed declared:

. . . there were no wires fifty years ago over which intelligence could pass with lightning speed, but the visit of Lafayette was expected, and the pulses and hearts of the people were quickened and warmed simultaneously through some mysterious medium throughout the whole Union. Citizens rushed from neighboring cities and villages to welcome the French nobleman, who, before he was twenty-one years old, had devoted himself and his fortune to the American colonies in their wonderful conflict with the mother country for independence. . . .

General Lafayette was now sixty-seven years of age, with some physical infirmities, but intellectually strong, and in manners and feeling cheerful, elastic, and accomplished.

The general's landing on the Battery, his reception by the military under General Martin, his triumphant progress through Broadway, his first visit to the City Hall, awakened emotions which cannot be described. I have witnessed the celebration of the completion of the Erie Canal and the mingling of the waters of Lake Erie with the Atlantic Ocean, the completion of the Croton Water Works celebration, the reception of the Prince of Wales, and other brilliant and beautiful pageants, but they all lacked the heart and soul which marked and signalized the welcome of Lafayette. [3]

The extraordinary demonstration never abated until Lafayette took leave of America some thirteen months later. He visited every state in the Union and almost every major city at least once during his triumphal tour. He was the personal guest of Jefferson at Monticello, of Jackson at the Hermitage. He sailed the Mississippi, ascended Bunker Hill, admired Niagara; and everywhere he went his appearance provoked a frenzied enthusiasm without parallel or precedent in American history.

18. *Landing of Lafayette at Castle Garden, 1825,* anonymous lithograph; courtesy of The New-York Historical Society.

"The general's landing on the Battery . . . awakened emotions which cannot be described."

The ruins of Castle Garden may still be seen at the tip of Manhattan, though now surrounded by a landfill that has extended the park land of the Battery as far as the sailing vessels on the left.

The five days Lafayette spent on the Hudson in September, 1824, were no exception to this unprecedented outburst of idolatrous hero worship—unless it was even more intense, for the new mode of steamboat travel permitted a rapid exposure to untold multitudes on a prearranged schedule that embraced 150 miles of towns and villages. The feat would have been inconceivable during the era of the sailing vessel, and it lent a distinctly modern note to the following account written by Frederick Butler (1766–1843), an enthusiastic American historian.

IN PURSUANCE OF THE arrangements made for that purpose, General Lafayette, his son, and suite, together with a select party of ladies and gentlemen, repaired on board of the steamboat *James Kent*,[1] directly on retiring from the Grand Fete of Tuesday evening, and proceeded up the Hudson river, to visit Albany, and the intermediate towns upon the river. The party embarked a few minutes after 2 o'clock, Wednesday morning; among the guests were members of the Cincinnati, with their President, Colonel [Richard] Varick; His Honour the Recorder, and several of the Corporation [of the City of New York]; Governor [Henry] Johnson, of Louisiana; Mrs. Lewis of Virginia [granddaughter of George Washington]; Colonel Alexander Hamilton, and his mother, (widow of the late General Hamilton); General Morton, Colonel [Charles L.] Platt, and a number of others.[2]

The boat made very good progress until she arrived off Tarry-Town, where a dense fog came on; but such was the anxiety of General Lafayette to reach West Point at the appointed time, (10 o'clock), that Commodore Wiswall determined to push slowly on. It was impossible for the pilot to see five rods ahead. The result was, that at about 7 o'clock the boat ran aground upon what is called the Oyster Bank. Here she was obliged to remain for several hours—to the great disappointment of those on board, and also of the thousands who had collected at West Point, to witness his reception, and the tens of thousands at the villages above, which he was expected to pass before dark. As soon as it cleared off, so that the shores were discernible, it was found that every height and cliff were covered with people, anxious to do their utmost in honouring the Guest of the Nation. At Stony Point, in particular, there was a large collection of people, a flag was hoisted, and a salute fired from a field piece stationed there for that purpose. One man, more eager than the rest, clambered down the rocks with the agility of a mountain goat, armed with a large musket, which a loud explosion gave us to understand was heavily charged. The boat was near in shore, and as the smoke cleared away, he waved his hand and exclaimed, "There, General, I give you the best I can!"

The population at West Point, including the officers, professors, cadets, the artisans, and their families, etc., etc., ordinarily amount to about one thousand persons. But from daylight yesterday morning, until ten o'clock, the ladies and gentlemen from the country adjacent, continued to flock in sloops and other craft, in great numbers. The suspense from the hours of 9 till 12 was very anxious; but at about fifteen minutes after 12, the welcome signal of his approach was given; and there was instantly more bustle and confusion than there has been before witnessed on the Point since the army of the revolution; the clangour of arms, the thrilling notes of the bugle, and the spirit-stirring drum, imparted life and animation to this wild and magnificent region.—The lofty bank of the Hudson was lined with spectators; and the Cadets were in line, as if they had been summoned from their barracks by the wand of a magician.

The *James Kent,* gorgeously decorated with flags, came proudly on, cutting away the foaming current, as though she dared Neptune and all his host to strife; and came majestically along side of the dock at half past 12. The General was here received by Colonel [Sylvanus] Thayer, the commander of the post,[3] accompanied by Major-Generals [Jacob Jennings] Brown [4] and [Winfield] Scott,[5] with their respective suites, together with the officers and professors upon the station, under a salute of twenty-one guns from a detachment of artillery, posted upon the bluff, directly north of the old barracks. A landeau was in readiness to receive the General as he stepped ashore, in which he ascended the hill to the plain, followed by a long procession, consisting of the Cincinnati, the officers of the station, gentlemen from New-York, and from the river towns above, delegates from the towns of Newburgh, Poughkeepsie, Clermont, Hudson, and Albany, etc., etc. He was received on the plain by the corps of Cadets, whom he reviewed; and afterwards received the marching salute in front of the marquee erected for him, and witnessed several evolutions, which evinced the perfection of discipline. From the parade ground the General repaired for a few moments to the quarters of Generals Brown and Scott, at Mr. Cozzen's,[6] where the ladies assembled in a spacious room adjoining the library, and partook of refreshments prepared for the occasion. At half past two, the General was conducted by Colonel Thayer to the splendid library of the institution, where the corps of Cadets were individually presented to him by Major Worth; the gentlemen upon the Point who had not previously been introduced, were then presented; after which the ladies were severally introduced.

From the library, the General repaired to the Mess-room of the Cadets, elegantly fitted up for the occasion, and sat down to dinner, which, whether we regard the quantity, quality, the variety, or the style in which it was served up, we may at once pronounce a sumptuous one.—Including the Officers, Cadets, the Cincinnati, Corporation from New-York, and guests, more than four hundred persons sat down at the table. Colonel Thayer presided, assisted by Major Worth. General Lafayette and General Scott were seated on the right of the President, and General Brown and Colonel Varick on his left. At a cross table at the head, were seated the members of the Cincinnati, and at another similar table, at the other end of the hall, were the members of the Corporation of New-York, with Mr. George Washington Lafayette, on the right of the Vice-President. The room was tastefully and elegantly decorated. Festoons of evergreen were suspended from pillar to pillar, in every direction through the spacious hall. Back of the President's chair hung the star-spangled banner. Over the chair was a large spread, and elegantly wrought, eagle, with the words "September, 1777," issuing from the streamer in his beak, and "York-Town" grasped in his claws. A crown of laurel, interwoven with roses, was suspended over the General's head. Over the window on his right, was the name of Washington, wrought in leaves of ever-green, and on the left that of Lafayette. At the other end of the hall hung a full-length portrait of "the Father of his Country"; and upon the right wall, in the centre, that of Jefferson, and on the left, President Adams.

At 6 o'clock, the company rose from the table, and the General and his friends re-embarked on board the *James Kent,* and proceeded to Newburgh.

Through the whole distance of the Highlands, the hardy mountaineers who inhabit many of the glens manifested their respect by showing themselves ever and anon, and discharging their muskets from the crags and cliffs which in some places seem to frown over the heads of the passing traveller, as the steam-boat ploughs her way close at the base of the mountains. In passing Cold-Spring, a salute was fired from a piece of artillery stationed near the shore for that purpose. A salute was also fired from New-Windsor, (near the old Encampment of the Revolutionary Army). Unfortunately, however, the delay occasioned by the morning accident, had detained the party so long that the shades of night now began to close in, and on the arrival of the steam-boat at New-burgh the twilight had so far advanced as to render objects indistinct at a very short distance. A corps of infantry were drawn up in handsome array upon the wharf, to receive the General, by whom he was escorted to the Orange Hotel, where he was received by the corporation of the village, by the President of which he was addressed.

The General made a brief and pertinent reply to this address; after which he entered an open carriage and was escorted through the principal streets of the village, which were thronged with people, who were delighted with a glimpse of the General's face, caught even by the aid of a flickering lamp; over the streets, at short distances, arches had been erected which were tastefully festooned with ever-greens and flowers, and on several of them were suspended appropriate inscriptions. On one of these arches was the following inscription:—"Thrice welcome Lafayette, Columbia's bright Occidental Star." Another arch was formed by the planting of two well grown forest trees, and bending their tops together. The inscription suspended from this lofty arch was too high for the rays of our feeble lamp. The inscription upon another arch was, "Lafayette and Liberty—Welcome Illustrious Chief." But the arch which was far the most beautiful, was erected by the ladies; it extended from the houses on each side of the street, and formed one grand and two smaller arches; these were so richly and beautifully ornamented with festoons and flowers, that

they would have answered well for decorations to the portals of the temple of Flora herself; the inscription here was "Welcome to our hero, Lafayette." Having returned to the Orange Hotel, an address was presented to the General by Johannis Miller, Esq., President of the Orange county Agricultural Society, in behalf of said Society.

The General was then ushered into the grand saloon of the Orange Hotel, attended by the Committee of Arrangements, consisting of Messrs. Rose, Ruggles, Smith, Fisk, and others, together with the Trustees of the village. The ladies and gentlemen of the village, and several hundreds from the adjoining towns, had then the honour of a presentation, and were received with the accustomed affability and kindness of our illustrious guest, until, completely exhausted with the fatigues of the day, and of the preceding night, he was compelled to seek a few hours repose. The hall of audience was ornamented with much taste, and it was in this room that the supper-table was bountifully spread, at 11 o'clock, when the General was sufficiently refreshed to take a seat at the table.[7] On the right of the chair were the words—"Brandywine, 11th September, 1777," encircled by a wreath of ever-greens, and on the left, the words "York-Town, 19th October, 1781," formed in the same manner. At the other end of the hall was a portrait of Washington, and the whole apartment was splendidly decorated with festoons and flowers of every variety of the season, and brilliantly illuminated by the light of several chandeliers, reflected from a large number of elegant mirrors.

The arrangements at this place were extensive and unusually imposing, but the time of the General's arrival was so late, that much derangement was the consequence. His arrival having been expected the day before, the people had been assembling for nearly two days; and it was computed that, independently of the troops on duty, there were at least 10,000 persons in the village. The public houses were all illuminated; and a splendid ball was given at Crawford's Hotel.

At 12 o'clock, the steam-boat *Chancellor Livingston* [8] which had also been detained on her passage up by the fog, made her appearance from Albany, when most of the guests from New-York, both ladies and gentlemen, returned to the city. Among the former were the two Miss Wrights, who have lately arrived from France, and whose "View of the American Society and Manners," has acquired some considerable notoriety.[9] The General and his suite came on board of the *Kent* at about the same hour, and retired to rest, when the boat made sail, and before day-light anchored off Poughkeepsie.

Our National Guest has no where received a more flattering reception, than at the beautiful, ancient, and patriotic village of Poughkeepsie; nor has more promptitude, vigour, and taste, been displayed in the arrangements at any other place. At sunrise all hands were "piped" on deck, and a more imposing spectacle has rarely been presented. The high bluffs below the landing place, were covered with troops, and thousands of citizens were crowding the wharves, showing themselves in large groups from the neighbouring heights, and windows of the houses standing within view of the river. All ages and sexes seemed to press anxiously forward to show their gratitude to their welcome visitor. At half past 6 o'clock, the boat got under way, and took a turn upon the river, while a salute was fired by a corps of artillery stationed upon one of the heights. When the General appeared upon the deck, the welkin rang with the cheers from the crowds upon the shore, which were returned from the boat. The boat was then drawn up to the wharf, where a company of horse, many of the officers of General Brush's division on horseback, all

mounted on elegant horses, and in complete uniform, together with several uniform companies, were drawn up in great order under the direction of Major-General Brush, assisted by Colonel Cunningham. General Lafayette was then conducted by Thomas T. Oakley,[10] General James Tallmadge,[11] Judge [James] Emott,[12] and Philo Ruggles, Esq., to a barouche, with four beautiful white horses, in which the General took his seat, attended by Colonel [Francis Kinloch] Huger, of South Carolina,[13] General [Philip] Van Courtland,[14] General [Nicholas] Fish,[15] and General [Morgan] Lewis.[16] A barouche, also drawn by four white horses, was then drawn up, which was occupied by the son of General Lafayette, and gentlemen attending them. After being conducted to the pleasant and extensive piazza in front of Mr. Forbus' house, and after being introduced to the clergy and gentlemen attending, he was cordially addressed by Colonel Henry A. Livingston.[17]

To this address, the General returned a neat and feeling reply.

A procession was then formed under the direction of the committee, to the Poughkeepsie hotel, at about 8 o'clock, where the General sat down to a sumptuous breakfast, handsomely served up by Mr. Myer. At the head of the table hung the well-known and venerated portrait of Washington, and at the opposite end, the Grand Banner of St. Tammany. On each side of the hall, at suitable distances, were suspended banners, with the arms, name, and motto, of each state in the union. Over the centre of the table, hung a canopy formed of festoons of flowers and ever-greens, of various kinds, belted by a riband, on which was inscribed the names of the thirteen original States. Over the folding doors, were the well-known words of "Welcome Lafayette" made with great accuracy, wholly of pink-coloured blossoms of china-astor, and on one of the walls, were inscribed the names of Washington and Lafayette, wrought in laurel leaves, and encircled in garlands of flowers. Directly in front of the General's seat, stood a representation of the temple of Fame; and the whole suite of apartments were decorated in a style to correspond with the above.

Immediately after breakfast, and with a praise-worthy promptness, the escort was formed, and the General was attended to the boat with every possible mark of respect; the troops again repaired to the heights; and on hauling into the stream, another salute was fired from the artillery, and afterwards several vollies of musketry were fired, with a precision which the General was pleased to say resembled very much the firing of regular troops. The shores were again lined with people, who cheered in all directions.

Passing rapidly up the river, preparations were made for the landing with Governor Lewis,[18] at the dock, near his elegant country seat. The boat arrived at about 12 o'clock, and on coming along side, carriages were found in readiness to convey the party to the mansion which stood at some distance from the road, which wound through a beautiful copse to the house. On alighting, the General and suite were introduced to the family, and were shortly after introduced into an apartment, where an elegant collation was provided: peaches, grapes, and melons, were mingled with more substantial fare, and every variety of wine sparkled on the table. After remaining an hour and a half, the General took leave of this hospitable family, and embarked, in order to continue his voyage to Albany.

Soon afterwards, in passing the seat of James Thompson, Esq., a boat came off with a large basket of peaches, of enormous size, and excellent flavour, and with several elegant bouquets of flowers.

In passing the landing at Kingston, (four miles from the village), a large collection were found to have assembled; a salute was fired from the shore, and hearty cheers given and returned. At this place, Colonel Henry Livingston,[19] who commanded a regiment under Lafayette in Rhode Island, and at Valley Forge, came on board. The General had just been inquiring of Colonel Fish, what had become of his old friend Henry Livingston, and received him most affectionately.[20]

The steam-boat arrived at Clermont at about 4 o'clock in the afternoon, and came to anchor off the elegant mansion of Robert L. Livingston, Esq. formerly the seat of the late Chancellor Livingston.[21] Before the boat arrived at the dock, it was discovered that the groves were literally alive with people, of all ages and sexes, equally anxious with the hospitable proprietor, to manifest their respect for their expected guest, and greet his landing. But while the rocks and glens, and even trees to their topmost branches, presented this animated spectacle, the General, his suite, and friends, were still more surprised by the appearance upon the lawn of this romantic and secluded place, of a regiment of well-disciplined troops, drawn up to receive him.—There were several vessels at anchor in the stream, one of which (a large sloop) was decorated with flags, and a streamer floated from her mast, with the motto of "Welcome Lafayette," in large letters. On landing, a salute was fired from this vessel, which was unexpectedly returned from a field piece planted in a thick copse of trees upon the shore. The General then ascended the shore, and was conducted by General Lewis and Fish, to the mansion of Mr. Livingston, where he was received by that gentleman with the utmost courtesy and cordiality.—After the friends of Mr. Livingston, assembled on the occasion, had been presented, the General reviewed the troops upon the lawn, by whom he was honoured with a *feu de joie*. At this moment, a long procession of the ancient and honourable fraternity of Freemasons, consisting of a Chapter of Royal Arch Masons, and the members of "Widow's Son Lodge," of Redhook, emerged from a grove, and on being presented to the General, an appropriate address was delivered by Palmer Cook, Esq., W.M. of the aforementioned lodge.

After a brief and pertinent reply, the General accepted of an invitation to visit the seat of Edward P. Livingston, Esq.,[22] which is situated but a short distance to the north, upon the same elevated and beautiful plain. His reception was equally cordial and flattering as before. An excellent cold collation, together with refreshments of every suitable kind, were served up. And while the company were partaking of these, the steamboat *Richmond,*[23] Captain William Wiswall, came gayly down, and anchored along side of the *James Kent,* having on board Major-General Jacob Rutsen Van Rensselaer,[24] and suite, Brigadier-General Fleming, and suite, the Mayor of Hudson, (Rufus Reed, Esq.) Dr. Tallman, late Mayor, and Colonel Strong, as delegates from the city of Hudson, together with the Hudson Band, and two elegant uniform companies, under the command of Colonel Edwards. This addition to the company already on the ground, repaired immediately to the seat of Mr. E. P. Livingston, from whence, after refreshments were served out to them by Mr. L. and Commodore Wiswall in person, General Lafayette was escorted back to the seat of his liberal entertainer. As night came on, the troops and crowd from the country dispersed, and the Hudson troops were taken on board of the steam-boat *James Kent,* where refreshments were ordered, and the forward deck and cabin assigned to them for the night. In the evening the whole of Mr. L.'s splendid suite of apartments [at Clermont] were brilliantly lit up, and an elegant ball was given in honour of the General's company. The assemblage was very numerous, and a brilliant

circle of ladies, arrayed in all the charm of health, beauty, and rich and elegant dresses, were contributing to the festivity and joy of the occasion, by "tripping the light fantastic toe," or by conversation sparkled with wit, or adorned by the graces of polished manners and education. Among the guests this evening, in addition to those already named, were the Honourable Edward Livingston,[25] of New Orleans, the Honourable Walter Patterson, Captain Ridgeley, of the Navy, the Honourable Peter R. Livingston,[26] A. Vanderpool, Esq., of Kinderhook, Mrs. Montgomery,[27] (widow of the gallant General who fell at Quebec,) and many others whose names are not recollected. During the evening a sumptuous supper was served up in a style of magnificence rarely, if ever equalled in this country. The room selected for this part of the *fête,* was an extensive Greenhouse, or Orangery, and the effect was indescribably fine. The tables had been made and fitted for this occasion, and were spread beneath a large grove of Orange and Lemon trees, with bending branches of fruit, and many other species of exotic shrubs and plants. Flora also, had profusely scattered her blossoms; and the whole scene seemed to partake of enchantment. The beholder stood gazing, as if bound by the wizard spell of the Magician. The night was dark and rainy; but this contributed to the general effect of the *fête,* inasmuch as the darkness heightened the effect of the thousand lamps by which the surrounding groves were illuminated. There was also a fine exhibition of fireworks, which had been prepared and brought from New York for the occasion. It having been found inconvenient to provide suppers for so many on board of the boat, the whole detachment of troops were invited by Mr. L. to supper in the Green house, which invitation was accepted. At 10 o'clock, General Lafayette retired from this scene of gayety and beauty, and at two the hall was closed, and the company separated, not only highly gratified with the entertainment, but with the manner in which it was got up and imparted to his guests by Mr. L. whose style of living closely approximates that of the real English gentleman, and whose wealth is equalled by his kindness and liberality.

At 9 o'clock on Friday, the General again embarked, and proceeded on his way, and before 10 o'clock, was in sight of Catskill.[28] The long wharf which projects half a mile into the river, was occupied by two battalions of troops.—The highlands which nearly exclude the whole village from a view of the river, were covered with people, and on the arrival of the *James Kent* at the dock, a salute of 13 guns was fired from the artillery on one of the heights. The arrangements of General Lafayette rendered it absolutely necessary that he should be at Albany on that day to dinner, and hence it was utterly impossible for him to make any stay at Catskill, although he was earnestly pressed to dine by a very respectable delegation. The General, to gratify the feelings of thousands who were assembled at the landing to hail his arrival and bid him welcome, consented to land and pass through the principal streets, in an elegant carriage, accompanied by the Committee of Arrangements, and escorted by the military, and a large assemblage of citizens in procession. In front of Crowell's Hotel the procession halted, and the General was received by the acclamations of a large concourse of people, eager to see, and embrace the Nation's Guest. Amongst the company was a body of the heroes of the revolution, whose furrowed features, silver locks, and tottering steps, bespoke age and hard service. But at the sight of their old General, they rushed forward to meet the quick-extended grasp of their old Commander. Among the number, was an old servant who was with Lafayette when he was wounded at the battle of Brandywine. This was a touching scene, few eyes were dry, either among the actors or spectators; but

the General's time was so short, that he was constrained to leave the further honours that awaited him in this place, bid adieu to the citizens, and embark for Hudson.

The boat arrived at Hudson a few minutes before 2 o'clock; but the same reason that prevented a longer stay at Catskill, also rendered it impossible, consistent with his arrangements, to make any considerable stay here. On landing, the crowd was so great that it was almost impossible to proceed, notwithstanding the active exertions of Colonel Darling, the Marshal of the day, assisted by the military. The General was conducted to an elegant barouche, drawn by four beautiful black horses, attended by four grooms in a special livery. After the General, followed a number of other carriages, with his retinue, and the different delegates from the river towns. The procession passed up Ferry to Warren-street, where an arch was erected, which for its size and elegance of construction, exceeded any that had been previously seen on the tour. The whole street, which is more than a mile in length, was choked with the crowd. And the windows, as at Catskill, were filled with ladies, whose snowwhite hands and handkerchiefs, were gracefully waved in the air, while the crowd in the streets were cheering, and the General, with his usual condescension, was bowing, or endeavouring to bow, to every individual in the multitude. About half-way up the street, stood another arch, elegantly adorned; and at the head of the town was a third, superior to all, on the top of which stood a colossal figure of the Genius of Liberty, well proportioned and painted, holding in her hand the American standard, which being of unusual size, floated in the air with an imposing effect. To each of the arches of which we have spoken, were suspended appropriate inscriptions. On arriving at the square, at the head of Warren-street, the procession wheeled and returned to the Court-house, when the troops and citizens opened to the right and left, and all that could, passed through, and up to the Court-room. All the seats without the bar were filled with the "Daughters of Columbia," forming a large and interesting group of well-dressed and beautiful females. The Court-room was superbly decorated—displaying more labour, taste, and skill, than any decorations of the kind that were seen on the route. At the entrance of the bar, on either side, stood a beautiful Corinthian pillar, with caps and cornices of the composite order of architecture, elegantly wrought and ornamented with leaves and gold. On the top of each of these pillars was placed a globe, and the whole were united at the top by a chain of flowers of every hue, festooned with laurel and roses. The General was conducted to this rich and beautiful portal, where His Honour the Mayor delivered an interesting address.

General Lafayette briefly replied to the address, after which the members of the Common Council were severally presented to him. A most interesting and affecting spectacle was then presented; sixty-eight veterans of the revolution, who had collected from the different parts of the country, formed a part of the procession, and were next presented; and it so happened that several of them were officers, and many of them soldiers who had served with Lafayette. Notwithstanding that they were admonished that the greatest haste was necessary, yet every one had something to say; and when they grasped his friendly hand, each seemed reluctant to release it. One of them came up with a sword in his hand, which, as he passed, he remarked was "given to him by the Marquis," at such a place, "in Rhode Island." Another, with a tear glistening in his eye, as he shook the hand of the General, observed—"You, Sir, gave me the first guinea I ever had in my life—shall never forget that."

The officers of the militia were next presented, and after them, the ladies. But time would not allow of de-

lay; and many thousands who were eagerly pressing forward, were disappointed in not being introduced to the man whom they had assembled to honour. In passing down the street, however, on arriving opposite Allen's hotel, where arrangements had been made for the dinner, the solicitations were so warm and earnest, that the General was constrained to alight and take a glass of wine in the long room. And here, again, was presented a specimen of Hudson taste, which deserves every commendation. The hall was decorated in a style of elegance, that would compare only with the Court-house. The General stopped but for a moment, when he re-entered his carriage, and returned to the boat, followed by the shouts and blessings of thousands. On leaving the dock, three cheers were given by the multitude, and returned from the boat—after which a salute was fired from the hill near the Observatory. In passing up the river, the docks at the villages of Coxsackie, New-Baltimore, and Coeymans, were crowded with people, who cheered the General repeatedly, and with as much enthusiasm as though they had had a nearer view. At Castleton, a large collection of people had assembled, and a salute was fired from a six pounder.

In consequence of the unavoidable delays on the way, a freshet in the river, the contrary winds and tide, the *James Kent* did not arrive at her moorings at the Overslaugh, until five o'clock (on Friday)—three hours later than was originally contemplated. The consequence was, that the arrangements of the committee for the city of Albany were deranged; the committee themselves, consisting of Alderman Townsend and Humphrey, Colonel Bacon, and others, (in addition to the New-York delegation, which had accompanied the General from New-York,) who had been waiting to receive their guest, were much fatigued; and the troops, who had been on duty since 7 o'clock in the morning, without refreshment, were nearly exhausted. On landing, the General was conducted to a superb landeau, drawn by four white horses, and carriages were in readiness for the gentlemen accompanying him. The procession was quickly formed, and moved rapidly on to Greenbush, escorted by a detachment of horse, commanded by Major General Solomon Van Rensselaer,[29] Marshall of the day, assisted by Colonel [J. Taylor] Cooper. On arriving at the centre of the village, the General was conducted to a large marquee, erected beneath an arch, similar to those heretofore described, and bearing appropriate inscriptions, where he was received by the members of the Corporation, who welcomed him with an appropriate address; after which, refreshments were served, and the procession moved on. Night was now rapidly setting in; and the delay at the Ferry, for the want of a sufficient number of boats, rendered it quite dark when the General landed in Albany.[30] It was, however, easy to discern, that the preparations for the event had been extensive, and that a prodigious assemblage of people were yet impatiently awaiting his approach. He was welcomed, in behalf of the citizens, by Stephen Lush, Esq., one of the oldest and most respectable of the inhabitants of Albany, who rode in the carriage with him. A large detachment of troops were on duty, and a salute was fired by a corps of artillery, stationed near the Ferry-stairs, which was answered by the old Clinton field-piece, which has long stood upon the hill back of Albany, to send its thunder forth, echoing among the distant hills, on all patriotic occasions. On entering the city, the procession passed under an arch, inscribed "The Hero is Welcome." At the junction of Church and South Market streets, stood another arch, large and beautiful, inscribed, "We remember thy deeds—We revere thy worth—We love thy virtues." At the foot of Beaver-street, near the Museum, stood a stupendous arch, displaying by its festoons and the disposition and

variety of flowers interwoven with ever-greens, much beauty in itself, and taste in the ladies, whose delicate fingers had formed and ornamented it.—On entering the foot of State-street, on the site of the Old Dutch Church, stood a temple, richly ornamented, around the pillars of which the ivy was gracefully entwined. On the top of the temple, stood a large living eagle, who proudly flapped his wings as the chieftain passed. Many of the houses were illuminated, among which were the capitol, and the whole block of Gregory's buildings, including the houses of Chancellor [Nathan] Sanford,[31] Mr. Gregory, Isaac Hamilton, Esq., and the extensive establishment of Mr. Cruttenden. On the front of the latter was a transparency, executed by [Henry] Inman,[32] of this city, representing the reception of General Lafayette by the Genius of Liberty, who proffers him a scroll; and in the back ground was seen the ship *Cadmus,* in which he made his passage from France. The elevated situation of these lofty buildings, contributed to give the illumination a splendid and elegant appearance; and the effect was greatly heightened by the bright light cast upon the military, the cavalcade, and the immense concourse of people, who otherwise would only have been felt instead of seen. On alighting at the capitol, the General was conducted to the Senate Chamber, where he was received by the Honourable Ambrose Spencer,[33] Mayor of the city, and the members of the Corporation. He was addressed by the Mayor in the following words:—

"Sir—Your visit to this country is received with universal and heartfelt joy. Your claims upon the gratitude and the friendship of this Nation, arise from your heroic devotion to its freedom, and your uniform assertion to the rights of man. The progress of time has attested the purity of your character, and the lustre of your heroism; and the whole course of your life has evinced those exalted virtues, which were first displayed in favour of the independence and liberty of America.

"In the hour of difficulty and peril, when America, without allies, without credit, with an enfeebled government, and with scanty means of resistance, confiding in the justice of her cause and the protection of Heaven, was combating for her liberties, against a nation, powerful in resources and all the materials for war, when our prospects of success were by many considered more than doubtful, if not desperate, you devoted all your energies and all your means to our defence; and after witnessing our triumphant success, your life has been consecrated to the vindication of the liberties of the old world.

"When Franklin, the wisest man of the age, pronounced you the most distinguished person he ever knew, when Washington, the illustrious hero of the new world, honoured you with friendship the most sincere, and with confidence the most unlimited, they evinced their just discernment of character, and foresaw the further display of faculties and virtues which would identify your name with liberty, and demonstrate your well founded claims to the gratitude, the love, and the admiration of mankind.

"The few surviving statesmen and soldiers of the Revolution have gathered around you as a friend and brother —the generation that has risen up since your departure, cherish the same feelings, and those that will appear in the successive future ages, will hail you as the benefactor of America, and the hero of liberty. In every heart you have a friend, and your eulogium is pronounced by every tongue. In behalf of the inhabitants of this ancient city, I welcome you most cordially, and tender to you their civic honours. I salute you as an illustrious benefactor of our country; and I supplicate the blessing of Heaven on a life sanctified in the sublime cause of heroic virtue and disinterested benevolence."

To this address, which we beg leave to pronounce forcible and elegant, the General returned the following reply:—

"Sir—The enjoyments of my visit to the beautiful and happy shores of the North River, cannot but be highly enhanced by the affectionate reception, the civic testimonies of esteem, which are conferred upon me in this city, and by the manner in which you are pleased to express sentiments so gratifying to my heart. Not half a century has elapsed since this place, ancient, but small, was my headquarters, on the frontiers of an extensive wilderness, since as commander in the northern department, I had to receive the oath of renunciation to a royal distant government, of allegiance to the more legitimate sovereignty of the people of the United States. Now, Sir, Albany has become a considerable city; is the central seat of the authorities of the state of New-York. Those wildernesses rank among the most populous, the best cultivated parts of the union. This rising generation, has, in two glorious wars, and still more so in her admirable institutions, asserted an indisputable superiority over the proud pretenders to a control upon her.

"To these happy recollections, Sir, you have the goodness to add remembrances of my early admission among the sons and soldiers of America, of friendships the most honourable and dear to me. I will not attempt to express the feelings that crowd on my mind, and shall only beg you, Sir, and the gentlemen of the Corporation, to accept the tribute of my respectful and devoted gratitude, for the city of Albany and her worthy magistrates."

The members of the Common Council, and those friends who had been specially invited, having been introduced, the General was then conducted to the Governor's apartment, where he was received by his Excellency Governor [Joseph C.] Yates.[34] . . .

The suite of the Governor having been presented to

the General, together with his Excellency's particular friends, he was conducted from the capitol to the residence of Matthew Gregory, Esq. (who mounted the ramparts with Lafayette and Hamilton at York-Town,) where many of the most distinguished gentlemen of the city and state, were assembled to pay him their respects. Among them were Governor [De Witt] Clinton,[35] the Chancellor, and Judges of the Supreme Court, the Lieut. Governor, and principal officers of the state, etc., etc. After remaining here for the space of an hour, the General was attended to the lodgings prepared for him at Cruttenden's, and where a rich and bountiful supper was spread for the Corporation and its guests. The Mayor presided at this entertainment, assisted by Alderman Van Ingen; and a number of toasts were drank by way of concluding the banquet.

Over head, in front of the chair of the president, was the painted inscription—"Lafayette the Guest of the Nation," and on the reverse—"York-Town, October 19th, 1781." Among the festoons were the words wrought in flowers—"Flora's Tribute." On the right of the chair hung the portrait of Lafayette, painted in 1783; and on the left that of the late Robert Morris.[36] Farther down the room stood a marble pedestal, surmounted with the bust of Washington, crowned with a wreath of laurel; and an American Bald Eagle hovered over the door. After remaining a short time in the drawing room, the General, accompanied by the distinguished gentlemen before mentioned, (excepting Governor Clinton, who did not attend, in consequence of the recent death of his son,) repaired to the Assembly Chamber of the Capitol, which was echoing to the music and the dance of a splendid ball, given in honour of the "Nation's Guest." The room was handsomely, though not profusely, decorated with wreaths and festoons, and the pillars entwined with ivy. The Speaker's Chair was entirely shrouded or enveloped

in shrubbery of ever-greens and flowers, and in front, in the centre of a large and beautiful garland, was the following inscription:—"Welcome brave Lafayette; we hail thee as the Nation's Guest and early Friend." From the staff projecting forward from the gallery, floated a broad streamer, bearing the hero's name. Over the Speaker's chair, the well known full length portrait of Washington preserved its place, encircled by a wreath of laurel; and the walls were hung round with banners, inscribed with the names of the following Generals of the Revolution, viz. Schuyler, Lincoln, Hamilton, Lingan, Wayne, Warren, Montgomery, Greene, Knox, Wooster, Heath, Gates, Clinton, M'Dougall, and Gansevoort. General Lafayette stayed but about an hour amidst this scene of pleasure and gayety, during which time the ladies and gentlemen moved in procession before him, and were severally honoured with an introduction. At 1 o'clock, he retired to obtain that repose which the incessant fatigues of the week must have rendered not only desirable, but highly necessary.

On Saturday morning, the General rose in excellent health and spirits, at an early hour; and as the arrangements of the day required that no time should be lost, the calls of the gentlemen commenced at a most unfashionable time. Among other gentlemen, Mr. [De Witt] Clinton called, pursuant to a request from the New-York Literary and Philosophical Society, of which he is President, to present the General with a diploma of membership. And in performing this duty, he addressed the General in an appropriate manner.

In replying to this forcible and elegant address of our distinguished fellow-citizen, General Lafayette remarked in substance, "that the honour conferred on him was rendered the more gratifying to his feelings by the reflection, that the evidence of it was presented to him by the highly respected son and nephew of two of his departed brothers in arms, and warm and personal friends and companions." [37]

At 8 o'clock the military were again under arms, and appeared before the General's lodgings, to escort him through a number of the principal streets, and thence to one of the elegant canal packet-boats, in which the Corporation had invited him to take a trip to Troy, and thence by land to Lansingburg, Waterford, and home by way of the Cohoose Falls, where the boat was in readiness to receive him. [38] The procession moved down State, South, Pearl, and Lydius-streets, to South Market-street, and thence up the second lock, near the seat of the Patroon. [39] The day was uncommonly fine, and the military appeared to excellent advantage.—The crowd was very great; the whole mass of citizens being in motion, and multitudes having flocked in from the surrounding country. It was 12 o'clock before the General, together with the Corporation and their guests, embarked on board of the *Schenectady Packet,* which was gayly dressed for the occasion. The embarkation was announced by a salute from cannon stationed on the hill, near the seat of Elias Kane, Esq. The Albany Band occupied a boat which preceded the packet, and a boat which followed was occupied by the officers of the Albany Military Association and their friends. Next followed two or three large packet boats filled with spectators, and the banks, the whole distance, were lined with people. Among the guests of the Corporation were Governor Yates, Mr. Clinton, the Chancellor and Judges, General Lewis, Colonel Fish, Colonel Huger, the Hon. Peter R. Livingston, and many others. The boats were briskly propelled onward by six horses each, selected for the occasion. In passing the Half-way-House, [40] a large basket of delicious grapes, in rich clusters, and adorned with flowers, was sent on board as a present to the General, from the Shakers at Neskayuna. [41] At the United States garrison, at Gibbons-

ville, [42] the General stopped, and was received within the walls of the arsenal by a salute of 21 guns. Having returned to the packet, the party moved on to the lateral canal, leading to the river, through which they descended and entered the Hudson by one of the "sprouts" which form the Delta of the Mohawk. At this place eight row-boats, all dressed with flags, the broadest of which bore the popular name of *Clinton,* were in readiness to tow the packet across the river, which service was expeditiously performed.

The General landed at Troy on a platform, erected and carpeted for the occasion, and a salute was fired. He was received by a deputation of the citizens, consisting of Messrs. Tibbitts, Russell, Mallory, Dickinson, Cushman, Paine, and others, by the former of whom he was presented with a handsome address.

The crowd was here very great, but they were orderly; and the military parade was rendered more formidable by the addition of two companies of uniform from Albany. A procession was here formed, which was escorted through the principal streets; the General riding, as usual, in an open carriage, attended by Colonel Lane, to the "Troy House," kept by Mr. Titus. On arriving here, he was received by the Common Council of the city, and an address was delivered to him by Mr. Recorder Clowes.

The concourse of people was immensely great; and such was the anxiety to see the illustrious visiter, that he went out upon the piazza, and gratified the multitude as long as his time would allow. The piazza was handsomely adorned with festoons of ever-greens and roses, and in the centre was perched a large living eagle, with a miniature of Lafayette upon his neck. While standing here, a deputation from the Troy Royal Arch Chapter of Masons were introduced to him. They came with a request that he would favour the Chapter, then in session in the tabernacle above, with the honour of a visit. The

19. *Entrance of the Canal into the Hudson at Albany,* anonymous engraving, 1823; courtesy of The New-York Historical Society.

"The party moved on to the lateral canal, leading to the river, through which they descended and entered the Hudson."

The building on the right is probably the Van Rensselaer Manor House.

20. *Troy, Rensselaer County, N.Y.*, engraving by W. J. Bennett, 1837; courtesy of The New-York Historical Society.

"The General landed at Troy on a platform, erected and carpeted for the occasion, and a salute was fired."

request was immediately assented to; and he was received, together with his son, with masonic honours.

The officers and members having been severally presented, the General retired to the dining-hall below, where a cold collation was handsomely and bountifully provided. While partaking of a little refreshment, the following note was presented to him, and the invitation promptly and cheerfully accepted:—

"To General Lafayette.—The Ladies of Troy, having assembled at the Female Seminary,[48] have selected from their number a committee to request General Lafayette that he would grant them an opportunity of beholding his person, their own, and their country's generous and beloved benefactor."

The General, prompt in his movements, together with those gentlemen of the party who chose, repaired to the Seminary; and here a scene of deep and delightful interest transpired. On arriving at the gate of the institution, an arbour of ever-greens, which, like Jonah's gourd, sprang up in a night, was found to extend the whole distance to the building, which is about 200 feet. At the entrance of this arbour was the following inscription:— "America commands her Daughters to welcome their Deliverer, Lafayette." At this place the General was met by the Committee of Arrangements, and Mrs. Colonel Pawling pronounced a pleasing address—which, as usual, received a brief and pertinent reply.

On entering the institution, the General was presented to Mrs. Willard, the principal, and afterwards the pupils were presented by her, for which purpose they were arranged in two lines along the hall leading directly from the arbour.—Two of the pupils, daughters of the Governors of Vermont and Michigan, then advanced and presented the following lines, entitled "Lafayette's Welcome," and written for the occasion by the principal:—

And art thou, then, dear Hero, come?
And do our eyes behold the man,
    Who nerved his arm and bared his breast
For us, ere yet our life began?
    For us and for our native land,
Thy youthful valour dared the war;
    And now, in winter of thine age,
Thou'st come, and left thy lov'd ones far.
        Then deep and dear thy welcome be;
        Nor think thy daughters far from thee:
        Columbia's daughters, lo! we bend,
        And claim to call thee Father, Friend!

But was't our country's rights alone
Impell'd Fayette to Freedom's van?
    No! 'twas the love of human kind—
It was the sacred cause of man—
    It was benevolence sublime,
Like that which sways the Eternal mind!
    And, benefactor of the world,
He shed his blood for all mankind!
        Then deep and dear thy welcome be;
        Nor think thy daughters far from thee!
        Daughters of human kind, we bend,
        And claim to call thee Father, Friend!

These lines were afterwards, by particular request, sung with great sweetness and pathos, by Miss Eliza Smith, of Worcester, Massachusetts, in the choruses of which the young ladies generally joined, and the whole was executed with much effect. The General was much affected, and at the close of the singing, with eyes suffused in tears, he said—"I cannot express what I feel on this occasion; but will you, madam, present me with three copies of those lines, to be given by me, as from you, to my three daughters."—It is wholly unnecessary to add that the request was complied with. The General then retired, and was conducted by the Committee of Arrangements back, through the arbour, along the sides of which the pupils had formed themselves in close order, to the number of about 200. It was a most interesting spectacle, thrilling the soul with delightful anticipations. . . . The visit of the General to Troy, short as it was, afforded him great satisfaction. He talked much about it, and frequently spoke of his visit to the Seminary, as one of the most interesting and delightful moments of his life.

By this time the day was so far advanced that the visit to Lansingburgh, Waterford, and the Falls, was necessarily relinquished, though with great reluctance, particularly on the part of General Lafayette, as he wished both to gratify the wishes of those villages, and to enjoy a further opportunity of examining that great work [the Erie Canal],[44] from a short section of which he had that morning derived so much pleasure. It was, however, necessary to embark and return to Albany, which was accordingly done—the whole party partaking of an excellent dinner on board of the boat.

On landing at the head of the Basin, he was escorted as before, but through different streets, back to his lodgings. In the evening he visited Governor Clinton, and afterwards his Excellency Governor Yates,[45] whence he was escorted to the steamboat, where he embarked on his return to New-York, at about 12 o'clock. General Muir was detached by the Governor, with Majors Henry and Webster, aids of Major General Stephen Van Rensselaer,

to accompany General Lafayette to New-York as an escort.

On Sunday morning, the General stopped at Red-Hook and visited Mrs. [Richard] Montgomery,[46] wife of General Montgomery, who fell in storming the city of Quebec, December 1775, where he met a numerous collection of friends, and partook of a sumptuous dinner. About 2 o'clock, the General took an affectionate leave of Mrs. Montgomery and guests, and retired on board of the steamboat, on his way to New-York. At 7 o'clock the boat came to at Fishkill landing, and the General called on Mrs. Dewitt, granddaughter of the former President Adams, where he was courteously as well as splendidly received, amidst a numerous collection of friends assembled to greet their country's guest. To add to the enjoyments of this interview, the General had the pleasure of shaking cordially by the hand another of his brave Light Infantry, adding, "the Light Infantry were a brave corps, and under my immediate command." "Yes," returned the old soldier, "and you gave us our swords and plumes." The General made but a short stay, took leave of his friends, and returned to the boat under a salute of three hearty cheers.

The boat arrived at Courtlandt-street wharf, New York, at 3 o'clock in the morning, and at 5 the General returned to his lodgings, after a most delightful excursion.

11.
Opening of the Erie Canal
1825 *

BY WILLIAM L. STONE

INTRODUCTION: One of the greatest celebrations in the history of the Hudson River began on the morning of October 26, 1825, amidst the booming of cannon from Buffalo on Lake Erie to Sandy Hook on the Atlantic Ocean. On that auspicious morning, as the echo of cannon fire reverberated through each successive town and village of the Mohawk and Hudson Valleys, four gaily caparisoned vessels entered the western terminus of the newly-completed Grand Erie Canal and started on an epoch-making voyage to New York City and the Atlantic Ocean. By the time the flotilla reached the mouth of the Hudson ten days later it had become the largest and most spectacular fleet of barges, steamboats, sloops, and men-of-war that had ever graced the waters of New York harbor. A great event had come to pass with a commensurate grandeur of public inauguration.

The opening of the Erie Canal coincided with an historical shift in the geographical axis of American development. From the early seventeenth to the early nineteenth centuries the prevailing axis of American history was the north-south axis of the great land masses (the Appalachian Mountains, the coastal plains) of the Atlantic seaboard. Most of the major events of the French and Indian Wars, the American Revolution, and even the War of 1812 were fought along this north-south axis from Canada to the Carolinas. The importance of the Hudson during these two centuries of growth and con-

flict may be attributed to the fact that it combined with the Champlain Valley to form a major thoroughfare along this abiding axis of American history. A great change occurred after the War of 1812. Finally free of all threat of foreign invasion and domination, America was now ready to turn its back on Europe and look westward with Lewis and Clark to the undeveloped empire that had been acquired with the Louisiana Purchase. The early stages of the Westward Movement, however, were frustrated by one formidable, irreducible fact of American geography—the great barrier of the Appalachian Mountains. Cumberland Gap and one or two other openings in the mountains provided primitive wagon roads through the barrier; but transportation over such roads was cumbersome, slow and expensive; what was needed was an all-water route that could take advantage of the new steamboats and carry freight and passengers in bulk and mass, and with minimum cost and effort. The only such route that pierced the 1,300-mile barrier of the Appalachian Mountains was in the state of New York in the confluence of the Mohawk and Hudson Rivers. Inspired by the vision of an all-water route between the Atlantic Ocean and the Great Lakes, the people of New York State raised the extraordinary sum of $7,600,000, and in eight years' time built a canal the full 363-mile length of the Mohawk River. The resulting all-water route between New York and Lake Erie became the path of American Empire.

The Erie Canal has been called "in its significance one of the greatest undertakings in American history." † It is indeed difficult to exaggerate its achievement. It laid the foundations of American engineering, both as a science and a profession, and inaugurated an epoch of canal-

* Excerpt from William L. Stone's *Narrative of the Festivities observed in Honor of the Completion of the Grand Erie Canal, uniting the Waters of the Great Western Lakes with the Atlantic Ocean, begun at Buffalo on the Twenty-Sixth of October, A.D. Eighteen Hundred and Twenty-Five, and ended in the City of New York, on the Fourth Day of November following.* Stone's *Narrative* appears as an "Appendix" in D. Cadwallader Colden's *Memoir . . . of the Completion of the New York Canals* (New York: 1825), 293–331.

† Dorothie Bobbé, "The Erie Canal," *Dictionary of American History* (New York: 1946), Vol. II, p. 226.

21. *The Erie Canal Celebration, November 4, 1825,* line engraving by J. L. Morton and W. H. Douglas; courtesy of the Museum of the City of New York.

"The spectacle was beautiful beyond measure . . . Castle Garden, the Battery, and every avenue to the water, were thronged to a degree altogether beyond precedent. The ships and vessels in the harbor were filled, even to their riggings and tops."

building throughout the nation. It linked the North and West, created new bonds of Union, and profoundly affected the outcome of the Civil War. Its phenomenal success raised the stock of American prestige throughout the skeptical capitals of Europe. It hastened the rise of such midwestern cities as Cleveland, Detroit, and Chicago. It established steamboat traffic on all the far-flung waters of the Great Lakes. It literally created the city and port of Buffalo. It influenced the rise of New York City as the leading commercial metropolis of the Western Hemisphere. It made New York the Empire State.

The following account of the remarkable festivities commemorating the opening of the Erie Canal was written by William L. Stone (1792–1844), a journalist and historian who had also accompanied Lafayette on his triumphant tour of the previous year. Stone was commissioned by the Committee of the Corporation of the City of New York to write the official account of the ten days' celebration. It is a graphic eyewitness account of one of the most significant and colorful episodes in the 300-year history of the Hudson Valley.

INTELLIGENCE HAVING BEEN received by the Corporation of New York, from the acting Canal Commissioners, that the gigantic work would be completed and prepared for navigation on the twenty-sixth of October, measures were immediately taken by that body, in connexion with the principal cities and villages along its extended line, for the celebration of the event, in a manner corresponding with its magnitude and importance; and in order that our fellow-citizens at the West might be duly apprised of the feelings of the metropolis on the occasion, a Committee, consisting of Alderman [Elisha W.] King[1] and Alderman [William A.] Davis, was dispatched to Buffalo,

to tender the hospitalities of our City to the several Committees which might be appointed on the route, to participate in the festivities of the occasion. But to guard against the disappointment that might arise from any unforeseen accident, which might have retarded the work beyond the specified time, arrangements were made for the firing of a grand salute, to be commenced at Buffalo, at a given hour, and continued to New York, by guns stationed at suitable points along the whole intermediate distance. The Committee arrived safely at Buffalo, where they were received with a cordial welcome, and found the Canal completed, and every thing prepared for the commencement of the celebration.

Early on the morning of the twenty-sixth of October, the appointed day, the village thronged with the yeomanry of the country, who, alive to the subject, had assembled in vast numbers to witness the attendant ceremonies of the departure of the first boat. At about nine o'clock the public procession was formed in front of the Court House, in which the various societies of mechanics appeared, with appropriate badges and banners to distinguish each; the whole preceded by the Buffalo band, and Capt. Rathbun's Company of Riflemen, and followed by the Committees, strangers, etc. Thus formed, the procession moved through the street to the head of the Canal, where the boat, *Seneca Chief*, elegantly fitted, was in waiting. Here the Governor [De Witt Clinton] and Lieut. Governor of the State,[2] the New York Delegation,[3] with the various Committees from different villages, including that of Buffalo, were received on board, and after mutual introductions in the open air, Jesse Hawley, Esq. delivered an Address, brief, and peculiarly appropriate, in behalf of the citizens of Rochester. He was deputed "to mingle and reciprocate their mutual congratulations with the citizens of Buffalo on this grand epoch." The Canal, as a matter of State pride, was spoken of with much felicity—"A work that will constitute the lever of industry, population, and wealth to our Republic—a pattern for our Sister States to imitate—an exhibition of the moral force of a free and enlightened people to the world. . . ."

Every thing being prepared, the signal was given, and the discharge of a thirty-two pounder from the brow of the terrace announced that all was in readiness, and the boats under way! The *Seneca Chief,* of Buffalo, led off in fine style, drawn by four grey horses, fancifully caparisoned, and was followed by the *Superior,* next to which came the *Commodore Perry,* a freight boat; and the rear was brought up by the *Buffalo,* of Erie. The whole moved from the dock under a discharge of small arms from the Rifle Company, with music from the band, and the loud and reiterated cheers from the throng on the shore, which were returned by the companies on board the various boats. The salute of artillery was continued along from gun to gun, in rapid succession, agreeably to previous arrangements; and, in the short space of one hour and twenty minutes, the joyful intelligence was proclaimed to our citizens [in New York City].

The news having been communicated in the same manner to Sandy Hook,[4] and notice of its reception returned to the City, the return salute was commenced at Fort La Fayette [in the Narrows] by a national salute, at twenty-two minutes past eleven o'clock. After the national salute from that fortress, at thirty minutes past eleven o'clock, a repeating gun was fired from Fort Richmond [now Fort Wadsworth, also on Staten Island], and followed at Governor's Island and the Battery, at thirty-one minutes past eleven o'clock, A.M.; and the sounds of our rejoicing were then sent roaring and echoing along the mountains and among the Highlands, back to Buffalo, where the answer was received in about the same time occupied by the sound in travelling to the Ocean. Mean-

time, at Buffalo, the festivities proceeded. The boats having departed, the procession returned to the Court House, where a finished Address was delivered by Sheldon Smith, Esq., after which an original Ode, written for the occasion, was sung to the tune of "Hail Columbia." A public dinner succeeded; and the festivities of the day were closed by a splendid Ball, at the Eagle Tavern, where beauty, vieing conspicuously with elegance and wit, contributed to the enlivening enjoyment of the scene.

The *Seneca Chief* was superbly fitted up for the occasion, and among other decorations her cabin was adorned with two paintings, of which the following is a description.—One was a view of Buffalo Harbour, a section of Lake Erie, Buffalo Creek, and its junction with the Canal, etc; the whole representing the scene exhibited at the moment of the departure of the *Seneca Chief.* The other was a classic emblematical production of the pencil. This piece, on the extreme left, exhibited a figure of Hercules in a sitting posture, leaning upon his favorite club, and resting from the severe labor just completed. The centre shows a section of the Canal, with a lock, and in the foreground is a full length figure of Gov. Clinton, in Roman costume; he is supposed to have just flung open the lock gate, and with the right hand extended, (the arm being bare,) seems in the act of inviting Neptune, who appears upon the water, to pass through and take possession of the watery regions which the Canal has attached to his former dominions; the God of the Sea is upon the right of the piece, and stands erect in his chariot of shell, which is drawn by sea-horses, holding his trident, and is in the act of recoiling with his body, as if confounded by the fact disclosed at the opening of the lock; Naiades are sporting around the sea-horses in the water, who, as well as the horses themselves, seem hesitating, as if half afraid they were about to invade forbidden regions, not their own. The artist is a Mr. [George] Catlin, miniature-portrait painter.[5] Besides the paintings, the boat carried two elegant kegs, each with an eagle upon it, above and below which were the words—"Water of Lake Erie." [6] These were filled from the Lake, for the purpose of being mingled with the Ocean on their arrival in New York. . . .

In addition to the boats above enumerated, was another, which, with its cargo, was more novel than the whole. This was "Noah's Ark," literally stored with birds, beasts, and "creeping things." She was a small boat, fitted for the occasion, and had on board, a bear, two eagles, two fawns, with a variety of other animals, and birds, together with several fish—not forgetting two Indian boys, in the dress of their nation—*all products of the West.*

At *Black Rock* [7] the Celebration was commenced previously to the arrival of the *Seneca Chief.* Early in the morning a very handsomely fitted boat, called the *Niagara,* of Black Rock, started down the Canal, with several respectable citizens and some distinguished guests on board.

This boat remained at Lockport [8] until the *Seneca Chief* arrived, when it fell into the rear. The *Seneca Chief,* with the Governor, Lieutenant-Governor, and the several Committees on board, arrived at a little after ten o'clock, when a salute was fired; the boat remained a few minutes, and when she departed, hearty cheers were exchanged. . . .

At *Lockport*—"the spot where the waters were to meet when the last blow was struck, and where the utility of an immense chain of locks was for the first time to be tested," the Celebration was in all respects such as to do honor to the work itself, and the patriotic feelings of the people. It is here that nature had interposed her strongest barrier to the enterprise and the strength of man. But the massive granite of the "Mountain Ridge"

was compelled to yield. The rocks have crumbled to pieces and been swept away, and the waters of Erie flow tranquilly in their place.

At sunrise, on the morning of the twenty-sixth, a salute was fired from the mountain adjoining the locks, and ere long the place was crowded with the citizens of the surrounding country; many individuals, too, from distant parts of this state, and from other states, attended the celebration at this interesting place. At nine o'clock, A.M., a procession was formed . . . which marched to the grand natural basin at the foot of the locks, where the President and Vice-President of the day, the Canal Commissioners and Engineers, the Visiting Committee, and several distinguished citizens from abroad, embarked on board the packet-boat *William C. Bouck;* [9] at the same time two hundred ladies were received on board the boat *Albany;* the rest of the procession embarked in the several boats lying in the Basin. This Basin, connected with the stupendous succession of locks, and the chasm which has been cut through the mountain, is one of the most interesting places on the route, if not in the World, and presents one of the most striking evidences of human power and enterprise which has hitherto been witnessed. A double set of locks, whose workmanship will vie with the most splendid monuments of antiquity, rise majestically, one after the other, to the height of sixty-three feet: the surplus water is conducted around them, and furnishes some of the finest mill-seats imaginable. A marble tablet modestly tells the story of their origin; and, without that vanity, which, though frequently laudable, is often carried to excess, imputes their existence to our Republican institutions.

When the grand salute from Buffalo East, had passed, the boats commenced ascending through the locks; and during their ascension they were greeted by a continued discharge of artillery, and the cheers of hundreds of joyous citizens. . . .

Night set in before the expedition left the rugged scenery of Lockport; but continuing on their way the boats were welcomed at *Holley*,[10] on the morning of the twenty-seventh, by the firing of cannon, and other testimonials of joy. After an Address, the Committee received the congratulations of a number of ladies and gentlemen. At nine o'clock they reached *Brockport*,[11] where similar ceremonies were observed. The bank of the Canal was for some distance lined with spectators, who received the Committees with the most enthusiastic huzzas, and the discharge of cannon. . . .

At *Rochester*, too, a rich and beautiful town, which, disdaining, as it were, the intermediate grade of a village, has sprung from a hamlet to the full grown size, wealth, and importance of a city, the interesting period was celebrated in a manner equally creditable to the country and occasion. There was considerable rain at Rochester on the day of the Celebration; yet such was the enthusiasm of the people, that at two o'clock, eight handsome uniform companies were in arms, and an immense concourse of people had assembled. The companies were formed in line upon the Canal, and on the approach of the procession of boats from the West, commenced firing a *feu de joie*, which was continued until they arrived at the aqueduct, where the boat called the *Young Lion of the West*, was stationed to "protect the entrance." The Pioneer boat on approaching was hailed from the *Young Lion*, and the following dialogue ensued:—

Question.—Who comes there?

Answer.—Your brothers from the West, on the waters of the great Lakes.

Q.—By what means have they been diverted so far from their natural course?

A.—By the channel of the Grand Erie Canal.

Q.—By whose authority, and by whom, was a work of such magnitude accomplished?

A.—By the authority and the enterprise of the patriotic People of the State of New York.

Here the *Young Lion* gave way, and "the brethren from the West" were permitted to enter the spacious basin, at the end of the aqueduct. The Rochester and Canandaigua Committees of Congratulation then took their places under an arch surmounted by an eagle, and the *Seneca Chief,* having the Committees on board, being moored, General [Vincent] Matthews,[12] and the Honorable John C. Spencer,[13] ascended the deck and offered to the Governor the congratulations of the citizens of their respective villages, to which an animated and cordial reply was given. The gentlemen from the West then disembarked, and a procession was formed, which repaired to the Presbyterian Church, where an appropriate prayer was made by the Rev. Mr. Penny, and an address pronounced by Timothy Childs, Esq. . . . After the address, the company repaired to Christopher's Mansion House, partook of a good dinner, and drunk a set of excellent toasts. . . . At half-past seven, the time fixed for the departure of the guests, the company reluctantly rose from a board where the most generous sentiments were given and received with unequalled enthusiasm, and the Governor and the several Committees were escorted to the Basin, and embarked amidst the congratulations of their fellow-citizens. The celebration was concluded with a grand ball, and a general illumination; and nothing occurred to mar the pleasure of the day. . . .

Little Falls.—From Utica to Little Falls, a distance of twenty-three miles, the country is rich and populous; but there are no villages at which any combined or formal manifestations of respect for the passing strangers, or joy for the completion of the great work, could be exhibited. Hundreds of the yeomanry, however, flocked to the banks of the Canal; and where groups were collected did not fail to send forth the cordial and loud huzza. Next to the Mountain Ridge, before described, the construction of the Canal at the Little Falls, was the most formidable labor executed. During some mighty convulsion of nature, the waters of the West, at a former period, evidently tore for themselves a passage through what previously had been a barrier of mountain granite. The hills rise on either side to a height of near five hundred feet, and at one point the cragged promontories approximate nearly to the toss of a biscuit. Through this chasm the Mohawk tumbles over a rocky bed, and falls, in the distance of half a mile to the depth of forty feet. The old Canal of the Inland Lock Navigation Company,[14] was constructed on the north side of the Rapids, which affords a far more favorable route. The Erie Canal runs upon the south side, the bed of which was excavated in the solid rock. The view is exceedingly wild and picturesque. Above, the rocks impend in rugged and fearful grandeur; while beneath, the foaming torrent of the Mohawk dashes from rock to rock, until it leaps into a basin of great depth, and then steals tranquilly through the rich vale extending to the falls of the Cahoos. The village stands upon the north side, and is connected with the Canal by a stupendous aqueduct, thrown over the river by means of three arches, viz—an eliptical one of seventy feet, embracing the whole stream in an ordinary state of its waters, with one on each side of fifty feet span, elevating the surface of the Canal thirty feet above that of the river. It was already evening when the boats reached this interesting region; but bonfires blazed upon the crags and brows of the mountains, and at the junction of the aqueduct with the Canal, they were met by a Committee, and an able address was delivered by George H. Feeter, Esq., to which a suitable reply was made. The party

was then invited over to the village, where a banquet was spread at M'Kinnister's Hotel. Having tarried as long as their time would allow, they took their leave amidst the cheers of the citizens, and departed under a salute of artillery.

Leaving Little Falls, and pursuing their journey in the dead of night, several of the ancient villages, such as Fort Plain, Paletine, etc., were deprived of the opportunity of giving utterance to their feelings; but on the morning of the first of November, which was a clear and delightful day, the people of the intermediate towns, to Schenectady, manifested great joy and enthusiasm, which was proclaimed by every means within their power.

At *Schenectady*, according to the published arrangements, the boats were to have arrived at five o'clock, P.M. of Tuesday. Here, however, it seems there were some "private griefs," which we "know not of," and which induced the publication of the leading paper of that city, of the *project* of a funeral procession, or some other demonstrations of mourning, and no preparations for the reception were made by the Corporation.[15] Yet it does not follow that there was a general want of good feeling; on the contrary, news was received that the arrival would be some hours sooner than had been anticipated. The result was, that a goodly concourse of people were speedily assembled; some field-pieces were stationed at a suitable point to honor the strangers with a salute, and the "College Guards," were quickly in uniform and on duty. This corps is formed of students in Union College,[16] and appeared in a handsome grey uniform. At about three o'clock the boats hove in sight—they were welcomed by a salute—and the literary soldiers fired a *feu de joie*. The Governor, Lieutenant Governor, and Committees were respectfully received by the principal citizens, and conducted to Given's Hotel, where a well provided table was spread, and the company partook of a dinner, at which Mr. De Graaf presided. There were no cheers, nor, on the contrary, any audible murmurs. On the whole it was rather a grave reception. At four o'clock the company re-embarked, and proceeded on their way. A drizzling rain came on; but the College Guards, who accompanied the boats to the street which leads to the buildings of this flourishing University, were not unprovided with a defence; each drew a blanket from his knapsack, and in a moment the graceful youths were metamorphosed in their apparel to the appearance of a band of Indians.

The shades of night set in soon after the boats crossed the aqueduct leading over the Mohawk, into the county of Saratoga. The night was dark and dreary, and a view of the sublime scenery of the Cahoos Falls, and the formidable range of locks by which the Canal descends into the vale of the Hudson, was entirely lost, much to the regret of those who were not already familiar with that region of rich and picturesque scenery. At two o'clock, A.M., the boats made a halt, and day-light found the company at the half-way house between Troy and Albany,[17] lately, and for a long time, kept by the heroic landlady, who several years since shot a desperate robber, in the act of plundering her house, in the night.

> "The dawn was overcast, the morning lowered
> "And heavily in clouds brought on the day
> "——big with fate"

of multitudes who had long been anticipating the pleasure of a visit to the capital of the State, and a participation in the festivities of the day. A cold north-west wind, however, soon sprung up, sweeping the mists before it, and rolling away the clouds. The consequence was, that even at this distance from the city, the indications betokened a large assemblage.

The company remained at this spot until near ten o'clock, and, in the mean time, an excellent and plentiful breakfast was served up by the landlord. A message was also received at an early hour, from Major Talcott, commanding the United States Arsenal at Gibbonsville,[18] expressing his regret that the boats should have passed that station so many hours before the expected time, as it had been his intention to honor them with a salute. An answer was returned with an invitation for the Major and his Officers to join the expedition, which was promptly accepted. Departing for Albany, it was soon found that there was a general ingathering in the direction of the ancient capital. The banks of the Canal were lined with people, and the roads were filled with horses and carriages, galloping and whirling towards the scene of the anticipated festivities.

Albany.—At the lock above the mansion of the Patroon (General Stephen Van Rensselaer) [19] the boats were met by Alderman [Henry I.] Wyckoff, and Assistant Alderman [Philip] Hone,[20] of the Committee of the New York Corporation, who were received on board, and the boats proceeding rapidly on, arrived at the last lock at half-past ten, A.M. Twenty-four pieces of cannon were planted on the pier, from which a grand salute was fired as the boats passed from the Canal into the basin, down which they proceeded, towed by yawls manned by twenty-four masters of vessels, and cheered onward by bands of music, and the huzzas of thousands of rejoicing citizens, who crowded the wharves, the south bridge, the vessels, and a double line of Canal boats, which extended through the whole length of the basin. Having passed the sloop lock, they returned up the river as far as the south bridge. Here the company were received by the city committee, and escorted to Rockwell's Mansion House, where congratulations were exchanged. A procession was then formed under the direction of Maj.

Taylor, Capt. Bradt, and W. Esleeck, Esq. in the following order:—Twenty-four cartmen, with carts loaded with eastern produce, each with a flag designating the articles conveyed;—cartmen on horseback, preceded by their Marshal, R. M'Clintock;—a band of music; Sheriff and Staff; Corporation; Governor and Lieutenant Governor; Canal Commissioners; Engineers and Assistants; Collector of Tolls; Revolutionary Officers and Cincinnati; Surveyor of the Port; Committees; Judicial Officers of the State and of the United States; Secretary of State and Surveyor-General; Attorney General; Comptroller; Treasurer; Adjutant General and Judge Advocate General; Officers of the Army and Navy; Chamber of Commerce; Military Association; Societies; Strangers and Citizens. The procession passed through several of the principal streets, to the Capitol. Here the exercises commenced in the Assembly Chamber, with an appropriate prayer. An ode was then sung, written for the occasion by John Aug. Stone, of the Albany Theatre. The vocal arrangements were under the direction of Mr. Harris, Professor of Music, aided by the orchestra of the Theatre. Philip Hone, Esq. in behalf of the Corporation of New York, then rose and addressed the Chairman and the assembled citizens. He glanced rapidly at the history of the great work, from its conception to its completion, and in conclusion tendered the congratulations of the Corporation of New York, and declared his instructions to invite the Corporation of Albany, together with the several Committees then assembled, to proceed with the boats to the city which he had the honor in part to represent. In performing this office, he assured them they would be received as welcome guests, and requested to unite with the municipal authorities in the celebration of the joyful event. . . .

The Assembly Chamber, in which these exercises took place, was tastefully decorated for the occasion. On the right of the Speaker's chair, hung a portrait of George Clinton, and on his left that of De Witt Clinton. Over the chair hung a full-length portrait of "The Father of his Country," surmounted by the bird of victory grasping his thunder. The benediction was pronounced by the Reverend Mr. Lacy; after which the procession was again formed, and moved through various streets, to the bridge, which was superbly decorated, to partake of a collation.

At the west end of the bridge was the entrance, composed of five pointed arches, rising above each other on each side of the grand centre arch. Those on the extreme right, and left, were twelve feet in height, and six feet in width, and presented a full view to the spectator. The two intermediate arches on either side of the centre, were fourteen feet in height by seven feet in width, and formed an angle with the others, thus showing a kind of perspective, and causing the centre arch to recede about six feet. The arches were supported by two pilasters, capped with gothic turrets, and the pannels decorated with delicate evergreens, in a style corresponding to that highly ornamental order. The centres of all the arches terminated in richly gilded and appropriate ornaments. The background of all, except the centre, was filled with shrubbery, presenting to the view a resemblance to the entrance of a garden. Passing through the arch were found lines of shrubbery fancifully arranged on both sides of the bridge, and forming curves from the arch to the draw-bridge. Standards, bearing the national arms, waved on both sides of the bridge. At the four corners of the draw-bridge were erected four masts, forty feet in height, decorated with evergreens, and rigged with flags, arranged as sails, emblematical of the termination of the Canal, and of the commencement of river navigation. Proceeding onward, the guests passed under three circular arches, the centre one of which bore the words,

"Grand Erie Canal"; that on the left hand was inscribed, "July 4th, 1817"; and that on the right, "October 26th, 1825." They were all ornamented in a similar manner, with evergreens, and formed the entrance to an immense hall, covered with an awning, and furnished with two lines of tables, each one hundred and fifty feet in length, and sufficient for the accommodation of six hundred guests. This terminated in an elegant circular marquee, surmounted with the national flag, calculated to contain about sixty persons. One part of the design struck the writer as remarkably beautiful. The two lines of tables were placed at such distances from the sides of the bridge, as to allow the marshals to conduct the procession, formed in double files, up the centre avenue between the tables, to the marquee, and there separating to the right and left countermarching to their respective seats at the table; thus placing the marshals in such a situation as to allow them to form the procession on retiring, in the same order as it entered, without any change of companions on the part of the guests. . . .

In the evening the Capitol and Theatre were brilliantly illuminated. In front of the Capitol was a large transparency, with the motto—"Peace and Commerce." It represented a wide landscape, exhibiting the varieties of field and meadow, hill and dale. Winding its way through this, was a Canal, on the bosom of which were two boats, drawn by three horses each. Over the door, within the portico, was another transparency, representing an Eagle, with emblems of war and peace. Motto—"1776." Over the stairway, within the great hall, as you ascend to the gallery, were the words—"The Grand Work is Done!" And at the head of the first flight of stairs, hung a broad painting of the Arms of New York, enwreathed with evergreens. The several Committees collected in Albany on this occasion, attended the Theatre in the evening. During an interval between the acts, a beautiful Canal scene, got up for the occasion by Mr. Gilfert, was exhibited and warmly cheered. The representation of locks, canals, etc., with boats and horses actually passing, was admirably done. Between the pieces which composed the evening's entertainment, an ode was recited by Mr. Barrett,[21] in his happiest manner, written for the occasion by James Ferguson, Esq. Thus terminated a day which will long be remembered in Albany as the memorable second of November, eighteen hundred and twenty-five.

Thursday morning arrived, and a more beautiful day never dawned upon our land. It seemed as though a benignant Providence, smiling upon the labors and triumphs of human genius and enterprise, had purposely chained the storms in their caverns. The hour of nine was appointed for the departure of the fleet, but by some unavoidable delays it was near ten before every thing was prepared. In the meantime the city and surrounding country poured forth its population in immense numbers, to view the beautiful spectacle. There were by thousands and thousands more people out than on the preceding day. The docks, stores, vessels, along the whole river in front of the city, presented thick masses of people. The several steam-boats formed in their proper order, gorgeously decorated, were ranged into a line, and a brisk northwest wind caused the gay banners and streamers to flutter in the air, so as to be seen to the best possible advantage. And the beauty of the scene was still further heightened by the large columns of steam rushing from the fleet, rising majestically upwards, and curling and rolling into a thousand fantastic and beautiful forms, until mingled and lost in surrounding vapors. Every boat was filled with passengers, and each was supplied with a band of music. The delight, nay, enthusiasm, of the people, was at its height. Such an animating, bright, beauteous, and glorious spectacle had never been seen at that place; nor, at that time, excelled in New York. About fifteen minutes before the departure of the fleet, the *Chief Justice Marshall*,[22] from Troy, came gaily down the river, as richly decorated as the ship of the Admiral himself, having the *Niagara*, of Black Rock, in tow. On board of this boat, also, was a fine band, and a large number of the most respectable citizens of Troy. At a given signal, the fleet was underway in a moment; and the Albanians, with long and reiterated cheers, took leave of such a spectacle as their eyes will never more behold.

The fleet consisted of the following steam-vessels, viz.: —The *Chancellor Livingston*,[23] Capt. Lockwood, under the special direction of Charles Rhind, Esq.,[24] acting as Admiral, assisted by Commodore Wiswall, as Captain of the fleet, having in tow the elegant Canal packet-boat, the *Seneca Chief*, of Buffalo; the *Constitution*,[25] Captain Bartholomew, having in tow the Rochester boat *Young Lion of the West*.—On board of this boat, among other productions of the West, were two living wolves, a fawn, a fox, four racoons, and two living eagles. *Noah's Ark*, from Ararat, having the bears and Indians, fell behind, and did not arrive in Albany in season to be taken in tow. Next came the *Chief Justice Marshall*, Captain [Richard W.] Sherman, having in tow the *Niagara*, from Black Rock. Then followed the *Constellation*,[26] Captain [Robert G.] Cruttenden; the *Swiftsure*,[27] Captain Stocking; the *Olive Branch*,[28] Captain [James] Moore, having in tow the safety-barge, *Matilda*; and the *Richmond*,[29] Captain Cochran. The *Saratoga*,[30] Captain [James] Benson, being a small and swift boat, acted as a tender on the voyage from Albany—landing and taking in passengers from all the boats and landing places. She sported about like a dolphin—now in the wake of one boat, now along side of another, and now shooting a-head of the whole, with her flags streaming gracefully in the breeze.

The appearance of the fleet from the different points along the shore was gay and animating. As it passed down the river, the boats, constantly varying their relative positions,—the foremost lying by to wait for the others to come up, and all of them decorated with flags and streamers,—presented a grand and splendid spectacle. This was particularly the case among the group of islands between Albany and Coeymans; and the scene from the Admiral's boat, as the passengers looked back among the islands, and along the crooked channels, was truly enchanting. Now a vessel in the richest attire, shot from behind a copse upon some little island,—and now another disappeared behind a second. At times, a boat, at some distance astern, appeared to be swiftly darting across the river; and again, at another point could only be discovered the variegated flags and streamers through the intervening though scattered shrubbery, whose verdure had lost its freshness, and been speckled with pale red and yellow by the early autumnal frosts. And now again, when the broad bosom of the Hudson was unbroken from bank to bank, the whole squadron appeared in a line, like a fleet from the dominion of the fairies. Thousands of the inhabitants crowded to the shore to admire and welcome the novel procession. Signal guns were posted on various heights, to give notice of its approach; and salutes from cannon or musketry were fired from every village. At Coeymans, New Baltimore, Kinderhook-Landing, and Coxsackie, great numbers of people were assembled, who cheered the passing multitude. Indeed, after Alexander of Macedon had carried his arms into India, he did not descend the Indus with greater triumph, or make a prouder display.

At *Hudson*, which is finely situated for such an exhibition, many thousands of citizens had collected. The shores, and the brow of Prospect Hill, were covered with people; and the colonnades of the "round house," were filled with ladies, whose snow-white handkerchiefs fluttered briskly in the breeze.[31] The river here expands to a breadth of nearly two miles. The country on both sides rises gradually from the river—particularly on the west, to the base of the Catskill Mountains. No finer view of these lofty mountains is obtained than at Hudson; and when we include Mount Marino, on the eastern side of the river, with the broad sweep of woods, and meadows and fields on either side, the landscape, embracing mountain, wood, and water scenery, uniting at once the sublime and beautiful, is perfect. The frost had changed its soft and early verdure, and decked it in the richly variegated and changing livery of autumn. It was not viewed, however, in a cold and cheerless day, but gazed upon under the genial influence of a mild autumnal sun, amidst a scene of gaiety and animation which imparted life and beauty and sublimity to all. The *Saratoga* touched at the dock, where the municipal authorities were in waiting, hoping that the fleet would stop a short time, and allow the committees to go ashore, and partake of a collation which had been provided for the occasion. But time would not permit, and the fleet passed down under a salute of artillery posted on the hills, which was answered from the cannon at Athens, directly opposite.

At *Catskill,* a salute was fired from the hill behind which, and almost invisible from the river, this busy and thriving village is entrenched. A military company was paraded on the point (so called), and fired repeatedly, while the boats lay to for the *Saratoga* to take off passengers. The afternoon was fine, and the banners waving gracefully in the breeze, and gaily dancing in the sunbeams, presented a scene of beauty at once novel and picturesque.

While passing *Redhook Landing,*[32] where the same curiosity and interest were exhibited by the assembled people, dinner was announced. . . . The fare was sumptuous, and wines good, and many a bumper was turned off to the patriotic sentiments elicited by the occasion, intermingled with national and other appropriate songs. Immediately after dinner, a committee from the *Chancellor Livingston,* (the flag ship,) was put off in a small boat, to pay complimentary visits to the other boats of the squadron, and the like civilities were returned.

Before reaching *Hyde Park,* evening had thrown her shadows over us; and instead of the gay attire which had rendered the fleet so beautiful by day, the boats were now decorated with lights, each having a different number for the sake of distinction. The flag ship, the *Chancellor,* bore a great number of lanterns, arranged in the form of a triangle, and must have made a brilliant appearance. And if the spectators on shore had been gratified during the day by views of the flotilla, the passengers on board the latter were now amply repaid by the splendor of bonfires and illuminations along the shore. The first of the kind which was seen, was the mansion of James D. Livingston, Esq.,[33] of Hyde Park, the whole front of which was illuminated. Capt. Sherman moreover, of the *Chief Justice Marshall,* had timely provided himself with a supply of rockets, which being thrown up at intervals, now sporting through the gloom like a comet, and now bursting and descending in showers of dazzling stars, produced a fine effect. At several points along the river, bonfires were blazing, and the flash and roar of cannon were seen and heard, which were answered by cheers from the boats and the firing of cannon in return.

As the flotilla approached *Poughkeepsie,* it was apparent that the citizens of that flourishing village were prepared to welcome it with the warmest demonstrations of joy. Upon an eminence on each side of the landings, huge signal-fires were lighted, which cast a broad red glare over the hills, and gleamed widely upon the waters. The effect, as seen from the water, was very grand. The red light bursting fitfully through the trees as the boats glided by, the human figures moving in every direction athwart the fires, the illuminated buildings, the thunder of cannon, the brilliant moving lights of the steam-boats, all seen and heard in the silence and darkness of night, could not fail to make an impression on every beholder, such as will not soon be forgotten.

At *Newburgh* cannon were fired; the village was partially illuminated, and a committee of congratulation came on board.

At *West Point,* a salute of twenty-four guns greeted the arrival of the first boats in the line; and another of the same number was fired while the last boats were passing. In the meantime, great numbers of rockets were sent up; and cheers resounded merrily, both from the hills and the boats. During these tokens of rejoicing, some of the boats were busily engaged in receiving on board the officers, as guests of the Corporation; and as soon as this was accomplished, the whole flotilla proceeded with all expedition to New York. The guests and passengers on board now retired, and in the morning awoke opposite the city, to greet the beautiful dawn of a day long to be remembered in the annals of our state and country.

The long expected fourth of November—a day so glorious for the city and state, with all its "pomp and circumstance," came and passed; and the incidents, like the fragments of a splendid vision, are yet floating, in bright and glowing masses, through the imagination. But the pageant was too brilliant, and the scene too various, for the memory to retain more than certain vague impressions, no less beautiful than indistinct.

Those who saw the magnificent scene, will at once admit that it cannot be painted in language; and those who had not that happiness, must content themselves with the assurance, that the best endeavours of the writer to convey to them an adequate idea of its grandeur, will fail. The poet, by giving full sway to his imagination, may perhaps partially succeed in conveying the various impressions imbibed on the occasion, and some detached parts of the scene might possibly be used to advantage by the painter who unites skill with genius. But we repeat, that the narrative, in humble prose, will fall short of a just representation.

The grand fleet arrived in our waters from Albany before daylight, and came to anchor near the State Prison [in Greenwich Village]. The roar of cannon from different points, and the merry peals of our numerous bells, greeted the sun as he rose in a cloudless sky. In a few moments afterwards, signals were given by the flag ship, and the various flags, banners, and other decorations, were run up as if at the sudden command of a magician. Shortly afterwards, the new and superb steam-boat *Washington,* Captain E. S. Bunker, bore proudly down upon the fleet, heaving up the foaming billows as though she spurned the dominion of Neptune. In the language of the Noble Bard—

"She walked the waters like a thing of life,
"And dared the very elements to strife."

She bore the great banner of the Corporation, representing in dark figures, the arms of the city upon a snow-white ground. The *Washington* was an entirely new boat, chartered for the occasion, of large dimensions, beautiful model, and superbly finished throughout,—uniting all the improvements in steam-boat architecture. The design of the taffrail represented the renown of Washington and Lafayette. The centre was a trophy

23. *The Hudson from West Point,* colored lithograph by
Currier & Ives, 1862; courtesy of The New-York Historical
Society.

"At West Point, a salute of twenty-four guns greeted the
arrival of the first boats in the line."

of various emblems—the laurel and olive—standards—swords—the balance—the caduceus of Mercury, etc. The trophy was surmounted with a bald eagle. Each side of it was decorated with a bust—on the right, that of Washington—on the left, the bust of Lafayette. The former was crowned with the civic wreath and the laurel—the latter with the laurel only. The Genius of America was crowning her hero, and the spirit of Independence, waving the flaming torch, binding the brow of Lafayette. Each of these figures was attended with emblematic medallions of Agriculture and Commerce. The whole was based on a section of the globe, and the background was a glory from the trophy. The corners of the taffrail were each filled with a cornucopia, which gracefully completed the design, on which neither painting nor gilding had been spared to enhance the effect. She ran along side of the *Chancellor,* and a Committee of the Corporation, with the Officers of the Governor's Guard, came on board to tender his Excellency their congratulations on his arrival in our waters, from those of Lake Erie. . . .

This duty having been performed, and there being an hour to spare, the several boats entered their respective docks, and came to anchor at the places assigned them, to give their numerous passengers an opportunity to prepare for the enjoyments of the day agreeably to their various inclinations.

The escorting fleet got under way, and passed the British Sloops of War, *Swallow,* Captain Baldock, and *Kingfisher,* Captain Henderson, dressed for the occasion, and bearing the American flag in company with the cross of St. George. A salute was fired from these ships, which was returned from the fleet.

Not the least pleasing of this morning scene, was the packet-ship *Hamlet,* Captain Candler, prepared by the Marine and Nautical Societies, appearing at sunrise, in the North River, superbly dressed in the flags of various nations, interspersed with private signals, and the number-flags of the different members. She made a most splendid appearance during the whole day. . . .

At half-past eight o'clock, the Corporation, and their invited guests, assembled in the Sessions Room at the City Hall, and at a quarter before nine, proceeded to the steam-boats *Washington, Fulton,* and *Providence,* stationed at the foot of Whitehall Street. At the same place was also stationed the *Commerce,*[34] Capt. [George E.] Seymour, with the elegant safety-barge, *Lady Clinton.*[35] This barge, with the *Lady Van Rensselaer,* had been set apart by the Corporation, for the reception of the invited ladies, with their attendants. The *Lady Clinton* was decorated with a degree of taste and elegance which was equally delightful and surprising. From stem to stern she was ornamented with evergreens, hung in festoons, and intertwined with roses of various hues, China astres, and many other flowers alike beautiful. In one of the niches below the upper deck, was the bust of Clinton, the brow being encircled with a wreath of laurel and roses. Mrs. [Catherine J.] Clinton,[36] as well as many other distinguished ladies were on board of the barge, which, though the party was select, was much crowded. Capt. Seymour, however, paid every attention to his beautiful charge; every countenance beamed with satisfaction, and every eye sparkled with delight.

A few minutes after nine o'clock, the whole being on board, the fleet from Albany, as before mentioned, led by the flag ship of the Admiral, came round from the North, and proceeded up the East River to the Navy Yard,[37] where salutes were fired, and the sloop of war *Cyane,* was dressed in the colors of all nations. While here, the flag ship took on board the officers of the station, together with their fine band of music. The officers stationed at West Point, with the celebrated band from that place, having been received on board on the preceding evening, were likewise on board of the *Chancellor Livingston*. On returning from the Navy Yard, the steam-boat *Ousatonic*, of Derby, joined the fleet. The wharves and shores of Brooklyn, the Heights, and the roofs of many of the buildings, were crowded with people to an extent little anticipated, and only exceeded by the thick masses of population which lined the shores of New York, as far as Corlaer's Hook.[38] The fleet having arrived between the East end of the Battery and Governor's Island, was joined by the ship *Hamlet*, before-mentioned. While the commander was signalling the various vessels, and they were manoeuvring about to take their stations, the spectacle was beautiful beyond measure. Long before this time, however, our City had been pouring forth its thousands and tens of thousands; Castle Garden, the Battery, and every avenue to the water, were thronged to a degree altogether beyond precedent. The ships and vessels in the harbor were filled, even to their rigging and tops. And the movements, in forming the order of the aquatic procession, gave opportunity to all, to observe the several vessels in every advantageous and imposing situation. Loud cheers resounded from every direction, which were often returned. Every thing being in readiness, and every boat crowded to the utmost, the fleet, taking a semi-circular sweep towards Jersey City, and back obliquely in the direction of the lower point of Governor's Island, proceeded down the bay in the order detailed in the official report of the Admiral;—each boat and ship maintaining the distance of one hundred feet apart.

The ship *Hamlet* was taken in tow by the *Oliver Ellsworth*[39] and *Bolivar*, and assumed and maintained its place in splendid style. Four pilot-boats were also towed by other steam-boats, together with the following boats of the Whitehall Waterman, all tastefully dec-

orated, viz.—*The Lady of the Lake, Dispatch, Express, Brandywine, Sylph, Active,* and *Whitehall, Junior.*

The sea was tranquil and smooth as the summer lake; and the mist, which came on between seven and eight in the morning, having partially floated away, the sun shone bright and beautiful as ever. As the boats passed the Battery they were saluted by the Military, the Revenue Cutter, and the Castle on Governor's Island;[40] and on passing the Narrows, they were also saluted by forts Lafayette and Tompkins.[41] They then proceeded to the United States schooner *Porpoise*, Captain Zantzinger, moored within Sandy Hook, at the point where the grand ceremony was to be performed. A deputation, composed of Alderman [Elisha W.] King and [Jacob B.] Taylor, was then sent on board the steam-boat *Chancellor Livingston,* to accompany his Excellency the Governor, the Lieutenant Governor, and the several Committees from Buffalo, Utica, Albany, and other places, on board the steam-boat *Washington.*

The boats were thereupon formed in a circle around the schooner, preparatory to the ceremony; when Mr. [Charles] Rhind, addressing the Governor, remarked "that he had a request to make, which he was confident it would afford his Excellency great pleasure to grant. He was desirous of preserving a portion of the water to be used on this memorable occasion, in order to send it to our distinguished friend, and late illustrious visitor, Major General Lafayette; and for that purpose Messrs. Dummer and Co. had prepared some bottles of American fabrick for the occasion, and they were to be conveyed to the General in a box made by Mr. D. Phyfe,[42] from a log of cedar, brought from Erie in the *Seneca Chief*." The Governor replied, that a more pleasing task could not have been imposed upon him, and expressed his acknowledgments to Mr. Rhind, for having suggested the measure.

His Excellency Governor Clinton then proceeded to perform the ceremony of commingling the waters of the Lakes with the Ocean, by pouring a keg of that of Lake Erie into the Atlantic; upon which he delivered the following Address;—

"This solemnity, at this place, on the first arrival of vessels from Lake Erie, is intended to indicate and commemorate the navigable communication, which has been accomplished between our Mediterranean Seas and the Atlantic Ocean, in about eight years, to the extent of more than four hundred and twenty-five miles, by the wisdom, public spirit, and energy of the people of the state of New York; and may God of the Heavens and the Earth smile most propitiously on this work, and render it subservient to the best interests of the human race."

Doctor [Samuel Latham] Mitchill,[43] whose extensive correspondence with almost every part of the world, enables him to fill his cabinet with every thing rare and curious, then completed the ceremony by pouring into the briny deep, bottles of water from the Ganges and Indus of Asia; the Nile and the Gambia of Africa; the Thames, the Seine, the Rhine, and the Danube, of Europe; the Mississippi and Columbia of North, and the Oronoko, La Plata, and Amazon of South, America. . . .

Never before was there such a fleet collected, and so superbly decorated; and it is very possible that a display so grand, so beautiful, and we may even add, sublime, will never be witnessed again. We know of nothing with which it can be compared. The naval fete given by the Prince Regent of England, upon the Thames, during the visit of the Allied Sovereigns of Europe to London, after the dethronement of Napoleon, has been spoken of as exceeding every thing of the kind hitherto witnessed in Europe. But gentlemen who had an opportunity of witnessing both, have declared, that the spectacle in the waters of New York so far transcended that in the metropolis of England, as scarcely to admit of comparison. The day, as we have before remarked, was uncommonly fine. No winds agitated the surface of the mighty deep, and during the performance of the ceremonies, the boats with their gay decorations, lay motionless in beauty. The orb of day darted his genial rays upon the bosom of the waters, where they played as tranquilly as upon the natural mirror of a secluded lake. Indeed, the elements seemed to repose, as if to gaze upon each other, and participate in the beauty and grandeur of the sublime spectacle. Every object appeared to pause, as if to invite reflections, and prepare the mind for deep impressions—impressions, which, while we feel them stealing upon the soul, impart a consciousness of their durability. It was one of those few bright visions whose evanescent glory is allowed to light up the path of human life—which, as they are passing, we feel can never return, and which, in diffusing a sensation of pleasing melancholy, consecrates, as it were, all surrounding objects, even to the atmosphere we inhale! . . .

Everything being made ready for returning to the City, salutes were fired from the Revenue Cutter, the pilot-boats, several of the steam-boats, and from the "Young Lion of the West," who, having prepared himself with a pair of brazen lungs at Rochester, often mingled his roar with that of the artillery with which he was saluted on his passage down. While passing up the Narrows, the passengers on board of the different boats partook of elegant collations. The Corporation, with their guests, dined on board of the *Washington*—the Mayor presiding, assisted by Aldermen King and Taylor.

When approaching the British armed vessels before mentioned, the latter fired another salute. In consequence of this compliment, a signal was immediately made from the flag ship, and the whole squadron passed

24. *Erie Canal Celebration, New York, 1825,* oil painting by Anthony Imbert; courtesy of the Museum of the City of New York.

"Never before was there such a fleet collected, and so superbly decorated."

round them in a circle. The United States Schooner *Porpoise,* manned her yards, and gave the Britons three cheers, which were returned. While performing this circular manoeuvre, the British bands struck up *"Yankee Doodle";* in return for which act of courtesy, the American bands, as they passed the other side, successively played *"God save the King."* . . .

The head of the land procession, under Major General [Augustus] Fleming, Marshal of the day . . . had already arrived on the Battery, where it was designed the whole should pass in review before the Corporation and their guests, and the spectators on board of the other boats, which lay to near the shore, to afford an opportunity of witnessing the cars, and banners, and other decorations of the several societies, professions, and callings, who had turned out in the city in honor of the event commemorated. The *Washington* and *Chancellor Livingston,* ran into the Pier No. 1, in the East River, and landed the Corporation and their friends, at the proper time for them to fall into the rear of the procession. The fleet dispersed, each vessel repairing to its own moorings. . . .

Thus passed a day so glorious to the state and city, and so deeply interesting to the countless thousands who were permitted to behold and mingle in its exhibitions. We have before said that all attempts at description must be utterly in vain. Others can comprehend the greatness of the occasion; the Grand Canal is completed, and the waters of Lake Erie have been borne upon its surface, and mingled with the Ocean. But it is only those who were present, and beheld the brilliant scenes of the day, that can form any adequate idea of their grandeur, and of the joyous feelings which pervaded all ranks of the community. Never before has been presented to the sight a fleet so beautiful as that which then graced our waters. The numerous array of steam-boats and barges, proudly breasting the billows and dashing on their way regardless of opposing winds and tides; the flags of all nations, and banners of every hue, streaming splendidly in the breeze; the dense columns of black smoke ever and anon sent up from the boats, now partially obscuring the view, and now spreading widely over the sky and softening down the glare of light and color; the roar of cannon from the various forts, accompanied by heavy volumes of white smoke, contrasting finely with the [black] smoke from the steam-boats; the crowds of happy beings who thronged the decks, and the voice of whose joy was mingled with the sound of music, and not unfrequently drowned by the hissing of the steam; all these, and a thousand other circumstances, awakened an interest so intense, that "the eye could not be satisfied with seeing, nor the ear with hearing." . . .

Thus has closed one of the greatest, happiest, proudest, most propitious scenes, our state has ever witnessed. Excepting that day on which she joined the national confederacy, there is none like it. What visions of glory rush upon the mind, as it attempts to lift the curtain of futurity and survey the rising destiny of New York through the long vista of years to come! For, whatever party rules, whatever political chief rises or falls, agriculture, manufactures and commerce, must still remain the greatest of our concerns; and by the opening of the Canal, these three great vital interests are all most eminently promoted. What a wide spread region of cultivated soil has already been brought within the near vicinity of the greatest market on our continent! How many manufacturing establishments have had the value of every thing connected with them doubled by this "meeting of the waters!" How vastly have the internal resources of this metropolis been in one day practically extended! Without adverting to the cheering prospects of future times, how much has been already effected at this present hour, in the enhancement of the total value of the whole state! . . .

The authors and builders—the heads who planned, and the hands who executed this stupendous work, deserve a perennial monument; and they will have it. To borrow an expression from the highest of all sources, "the works which they have done, these will bear witness of them." Europe begins already to admire—America can never forget to acknowledge, that THEY HAVE BUILT THE LONGEST CANAL IN THE WORLD IN THE LEAST TIME, WITH THE LEAST EXPERIENCE, FOR THE LEAST MONEY, AND TO THE GREATEST PUBLIC BENEFIT.

12.

Fanny Kemble 1832–33*

INTRODUCTION: What it meant to travel by steamboat during the era immediately following the opening of the Erie Canal has been imperishably recorded in the *Journal of a Residence in America,* penned by Frances Anne Kemble (1809–1893), the immortal "Fanny Kemble" of the British and American stage.

Fanny was all but unknown when she arrived in New York on September 3, 1832, with her father, the actor Charles Kemble, and her Aunt Adelaide De Camp (the "Dall" of the *Journal*). But from the time she first appeared on a stage in New York City and received a standing ovation from the audience, she became an idol of the people; and by the time she gave up the stage, in June 1834, to marry a Georgia planter, she was one of the most famous women in America. Statesmen admired her; Longfellow wrote a sonnet to her; students at Harvard saved money for weeks to purchase tickets to one of her plays. In the late 1830s, when she began to spend her summers in Lenox, Massachusetts, her very presence was sufficient to start a fashionable summer resort in the area. Fanny subsequently left her husband (revealing the reasons why in her *Journal of a Residence on a Georgian Plantation*) and returned to the stage in England in 1841. But by 1849 she was back in America waging a famous court battle (with Rufus Choate as her lawyer) to win her freedom from her husband and thrilling her audience once again by giving public readings from Shakespeare. After 1869 she gave up the stage altogether—for, in spite of her success, she never really liked it—and spent the remainder of her life writing books and visiting her two daughters, one of whom resided in England and the other of whom married Dr. Owen J. Wister of German, Pennsylvania, father of Fanny's famous grandson, Owen Wister.

* Excerpt from Frances Anne [Kemble] Butler's *Journal* (Philadelphia: 1835), Vol. I, pp. 198–217; Vol. II, pp. 160–170.

Fanny's writing career began literally as an accident. While traveling through the Mohawk Valley during the first acting tour of 1833, the stagecoach in which Fanny and her father and aunt were riding overturned, causing serious injury to the beloved Aunt Dall. A few weeks later it became apparent that the aunt would be totally incapacitated for the rest of her life, and with deep feelings of guilt and anguish (the aunt had lived with the Kembles ever since Fanny was a girl), Fanny determined to raise enough money to provide for her aunt's future in as comfortable a manner as possible. Remembering that a Philadelphia publisher had once begged her to permit him to print the lively journal she was keeping of her American tour (with all names deleted!), she now eagerly embraced his generous offer and in 1835 became the avidly read—and occasionally maligned—authoress of the *Journal of a Residence in America.*

The following extracts from this spirited work recount two voyages Fanny took up the Hudson—the first on November 10, 1832, when she made a one-day excursion to West Point; the second between June 30 and July 2, 1833, when she revisited West Point, spent two days at Cold Spring, and then went on to Albany to keep a theatrical appointment. Traveling with Fanny Kemble is something of a magical experience: time dissolves, the intervening years disappear from view, and we are immediately immersed in the sights and sounds of the Hudson Valley during the Golden Age of steamboating.

First Excursion to West Point

Sat., Nov. 10, 1832

At six o'clock D——— [Dall] roused me; and grumpily enough I arose. I dressed myself by candlelight in a hurry. Really by way of a party of pleasure, 'tis too abominable to get up in the middle of the night this fashion. At half past six, Colonel ——— came, and as soon as I could persuade myself into my clothes, we set off to walk to the quay. Just as we were nearing the bottom of Barclay street,[1] the bell rang from the steamboat, to summon all loiterers on board; and forthwith we rushed, because in this country steam and paddles, like wind and tide in others, wait for no man. We got on board in plenty time, but D——— [Dall] was nearly killed with the pace at which we had walked, in order to do so. One of the first persons we saw was Mr. ———, who was going up to his father's place beyond West Point, by name Hyde Park, which sounds mighty magnificent. I did not remain long on the second deck, but ascended to the first with Colonel ———, and paced to and fro with infinite zeal till breakfast time. The morning was gray and sad looking, and I feared we should not have a fine day: however, towards eight o'clock the gray clouds parted, and the blue serene eyes of heaven looked down upon the waters, the waves began to sparkle, though the sun had not yet appeared; the sky was lighter, and faint shadows began to appear beside the various objects that surrounded us, all which symptoms raised our hopes of the weather. At eight o'clock we went down to breakfast. Nobody who has not seen it, can conceive the strange aspect of the long room on one of these fine boats at meal-time. The crowd, the hurry, the confusion of tongues, like the sound of many waters, the enormous consumption of eatables, the mingled demands for more, the cloud of black waiters hovering down the sides of the immense tables, the hungry, eager faces seated at them, form altogether a most amusing subject of contemplation, and a caricaturist would find ample matter for his vein in almost every other devouring countenance. As far as regards the speed, safety, and convenience with which these vessels enable one to perform what would be in any other conveyance most fatiguing journeys, they are admirable inventions. The way in which they are conducted, too, deserves the highest commendation. Nothing can exceed the comfort with which they are fitted up, the skill with which they are managed, and the order and alacrity with which passengers are taken up from, or landed at the various points along the river. The steamer goes at the rate of fifteen miles an hour, and in less than two minutes when approaching any place of landing, the engine stops, the boat is lowered—the captain always convoys his passengers himself from the steamer to the shore—away darts the tiny skiff, held by a rope to the main boat; as soon as it grazes the land, its freight, animate and inanimate, is bundled out, the boat hauls itself back in an instant, and immediately the machine is in motion, and the vessel again bounding over the water like a racehorse.[2] Doubtless all this has many and great advantages; but to an English person, the mere circumstance of being the whole day in a crowd is a nuisance. As to privacy at any time, or under any circumstances, 'tis a thing that enters not into the imagination of an American. They do not seem to comprehend that to be from sunrise to sunset one of a hundred and fifty people confined to a steamboat, is in itself a great misery, or that to be left by oneself and to oneself, can ever be desirable. They live all the days of their lives in a throng, eat at ordinaries of two or three hundred, sleep five or six in a room, take pleasure in droves, and travel by swarms.[3]

In spite, therefore, of all its advantages, this mode of journeying has its drawbacks. And the greatest of all, to me, is the being *companioned* by so many strangers, who crowd about you, pursue their conversation in your very ears, or, if they like it better, listen to yours, stare you out of all countenance, and squeeze you out of all comfort. It is perfectly intolerable to me; but then I have more than even the national English abhorrence of coming in contact with strangers. There is no moment of my life when I would not rather be alone, than in a company; and feeling, as I often do, the society of even those I love a burthen, the being eternally surrounded by indifferent persons, is a positive suffering that interferes with every enjoyment, and makes pleasure three parts endurance. I think this constant living in public is one reason why the young women here are much less retiring and shy than English girls. Instead of the domestic privacy in which women among us are accustomed to live and move, and have their being, here they are incessantly, as Mr. ——— says, *"en evidence."* Accustomed to the society of strangers, mixing familiarly with persons of whom they know nothing earthly, subject to the gaze of a crowd from morning till night, pushing, and pressing, and struggling in self-defence, conversing, and being conversed with, by the chance companions of a boarding-house, a steamboat, or the hotel of a fashionable watering-place; they must necessarily lose everything like reserve or bashfulness or deportment, and become free and familiar in their manners, and noisy and unrefined in their tone and style of conversation. An English girl of sixteen, put on board one of these Noah's arks, (for verily there be clean and unclean beasts in them,) would feel and look like a scared thing. To return to our progress. After losing sight of New York, the river becomes narrower in its bed, and the banks on either side assume a higher and more rocky appearance. A fine range of basaltic rock, called the Palisadoes, rising to a height of some hundred feet, (I guess,) [4] immediately from the water on the left, forms a natural rampart, over-hanging the river for several miles. The colour of the basalt was greenish grey, and contrasted finely with the opposite shore, whose softer undulations were yet clothed with verdure, and adorned with patches of woodland, robed in the glorious colours of an American autumn. While despatching breakfast, the reflection of the sun's rays on the water flickered to and fro upon the cabin ceiling, and through the loop-hole windows we saw the bright foam round the paddles sparkling like frothed gold in the morning light. On our return to the deck, the face of the world had become resplendent with the glorious sunshine that now poured from the east; and rock and river, earth and sky, shone in intense and dazzling brilliancy. The broad Hudson curled into a thousand crisp billows under the fresh north-wester that blew over it. The vaporous exhalations of night had melted from the horizon, and the bold, rocky range of one shore, and exquisite rolling outline of the other, stood out in fair relief against the deep serene of the blue heavens.

I remained on deck without my bonnet, walking to and fro, and enjoying the delicious wind that was as bracing as a shower-bath. . . . As we passed the various points of the river, to which any interest, legendary or historical, attached, each of my three companions,[5] drew my attention to it; and I had, pretty generally, three variations of the same anecdote at each point of observation. On we boiled past Spitendevil [*sic*] creek, where the waters of the broad Hudson, join those of the East river, and circle with their silver arms the island of Manhattan. Past the last stupendous reach of the Palisadoes, which, stretching out into an endless promontory, seems to grow with the mariner's onward progress, and bears witness to the justice with which Hudson, on his exploring voyage up the river, christened it, "the weary point." Past the thick masses of wood that mark the shadowy side of Sleepy Hollow. Past the marble prison of Sing Sing; and Tarrytown, where poor André was taken, and on the opposite shore, saw the glimmering white buildings, among which his tomb reposes.—By and bye, for a bit of the marvellous, which I dearly love. I am credibly informed, that on the day the traitor Arnold died, in England, a thunderbolt struck the tree that grew above André's tomb here, on the shores of the Hudson —nice, that! Crossed the broad, glorious, Tappan Sea, where the shores receding, from a huge basin, where the brimming waters roll in an expanse of lake-like width, yet hold their rapid current to the ocean, themselves a running sea. The giant shadows of the mountains on the left, falling on the deep basin at their feet, the triumphant sunlight that made the restless mirror that reflected it too bright for the eye to rest upon, the sunny shores to the right, rising and falling in every exquisite form that hill and dale can wear, the jutting masses of granite, glittering like the diamond rocks of fairy-land, in the sun, the golden waves flinging themselves up every tiny crevice, the glowing crimson foliage of the distant woods, the fresh vivid green of the cedars, that rifted their strong roots in every stony cleft, and threw a semblance of summer over these November days—all, all was beautiful, and full of brightness. We passed the light-house of Stony Point, now the peaceful occupant of the territory, where the blood in English veins was poured out by English hands, during the struggle between old established tyranny and the infant liberties of this giant world. Over all and each, the blessed sky bent its blue arch, resplendently clear and bright, while far away the distant summits of the Highlands rose one above another, shutting in the world, and almost appearing as though each bend of the river must find us locked in their shadowy circle, without the means of onward progress.

At every moment the scene varied; at every moment new beauty and grandeur was revealed to us; at every moment the delicious lights and shadows fell with richer depth and brightness upon higher openings into the mountains, and fairer bends of the glorious river. At about a quarter to eleven the buildings of West Point

were seen perched upon the rock side, overhanging the water; above, the woody rise upon whose summit stands the large hotel, the favourite resort of visitors during the summer season; [6] rising again above this, the ruins of Fort Putnam, poor André's prison-house, overlooking the Hudson and its shores; and towering high beyond them all, the giant hills, upon whose brown shoulders the trees looked like bristles standing up against the sky. We left the boat, or rather she left us, and presently we saw her holding her course far up the bright water, and between the hills; where, framed by the dark mountains with the sapphire stream below and the sapphire sky above, lay the bright little town of Newburgh, with its white buildings glittering in the sunshine.

We toiled up the ascent, which, though by comparison with its overpeering fellows inconsiderable, was a sufficiently fatiguing undertaking under the unclouded weather and over the unshaded downs that form the parade ground for the cadets. West Point is a military establishment containing some two hundred and fifty pupils; who are here educated for the army under the superintendence of experienced officers. The buildings in which they reside and pursue their various studies, stand upon a grassy knoll holding the top of the rocky bank of the river, and commanding a most enchanting view of its course. They are not particularly extensive; but commodious and well-ordered. I am told they have a good library, but on reaching the dwelling of Mr. Cozzens (proprietor of the hotel, which being at this season shut, he received us most hospitably and courteously in his own house), I felt so weary, that I thought it impossible I should stir again for the whole day, and declined seeing it. I had walked on the deck at an amazing pace, and without once sitting down from eight o'clock till eleven; and I think must nearly have killed Colonel ————, who was my companion during this march. How-

25. *West Point from Phillipstown*, engraving by W. J. Bennett from his own painting, 1831; courtesy of The New-York Historical Society.

"The buildings of West Point were seen perched upon the rock side . . . upon whose summit stands the large hotel, the favourite resort of visitors during the summer season."

Cozzens Hotel on the left faces the point of Constitution Island across the river. Beyond the island, Storm King Mountain and Breakneck Mountain form the northern gateway to the Highlands.

ever, upon finding that it wanted full an hour till dinner time, it was agreed that we should go up to the fort, and we set off under the guidance of one of Mr. Cozzen's servants, who had orders not to go too fast with us. Before turning into the woods that cover the foot of the mountain, we followed a bit of road that overhung the river; and stealing over its sleepy-looking waters, where shone like stars, the white sails of many a tiny skiff, came the delicious notes of a bugle-horn. The height at which we stood above the water prevented the ear being satisfied with the complete subject of the musician, but the sweet, broken tones that came rising from the far down thickets that skirted the river, had more harmony than a distinct and perfect strain. I stood entranced to listen—the whole was like a dream of fairyland: but presently our guide struck into the woods, and the world became screened from our sight. I had thought that I was tired, and could not stir, even to follow the leisurely footsteps of our cicerone; but tangled brake and woodland path, and rocky height, soon roused my curiosity, and my legs followed therewith, I presently outstripped our party, guide and all, and began pursuing my upward path. Through close growing trees and shrubs, over pale, shining ledges of granite, over which the trickling mountain springs had taken their silvery course, through swampy grounds where the fallen leaves lay like gems under the still pools that here and there shone dimly in little hollow glens. Over the soft starry moss that told where the moist earth retained the freshening waters, over sharp hard splinters of rock, and rough masses of stone. Alone, alone, I was alone and happy, and went on my way rejoicing, climbing and climbing still, till the green mound of thick turf, and ruined rampart of the fort arrested my progress. I coasted the broken wall, and lighting down on a broad, smooth table of granite fringed with young cedar bushes, I looked down, and for a moment my

breath seemed to stop, the pulsation of my heart to cease—I was filled with awe. The beauty and wild sublimity of what I beheld seemed almost to crush my faculties,—I felt dizzy as though my senses were drowning,—I felt as though I had been carried into the immediate presence of God. Though I were to live a thousand years, I never can forget it. The first thing that I distinctly saw, was the shadow of a huge mountain, frowning over the height where I stood. The shadow moved down its steep sunny side, threw a deep blackness over the sparkling river, and then passed off and climbed the opposite mountain on the other shore, leaving the world in the full blaze of noon. I could have stretched out my arms and shouted aloud—I could have fallen on my knees and worshipped—I could have committed any extravagance that ecstacy could suggest. I stood filled with amazement and delight, till the footsteps and voices of my companions roused me. I darted away, unwilling to be interrupted. Colonel ———— was following me, but I preemptorily forbade his doing so, and was clambering on alone, when the voice of our guide assuring me that the path I was pursuing was impassable, arrested my course. My father beckoned to me from above not to pursue my track; so I climbed through a break, which the rocky walls of nature and the broken fortifications of art rendered tolerably difficult of access, and running round the wall joined my father on his high stand, where he was holding out his arms to me. For two or three minutes we mingled exclamations of delight and surprise; he then led me to the brink of the rampart, and looking down the opposite angle of the wall to that which I was previously coasting, I beheld the path I was then following break suddenly off, on the edge of a precipice several hundred feet down into the valley: it made me gulp to look at it. Presently I left my father, and after going the complete round of the ruins, found out for myself a grassy knoll commanding a full view of the scene, sufficiently far from my party not to hear their voices, and screened from seeing them by some beautiful young cedar bushes; and here I lay down and cried most abundantly, by which means I recovered my senses, which else, I think, must have forsaken me. How full of thoughts I was! Of God's great might, and gracious goodness, of the beauty of this earth, of the apparent nothingness of man when compared with this huge inanimate creation, of his wondrous value, for whose delight and use all these fair things were created. I thought of my distant home; that handfull of earth thrown upon the wide waters, whose genius has led the kingdoms of the world—whose children have become the possessors of this new hemisphere. I rejoiced to think that when England shall be, as all things must be, fallen into the devouring past, her language will still be spoken among these glorious hills, her name revered, her memory cherished, her fame preserved here, in this far world beyond the seas, this country of her children's adoption. Poor old mother! how she would remain amazed to see the huge earth and waters where her voice is heard, in the name of every spot where her descendants have rested the soles of their feet. This giant inheritance of her sons, poor, poor, old England!

Where are the poets of this land! Why such a world should bring forth men with minds and souls larger and stronger than any that ever dwelt in mortal flesh. Where are the poets of this land? They should be giants too; Homers and Miltons, and Goethes and Dantes, and Shakespeares. Have these glorious scenes poured no inspirings into hearts worthy to behold and praise their beauty? Is there none to come here and worship among these hills and waters till his heart burns within him, and the hymn of inspiration flows from his lips, and rises to the sky? Is there not one among the sons of such a soil to send forth its praises to the universe, to throw new glory round the mountains, new beauty over the waves? Is inanimate nature, alone, here "telling the glories of God?" Oh, surely, surely, there will come a time when this lovely land will be vocal with the sound of song, when every close-locked valley, and waving wood, rifted rock and flowing stream shall have their praise. Yet 'tis strange how marvellously unpoetical these people are! How swallowed up in life and its daily realities, wants, and cares; how full of toil and thrift, and money-getting labour. Even the heathen Dutch, among us the very antipodes of all poetry, have found names such as the Donder Berg for the hills, whilst the Americans christen them Butter Hill,[7] the Crows Nest, and *such like*. Perhaps some hundred years hence, when wealth has been amassed by individuals, and the face of society begins to grow chequered, as in the old lands of Europe, when the whole mass of population shall no longer go running along the level road of toil and profit, when inequalities of rank shall exist, and the rich man shall be able to pay for the luxury of poetry, and the poor man who makes verses, no longer be asked, "Why don't you cast up accounts;" when all this comes to pass, as *perhaps* some day it may, America will have poets. It seems strange to me that men such as the early settlers in Massachusetts, the Puritan founders of New England, the "Pilgrim Fathers," should not have had amongst them some men, or at least man, in whose mind the stern and enduring courage, the fervent enthusiastic piety, the unbending love of liberty, which animated them all, become the inspiration to poetic thought, and the suggestion of poetical utterance. They should have had a Milton or a Klopstock amongst them. Yet after all, they had excitement of another sort, and moreover, the difficulties, and dangers, and distresses of a fate of unparalleled hardship, to engross all the energies of their minds; and I am half inclined to believe that poetry is but a hot-house growth, and yet I don't know; I wish somebody would explain to me every thing in this world that I can't make out.

We came down from the mountain at about half past one, our party [having] been joined by Colonel ——— [Sylvanus Thayer], Governor of the College,[8] who very courteously came toiling up to Fort Putnam,[9] to pay his compliments to us. I lingered far behind them, return-ing, and when they were out of sight turned back and once more ascended the ruin, to look my last admiration and delight, and then down, down, every step bringing me out of the clouds, farther from heaven, and nearer this work i'day world. I loitered, looking back at every step, but at last the hills were shut out by a bend in the road, and I came into the house, to throw myself down on the floor, and sleep most seriously for half an hour, at the end of which time we were called to dinner.

In England, if an inn-keeper gives you a good dinner, and places the first dish on the table himself, you pay him, and he's obliged to you. Here, an inn-keeper is a gentleman, your equal, sits at his table with you, you pay him, and are obliged to him besides. 'Tis necessary therefore for a stranger, but especially an Englishman, to understand the fashions of the land, else he may chance to mistake that for an impertinent familiarity, which is in fact the received custom of the country. Mr. Cozzens very considerately gave us our dinner in a private room, instead of seating us at an ordinary with all the West Point officers. Moreover, *gave* in the literal sense, and a very good dinner it was. He is himself a very intelligent, courteous person, and during the very short time that we were his guests, showed us every possible attention and civility. We had scarce finished our dinner, when in rushed a waiter to tell us that the boat was in sight. Away we trotted, trailing cloaks and shawls, any-how fashion, down the hill.

The steamer came puffing up the gorge between the mountains, and in a moment we were bundled into the boat, hauled alongside, and landed on the deck; and presently the glorious highlands all-glowing in the rosy sunset, began to recede from us. Just as we were putting off from the shore, a tiny skiff with its graceful white sail glittering in the sun, turned the base of the opposite hill, evidently making to the point whence we embarked. I have since learned that it contained a messenger to us, from a gentleman bearing our name, and distantly con-nected with us, proprietor of some large iron works on the shore opposite West Point.[10] However, our kinsman was too late, and we were already losing sight of West Point when his boat reached the shore. Our progress homeward was if anything more enchanting than our coming out had been, except for leaving all this loveli-ness. The sun went down in splendour, leaving the world robed in glorious beauty. The sky was one glowing ger-anium curtain, into which the dark hills rose like shadow-land, stretching beyond, and still beyond, till they grew like hazy outlines through a dazzling mist of gold. The glory faded; and a soft violet colour spread downwards to the horizon, where a faint range of clouds lay floating like scattered rose leaves. As the day fell, the volumes of smoke from our steamboat chimneys, became the streams of fiery sparks, which glittered over the water with a strange unearthly effect. I sat on deck watching the world grow dark, till my father, afraid of the night air, bade me go down; and there, in spite of the chattering of a score of women, and the squalling of half as many children, I slept profoundly, till we reached New York, at a quarter to seven.

Second Visit to West Point

Sunday, June 30, 1833

Rose at four, but after looking at my watch, resumed my slumbers until six, when I started up, much dismayed to find it so late, and presently, having dressed as fast as ever I could, we set off for the steam-boat. The morning was the brightest possible, the glorious waters that meet before New York were all like rivers of light blazing with the reflected radiance of the morning sky. We had no sooner set foot on board the steam-boat, than a crowd of well-known faces surrounded us: I was introduced to Mr. ——— [Edward Trelawny],[11] and Mr. ——— [William Kemble], the brother of our host at Cold Spring.[12] Mr. ——— [Trelawny] came and stood by me for a considerable time after we started. It is agreeable to talk to him, because he has known and seen so much; traversed the world in every direction, and been the friend of Byron and Shelley; a common mind that had enjoyed the same opportunities, (that's impossible by the bye, no common mind would have sought or found them) must have acquired something from intercourse with such men, and such wide knowledge of things; but he is an uncommon man, and it is very interesting to hear him talk of what he has seen, and those he has known.

When we reached West Point, Mr. ——— [Gouverneur Kemble] was waiting with his boat to convey us over to Cold Spring, and accordingly bidding our various acquaintances and companions farewell, we rowed over out of the course of the river, into a sunny bay it forms among the hills, to our kinsman's abode. Mr. ———'s [Kemble's] place is a lovely little nook, situated on the summit of a rise, on the brink of the placid curve of water formed here by the river, and which extends itself from the main current about a mile into the mountains, ending in a wide marsh.[13] The house, though upon a hill, is so looked down upon, and locked in by the highlands around it, that it seems to be at the bottom of a valley. From the verandah of his house, through various frames which he has had cut with exceeding good judgment among the plantations around the lawn, exquisite glimpses appeared of the mountains, the little bay, the glorious Hudson itself, with the graceful boats, for ever walking its broad waters, their white sails coming through the rocky passes, where the river could not be detected, as though they were sailing through the valleys of the earth. The day was warm; but a fresh breeze stirred the boughs, and cooled the air. My father, and D——— [Dall] seemed overcome with drowsiness, and lay in the verandah with half-closed eyes, peeping at the dream-like scene around them. I was not inclined to rest, and Mr. ——— [Kemble] having promised to show me some falls [14] at a short distance from the house; he and his brother, and I, set forth thither. We passed through the iron-works: 'twas Sunday, and everything except a bright water-course, laughing and singing as it ran, was still. They took me over the works, showed me the iron frames of large mill wheels, the machinery and process of boring the cannon, the model of an iron forcing pump, the casting houses, and all the wonders of their manufactory.[15] All mechanical science is very interesting to me, when I have an opportunity of seeing the detail of it, and comprehending, by illustrations presented to my eyes, the technical terms used by those conversing with me. We left these dark abodes, and their smouldering fires, and strange, powerful-looking instruments, and taking a path at the foot of the mountains, skirted the marsh for some time, and then struck into the woods, ascending a tremendous stony path, at the top of which we threw ourselves down to pant, and looked below through a narrow rent in the curtain of leaves around us,

26. *West Point Foundry, Cold Spring, N.Y.*, engraving by
Currier & Ives, 1862; courtesy of The New-York Historical
Society.

"They took me over the works, showed me the iron frames
of large mill wheels, the machinery and process of boring
the cannon."

The ruins of this famous foundry may still be seen, hidden
in the rich foliage of the east bank.

on the river, and rocks, and mountains, bright with the noon-day splendour of the unclouded sky.

After resting here a few moments, we arose and climbed again, through the woods, across a sweet clover field, to the brow of the hill, where stands the highland school,—a cheerful-looking cottage, with the mountain tops all round, the blessed sky above, and the downward sloping woods and lake-like river below. Passing through the ground surrounding it, we joined a road skirting a deep ravine, from the bottom of which the waters called to me. I was wild to go down, but my companions would not let me. It was in vain that I strained over the brink, the trees were so thickly woven together, and the hollow so deep, that I could see nothing but dark boughs, except every now and then, as the wind stirred them, the white glimmer of the leaping foam, as it sprang away with a shout that made my heart dance. We followed the path, which began to decline, and presently a silver thread of gushing water, ran like a frightened child across our way, and flung itself down into the glen. At length we reached the brown, golden-looking stream.[16]

Mr. ———— [Gouverneur Kemble] was exhorting us to take an upper path, which he said would bring us to the foot of the fall; but I was not to be seduced from the side of the rivulet, and insisted upon crossing it then and there, through the water, over moss-capped stones, across fallen trees, which, struck by the lightning, or undermined by the cold-kissing waters, had choked up the brook with their leafy bridges. So, striving on, as best we might, after wading through the stream two or three times, we reached the end and aim of our journey, the waterfall. We stood on the brink of a pool, about forty feet across, and varying in depth from three to seven or eight feet: it was perfectly circular, and except on the south,—where the waters take their path down the glen, —closed round with a wall of rock about thirty feet high,

in whose crevices trees, with their rifted roots, hung fearlessly, clothing the grey stone with a soft curtain of vivid green. . . . As I gazed up in perfect ecstacy, an uncontrollable desire seized me to clamber up the rocks by the side of the fall, and so reach the top of it. My companions laughed incredulously as I expressed my determination to do so, but followed where I led, until they became well assured that I was in earnest. Remonstrance and representation of impossibility having been tried in vain, Mr. ———— [William Kemble] prepared to guide me, and Mr. ———— [Gouverneur Kemble], with my bag, parasol, and bonnet in charge, returned to the edge of the pool to watch our progress. Away we went over the ledges of the rocks, with nothing but damp leaves, and slippery roots of trees for footing. At one moment the slight covering of mould on which I had placed my foot, crumbled from beneath it, and I swung over the water by a young sapling, which upheld me well, and by which I recovered footing and balance. We had now reached the immediate side of the waterfall, and my guide began ascending the slippery, slanting rocks down which it fell. I followed: in an instant I was soaked through with the spray,—my feet slipped,—I had no hold; he was up above me—the pool far below. With my head bowed against the foam and water, I was feeling where next to tread, when a bit of rock, that my companion had thought firm, broke beneath his foot, and came falling down beside me into the stream. I paused, for I was frightened. I looked up for a moment, but was blinded by the water, and could not see where my guide was; I looked down the slanting edge we had climbed, over which the water was churning angrily. "Shall I come down again?" I cried to Mr. ———— [Gouverneur Kemble] who was anxiously looking up at our perilous path. "Give me your hand!" shouted his brother above me. I lifted my head, and turned towards him, and a dazzling curtain of spray and foam fell over my face. "I cannot see you," I replied; "I cannot go on—I do not know what to do." "Give me your hand!" he exclaimed again; and I, planting one foot upon a ledge of rock so high as to lift me off the other, held up my arm to him; but my limbs were so strained from his height above me, that I had no power to spring or move, either up or down. However, I felt my presence of mind going; I knew that to go down was impossible, except headlong,—the ascent must therefore be persevered in. "Are you steady, quite, quite steady?" I inquired: he replied, "Yes"; and holding out his hand, I locked mine in it, and bade him draw me up. But he had not calculated upon my weight,—my slight appearance had deceived him, and as I bore upon his arm, we both of us slipped—I turned as sick as death, but only cried out, "Recover yourself! recover yourself!—I am safe!" which I was, upon a rocky rim about three inches wide, with my arm resting on the falling stump of the blasted tree. He did recover his balance, and again holding out his hand, drew me up beside where he was sitting, on the edge of the rocks, in the water. We pledged each other in the clear stream, and standing on the top of our hardly gained eminence, in the midst of the rushing brook, I wrang my handkerchief triumphantly at Mr. —— [Gouverneur Kemble]; which was rather a comical consideration, as I was literally dripping from head to foot,—no Naiad ever looked so thoroughly watery, or could have taken more delight in a ducking. As soon as he saw us safe, he scrambled up through the woods to the road, and we doing the same, we presently all met on the dusty highway, where we congratulated each other on our perseverance and success, and laughed very exceedingly at my soaked situation.

We determined not to pass through the Highland school ground, but kept the main road for the advantage of sun and wind, the combined influences of which presently dried my frock and handkerchief. When I reached home, ran up stairs, and dressed myself for dinner, which we sat down to at about four. After dinner came up to my room, and slept very profoundly until summoned to coffee, which we drank in the verandah. At about eight o'clock the sun had left the sky, but his warm mantle lay over the western clouds, and hung upon the rocks and woody mountain sides; a gentle breeze was stirring the trees round where we sat; and through the thick branches of a chestnut tree, as they waved to and fro, the silver disk of the full moon looked placidly down upon us. We set out strolling through the woods: leisurely as foot could fall, we took our way through the twilight paths; and when we reached the Roman Catholic chapel our host is building by the river side, the silent, thoughtful mountains were wrapped in deep shadows, and the broad waters shone like a sheet of silver in the moonlight. We sat down on the cannon lying on the pebbly shore, and Mr. —— ran off to order the boat, which presently came stealing round over the shining waters. We got in, —— rowing, and they put me at the helm; but owing to Mr. ——'s misdirections, (who seemed extremely amused at my awkwardness, and took delight in bothering poor —— by making me steer all awry,) we made but little progress, and that rather crab-wise, backing, and sideling, and turning, as though the poor boat had been a politician.

Full of my own contemplations, I kept steering round and round, and so we wandered, as purposeless as the night air over the smooth waters, and beneath the shadows of the solemn hills, till near eleven o'clock, when we made for shore, and slowly turned home. We sat for a length of time under the verandah: the gentlemen were discussing the planetary system as accepted in the civilized world; and Mr. —— maintained, with sufficient plausibility, that we knew nothing at all about it, in spite of Newton; for, that though his theories were borne out by all observation, it did not follow therefore that another theory equally probable might not exist. . . . And so they went on, the end of all being, to my mind as usual, utter unsatisfactoriness, and as the mosquitoes were stinging me, I left them to their discussions, and came to bed.

Monday, July 1, 1833

Major ———, and Mr. ———, came over from West Point; they were going to prove some cannon, that had not yet been fired, and some time passed in the various preparations for so doing. At length we were summoned down to the water side, to see the success of the experiment. The cannon lay obliquely, one behind the other, at intervals of about six yards, along the curve line of the little bay: their muzzles pointed to the high gravelly bank, into which they fired.[17] The guns were double loaded with very heavy charges, and as soon as we were safely placed so as to see and hear, they were fired. The sound was glorious: the first heavy peal, and then echo after echo, as they *rimbombavano* among the answering hills, who growled aloud at the stern voice waking their still, and noon-day's deep repose. I pushed out in the boat from shore to see the thick curtain of smoke, as it rolled its silver, and brassy, and black volumes over the woody mountain sides; parting in jagged rents as it rose, through which the vivid green and blessed sky smiled in their peaceful loneliness. They ended in discharging all the cannon at once, which made a most glorious row, and kept the mountains grumbling with its echoes for some minutes after the discharge. All the pieces were sound, which was highly satisfactory; as upon each one that flaws in the firing, Mr. ——— [Kemble] loses the cost of the piece.

Just as the smoke cleared off from the river, we saw the boat making to shore; and presently, Mr. ———, his wife, and children, and a young Mr. ——— landed. After introductions, and one or two questions, Mrs. ——— went up to her cottage to put things in order there, Mr. ——— betook himself to Froissart [18] and the shade, Mr. ——— [Gouverneur Kemble] to his business; and D——— [Dall], my father, Mr. ——— [Trelawny?] and myself set forth to the fountain in the glen. The weather was intensely hot: the thermometer above 90° in the shade; it was about half past twelve, and we toiled and gasped on like so many Indians up the steep path. The walk had been so laborious, that neither D——— [Dall] nor my father were willing at first to admit that the object was a sufficient one. We sat for some time by the dark shady pool, and they by degrees recovered their breath and complacency, and began to perceive how beautiful the place really was. My father said the waterfall looked like a fine lace veil torn by the rocks, which pleased me, because it did look like that. Mr. ——— [Trelawny?] proposed an admirable plan, that of walking down the water's side, and taking a boat upon the Hudson, and so avoiding the long hot walk home. We called at the Highland School, where the worthy man who keeps it, received us with infinite civility, put us into a delicious cool room, and gave us some white hermitage and water to drink, which did us all manner of good. We then descended to the river, after some delay and difficulty, got a boat and rowed home.

Tuesday, July 2, 1833

Packed up my bag, took a cup of tea, went and gathered some flowers, and gave the poor lamb some heads of clover, bade a very unwilling farewell to the pretty place, and rowed over to West Point, where Mr. ———

was waiting for us. We breakfasted at ten, and went down to meet the boat. Young Mr. ——— came over to see us off, and brought me some lovely fresh flowers. . . . When the boat came up, the rush to and from it was without exception the most frightful thing I ever saw. . . . Safely on board, I again found myself surrounded by familiar faces; I took out my work, and Mr. ——— [Trelawny] sat down by us. As a nuisance, which all unsought-for companionship is, he is quite the most endurable possible, for he has seen such things, and known such people, that it is greatly worth while to listen to him. Everything he says of Byron and Shelley confirms my impression of them.

The scenery of the Hudson immediately beyond West Point loses much of its sublimity, though no beauty. The river widens and the rugged summits of the Highlands melt gradually into a softer and more undulating outline. The richness, and swelling, and falling of the land, reminded me occasionally of England. The yellow grain was giving diversity and warmth to the green landscape, and the shadowy woods fencing the cornfields, threw over the whole picture a sheltering peaceful charm. On the left, we presently began to see the blue outline of the Catskill mountains towering into the hot sky, and looking most blessedly cool and dark amid the fervid glowing of the noon-day world. . . .

At about halfpast three in the afternoon, the sky became suddenly and thickly overcast, the awning which sheltered the upper deck was withdrawn, and every preparation made for the storm. The pale angry-looking clouds heaped like chalk upon a leaden sky, and presently one red lightning dipped down into the woods like a fiery snake falling from the heavens. At the same time, a furious gust of wind and torrent of rain rushed down the mountain side. We scuttled down to the lower deck as fast as ever we could, but the storm met us at the bottom of the stairs, and in an instant I was drenched; chairs, tables, every thing was overturned by the gust, and the boat was running with water in every direction. It thundered and lightened a little, but the noise of the engine was such that we scarce heard the storm. I stood by the door of the furnace, and dried leisurely, talking the while to Mr. ——— [Trelawny], who is sunburnt enough to warm one through with a look. During our progress, one of the wheels, or paddles, as they are properly called, took it into its head to knock its case to pieces, and banged the boards about in a strange way. Accident the second: one of the men, a black, who was employed in tending the fire, got so dreadfully heated with the intense furnace, that he rushed out of the engine room, and swallowed two or three draughts of cold water; the effect was instantaneous, he fell down in violent internal spasms, and died, poor wretch! before we arrived in Albany. We reached that town at about half past five in the afternoon, and went to a house the ———'s recommended to us. At about seven they gave us dinner, and immediately after I came up to my own room. I was so exhausted with fatigue and a violent cold and cough, that I literally fell down on the floor, and slept till dark.

13.
Harriet Martineau 1835*

INTRODUCTION: Fanny Kemble's enthusiasm for the beauties of the Hudson was shared by an incredible number of her compatriots during the 1830s. Half the population of Great Britain, it seems, descended upon the New World during this period of rising American nationalism and self-confidence. Drawn by the ambivalent magnet of American success—for the *fait accompli* of American independence was still a source of embarrassment to the English Establishment—many visitors came with malice aforethought and were notably attentive to the harsher aspects of American life and environment. Armed with the new tenets and concepts of European Romanticism, English travelers were especially sensitive to the "unpicturesqueness" of the raw American landscape. The one region, however, that proved exceptional to this general indictment was the Hudson Valley. Since the Hudson had become the busiest and most highly developed thoroughfare in the nation during this period, it soon became a "must" of foreign travel. And whether the traveler was the master-of-household and privy councillor at the court of Queen Victoria, Charles Augustus Murray (who was on the Hudson in 1834 and 1836), or the Scotsman David Wilkie (1836), or the arrogant Captain Frederick Marryat (almost lynched by an American mob in 1837), or James Silk Buckingham, editor and member of Parliament (whose visit of 1838 is recorded in Chapter 14)—all supported Harriet Martineau's contention of 1835 that "however widely European travelers have differed about other things in America, all seem to agree in their love of the Hudson."

Some of the reasons for this adulation found eloquent expression in Fanny Kemble's account of the early 1830s.

More are revealed in the present narration of Harriet Martineau and the following account by James Silk Buckingham. All three accounts span the complete decade of the 1830s and portray the Hudson when it became not only the busiest thoroughfare in America, but a burgeoning region of country estates and summer resorts, the chief inspiration of the first school of American landscape painting, and the scenic wonder of the nation.

Harriet Martineau (1802–1876) was a prolific writer on social, philosophic, and economic subjects who visited America during the years 1834–1836. In 1837, after returning to England, she published *Society in America,* a work that aroused considerable enmity because of its very early, outspoken support of the radical abolitionist movement, and *Retrospect of Western Travel* (1838), a much more popular work that contains the following consolidated account of three separate voyages she made up the Hudson, mostly in the year 1835. The account terminates with her visit to the Catskill Mountain House, a famous hotel overlooking the Hudson Valley, that was the goal of innumerable travelers during the fashionable era of steamboat travel.

I WENT THREE TIMES up the Hudson; and, if I lived at New-York, should be tempted to ascend it three times a week during the summer. Yet the greater number of ladies on board the steamboat remained in the close cabin among the crying babies, even while we were passing the finest scenery of the river. They do not share the taste of a gentleman who, when I was there, actually made the steamboat his place of abode during the entire summer season, sleeping on board at Albany and New-York on alternate nights, and gazing at the shores all the day long with apparently undiminished delight.

* Excerpt from Harriet Martineau's *Retrospect of Western Travel* (London: 1838), Vol. I, pp. 43–63. All bracketed material is by the present editor.

The first time we went up the early part of the morning was foggy, and the mist hung about the ridge of the Palisades, the rocky western barrier of the river. There were cottages perched here and there, and trees were sprinkled in the crevices, and a little yellow strand, just wide enough for the fisherman and his boat, now and then intervened between the waters and the perpendicular rock. In the shadowy recesses of the shore war sloops moored. Seagulls dipped their wings in the gleams of the river, and the solitary fishhawk sailed slowly over the woods. I saw on the eastern bank a wide flight of steps cut in the turf, leading to an opening in the trees, at the end of which stood a white house, apparently in deep retirement. Farther on the river widened into the Tappan Sea, and then the hills rose higher behind the banks, and wandering gleams lighted up a mountain region here and there. The captain admitted us, as strangers (of course without any hint from us), into the wheel-room, which was shady, breezy, roomy, and commanding the entire view. Hence we were shown Mr. [Washington] Irving's cottage, the spot where André was captured, and the other interesting points of the scenery. Then the banks seemed to close, and it was matter for conjecture where the outlet was. The waters were hemmed in by abrupt and dark mountains, but the channel was still broad and smooth enough for all the steamboats in the republic to ride in safety. Ridges of rock plunged into the waters, garnished with trees which seemed to grow without soil; above them were patches of cultivation on the mountain sides, and slopes of cleared land, with white houses upon them. Doves flitted among the nearest trees, and gay rowboats darted from point to point from one island to another.

West Point, beautiful as it is, was always visible too soon. Yet to leave the boat was the only way to remain in sight of the Highlands; and the charms of the place itself are scarcely to be surpassed. The hotel is always full of good company in the season.[1] Mr. Cozens [*sic*] keeps a table for the officers, and is permitted to add as many guests as his house will hold; but, under such circumstances, he takes pains to admit only such as are fit company for his permanent boarders. The views from the hotel are fine, and there is such a provision of comfort and entertainment, that there would be no hardship in sitting within doors for a week; but we made the best use we could of our opportunities, and saw and achieved everything pertaining to the place, except mounting the Crow's Nest;[2] an expedition which the heat of the weather prevented our undertaking.

In some solitary spots of this settlement the stranger cannot help meditating on the vast materials of human happiness which are placed at the disposal of the real administrators of this great country. How great is the apparatus to be yet put to use! Here, where life is swarming all around, how few are the habitations of men! Here are woods climbing above woods to the clouds and stretching to the horizon, in which myriads of creatures are chirping, humming, and sporting; clefts whence the waters gush out; green slopes ready for the plough and the sickle; flat meadows with a few haycocks lying at the foot of mountains as yet untouched. Grasshoppers spring at every step one takes in the rich grass, and many a blue dragon-fly balances itself on the tips of the strongest blades; butterflies, green, black, white, and yellow, dazzle the eye that would follow them; yet how few men are near! A gay group on the steps of the hotel, a company of cadets parading on the green, the ferryman and his fare, and the owners of this, and that, and the other house perched upon the pinnacles of the hills; these are all as yet visible in a region which will hereafter be filled with speech and busy with thought.

27. *Hudson River Valley from Fort Putnam,* oil painting by George A. Boughton, n.d.; courtesy of The New-York Historical Society.

"The beauty from this elevated platform is really oppressive to the sense."

The view looking northeast to Cold Spring, N.Y., and Mount Taurus (Bull Hill) and Breakneck Mountain (Turk's Face).

On the steep above the landing-place I was introduced to Mr. [Washington] Irving, with whom I had a few minutes' conversation before he stepped into the ferry-boat which was to take him over to the [Cold Spring] foundry to dinner.[3] Many other persons with whom I was glad to have the opportunity of becoming acquainted were at the hotel. Mr. and Mrs. Morris[4] were our guides to Fort Putnam[5] after dinner; walkers as active and resolute as ourselves. The beauty from this elevated platform is really oppressive to the sense. One is glad to divert one's attention from its awful radiance by walking in precipitous places, by visiting the cell in which it is said, but doubtfully, that André was confined, or even by meditating on the lot of the solitary cow that has the honour of grazing in the midst of the only ruins that adorn American scenery.

A lady in the hotel offered to meet me on the housetop at five o'clock in the morning to see the sun rise. I looked out at three; there was a solitary light twinkling in the academy, and a faint gleam out of a cloudy sky upon the river. At five the sky was so thickly overspread with clouds that the expedition to the housetop had to be abandoned. The morning afterward cleared, and I went alone down to Kosciusko's Garden.[6] I loved this retreat at an hour when I was likely to have it to myself. It is a nook scooped, as it were, out of the rocky bank of the river, and reached by descending several flights of steps from the platform behind the hotel and academy. Besides the piled rocks and the vegetation with which they are clothed, there is nothing but a clear spring, which wells up in a stone basin inscribed with the hero's name. This was his favourite retreat; and here he sat for many hours in a day with his book and his thoughts. After fancying for some time that I was alone, and playing with the fountain and the leaves of the red beech and the maple, now turning into its autumnal scarlet,

I found, on looking up, that one of the cadets was stretched at length on a high projection of rock, and that another was coming down the steps. The latter accosted me, offering to point out to me the objects of interest about the place. We had a long conversation about his academical life.

The students apply themselves to mathematics during the first and second years; during the third, to mathematics, chemistry, and natural philosophy; and during the fourth, to engineering. There is less literary pursuit than they or their friends would like; but they have not time for everything. Their work is from seven in the morning till four in the afternoon, with the exception of two hours for meals. Then come drill and recreation, and then the evening parade. During six weeks (I think) of the summer they camp out, which some of the youths enjoy, while others like it so much less than living under a roof, that they take this time to be absent on furlough. The friends of others come to see them while the pretty spectacle of a camp is added to the attractions of the place. Every care is used that the proficiency should be maintained at the highest point that it can be made to reach. The classes consist of not less than one hundred and forty, of whom only forty graduate. Some find the work too hard; some dislike the routine; others are postponed; and by this careful weeding out the choicest are kept for the public service. This process may go some way towards accounting for the present unpopularity of the institution, and the consequent danger of its downfall. The number of disappointed youths, whose connexions will naturally bear a grudge against the establishment, must be great. There is a belief abroad that its principle and administration are both anti-republican; and in answer to an irresistible popular demand, a committee of Congress has been engaged in investigating both the philosophy and practice of this national military academy; for some time previous to which there was difficulty in obtaining the annual appropriation for its support. I have not seen the report of this committee, but I was told that the evidence on which it is founded is very unfavourable to the conduct of the establishment in a political point of view. The advantages of such an institution in securing a uniformity of military conduct in case of war, from the young soldiers of all the states having received a common education; in affording one meeting point where sectional prejudice may be dissolved; and in concentrating the attention of the whole union upon maintaining a high degree of proficiency in science, are so great, that it is no wonder that an indignant and honest cry is raised against those who would abolish it on account of its aristocratical tendencies. I rather think it is a case in which both parties are more than commonly right; that it is an institution which can scarcely be dispensed with, but which requires to be watched with the closest jealousy, that there may be no abuse of patronage, and no such combination as could lead to the foundation of a military aristocracy. . . .

The manners of the cadets are excellent. They are allowed, under restrictions, to mix with the company at Mr. Cozens's, and thus to be frequently into ladies' society. There is a book kept at the hotel, where every cadet must, at each visit, enter his name at length, and the duration of his stay.

The second time I was at West Point was during the camping-out season. The artillery drill in the morning was very noisy and grand to the ladies, who had never seen anything of the "pomp and circumstances of glorious war." Then the cadets retired to their tents, and the ladies flitted about all the morning, making calls on each other. When we had discharged this first of a traveller's duties, we sauntered to the cemetery. Never

did I see such a spot to be buried in. The green hill projects into the river so that the monumental pillar erected by the cadets to the comrade who was killed by the bursting of a gun in 1817 is visible from two long reaches.[7] One other accident had occurred a little while before; a cadet had been killed by a comrade in fencing. The tombs are few, and the inscriptions simple. Broad, spreading trees overshadow the long grass, and the whole is hemmed in, so intensely quiet, that no sound is to be heard but the plash of oars from below and the hum of insects around, except when the evening gun booms over the heights, or the summer storm reverberates among the mountains.

Such a storm I had beheld the evening before from the piazza of the hotel. I stayed from the parade to watch it. As the thick veil of rain came down, the mountains seemed to retire, growing larger as they receded. As the darkness advanced, the scene became strangely compound. A friend sat with me in the piazza, talking of the deepest subjects on which human thought can speculate. Behind us were the open windows of the hotel, where, by turning the head, we might see the dancing going on; the gallant cadets and their pretty partners, while all the black servants of the house ranged their laughing faces in the rear. The music of the ballroom came to us mingling with the prolonged bursts of thunder; and other and grander strains rose from the river, where two large steamboats, with their lights, moved like constellations on the water, conveying a regiment from Pennsylvania which was visiting the soldiery of New-York State. They sent up rockets into the murky sky, and poured new blasts of music from their band as they passed our promontory. Every moment the lightning burst; now illuminating the interior of a mass of clouds; now quivering from end to end of heaven; now shedding broad livid gleams, which suddenly revealed a solitary figure on the terrace, a sloop on the waters, and every jutting point of rock. Still the dance went on till the hour struck which abruptly called the youths away from their partners, and bade them hie to their tents.

On returning from the cemetery we found Mr. and Mrs. [Gouverneur] Kemble, from the opposite side of the river, waiting to offer us their hospitality; and we agreed to visit them in the afternoon. Mr. Kemble's boat awaited us at the landing-place by three o'clock, and we rowed about some time before landing on the opposite bank, so irresistible is the temptation to linger in this scene of magical beauty. The Catholic chapel of Coldspring is well placed on a point above the river; and the village, hidden from West Point by a headland, is pretty. From Mr. Kemble's we were to be treated with a visit to the Indian Fall, and were carried within half a mile of it by water.[8] We followed the brawling brook for that distance, when we saw the glistening of the column of water through the trees. No fall can be prettier for its size, which is just small enough to tempt one to climb. A gentleman of our party made the attempt; but the rocks were too slippery with wet weed, and he narrowly escaped a tumble of twenty feet into the dark pool below.[9] The boys, after bringing us branches of the black cherry, clustered with the fruit, found a safe and dry way up, and appeared waving their green boughs in triumph at the top of the rocks. The tide had risen so that the river was brimming full as we returned, and soft with the mountain shadows; but we landed at West Point in time to see the sun set twice, as it happened. At the landing-place we stood to see it drop behind the mountain; but just after we had bidden it good-night, I saw that a meditative cadet, lying at length upon a rock, was still basking in the golden light, and I ran up the steep to the piazza. There, in a gap between two summits, was the broad disk, as round as ever; and once more we saw it sink in a tranquillity almost as grand as the stormy grandeur of the preceding night. Then ensued the evening parade, guitar music in the hotel, and dancing in the camp.

This evening a lady and her daughter steamed down from Fishkill with a request to us to spend a few days there; and a clergyman steamed up from New-York with an invitation from Doctor [David] Hosack to visit him and his family at Hyde Park. We could not do both; and there was some difficulty in contriving to do either, anxiously as we desired it; but we presently settled that Fishkill must be given up, and that we must content ourselves with two days at Hyde Park.

The next morning I experienced a sensation which I had often heard of, but never quite believed in; the certainty that one has awakened in another world. Those who have travelled much know that a frequent puzzle, on waking from sound sleep in new places, is to know where one is; even in what country of the world. This night I left my window open close to my head, so that I could see the stars reflected in the river. When I woke the scene was steeped in the light of the sunrise, and as still as death. Its ineffable beauty was all; I remarked no individual objects; but my heart stood still with an emotion which I should be glad to think I may feel again whenever I really do enter a new scene of existence. It was some time before my senses were separately roused; during the whole day I could not get rid of the impression that I had seen a vision; and even now I can scarcely look back upon the scene as the very same which, at other hours, I saw clouded with earth-drawn vapors, and gilded by the common sun.

At eleven o'clock we left West Point; and I am glad that we felt sure at the time that we should visit it again; a design which we did not accomplish, as the place was ravaged by scarlet fever at the season of the next year that we had fixed for our visit. Mr. [Edward] Livingston, who had just returned from his French mission, was on board the boat.[10] My letters of introduction to him were at the bottom of my trunk; but we did not put off becoming acquainted till I could get at them. . . .

During the whole preceding year I had heard Mr. Livingston's name almost daily in connexion with his extremely difficult negotiations between the United States and France, or, rather, between President Jackson and Louis Philippe. I had read his dispatches (some of which were made public that were never designed to be so), and had not been quite satisfied as to their straightforwardness, but concluded, on the whole, that he had done as much as human wits could well do in so absurd, and perplexed, and dangerous a quarrel, where the minister had to manage the temper of his own potentate as well as baffle the policy of the European monarch. A desire for peace and justice was evident through the whole of Mr. Livingston's correspondence; and under all, a strong wish to get home. Here he was, now ploughing his way up his own beloved river, whose banks were studded with the country-seats of a host of his relations. He came to me on the upper deck, and sat looking very placid with his staff between his knees, and his strong observing countenance melting into an expression of pleasure when he described to me his enjoyment in burying himself among the mountains of Switzerland. He said he would not now hear of mountains anywhere else; at least not in either his own country or mine. He gave me some opinions upon the government of the King of the French which I little expected to hear from the minister of a democratic republic. We were deep in this subject when a great hissing of the steam made us look up and see that we were at Hyde Park, and that Dr. Hosack and a party of ladies were waiting for me on

the wharf. I repeatedly met Mr. Livingston in society in New-York the next spring [1836], when a deafness, which had been slight, was growing upon him, and impairing his enjoyment of conversation. The last time I saw him was at the christening of a grand-niece, when he looked well in health, but conversed little, and seemed rather out of spirits. Within a month of that evening he was seized with pleurisy, which would in all probability have yielded to treatment; but he refused medicine, and was carried off after a very short illness [May 23, 1836]. Dr. Hosack died some months before him [December, 1835]. How little did I think, as I now went from the one to the other, that both these vigorous old men would be laid in their graves even before my return home should call upon me to bid them farewell!

The aspect of Hyde Park from the river had disappointed me, after all I had heard of it.[11] It looks little more than a white house upon a ridge. I was therefore doubly delighted when I found what this ridge really was. It is a natural terrace, overhanging one of the sweetest reaches of the river; and, though broad and straight at the top, not square and formal, like an artificial embankment, but undulating, sloping, and sweeping between the ridge and the river, and dropped with trees; the whole carpeted with turf, tempting grown people, who happen to have the spirits of children, to run up and down the slopes, and play hide-and-seek in the hollows. Whatever we might be talking of as we paced the terrace, I felt a perpetual inclination to start off for play. Yet, when the ladies and ourselves actually did something like it, threading the little thickets and rounding every promontory, even to the farthest (which they call Cape Horn), I felt that the possession of such a place ought to make a man devout if any of the gifts of Providence can do so. To hold in one's hand that which melts all strangers' hearts is to be a steward in a very serious sense of the term. Most liberally did Dr. Hosack dispense the means of enjoyment he possessed. Hospitality is inseparably connected with his name in the minds of all who ever heard of it; and it was hospitality of the heartiest and most gladsome kind.

Dr. Hosack had a good library; I believe, one of the best private libraries in the country; some good pictures, and botanical and mineralogical cabinets of value. Among the ornaments of his house I observed some biscuits and vases once belonging to Louis XVI, purchased by Dr. Hosack from a gentleman who had them committed to his keeping during the troubles of the first French Revolution.

In the afternoon Dr. Hosack drove me in his gig round his estate, which lies on both sides of the high road; the farm on one side and the pleasure-grounds on the other. The conservatory is remarkable for America; and the flower-garden all that it can be under present circumstances, but the neighboring country people have no idea of a gentleman's pleasure in his garden, and of respecting it. On occasions of weddings and other festivities, the villagers come up into the Hyde Park grounds to enjoy themselves; and persons who would not dream of any other mode of theft, pull up rare plants, as they would wild flowers in the woods, and carry them away. Dr. Hosack would frequently see some flower that he had brought with much pains from Europe flourishing in some garden of the village below. As soon as he explained the nature of the case, the plant would be restored with all zeal and care; but the losses were so frequent and provoking as greatly to moderate his horticultural enthusiasm. We passed through the poultry-yard, where the congregation of fowls exceeded in number and bustle any that I had ever seen. We drove round his kitchen-garden too, where he had taken pains to grow every kind of vegetable which will flourish in that cli-

mate. Then crossing the road,[12] after paying our respects to his dairy of fine cows, we drove through the orchard, and round Cape Horn, and refreshed ourselves with the sweet river views on our way home. There we sat in the pavilion, and he told me much of De Witt Clinton, and showed me his own *Life of Clinton,* a copy of which he said should await me on my return to New-York. When that time came he was no more; but his promise was kindly borne in mind by his lady, from whose hands I received the valued legacy.

We saw some pleasant society at Hyde Park: among the rest, some members of the wide-spreading Livingston family, and the Rev. Charles Stewart, who lived for some years as missionary in the South Sea Islands, and afterward published a very interesting account of his residence there. His manners, which are particularly gentlemanly and modest, show no traces of a residence among the savages, or of the shifts and disorder of a missionary life; nor of any bad effects from the sudden fame which awaited him on his return into civilized life.[13] I remember with great pleasure a conversation we had by the riverside, which proved to me that he understands the philosophy of fame, knowing how to appropriate the good and reject the evil that it brings, and which deepened the respect I had entertained for him from the beginning of our acquaintance.

The Livingston family, one of the oldest, most numerous, and opulent in the States, has been faithful in the days of its greatness to its democratic principles. In Boston it seems a matter of course that the "first people" should be federalists; that those who may be aristocratic in station should become aristocratic in principle. The Livingstons are an evidence that this need not be. Amid their splendid entertainments in New-York, and in their luxurious retirements on the Hudson, they may be heard going further than most in defence of President Jackson's idiosyncracy. Their zeal in favour of Mr. Van Buren was accounted for by many from the natural bias of the first family in the state of New-York in favour of the first president furnished by the state; but there is no reason to find any such cause. The Livingstons have consistently advocated the most liberal principles through all changes; and that they retain their democratic opinions in the midst of their opulence and family influence is not the less honourable to them for their party having now the ascendency.

Dr. Hosack and his family accompanied us down to the wharf to see Mr. Stewart off by one boat and our party by another, when, on the third day of our visit, we were obliged to depart. Our hearts would have been more sorrowful than they were if we had foreseen that we should not enjoy our promised meeting with this accomplished and amiable family at New York.[14] . . .

The steamboat in which we left Hyde Park landed us at Catskill (thirty-one miles) at a little after three in the afternoon. Stages were waiting to convey passengers to the Mountain House,[15] and we were off in a few minutes, expecting to perform the ascending journey of twelve miles in a little more than four hours. We had the same horses all the way, and therefore set off at a moderate pace, though the road was for some time level, intersecting rich bottoms, and passing flourishing farmhouses, where the men were milking, and the women looked up from their work in the piazzas as we passed. Haymaking was going on in the fields, which appeared to hang above us at first, but on which we afterward looked down from such a height that the haycocks were scarcely distinguishable. It was the 25th of July, and a very hot day for the season. The roads were parched up, and every exposed thing that one handled on board the steamboat or in the stage made one flinch from the burning sensation. The panting horses, one of them bleeding at the mouth,

stopped to drink at a house at the foot of the ascent; and we wondered how, exhausted as they seemed, they would drag us up the mountain. We did not calculate on the change of temperature which we were soon to experience.

The mountain laurel conveyed by association the first impression of coolness. Sheep were browsing among the shrubs, apparently enjoying the shelter of the covert. We scrambled through deep shade for three or four miles, heavy showers passing over us, and gusts of wind bowing the tree-tops, and sending a shiver through us, partly from the sudden chillness, and partly from expectation and awe of the breezy solitude. On turning a sharp angle of the steep road, at a great elevation, we stopped in a damp green nook, where there was an arrangement of hollow trees to serve for water-troughs.[16] While the horses were drinking, the gusts parted the trees to the left, and exposed to me a vast extent of country lying below, checkered with light and shadow. This was the moment in which a lady in the stage said, with a yawn, "I hope we shall find something at the top to pay us for all this." Truly the philosophy of recompense seems to be little understood. In moral affairs people seem to expect recompense for privileges, as when children, grown and ungrown, are told that they will be rewarded for doing their duty; and here was a lady hoping for recompense for being carried up a glorious mountainside, in ease, coolness, leisure, and society, all at once. If it was recompense for the evil of inborn *ennui* that she wanted, she was not likely to find it where she was going to look for it.

After another level reach of road and another scrambling ascent I saw something on the rocky platform above our heads like (to compare great things with small) an illuminated fairy palace perched among the clouds in opera scenery; a large building, whose numerous window-lights marked out its figure from amid the thunder-clouds and black twilight which overshadowed it. It was now half past eight o'clock and a stormy evening. Every-thing was chill, and we were glad of lights and tea in the first place.

After tea I went out upon the platform in the front of the house, having been warned not to go too near the edge, so as to fall an unmeasured depth into the forest below. I sat upon the edge as a security against stepping over unawares. The stars were bright overhead, and had conquered half the sky, giving promise of what we ardently desired, a fine morrow. Over the other half the mass of thunderclouds was, I supposed, heaped to-gether, for I could at first discern nothing of the champaign which I knew must be stretched below. Sud-denly, and from that moment incessantly, gushes of red lightning poured out from the canopy, revealing not merely the horizon, but the course of the river, in all its windings through the valley. This thread of river, thus illuminated, looked like a flash of lightning caught by some strong hand and laid along in the valley. All the principal features of the landscape might, no doubt, have been discerned by this sulphurous light; but my whole attention was absorbed by the river, which seemed to come out of the darkness like an apparition at the sum-mons of my impatient will. It could be borne only for a short time; this dazzling, bewildering alternation of glare and blackness, of vast reality and nothingness. I was soon glad to draw back from the precipice and seek the can-dlelight within.

The next day was Sunday. I shall never forget, if I live to be a hundred, how the world lay at my feet one Sun-day morning. I rose very early, and looked abroad from my window, two stories above the platform. A dense fog, exactly level with my eyes, as it appeared, roofed in the whole plain of the earth; a dusky firmament in which the stars had hidden themselves for the day. Such is the account which an antediluvian spectator would probably have given it. This solid firmament had spaces in it, however, through which gushes of sunlight were poured, lighting up the spires of white churches, and clusters of farm buildings too small to be otherwise distinguished; and especially the river, with its sloops floating like motes in the sunbeam. The firmament rose and melted, or parted off into the likeness of snowy sky-mountains, and left the cool Sabbath to brood brightly over the land. What human interest sanctifies a bird's-eye view! I suppose this is its peculiar charm, for its charm is found to deepen in proportion to the growth of the mind. To an infant, a champaign of a hundred miles is not so much as a yard square of gay carpet. To the rustic it is less bewitching than a paddock with two cows. To the philosopher, what is it not! As he casts his eye over its glittering towns, its scattered hamlets, its secluded homes, its mountain ranges, church spires, and untrodden forests, it is a pic-ture of life; an epitome of the human universe; the com-plete volume of moral philosophy, for which he has sought in vain in all libraries. On the left horizon are the Green Mountains of Vermont, and at the right ex-tremity sparkles the Atlantic.[17] Beneath lies the forest where the deer are hiding and the birds rejoicing in song. Beyond the river he sees spread the rich plains of Connecticut; there, where a blue expanse lies beyond the triple range of hills, are the churches of religious Massachusetts sending up their Sabbath psalms; praise which is too high to hear, while God is not. The fields and waters seem to him to-day no more truly property than the skies which shine down upon them; and to think how some below are busying their thoughts this Sab-bath-day about how they shall hedge in another field, or multiply their flocks on yonder meadows, gives him a taste of the same pity which Jesus felt in his solitude

28. *View from the Mountain House, Catskill,* engraving by
W. H. Bartlett, 1836; courtesy of The New-York Historical
Society.

"After tea I went out upon the platform in the front of the
house, having been warned not to go too near the edge, so
as to fall an unmeasured depth into the forest below."

The hotel was destroyed by fire in 1963, but hikers and
campers still seek out the famous view of fifty linear miles
of the Hudson Valley.

when his followers were contending about which should be greatest. It seems strange to him now that man should call anything *his* but the power which is in him, and which can create somewhat more vast and beautiful than all that this horizon encloses. Here he gains the conviction, to be never again shaken, that all that is real is ideal; that the joys and sorrows of men do not spring up out of the ground, or fly abroad on the wings of the wind, or come showered down from the sky; that good cannot be hedged in, nor evil barred out; even that light does not reach the spirit through the eye alone, nor wisdom through the medium of sound or silence only. He becomes of one mind with the spiritual [George] Berkeley, that the face of nature itself, the very picture of woods, and streams, and meadows, is a hieroglyphic writing in the spirit itself, of which the retina is no interpreter. The proof is just below him (at least it came under my eye), in the lady (not American) who, after glancing over the landscape, brings her chair into the piazza, and, turning her back to the champaign, and her face to the wooden walls of the hotel, begins the study, this Sunday morning, of her lapful of newspapers. What a sermon is thus preached to him at this moment from a very hackneyed text! . . . To him who is already enriched with large divine and human revelations this scene is, for all its stillness, musical with divine and human speech; while one who has been deafened by the din of worldly affairs can hear nothing in this mountain solitude.

The march of the day over the valley was glorious, and I was grieved to have to leave my window for an expedition to the [Kaaterskill] Falls a few miles off.[18] The Falls are really very fine, or, rather, their environment; but I could see plenty of waterfalls elsewhere, but nowhere else such a mountain platform. However, the expedition was a good preparation for the return to my window. The little nooks of the road, crowded with bilberries, cherries, and alpine plants, and the quiet tarn, studded with golden water-lilies, were a wholesome contrast to the grandeur of what we had left behind us.

On returning, we found dinner awaiting us, and also a party of friends out of Massachusetts, with whom we passed the afternoon, climbing higher and higher among the pines, ferns, and blue-berries of the mountain, to get wider and wider views. They told me that I saw Albany, but I was by no means sure of it. This large city lay in the the landscape like an anthill in a meadow. Long before sunset I was at my window again, watching the gradual lengthening of the shadows and purpling of the landscape. It was more beautiful than the sunrise of this morning, and less so than that of the morrow. Of this last I shall give no description, for I would not weary others with what is most sacred to me. Suffice it that it gave me a vivid idea of the process of creation, from the moment when all was without form and void, to that when light was commanded, and there was light. Here, again, I was humbled by seeing what such things are to some who watch in vain for what they are not made to see. A gentleman and lady in the hotel intended to have left the place on Sunday. Having overslept that morning's sunrise, and arrived too late for that on Saturday, they were persuaded to stay till Monday noon; and I was pleased, on rising at four on Monday morning, to see that they were in the piazza below, with a telescope. We met at breakfast, all faint with hunger, of course.

"Well, Miss M.," said the gentleman, discontentedly, "I suppose you were disappointed in the sunrise."

"No, I was not."

"Why, do you think the sun was any handsomer here than in New-York?"

I made no answer; for what could one say? But he

drove me by questions to tell what I expected to see in the sun.

"I did not expect to see the sun green or blue."

"What did you expect, then?"

I was obliged to explain that it was the effect of the sun on the landscape that I had been looking for.

"Upon the landscape! Oh! but we saw that yesterday."

The gentleman was perfectly serious; quite earnest in all this. When we were departing, a foreign tourist was heard to complain of the high charges! High charges! As if we were to be supplied for nothing on a perch where the wonder is if any but the young ravens get fed! When I considered what a drawback it is in visiting mountain-tops that one is driven down again almost immediately by one's bodily wants, I was ready to thank the people devoutly for harbouring us on any terms, so that we might think out our thoughts, and compose our emotions, and take our fill of that portion of our universal and eternal inheritance.

14.

James S. Buckingham

1838 *

INTRODUCTION: James Silk Buckingham (1786–1855), author, traveler, journalist, lecturer, and member of Parliament, followed his compatriot, Harriet Martineau, up the Hudson in 1838. Having failed to be reelected to the House of Commons after a four-year term in which he consistently advocated liberal social reforms, he decided to spend the next four years (1837–1841) traveling and lecturing in America. Buckingham had become something of a celebrity by this time; in 1823 he had been expelled from India because he had presumed to criticize the policies of the East India Company in the pages of his newspaper, the liberal *Calcutta Journal.* Upon returning to England he resumed his journalistic career by founding the *Athenaeum* (1828), the magazine that was later to become the vehicle for some of the greatest writers of the nineteenth century. In subsequent years Buckingham traveled throughout Europe and Asia as well as America, and built up considerable reputation as the author of innumerable travel books. His youngest son, Leicester Silk Buckingham, became a well-known playwright of the 1860s.

Buckingham's trip up the Hudson in the early summer of 1838 was not entirely voluntary. The previous year while traveling along the coast of the Atlantic seaboard he contracted a severe case of what was then called "the American plague," the little-understood malaria and yellow fever that tormented all American summers from the seventeenth to the end of the nineteenth century. Suffering from a recurrence of the disease in the late spring of 1838, Buckingham was advisd by his physician —as he tells us in the opening of the following narrative —to go up the Hudson and take refuge in the Catskill Mountains. It was a standard prescription. The belief that the higher elevations of the mountainous parts of the Atlantic seaboard were the safest places to go during the season of "the fevers" was universal to the age, and it had a strong influence on the development of the first American resorts in the upper Hudson Valley and the consequent rise in steamship travel during the two summer months. As early as 1827 Captain Basil Hall, another English traveler who ascended the Hudson, noted that "during the hot season of the year—when the greater part of the United States becomes unhealthy, or otherwise disagreeable as a residence, even to the most acclimated natives, as the local expression is—the inhabitants repair to the North, to those spots in particular [Saratoga and Ballston Spa], which are consequently much crowded during July and August, and sometimes during September." † The Catskills, as we have already noted, became at this time another favorite refuge of the well-to-do of the Atlantic seaboard—and especially the world-famous Catskill Mountain House, which we have already visited with Harriet Martineau and which we now visit again with the ailing James S. Buckingham.

AS THE WEATHER continued sultry, and I derived less benefit from medicine than it was thought likely I should do from change of air, I was advised by my physician to embark at once upon the Hudson river, and go straight to the village of Catskill, without halting at any intermediate point, but on landing there, to ascend the mountains, and pass a night or two at the Mountain House, the elevation of which secures a cool and bracing

* Excerpt from James Silk Buckingham's *America, Historical, Statistic, and Descriptive* (London: 1841), Vol. II, Chap. XIII, 236–267.

† Captain Basil Hall, *Lands in North America in the Years 1827 and 1828* (Edinburgh: 1830), 3 Vols., 3rd Edition, Vol. II, p. 9.

29. *A Brisk Gale, Bay of New York,* aquatint engraved by
W. J. Bennett, 1838; courtesy of the I. N. Phelps Stokes
Collection, Prints Division, New York Public Library.

"At every hundred yards, and often less, we met schooners and
sloops under sail . . . giving great life and animation to the
scene."

atmosphere, while all the lower parts of the country are steeped in sultry heat.

On the morning of Saturday, the 23rd of June, we [1] accordingly embarked at seven o'clock, on board the steamer for Albany, and found there between four or five hundred passengers bound up the river. The vessel was of large size, with ample accommodations, and engines of great power, so that her average speed when under way was not less than fourteen miles per hour.

Leaving the wharf at the foot of Barclay Street, we proceeded upwards on our course, having on our right the continuous lines of wharves, ships, steamers, and small craft, which fringe the western edge of New York, as the larger vessels do the banks of the East River on the other side of the town. [2] At every hundred yards, and often less, we met schooners and sloops under sail, coming down the Hudson, with a leading wind from the eastward, while as many were passed by us upward-bound; the number of these small craft—with their clean, well cut, and well trimmed sails, and vanes lengthened out into broad pennants, after the manner of the Dutch, from whom this custom is, no doubt, derived—being sometimes as many as a hundred all in sight at once, and giving great life and animation to the scene.

We passed the hills of Hoboken on our left; scattered over which, were many beautiful villas, the country-seats of opulent merchants and others from New York; the position of Hoboken combining the advantages of fine air, extensive view, beautiful woods, and close proximity to the city, there being a steam ferry-boat that crosses the Hudson at this point continuously throughout the day.

A little above this, on the same side of the river, and distant from the city about six miles, is a spot called Weehawken, which is memorable as the usual duel-ground of this quarter. It is close to the river's edge, and screened in from the land-view by surrounding rocks, which gives it the privacy usually sought in such encounters. Here it is that the well-known General [Alexander] Hamilton fell in a duel with the then notorious, and it may now be added, infamous Colonel [Aaron] Burr. The St. Andrew's Society of New York erected a monument to the memory of the General, which continued for some years to occupy the spot where he fell; but since the removal of his remains to the burial-ground of Trinity Church, in Broadway, the monument has been removed also, and one has been erected to his memory near the church named. [3]

About two miles beyond this, and eight from New York, the western bank of the river begins to assume a very remarkable appearance, presenting all along, on that margin of the stream, a perpendicular wall of rock, varying from 100 to 500 feet in height, sometimes perfectly bare, and sometimes partially covered with brushwood, but always showing the perpendicularity which constitutes its most striking feature, and carrying along on its summits the sharp and broken edge of a precipice, while at the foot of the cliff below there is often neither beach nor platform; so that the river bathes the solid wall of rock as it rises perpendicularly from the stream.

These cliffs extend for nearly twenty miles along the western bank of the Hudson, and are called "The Palisadoes," a name given, probably, from the ribbed appearance of some parts of the cliff, which seem like rude basaltic columns, or huge trunks of old and decayed trees, placed close together in a perpendicular form, for a barricade or defence. The water is deep close to their feet, being what is called, in nautical language "a bold shore"; and the small sloops and schooners that navigate the stream were often so close to the cliffs, that a biscuit might be thrown on shore from them; sometimes, indeed, it would seem as if they were determined to run their bowsprits into the rock, as they did not tack till their

30. *The Hudson Highlands from Peekskill & Cold Spring Road near Garrison's Landing,* colored lithograph by Currier & Ives, 1857; courtesy of The New-York Historical Society.

"The range of hills, called the Highlands, approach close to the water, and hem in the stream on either side."

stems were within a few feet of the cliff, making their evolutions interesting and picturesque.

Here and there, however, a break in the cliffs would show a little bit of lawn sloping down to the stream, and a pretty little cottage peeping out from the wood in which it was embosomed; and sometimes at the foot of a narrow ravine, would be seen a humble shed, either of a river-fisherman, a quarry, or some other labourer to whom this locality was acceptable. The opposite or eastern bank of the river was only of moderate height, cultivated, wood, and dotted over with dwellings at intervals, so as to contrast agreeably with the western cliffs.

In the course of our progress along the palisadoes, and about four miles after their commencement, there were pointed out to us the sites of two remarkable forts: one of them, called Fort Lee, which stood on the very edge and summit of the western cliffs, at an elevation of 300 feet above the level of the river; and the other called Fort Washington, which stood on the opposite side of the stream, on a moderately elevated hill.[4] This latter fort was taken by the British in 1776, and the garrison, consisting of 2,600 troops, were captured as prisoners of war. Fort Lee soon after surrendered also, but these were only temporary disasters in the glorious effort by which the oppressed colonists of Britain achieved their independence.

At the termination of the Palisadoes, the river, which hitherto continues its breadth of about a mile, suddenly expands to a width varying from two to five miles, and is here called Tappan Bay, the increased breadth continuing for a distance of about eight miles. This spot is also consecrated in American history, for, close by the little village of Tappan, which gives its name to the bay, is pointed out the grave of André, whose connection with the conspiracy of the traitor Arnold is well known; and whose remains, as that of a British officer, were given up at the request of the British government, and conveyed to England for interment there, a few years ago.[5]

On the eastern shore of the Hudson, and near the northern termination of Tappan Bay, is the state-prison for criminals, called Sing-Sing. It presents a very singular appearance from the river, being a mass consisting of several low ranges of buildings, quite close to the water's edge, and, from being built of white marble, it has a snowy, and, in some positions of the sun, even a dazzling appearance. It was my intention, had my health permitted, to have visited Sing Sing and West Point, in our progress up the river; but the interdict under which I was placed by my physician forbade it, and I was therefore compelled to reserve my examination of these two interesting spots—interesting, of course, from very different causes, the one as a place of punishment, the other as a place of education—till some future time.

About twenty miles beyond the bay of Tappan, and forty from New York, the scenery of the river becomes changed again, and the range of hills, called the Highlands, approach close to the water, and hem in the stream on either side. The entrance into this channel is strikingly picturesque; and, with the full-green foliage of the month of June, and the countless sailing and steam vessels going up and down the river, some of the latter like floating warehouses (laden with two or three tiers of decks filled with cargo) few prospects can be imagined more romantic, more stirring, or more beautiful. The hills rise abruptly in steep angles from the stream, and present, for a distance of nearly twenty miles, a succession of bluff headlands or promontories, all, however, clothed with underwood from their base to their summits; and the ravines or valleys between them are as beautiful as the hills themselves. The windings round the promontories present a series of lakes, in which the spectator seems land-locked, as the continuation of the

31. *View of West Point from the Landing at Garrison,* anonymous lithograph, 1860; courtesy of The New-York Historical Society.

"About half-past ten we arrived opposite to West Point."

river is not visible either above or below, from the overlapping or interlacing of the headlands of the one side with the projecting capes of the other. This is particularly the case at a spot called "the Horse Race," where the stream makes a bend, running nearly east and west, its general direction being north and south.[6] The hills on either side approach closer to each other here, and the contraction of the river's breadth, contrasted with the height of the overhanging hills which rise from 1,200 to 1,500 feet—higher than the highest peak of the rock of Gibraltar, and with almost as steep an angle of ascent—give the whole a very striking and imposing appearance.

Here, too, the recollections of the revolutionary war are preserved in the names of Fort Montgomery and Fort Clinton,[7] which were captured from General [Israel] Putnam by the British troops in 1777;[8] and in the name of a sheet of water in the rear of Fort Clinton, called "Bloody Pond," [9] from the crimson tinge given to the waters by the number of slain thrown into it after the sanguinary battle and dreadful carnage, of which that fort was the scene.

About half-past ten we arrived opposite to West Point, having performed the distance of fifty miles in about three hours and a half, making good the rate of fourteen miles an hour. The approach to this spot is highly interesting. On the west side of the Hudson, a promontory of moderate height, from 150 to 200 feet above the level of the river, projects into the stream, so as to require a sharp turn round its extremity to follow the course of the river on the other side. On the upper, or level part of this promontory, are placed the buildings of the Military Academy, at which all the cadets intended to form the officers of the United States are educated; and above these, on a commanding elevation of about 600 feet, are the ruins of Fort Putnam, one of the most impregnable of the American fortresses during the revolutionary war.

The position of the fortress, and of the batteries on West Point, gave them a complete command of the river up and down, as far as the range of the cannon could extend; and every effort of the British, during eight years of warfare, to wrest them from the brave hands that defended both, were unsuccessful.[10] Fort Putnam is dismantled and in ruins, there being no apparent necessity for such inland fortresses at present: and the policy and the interest of the country being pacific, centuries may elapse before they are ever required again.

The establishment at West Point is still, however, maintained with full efficiency, and the beauty, as well as the interesting nature of the spot, occasions it to be much frequented. To accommodate the large number of visitors here in the summer, a spacious and splendid hotel was built by the government, and leased out to a proper superintendent; but after a few years of trial, it became so attractive that it was thought injurious to the good discipline of the students to continue it; and, therefore, it was ordered to be shut up.[11] The building still occupies its original position, and forms a fine object from the river, but it is quite untenanted at present.

I had letters of introduction to Colonel De Russey and Colonel [Sylvanus] Thayer,[12] the officers in command at West Point, as I had originally intended to have passed a few days here; but my present debility rendered it imprudent to attempt it now. I therefore passed on, without landing, reserving my visit till another opportunity. We admired exceedingly, however, the beautiful appearance of the place, saw with pleasure the pillared monument erected to the memory of the brave Polish patriot, Kosciusko, who resided here, and tilled with his own hands a quiet little garden,[13] which he made his favourite retreat, and which is still carefully preserved; as well as an obelisk erected to the memory of General Brown, who was educated at West Point, and afterwards fell in the defence of Fort Erie,[14] in the last short American war with the English, in 1814.

The termination of the Highland scenery is about six miles above West Point, where two frowning hills over-hang the stream on either side; the one called Break-neck, and the other Butter Hill [Storm King]; and be-tween these, in the centre of the river, rises a mass of rock, called Pollopel Island.[15] The height of the over-hanging hills is here also from 1,200 to 1,500 feet, and the scene is one of great grandeur and beauty.

Beyond this, the character of the landscape changes into a softer and more subdued style. The river again expands in breadth; the shores on either side are well cultivated in rising slopes, and studded with small vil-lages, separate farm-houses, and private dwellings; while the incorporated town of Newburgh, just above the smaller village of New Windsor, displays itself on a com-manding elevation and presents a striking appearance from the river. It is a rising and flourishing place of trade, containing already a population of about 10,000, annually on the increase. The buildings have all that newness and freshness of appearance which is so char-acteristic of American settlements; and being built chiefly of wood (though there are many fine stone houses in Newburgh), and painted, with white walls, relieved by bright-green Venetian windows and blinds, they seem as if they were hardly a month old. There are several large hotels, an Episcopalian church with a lofty steeple, and a Presbyterian church with a gilded cupola or dome, the first I had seen in the country; and these, rising from the mass of well-built houses, symmetrically arranged, and sloping down the steep bank of the Hudson on the west, gave the whole town a commanding air, and pleas-ing aspect.

Among the whole is preserved, with great care, the "stone house" in which General Washington held his head-quarters when the revolutionary army was en-camped here;[16] and many continue to visit it, as a spot rendered sacred by its former occupier, and by the cause in which he fought. On the eastern bank of the river rises a lofty eminence called Beacon Hill, which is 1,500 feet high, and a little to the south of it is another peak, about 1,700 feet high. These are both called Beacon Hills [or North and South Beacon Hills], because, during the revo-lutionary war, signals were made from their summits by fires. They are often frequented by visitors, especially the former, as, from its summit the view extends into five different states, namely, Vermont, New Hampshire, Mas-sachusetts, Connecticut, and New York.[17]

About fifteen miles beyond Newburgh but on the op-posite side of the river, on the east, is another of those rising and flourishing towns of which America is so full, namely Poughkeepsie. It contains a population of about 10,000, but is even more rapidly augmenting its numbers than Newburgh. Occupying an elevated position, it is seen as a conspicuous object in the river scenery, both in ascending and in descending the stream. Its principal source of wealth is its manufactures, and of these the principal branch is silk, there being a company engaged in this, with a capital of 200,000 dollars. A variety of manufactures in hardware are also carried on, and a peculiarly beautiful screw has been manufactured here by machine, for which a patent has been taken out, which, from its mathematical precision in all its parts, is likely to supersede every other kind of screw in use, it being far superior to any other in quality, and quite as cheap in price. A little to the north of Poughkeepsie, and on the same side of the river, are several very pretty country-seats, at a spot called Hyde Park, which abounds in beautiful landscape views.

At three o'clock we arrived at the intended place of our debarkation, Catskill, and, having dined on board the boat, we landed here, and entered the stage-coach, which was waiting on the wharf, with a party of three or four fellow-passengers from New York, making, with Mrs. Buckingham, my son, and myself, six in all. The stage was a large open coach, designed for nine inside passengers, a front and back seat for three each, and a central cross seat, midway between these two, for three more; and we were heartily glad that it was not likely to be filled, as the heat was oppressive, and in my weak and exhausted condition I should have felt the pressure painfully.

The word "kill" signifies, it is said, in Dutch, "creek": and hence the number of names in the rivers of those parts of America settled by the Dutch, with this termination: such as Schuyl[er]kill, Fishkill, etc. This village stands on a small creek, which flows through it towards the Hudson, and contains about 5,000 inhabitants, the buildings being chiefly of wood.

We left the village, and rattled on, with four stout horses and a skilful driver, at a rate which soon made me long for the English roads instead of American ones. We had been told, on inquiry, that the road to the foot of the mountain, which is about nine miles, was level and excellent, and that it was only the ascent of the mountain itself, about three miles more, that was at all rough or disagreeable. The standard of excellence differs, however, in different countries and in different minds. In any part of Europe the road would have been thought bad, but in England it would have been called execrable. There was no remedy, however, but patience; though it required a large exercise of this to sustain the jolts and shocks, which were almost enough to dislocate a weak frame and shake it to pieces. The road was not only full of deep ruts and large masses of rock, by which elevation and depression sometimes succeeded each other so rapidly that the transition was fearful; but there was a perpetual succession of steep ascents and descents, instead of a level road, nearly all the way to the foot of the mountain.[18]

The country looked beautiful, however, on either side. The wood predominated in the track we passed: but at intervals small patches of cleared land appeared, the trunks of the felled trees still remaining a foot or two above the ground, and wheat, barley, rye, and grass occupying the general surface. Many rivulets crossed the road, and it was deemed a sufficient bridge over these to lay along a few rough trunks of trees, or a few loose planks; the sensation of passing over which, at a full trot, and sometimes a gallop, may be better imagined than described.

It took us about two hours and a half, over this rugged road, to reach the foot of the mountain; our rate of speed, upon the whole, therefore, being hardly four miles an hour. Here we drew up at an inn,[19] and supposed that a pair of fresh horses, if not the entire four, would have been put in, to complete our journey up the steep ascent; but it was not the custom to change at all, as it had been found, by experience, that the same horses could perform the whole distance without being distressed. We accordingly set forth again upon our way. We had scarcely commenced the ascent, however, before the clouds began to lower overhead, and there was every indication of an approaching thunder-storm. In less than half an hour it burst upon us with all its fury. The lightning was most vivid, the rattling of the thunder deafening, and its prolonged reverberation in the hollows of the surrounding mountains, grand in the extreme. The rain, too, fell in torrents, the drops being so heavy as to make an impression as large as a dollar on the rocky masses which formed part of our road; and these were succeeded by a rattling hail-shower, which completely chilled the air. During the first burst of the storm, the horses stopped; but there being a guard against the descent of the coach behind, in the shape of a large iron fork, which, as the coach receded backward, plunged into the road, and prevented its going farther, we were at ease respecting our safety. The driver managed his team not only with great skill, but with great tenderness also; for he permitted them to halt for breath in the steep ascent every five minutes at least; and when they had sufficiently rested, said to them, "Come, my joys, set out again," as if he had been addressing men instead of cattle; and the horses understood these good English phrases quite as well as the unmeaning sounds of "gee-whoap, gee-whoah, and meather-ho!" with which English carters and ploughmen accost their beasts; and once or twice he said, "Now mind, if you don't get us well up the hill, I must get others that will." They set out invariably at the word of command, and the whip was not once used, nor its sound ever heard, from the commencement to the end of our journey; and I confess, I thought the substitution of the vocal organs for the lash a great improvement, and one worthy of universal imitation.

Our road wound up the mountain-side with a steep rising or ascending slope of rock, clothed with wood on our right hand, or above us, and deep glens and ravines, with a similar or still greater profusion of wood on our left hand, or below us; the road often going on the very edge of the precipice, several hundred feet in depth, over which a timid traveller would every moment expect to be thrown. But no accident of any kind has occurred on this mountain road for many years past; an honourable testimony to the skill, sobriety, and care of the drivers.

About half-way up the ascent we became completely enveloped in a thin blue mist, so as to be unable to see a dozen yards before us. Patches of this would sometimes clear away, and then unfold to us peeps of beautiful views through the opening foliage below us. To this again succeeded a second thunder storm more violent, and with heavier rain than the first; until after two hours' tedious climbing—for our very slow and broken pace might aptly so be called—and with intervals of thunder, lightning, wind, rain, and momentary gleams of sunshine and mist, we reached the hotel called the Mountain House, about half-past seven, having been four hours and a half performing the distance of twelve miles from the landing. We found here a small party of about a dozen persons only, as the season was yet early, so that we had an ample choice of rooms; and our fatigue was so great, that we were glad to retire as early as possible, after we had taken refreshments, to rest.

We passed the whole of Sunday at the Mountain House, as completely shut out from the world below, as if we had been elevated to another planet; for the mist or fog continued so intense during the greater part of the day, that we could barely see the foundations of the house we occupied; and at some moments the mist so completely enveloped the house, that not a particle of the ground around or near it could be distinguished, so that our dwelling was like an aerial mansion suspended among the clouds. I never remember to have been placed in any situation in which I felt so strongly the impression of complete isolation from the world.

The hotel is a large edifice, built of wood, within a few feet only of the brink of a precipice of perpendicular rock, about 100 feet in depth, overhanging the brow of the mountain below. It thus stands on a level platform of rock, which occupies an area of about six acres, having a rising elevation on the south, and several higher peaks on the west; but the eastern slope of the mountain being continuous downward, from the Mountain House to the plain. The elevation of the hotel above the river Hudson, is 2,212 feet measured barometrically; but there are other peaks of the same range of mountains in the vicinity which have an altitude of 3,800 feet.[20]

The Mountain House has a frontage of 140 feet, with a depth of only 24;[21] so that it is extremely narrow in proportion to its length. A separate wing furnishes a series of drawing rooms, of the extent of about 50 feet by 20; and there is a large verandah, or piazza, with lofty wooden pillars in the eastern front of the house, for the promenade of visitors, with a long dining-room, divided by a range of central pillars, in the sub-area or lowermost story; but all the upper part of the house is subdivided into very small bed-rooms for the accommodation of large numbers, to the extent it is said of 200, which number of visitors they sometimes have in the months of July and August, but the present is considered the earliest part of the season, when few persons are here.

We found the accommodation more agreeable than we had anticipated, as the rooms and beds were perfectly clean, the servants numerous and attentive. The table, however, was, like all the American tables of hotels, steam-boats, and boarding houses that we had yet seen, more remarkable for the superabundance of food than skill or delicacy in preparing it. I had often thought that we might be too fastidious in our tastes, though my whole family were, like myself, partial to plain dishes and simple food, and in England were always classed among those least attached to the pleasures of the table; but though the native Americans are generally insensible to the defects of their culinary preparations, all persons who have travelled in Europe return deeply convinced of their national inferiority in this particular. . . .

On the morning of Monday the 18th [25th?] of June, we were all stirring at daylight, in order to enjoy the prospect of the rising sun. On looking out of the windows, the scene that presented itself was most remarkable, and totally different from any thing I had ever before witnessed.[22] The sky above us was a bright clear blue, slightly mottled with white fleecy clouds, as in the finest summer mornings of England. But of the earth beneath us, nothing was to be seen except the rocky platform on which our habitation was built, and a small portion of the brow of the hill on which this stood. All the rest of the great expanse before us, extending to a distance of from 40 to 50 miles, was covered with a thick sea of perfectly white billows, as if there had been a general deluge, and we were occupying the summit of the Ararat[23] which alone rose above the wide waste of waters around us. . . . It was altogether the most striking and impressive scene I had ever beheld, and could never be forgotten if life were prolonged to a thousand years.

While we were gazing with unspeakable admiration on this singular and beautiful cloudy sea, the increasing light of the eastern horizon, betokened the near approach of the sun. All eyes were accordingly turned in that direction, and in a few moments the bright and splendid orb rose up from his eastern bed, with a fulness of glory, that seemed like the dawn of a new creation. . . .

About an hour after sunrise, we began to discover a partial breaking away of the cloudy awning, or rather the opening of patches and spaces in it, which bespoke its approaching dissolution. The first place in which this was visible, was over the channel of the Hudson river, the track of which could be plainly traced, by a corresponding hollow, or long and winding valley in this misty sea. The next places were close by the sides of the mountain on which we stood, where little slits, or loop-holes, gradually opened, through which we could peep downward, and see, at a great distance below, the green fields, and thick woods, with little farm-houses, just visible as white spots on a speckled plain.

At ten o'clock the mist had so cleared away over the

Hudson, that its stream became visible, but no portion of the green banks of the river could be seen on either side, so that it was like a mighty stream winding its way through a bed of clouds. At eleven, large hollow patches in the mass of clouds opened in several places, so as to enable us to see corresponding portions of the earth's surface through them. . . .

By noon, the whole of the clouds below us were dissipated, and the full glory of a meridian sun beamed down upon one of the most extensive and beautiful landscapes that could be well conceived. Behind us, to the westward, rose the peaks of mountains higher by a thousand feet and more, than the summit of that on which we stood, and completely intercepting all further view in that direction. To the east, however, the prospect was almost boundless. At the foot of the steep slope of the range beneath our feet, commenced the cultivated plain, covered with cleared land, in farms of different sizes and in different degrees of cultivation, interspersed with patches of thick wood, or variegated trees, and dotted over with farm-houses, country residences, and other buildings. This plain continued for seven or eight miles in a straight line, till it reached the western bank of the Hudson.

Beyond that stream, the lands, equally fertile, and as extensively cleared and cultivated, rose gradually in an ascending slope till it terminated in a range of hills, at a distance of forty or fifty miles, intercepting the eastern horizon, and bounding the view in that direction. In the centre of the valley or plain, and between these distant ranges of eastern and western elevation, flowed down the noble river, which could be distinctly traced along its path for thirty miles at least, here contracting its channel between abrupt projecting bluffs—there expanding it into ample bays—and several times, throughout its length, having its current interrupted by beautifully-fertile islands; while its surface was studded with at least a hundred sails, as white as the fresh-fallen snow, floating on its glassy bosom, like so many buoyant pearls.

Altogether the prospect was enchanting, and worth going a hundred miles to see. . . .

Soon after noon, we left the Mountain House for the river, to embark for Albany. On our way down, the bright sunshine, clear atmosphere, and perpetual vistas of beauty through the trees, made a pleasant contrast to the thunder-storms and mists of our ascent. We found the way therefore more agreeable; but on the road from the foot of the mountain to the village—the dislocating jolts and shocks were repeated: and it seemed to me that I had been more bruised and beaten by this ride of twelve miles, than I could be in Europe by the longest journey that could be undertaken.

We reached the wharf at the landing-place about three; and the steam-boat from New York arriving soon after, we re-embarked and proceeded onward to Albany, with a still larger company of passengers, and in a larger and finer boat than that in which we had come thus far.

From Catskill to Albany the river appeared narrower than below, and the banks became more tame in scenery; but they everywhere preserve the most exuberant fertility, and are thickly interspersed with towns, villages, hamlets, and single dwellings.

About five miles beyond Catskill, to the north, are two towns, occupying opposite banks of the river, that on the east being the city of Hudson, of Dutch foundation, and called after the navigator who has given his name to the river; and that on the west being the incorporated village of Athens. The first of these, which contains about 6,000 inhabitants, exhibits in its architecture and the colouring of its houses, the origin from whence it has sprung. The latter, containing about 1,500 inhabitants, is of much more recent date, and exhibits, accordingly, a newness and freshness in the style and hue of its buildings, which makes it look gayer and lighter than its opposite neighbour.

To be called upon by some fellow passenger to look around and see Athens, appears at first like a joke; it seems too difficult to separate from the sound of that word the glories of the immortal city of Minerva, with its frowning Acropolis, its beautiful Parthenon, its Temple of Theseus, and its classically-sacred associations. . . . But all this dream of the imagination vanishes the moment the eye reposes on the humble village which here assumes this imposing name.

It is not peculiar, however, to any part of America more than another, thus to appropriate to itself the most renowned names of history for their cities, towns, and villages; everywhere this singularly ill-directed taste is apparent. From New York to Albany, within the compass of a single day's journey, including the valley of the Hudson and its neighbourhood, we have Babylon and Jericho, Salem, Lebanon, Gilboa, Carmel, Goshen, Athens, Troy, with a railroad to Syracuse, Utica, and Rome, from among the ancient cities and places of celebrity; and Oxford, Canterbury, Salisbury, Windsor, Hamburgh, Hyde Park, Kingston, Glasgow, Bristol, Durham, Cairo, Bath, Cambridge and Waterford, from among the modern. The evil of this is increased by the constant repetition of the same practice in different States, so that there are no less than 14 places bearing the name of Athens, and 9 of Rome, besides a Romeo and a Romulus, 14 Palmyras, 12 Alexandrias, 4 of Damascus, 2 of Joppa, and 3 of Jerusalem. . . .

At five o'clock we came in sight of Albany, having passed several small villages and landing-places on the way, and rapidly approached the town. The appearance presented by it was interesting, and full of promise. The slope of the western bank, on which it stands, represents a city rising upward from the shore of the river to an elevated ridge of land, and the number of towers and domes scattered among the general mass of dwellings, one of them, that of the City Hall, having its surface gilded, and several others of a burnished and dazzling white, being overlaid with plating of zinc and tin, gave to the whole a very brilliant aspect.

At half-past five we reached the wharf, the boat having accomplished her voyage from New York, of about 150 miles in a period of ten hours and a half, going, therefore, nearly fifteen miles an hour the whole way. This triumph of steam navigation is felt in its fullest force by a voyage upon the Hudson, and especially on arriving at Albany, as it is the very route on which the first experiment was made, the record of which is at once so affecting and so instructive that it cannot be made too widely known. . . .

If Fulton and his then doubting friends could but be raised from the dead, and witness now the triumphs of steam on the Hudson and the Mississippi, the Ganges, the Indus, the Tigris, the Euphrates, and the Nile, and still later, across the broad Atlantic, the sensations of both would be very different to those by which they were animated on the first experimental voyage.

PART V *The Upper River*

The Sources of the Hudson

The Upper River, 1836–1880

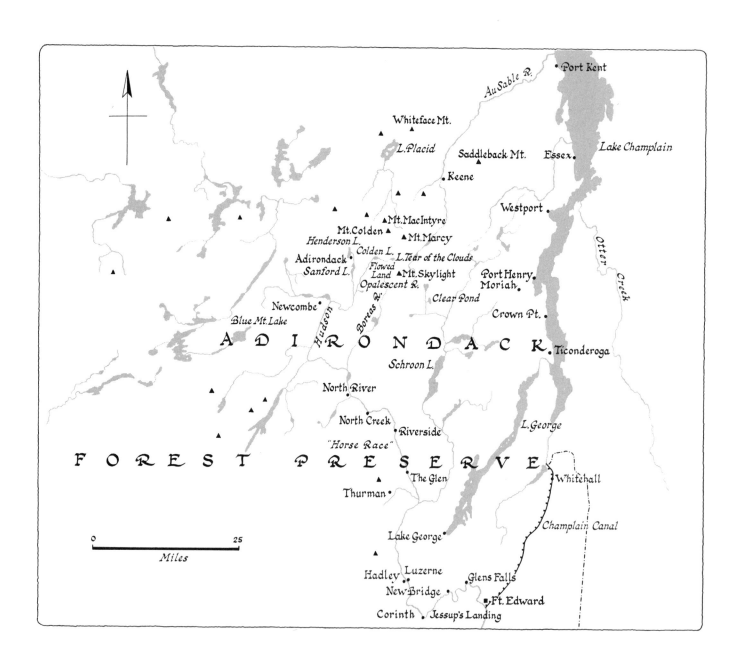

PART V *Introduction*

THE CHRONICLES of the Hudson follow the course of colonization and history up the navigable reaches of the river to Albany, thence west up the Mohawk or north to the deep waters of the Champlain corridor. Yet from Albany north the river has only traveled halfway from its source, and from Fort Edward, where pioneers left the Hudson for the overland trek to Lake Champlain, the river was still a hundred miles from its unknown origins. Thus a third of the total length of the Hudson has remained *fluvius incognitus* and outside the chronicles of recorded history. Discovery and exploration awaited the third decade of the nineteenth century. Why this is so becomes dramatically clear in the following two narratives of that portion of the Hudson which has never been tamed by human history.

15.
William C. Redfield 1836–37 *

INTRODUCTION: For more than two hundred years after the Dutch first established the colony of New Netherland the sources of the Hudson remained a well-kept secret of the unnamed peaks and passes of the Adirondack Mountains. The known river above tidewater terminated, as we have suggested, at Fort Edward or Glens Falls where pioneers left the Hudson for the portage to Lake George or the Woodcreek, thence on to Lake Champlain. Above Fort Edward the river became an unnavigable mountain stream that twisted and turned through an uncharted wilderness until it disappeared unknown miles later in the interior of Essex County. By 1820, when primitive settlements began to appear in the wilderness, the Hudson could be identified as far north as Newcombe near the middle of the western border of Essex County; but the surrounding mountain peaks were still unnamed, uncharted; and the actual sources of the Hudson, some miles farther to the north, remained a self-contained secret of what is still one of the largest and wildest forest preserves in all the continental United States.[1]

The heart of this wilderness, near two beautiful lakes later named Sanford and Henderson, was first penetrated by white men in October, 1826, when a young Indian led five prospectors to the site of some of the richest iron deposits in the state of New York. The five men, two of whose names are perpetuated in the lakes and mountains of the area (MacIntyre Mountain; Lake Henderson, and Henderson Mountain) soon acquired title to most of the land in the region and in a few years' time had erected a forge and village (first named Mac-

Intyre and later Adirondack), and eventually manufactured the first steel of completely American origin.[2] Though the enterprise was located deep in the heart of the Adirondacks, it led at the start to very little knowledge of the still-unexplored peaks and passes of the surrounding wilderness. MacIntyre and Henderson were businessmen, not explorers or mountain-climbers. Discovery awaited other developments.

Early in 1836 Governor William L. Marcy ordered the survey of the complete geological resources of the state of New York. Pursuant to this aim, the state was divided into a number of geological districts, and in early June of the same year Professor Ebenezer Emmons of Williams College was appointed geologist of the 2nd or northern district. Planning a trip to the northern Adirondacks in the late summer of 1836, Emmons apparently directed his assistant, James Hall, to spend the earlier part of the summer in the southern part of the mountains. In any event, the month of August found James Hall a guest of MacIntyre and Henderson at the Adirondack iron works and joining with the proprietors and several other men in an exploratory visit to the surrounding mountain peaks. Tentative discoveries were made of an extraordinary nature (reconfirmed, in part, by Hall's and Emmons's climb of Whiteface in the latter part of the summer); a second expedition was planned for the summer of 1837 in which both Emmons and Hall participated and which concentrated exclusively on the MacIntyre area. The proprietors of the Adirondack Iron Company again acted as hosts of the expedition. The results of this second expedition aroused excitement throughout the state. The two geologists had discovered not only the exact sources of the Hudson, but a great mountain peak—named Marcy by Emmons in honor of the governor—that lay within a thousand feet of those sources and turned out to be the highest peak in New

* Excerpt from W. C. Redfield's "Some Account of Two Visits to the Mountains in Essex County, New York, in the Years 1836 and 1837; with a Sketch of the Northern Sources of the Hudson," *American Journal of Science and Arts*, Vol. XXXIII, No. 2 (Jan., 1838), pp. 1–23. Bracketed material is by the present editor.

York State and the fifth largest peak east of the Rocky Mountains.

The following narrative of these two expeditions was written by William C. Redfield (1789–1857)—known as a promoter of steamboat, and later of railroad, travel in the Hudson Valley—who participated in both expeditions and became the official chronicler of their exciting discoveries.[3]

NOTWITHSTANDING THE INCREASE of population, and the rapid extension of our settlements since the peace of 1783, there is still found, in the northern part of the state of New York, an uninhabited region of considerable extent, which presents all the rugged character and picturesque features of a primeval wilderness. This region constitutes the most elevated portion of the great triangular district which is situated between the line of the St. Lawrence, the Mohawk, and Lake Champlain. That portion of it which claims our notice in the following sketches, lies mainly within the county of Essex, and the contiguous parts of Franklin, and comprises the head waters of the principal rivers in the northern division of the state.

In the summer of 1836, the writer had occasion to visit the new settlement at McIntyre, in Essex County, in company with the proprietors of that settlement, and other gentlemen who had been invited to join the expedition. Our party consisted of the Hon. Archibald McIntyre of Albany, the late Judge McMartin of Broadalbin, Montgomery County, and David Henderson, Esq., of Jersey City, proprietors, together with David C. Colden, Esq. of Jersey City, and Mr. James Hall, assistant state geologist for the northern district.[1]

First Journey to Essex

We left Saratoga on the 10th of August, and after halting a day at Lake George, reached Ticonderoga on the 12th; where at 1 P.M. we embarked on board one of the Lake Champlain steamboats, and were landed soon after 3 P.M. at Port Henry, two miles N.W. from the old fortress of Crown Point. The remainder of the day, and part of the 13th, were spent in exploring the vicinity, and examining the interesting sections which are here exhibited of the junction of the primary rocks with the transition series, near the western borders of the lake. . . .

On the 13th we left Port Henry on horseback, and, after a ride of six miles, left the cultivated country on the borders of the lake and entered the forest. The road on which we traveled is much used for the transportation of sawed pine lumber from the interior, there being in the large township of Moriah, as we were informed, more than sixty saw-mills. Four hours of rough traveling brought us to Weatherhead's, at West Moriah, upon the Schroon river, or East Branch of the Hudson, thirteen miles from Lake Champlain. An old state road from Warren County to Plattsburgh passes through this valley, along which is established the line of interior settlements, in this part of the county. Our further route to the westward was upon a newer and more imperfect road, which has been opened from this place through the unsettled country in the direction of the Black River, in Lewis County.[2] We ascended by this road the woody defiles of the Schroon mountain-ridge, which, as seen from Weatherhead's, exhibits, in its lofty and apparently continuous elevations, little indications of a practicable route. Having passed a previously unseen gorge of this chain, we continued our way under a heavy rain, till we reached the dwelling of Israel Johnson, who has established himself at the outlet of a beautiful mountain lake, called Clear Pond, nine miles from Schroon river. This is the only dwelling house upon the new road. . . .

We resumed our journey on the morning of the 15th, and at 9 A.M. reached the Boreas branch of the Hudson, eight miles from Johnson's. Soon after 11 A.M., we arrived at the Main Northern Branch of the Hudson, a little below its junction with the outlet of Lake Sanford.[3] Another quarter of an hour brought us to the landing at the outlet of the lake, nine miles from the Boreas. Taking leave of the "road," we here entered a difficult path which leads up the western side of the lake, and a further progress of six miles brought us to the Iron Works and settlement at McIntyre, where a hospitable reception awaited us.

At this settlement, and in its immediate vicinity, are found beds of iron ore of great, if not unexampled extent, and of the best quality. These deposits have been noticed in the first report of the state geologists, and have since received from Professor Emmons a more extended examination.[4] Lake Sanford is a beautiful sheet of water, of elongated and irregular form, and about five miles in extent.[5] The Iron Works are situated on the north fork of the Hudson, a little below the point where it issues from Lake Henderson, and over a mile above its entrance into Lake Sanford.[6] The fall of the stream between the two lakes is about one hundred feet. This settlement is situated in the upper plain of the Hudson, and at the foot of the principal mountain nucleus, which rises between its sources and those of the Au Sable. . . .

It has been noticed that the north branch of the Hudson, after its exit from Lake Sanford, joins the main branch of the river [or today's Opalescent River], about seven miles below the settlement at McIntyre. Having prepared for an exploration up the latter stream, we left McIntyre on the 17th of July, with three assistants, and the necessary equipage for encampment. Leaving the

north branch, we proceeded through the woods in a southeasterly direction, passing two small lakes [Lake Jimmy and Lake Sally], till, at the distance of three or four miles from the settlement, we reached the southern point of one of the mountains [probably Popple Hill], and assuming here a more easterly course, we came, about noon, to the main branch of the river. Traces of wolves and deer were frequently seen, and we discovered also the recent tracks of a moose deer or the American elk. We had also noticed on the 16th, at the inlet of Lake Sanford, the fresh and yet undried footsteps of a panther, which apparently had just crossed the inlet.

The beaches of the [Opalescent] river, on which, by means of frequent fording, we now traveled,[7] are composed of rolled masses of the labradoritic rock, and small opalescent specimens not unfrequently showed their beautiful colors in the bed of the stream. As we approached the entrance of the mountains, the ascent of the stream sensibly increased, and about 4 P.M., preparations were commenced for an encampment. A comfortable hut, of poles and spruce bark, was soon constructed by the exertions of our dexterous woodsmen. The campfire being placed on the open side, the party sleep with their heads in the opposite direction, under the lower part of the roof.[8]

On the morning of the 18th we resumed the ascent of the stream by its bed, in full view of two mountains, from between which the stream emerges.[9] About two miles from our camp, we entered the more precipitous part of the gorge through which the river descends.[10] Our advance here became more difficult and somewhat dangerous. After ascending falls and rapids, seemingly innumerable, we came about noon to an imposing cascade,[11] closely pent between two steep mountains, and falling about eighty feet into a deep chasm, the walls of which are as precipitous as those of Niagara, and

32. *The Hudson 20 miles from its Source,* engraving by Harry Fenn, 1874; courtesy of the New York Public Library.

"A comfortable hut, of poles and spruce bark, was soon constructed."

more secluded. With difficulty we emerged from this gulf, and continued our upward course over obstacles similar to the preceding, till half past 2 P.M., when we reached the head of this terrific ravine. From a ledge of rock which here crosses and obstructs the stream, the river continues, on a level which may be called the Upper Still Water,[12] for more than a mile in a westerly and northwesterly direction, but continues pent in the bottom of a deep mountain gorge or valley, with scarce any visible current. To this point the river has been explored by the proprietors on a former occasion.

Emerging from this valley, we found the river to have a meandering course of another mile, in a northwesterly and nearly northerly direction, with a moderate current, until it forks into two unequal branches. Leaving the main branch which here descends from the east,[13] we followed the northern tributary to the distance of two hundred yards from the forks, where it proved to be the outlet of a beautiful lake, of about a mile in extent. This lake, to which our party afterwards gave the name of Lake Colden,[14] is situated between two mountain peaks which rise in lofty grandeur on either hand. We made our second camp at the outlet of this lake, and in full view of its interesting scenery.[15]

Previous to reaching the outlet, we had noticed on the margin of the river, fresh tracks of the wolf and also of the deer, both apparently made at the fullest speed, and on turning a point we came upon the warm and mangled remains of a fine deer, which had fallen a sacrifice to the wolves; the latter having been driven from their savage repast by our unwelcome approach. There appeared to have been two of the aggressive party, one of which, by lying in wait, had probably intercepted the deer in his course to the lake, and they had nearly devoured their victim in apparently a short space of time.

The great ascent which we had made from our first encampment, and the apparent altitude of the mountain peaks before us, together with the naked condition of their summits, rendered it obvious that the elevation of this mountain group had been greatly underrated; and we were led to regret our want of means for a barometrical measurement. The height of our present encampment above Lake Sanford was estimated to be from ten to twelve hundred feet, and the height of Lake Colden, above tide, at from one thousand eight hundred, to two thousand feet, the elevation of Lake Sanford being assumed from such information as we could obtain, to be about eight hundred feet. The elevation of the peaks on either side of Lake Colden, were estimated from two thousand, to two thousand five hundred feet above the lake. These conclusions were entered in our notes, and are since proved to have been tolerably correct, except as they were founded on the supposed elevation of Lake Sanford, which had been very much underrated.[16]

August 19th. The rain had fallen heavily during the night, and the weather was still such as to preclude the advance of the party. But the ardor of the individuals was hardly to be restrained by the storm; and during the forenoon, Mr. Henderson, with John Cheney,[17] our huntsman, made the circuit of Lake Colden, having in their course beaten up the quarters of a family of panthers, to the great discomfiture of Cheney's valorous dog. At noon, the weather being more favorable, Messrs. McIntyre, McMartin and Hall, went up the border of the lake to examine the valley which extends beyond it in a N.N.E. and N.E. direction [Avalanche Pass], while the writer, with Mr. Henderson, resumed the ascent of the main stream of the Hudson.[18] Notwithstanding the wet, and the swollen state of the stream, we succeeded in ascending more than two miles in a southeasterly and southerly direction, over a constant succession of falls and rapids of an interesting character. In one instance, the river has assumed the bed of a displaced trap dyke, by which the rock has been intersected, thus forming a chasm or sluice of great depth, with perpendicular walls, into which the river is precipitated in a cascade of fifty feet.

Before returning to camp, the writer ascended a neighboring ridge for the purpose of obtaining a view of the remarkably elevated valley from which the Hudson here issues. From this point a mountain peak was discovered, which obviously exceeds in elevation the peaks which had hitherto engaged our attention.[19] Having taken the compass bearing of this peak, further progress was relinquished, in hope of resuming the exploration of this unknown region on the morrow.

On returning to our camp, we met the portion of our party which had penetrated the valley north of the lake, and who had there discovered another lake of nearly equal extent [Avalanche Lake], which discharges by an outlet that falls into Lake Colden. On the two sides of this lake, the mountains rise so precipitously as to preclude any passage through the gorge, except by water.[20] The scenery was described as very imposing, and some specimens of the opalescent rock were brought from this locality. Immense slides or avalanches had been precipitated into this lake from the steep face of the mountain, which induced the party to bestow upon it the name of Avalanche Lake.

Another night was passed at this camp, and the morning of the 20th opened with thick mists and rain, by which our progress was further delayed. It was at last determined, in view of the bad state of the weather and our short stock of provisions, to abandon any further exploration at this time, and to return to the settlement. Retracing our steps nearly to the head of the Still Water, we then took a westerly course through a level and

swampy tract [Flowed Land], which soon brought us to the head waters of a stream which descends nearly in a direct course to the outlet of Lake Henderson [Calamity Brook]. The distance from our camp at Lake Colden to McIntyre, by this route, probably does not exceed six miles.[21] Continuing our course, we reached the settlement without serious accident, but with an increased relish for the comforts of civilization.

This part of the state was surveyed into large tracts, or townships, by the colonial government as early as 1772, and lines and corners of that date, as marked upon the trees of the forest, are now distinctly legible. But the topography of the mountains and streams in the upper country, appears not to have been properly noted, if at all examined, and in our best maps, has either been omitted or represented erroneously. Traces have been discovered near McIntyre of a route, which the natives sometimes pursued through this mountain region, by way of Lakes Sanford and Henderson, and thence to the Preston Ponds and the head waters of the Racket.[22] But these savages had no inducement to make the laborious ascent of sterile mountain peaks, which they held in superstitious dread, or to explore the hidden sources of the rivers which they send forth. Even the more hardy huntsman of later times, who, when trapping for northern furs, has marked his path into the recesses of these elevated forests, has left no traces of his axe higher than the borders of Lake Colden, where some few marks of this description may be perceived. All here seems abandoned to solitude; and even the streams and lakes of this upper region are destitute of the trout, which are found so abundant below the cataracts of the mountains.

At a later period of the year, Professor Emmons, in the execution of his geological survey, and accompanied by Mr. Hall, his assistant, ascended the Whiteface Mountain, a solitary peak of different formation, which rises in the north part of the county. From this point, Prof. E. distinctly recognized as the highest of the group, the peak on which the writer's attention had been fastened at the termination of our ascent of the Hudson, and which he describes as situated about sixteen miles south of Whiteface. Prof. E. then proceeded southward through the remarkable Notch, or [Indian] pass, which is described in his Report, and which is situated about five miles north of McIntyre. The Wallface mountain, which forms the west side of the pass, was ascended by him on this occasion, and the height of its perpendicular part was ascertained to be about twelve hundred feet, as may be seen by reference to the geological Report which was published in February last [1837], by order of the legislature.[23] It appears by the barometrical observations made by Prof. Emmons, that the elevation of the table land which constitutes the base of these mountains at McIntyre, is much greater than we had been led to suppose.

Second Journey to Essex County

The interest excited in our party by the short exploration which has been described, was not likely to fail till its objects were more fully accomplished. Another visit to this alpine region was accordingly made in the summer of the present year. Our party on this occasion consisted of Messrs. McIntyre, Henderson and Hall, (the latter at this time geologist of the western district of the state,) together with Prof. Torrey, Prof. Emmons, Messrs. Ingham and Strong of New York, Miller of Princeton, and Emmons, Jr., of Williamstown.[24]

We left Albany on the 28th of July, and took steamboat at Whitehall on the 29th. At the latter place an opportunity was afforded us to ascend the eminence known as Skeenes' mountain, which rises about five hundred feet above the lake [Champlain]. Passing the interesting ruins of Ticonderoga and the less imposing military works of Crown Point,[25] we again landed at Port Henry and proceeded to the pleasant village of East Moriah, situated upon the high ground, three and a half miles west of the lake. This village is elevated near eight hundred feet above the lake, and commands a fine view of the western slope of Vermont, terminating with the extended and beautiful outline of the Green Mountains.

We left East Moriah on the 31st, and our first day's ride brought us to Johnson's at Clear Pond.[26] The position of the High Peak of Essex was known to be but a few miles distant, and Johnson informed us that the snow remained on a peak which is visible from near his residence, till the 17th of July of the present year. We obtained a fine view of this peak the next morning, bearing from Johnson's, N. 20° West, by compass, a position which corresponded to the previous observations; the variation in this quarter being somewhere between 8° and 9° West.

Descending an abrupt declivity from Johnson's, we arrive at a large stream which issues from a small lake farther up the country [Elk Lake], and receiving here the outlet of Clear Pond, discharges itself into the Schroon river. The upper portions of these streams and the lakes from which they issue, as well as the upper course of the Boreas and its mountain lakes, are not found on our maps. From the stream last mentioned, the road ascends the Boreas ridge or mountain chain by a favorable pass, the summit of which is attained about four miles from Johnson's. Between the Boreas and the main branch of the Hudson, we encounter a subordinate extension of the mountain group which separates the sources of the two streams [North River Mountains], through the passes of which ridge the road is carried by a circuitous and uneven route.

We reached the outlet of Lake Sanford about noon on the 1st of August, and found two small boats awaiting our arrival.[27] Having embarked we were able fully to enjoy the beauty and grandeur of the lake and mountain scenery which is here presented, all such views being, as is well known, precluded by the foliage while traveling in the forests. The echoes which are obtained at a point on the upper portion of this lake, are very remarkable for their strength and distinctness. The trout are plentiful in this lake, as well as in Lake Henderson and all the neighboring lakes and streams. We arrived at McIntyre about 4 P.M., and the resources of the settlement were placed in requisition by the hospitable proprietors, for our expedition to the source of the Hudson. . . .

We left the settlement on the 3d of August, with five woodsmen as assistants, to take forward our provisions and other necessaries, and commenced our ascent to the higher region in a northeasterly direction, by the route on which we returned last year [via Calamity Brook]. We reached our old camp at Lake Colden at 5 P.M. where we prepared our quarters for the night. The mountain peak which rises on the eastern side of this lake and separates it from the upper valley of the main stream of the Hudson [or Opalescent River], has received the name of Mount McMartin, in honor of one now deceased,[28] who led the party of last year, and whose spirit of enterprise and persevering labors contributed to establishing the settlement at the great Ore Beds, as well as other improvements advantageous to this section of the state.

On the 4th we once more resumed the ascent of the main stream, proceeding first in an easterly direction, and then to the southeast and south, over falls and rapids, till we arrived at the head of the Great Dyke Falls.[29] Calcedony was found by Prof. Emmons near the foot of these falls. Continuing our course on a more gradual rise, we soon entered upon unexplored ground,

and about three miles from camp, arrived at the South Elbow, where the bed of the main stream changes to a northeasterly direction, at the point where it receives a tributary which enters from south-southwest [Uphill Brook].[30] Following the former course, we had now fairly entered the High Valley which separates Mount McMartin [or Colden] from the High Peak [or Marcy] on the southeast, but so deeply enveloped were we in the deep growth of forest, that no sight of the peaks could be obtained. About a mile from the South Elbow we found another tributary entering from the south-southeast [Feldspar Brook], apparently from a mountain ravine which borders the High Peak on the west.[31] Some beautifully opalescent specimens of the Labradorite were found in the bed of this stream.

Another mile of our course brought us to a small tributary from the north, which from the alluvial character of the land near its entrance is called the High Meadow fork.[32] This portion of our route is in the center of this mountain valley, and has the extraordinary elevation of three thousand and seven hundred feet above tide. We continued the same general course for another mile, with our route frequently crossed by small falls and cascades, when we emerged from the broader part of the valley and our course now became east-southeast,[33] with a steeper ascent and higher and more frequent falls in the stream. The declivity of the mountain which incloses the valley on the north [Table Top] and that of the great peak [Marcy], here approximate closely to each other, and the valley assumes more nearly the character of a ravine or pass between two mountains, with an increasing ascent, and maintains its course for two or three miles, to the summit of the pass. Having accomplished more than half the ascent of this pass we made our camp for the night,[34] which threatened to be uncommonly cold and caused our axemen to place in requisition some venerable specimens of the white birch which surrounded our encampment.

A portion of the deep and narrow valley in which we were now encamped, is occupied by a longitudinal ridge consisting of boulders and other *debris,* the materials, evidently, of a tremendous slide or avalanche, which at some unknown period has descended from the mountain. . . . The slides still recur, and their pathway may often be perceived in the glitter of the naked rock, which is laid bare in their course from the summit of the mountain towards its base, and these traces constitute one of the most striking features in the mountain scenery of this region.

On the morning of the fifth we found that ice had formed in exposed situations. At an early hour we resumed our ascending course to the southeast, the stream rapidly diminishing and at length becoming partially concealed under the grass-covered boulders. At 8:40 A.M. we arrived at the head of the stream on the summit of this elevated pass, which here forms a beautiful and open mountain meadow, with the ridges of the two adjacent mountains rising in an easy slope from its sides. From this little meadow, which lies within the present limits of the town of Keene, the main branch of the Hudson and a fork of the east branch of the Au Sable commence their descending course in opposite directions, for different and far distant points of the Atlantic ocean.[35] The elevation of this spot proves by our observations to be more than four thousand seven hundred feet above tide water; being more than nine hundred feet above the highest point of the Catskill mountains, which have so long been considered the highest mountains in the state.[36]

The descent of the Au Sable from this point is most remarkable. In its comparative course to Lake Champlain, which probably does not exceed forty miles, its fall is more than four thousand six hundred feet! This, according to our present knowledge, is more than twice the entire descent of the Mississippi proper, from its source to the ocean. Water-falls of the most striking and magnificent character are known to abound on the course of this stream.

Our ascent to the source of the Hudson had brought us to an elevated portion [Little Marcy] of the highest peak, which was also a principal object of our exploration, and its ascent now promised to be of easy accomplishment by proceeding along its ridge in a W.S.W. direction.[37] On emerging from the pass, however, we immediately found ourselves entangled in the zone of dwarfish pines and spruces, which with their numerous horizontal branches interwoven with each other, surround the mountain at this elevation. These gradually decreased in height, till we reached the open surface of the mountain [above the timber line], covered only with mosses and small alpine plants, and at 10 A.M. the summit of the High Peak of Essex was beneath our feet.

The aspect of the morning was truly splendid and delightful, and the air on the mountain-top was found to be cold and bracing. Around us lay scattered in irregular profusion, mountain masses of various magnitudes and elevations, like to a vast sea of broken and pointed billows. In the distance lay the great valley or plain of the St. Lawrence, the shining surface of Lake Champlain, and the extensive mountain range of Vermont. The nearer portions of the scene were variegated with the white glare of recent mountain slides as seen on the sides of various peaks, and with the glistening of the beautiful lakes which are so common throughout this region. To complete the scene, from one of the nearest settlements a vast volume of smoke soon rose in majestic splendor, from a fire of sixty acres of forest clearing, which had been prepared for the "burning," and exhibiting in the vapor which it embodied, a gorgeous array of the prismatic colors, crowned with the dazzling beams of the midday sun.

The summit, as well as the mass of the mountain, was found to consist entirely of the labradoritic rock, which has been mentioned as constituting the rocks of this region, and a few small specimens of hypersthene were here procured. On some small deposits of water, ice was also found at noon, half an inch in thickness. The source of the Hudson, at the head of the High Pass [Little Marcy] bears N.70°E. from the summit of this mountain, distant one and a quarter miles, and the descent of the mountain is here more gradual than in any other direction. Before our departure we had the unexpected satisfaction to discover, through a depression in the Green Mountains, a range of distant mountains in nearly an east direction, and situated apparently beyond the valley of the Connecticut; but whether the range thus seen, be a portion of the White Mountains of New Hampshire or the mountains of Franconia, near the head of the Merrimack, does not fully appear.[38] Our barometrical observations on this summit show an elevation of five thousand four hundred and sixty seven feet. This exceeds by about six hundred feet, the elevation of the Whiteface Mountain, as given by Prof. Emmons; and is more than sixteen hundred and fifty feet above the highest point of the Catskill Mountains.[39]

The descent to our camp was accomplished by a more direct and far steeper route than that by which we had gained the summit, and our return to Lake Colden afforded us no new objects of examination.[40] The boulders which form the bed of the stream in the upper Hudson, are often of great magnitude, but below the mountains, where we commenced our exploration of last year, the average size does not exceed that of the paving stones in our cities;—so great is the effect of the attrition to which these boulders are subject in their gradual progress down the stream. Search has been made by the writer, among the gravel from the bottom and shoals of the Hudson near the head of tide-water, for the fragmentary remains of the labradoritic rock, but hitherto without success. We may hence infer that the whole amount of this rocky material, which, aided by the ice, and the powerful impulse of the annual freshets, finds its way down the Hudson, a descent of from two thousand to four thousand seven hundred feet, is reduced by the combined effects of air, water, frost, and attrition, to an impalpable state, and becomes imperceptibly deposited in the alluvium of the river, or continuing suspended, is transferred to the waters of the Atlantic.

On the 7th of August we visited Avalanche Lake, and examined the great dyke of sienitic trap in Mount McMartin [Colden], which cuts through the entire mountain in the direction from west-northwest to east-northeast. This dyke is about eighty feet in width, and being in part broken from its bed by the action of water and ice, an open chasm is thus formed in the abrupt and almost perpendicular face of the mountain. The scene on entering this chasm is one of sublime grandeur, and its nearly vertical walls of rock, at some points actually overhang the intruder, and seem to threaten him with instant destruction. With care and exertion this dyke may be ascended, by means of the irregularities of surface which the trap rock presents, and Prof. Emmons by this means accomplished some twelve or fifteen hundred feet of the elevation. His exertions were rewarded by some fine specimens of hypersthene and of the opalescent labradorite, which were here obtained. The summit of Mount McMartin [Colden] is somewhat lower than those of the two adjacent peaks, and is estimated at four thousand nine hundred and fifty feet above tide.[41]

The distance from the outlet of Lake Colden to the op-

33. *Source of the Hudson,* engraving by Harry Fenn, 1874; courtesy of The New-York Historical Society.

"The source of the Hudson, at the head of the High Pass [Little Marcy] bears N.70°E. from the summit of this mountain, distant one and a quarter miles."

posite extremity of Avalanche Lake is estimated at two and a quarter miles. The stream which enters the latter at its northern extremity, from the appearance of its valley, is supposed to be three-fourths of a mile in length, and the fall of the outlet in its descent to Lake Colden is estimated, as we have seen, at eighty feet. The head waters of this fork of the Hudson are hence situated farther north than the more remote source of the Main Branch [Opalescent], which we explored on the 4th and 5th, or perhaps than any other of the numerous tributaries of the Hudson.[42] The elevation of Avalanche Lake is between two thousand nine hundred and three thousand feet above tide, being undoubtedly the highest lake in the United States, east of the Rocky Mountains.[43]

The mountain which rises on the west side of this lake and separates its valley from that of the Au Sable, is perhaps the largest of the group. Its ridge presents four successive peaks [Iroquois, Boundary, Algonquin, and Wright], of which the most northern save one [Algonquin], is the highest [5,114], and is situated immediately above the lake and opposite to Mount McMartin [Colden]. It has received the name of Mount McIntyre [MacIntyre],[44] in honor of the late Controller of this state, to whose enterprise and munificence, this portion of the country is mainly indebted for the efficient measures which have been taken to promote its prosperity.

On the morning of the 8th, we commenced the ascent of Mount McIntyre through a deep ravine, by which a small stream is discharged into Lake Colden.[45] The entire ascent being comprised in little more than a mile of horizontal distance, is necessarily difficult, and on reaching the lower border of the belt of dwarf forest, we found the principal peak rising above us on our right, with its steep acclivity of naked rock extending to our feet. Wishing to shorten our route, we here unwisely abandoned the remaining bed of the ravine, and sustain-

ing ourselves by the slight inequalities of surface which have resulted from unequal decomposition, we succeeded in crossing the apparently smooth face of the rock by an oblique ascent to the right, and once more obtained footing in the woody cover of the mountain. But the continued steepness of the acclivity, and the seemingly impervious growth of low evergreens on this more sheltered side, where their horizontal and greatly elongated branches were most perplexingly intermingled, greatly retarded our progress. Having surmounted this region we put forward with alacrity, and at 1 P.M. reached the summit.

The view which was here presented to us differs not greatly in its general features from that obtained at the High Peak, and the weather, which now began to threaten us with a storm, was less favorable to its exhibition. A larger number of lakes were visible from this point, and among them the beautiful and extensive group at the sources of the Saranac, which are known by the settlers as the "Saranac Waters." The view of the still water of the Hudson, lying like a silver thread in the bottom of its deep and forest-green valley, was peculiarly interesting. The opposite front of Mount McMartin [Colden] exhibited the face of the great dyke and its passage through the summit, near to its highest point, and nearly parallel to the whitened path of a slide which had recently descended into Avalanche Lake. In a direction a little south of west, the great vertical precipice of the Wallface Mountain at the Notch [Indian Pass], distinctly met our view. Deeply below us on the northwest and north, lay the valley of the west branch of the Au Sable, skirted in the distance by the wooded plains which extend in the direction of Lake Placid and the Whiteface Mountain.[46]. . .

Our barometric observations show a height of near five thousand two hundred feet, and this summit is probably the second in this region, in point of elevation. There are three other peaks lying in a westerly direction, and also three others lying eastward of the main source of the Hudson, which nearly approach to, if they do not exceed, five thousand feet in elevation, making of this class, including Mount McMartin [Colden], Whiteface, and the two peaks visited, ten in all. Besides these mountains there are not less than a dozen or twenty others that appear to equal or exceed the highest elevation of the Catskill group.[47]

The descent of the mountain is very abrupt on all sides, and our party took the route of a steep ravine which leads into the valley of the Au Sable, making our camp at night-fall near the foot of the mountain. The night was stormy, and the morning of the 9th opened upon us with a continued fall of rain, in which we resumed our march for the Notch, intending to return to the settlement by this route. After following the bed of the ravine till it joined the Au Sable [north end of Indian Pass Brook], we ascended the latter stream, and before noon arrived at this extraordinary pass, which has been described by the state geologists, and which excites the admiration of every beholder. Vast blocks and fragments have in past ages fallen from the great precipice of the Wallface Mountain on the one hand, and from the southwest extension of Mount McIntyre on the other, into the bottom of this natural gulf. Some of these blocks are set on end, of a height of more than seventy feet, in the moss-covered tops and crevices of which, large trees have taken root, and now shoot their lofty stems high above the toppling foundation. The north branch of the Hudson [or today the Hudson proper], which passes through Lakes Henderson and Sanford, takes its

rise in this pass, about five miles from McIntyre, and the elevation of its source, as would appear from the observations taken by Prof. Emmons last year, is not far from three thousand feet above tide.[48]

Following the course of the valley, under a copious fall of rain, we descended to Lake Henderson, which is a fine sheet of water of two or three miles in length, with the high mountain of Santanoni rising from its borders, on the west and southwest. It is not many months since our woodsman, Cheney, with no other means of offense than his axe and pistol, followed and killed a large panther, on the western borders of this lake. Pursuing our course along the eastern margin of this lake, we arrived at the settlement about 3 P.M., having been absent on our forest excursion seven days. . . .

The source of the Hudson and the High Peak of Essex, can be most conveniently reached from Johnson's, at Clear Pond, by a course N. 20° W.; or by landing at Westport, or Essex [north of Port Henry on Lake Champlain] and proceeding to the nearest settlement in Keene. By landing at Port Kent, and ascending the course of the Au Sable to the southeast part of Keene [township], and from thence to the Peak, the most interesting chain of waterfalls and mountain ravines that is to be found, perhaps, in the United States, may be visited.[49] At Keene, Mr. Harvey Holt, an able woodsman, who was attached to our party, will cheerfully act as guide and assistant, in reaching the mountain. From the valley which lies southward of the peak, and near to the head waters of the Boreas and Au Sable, may be obtained, it is said, some of the best mountain views which this region affords. But travelers in these wilds, must be provided with their own means of subsistence, while absent from the settlements.

16.
Charles Farnham 1880*

INTRODUCTION: A turbulent mountain stream leaves little for history to say, and such is the Hudson during the first one hundred miles of its three-hundred-and-fifteen-mile journey to the Atlantic Ocean. The Hudson leaves the Adirondack State Park in the vicinity of Glens Falls. South of that point the chronicles of the Hudson offer an embarrassment of riches; north of it they are virtually nonexistent. History, as we must assert again, has followed the course of colonization westward up the Mohawk or northward up the deep navigable waters of Lake Champlain.

Yet if history has been silent along the upper reaches of the Hudson, nature has spoken with the eloquence of primeval creation. The state geologists of 1836 were impelled to chart the origins of the Hudson because of the historical importance of the lower river. Once in the heart of the Adirondacks, however, they realized they had discovered an upper region that has transcendent value precisely because of the absence of historical importance. The upper Hudson, they realized, belongs to the splendors of natural, rather than human, history. Writing soon after the geologists had reported their discoveries of 1836, a New York writer and editor declared:

Everybody was, indeed, aware that the Hudson rose among a group of mountains in the northern part of the state of New York; and if you looked upon the map, some of the lakes which formed its headwaters seemed to be laid down with sufficient peculiarity. Few, however, until the legislature instituted the geological survey which is now in progress, had any idea that the mountains upon which this noble river rises, overtopped the Katsbergs and the Alleghanies, and were among the loftiest in the United States; or that the lakes from which it draws its birth were equally remarkable for their prodigal numbers,

their picturesque variety, and their wild and characteristic beauty.

Tourists steamed upon the estuary of the Hudson, or loitered through the populous counties between the cities of New York and Albany, and, ignorant or unmindful that in ascending to the head of tide-water they had not seen quite one-half of the lordly stream, discussed its claims to consideration with an amiable familiarity, and, comparing its scenery with that of other celebrated rivers, they settled its whole character after a most summary fashion.

The worthy Knickerbockers were, therefore, not a little surprised when they learned from the first official report of the surveying corps that their famous river was fed by mountain snows for ten months of the year; and that there were a dozen cascades about its head-waters, to which Glen's Falls, however endeared to association by the genius of Cooper, must hereafter yield in romantic interest and attraction. Many were disposed at once to visit the sources of the Hudson. . . . †

Early visitors were such writers as the above, who together with the first landscape painters in America, always preceded the later invasion of tourists and vacationers into the newly-discovered wonderlands of nineteenth-century America. In time, a wealthy few attracted by the revelation of a sportsman's paradise began to arrive; private hunting clubs were established; primitive roads were built. The great era of development, however, occurred after the Civil War when cabins, hunting lodges, trails, and camps were built all over the Adirondacks and the region became one of the most popular vacationlands in America. Devoid of historical associations, the region of the upper Hudson thus fulfilled itself in the pleasurable and salutary associations of man and nature.

The few chronicles we have bear witness to this pre-

† Charles Fenno Hoffman, "The Sources of the Hudson," *Wild Scenes in the Forest and Prairie with Sketches of American Life* (New York: 1843), pp. 14–15. This was written after Hoffman visited Mt. Marcy in early September, 1837, in company with John Cheney. The narrative first appeared in the *New-York Mirror* (1837), of which Hoffman was the chief editor.

* Excerpt from Charles Farnham's "Running the Rapids of the Upper Hudson," *Scribner's Monthly*, Vol. XXI (April, 1881, No. 6), pp. 857–870.

eminent service of the untamable river of the north. About 1880 Charles Farnham, an intrepid sportsman, astounded the natives of the upper Hudson by plunging down the rapids of the river in a canoe "just for the fun" of it. He was the first of a legion of dedicated canoeists. Starting at a remote village that is now called "North River," about thirty-five miles south of Lake Tear of the Clouds, he successfully negotiated the turbulent rifts and rapids between that point and Glens Falls, and then drifted amiably down the main stream of the Hudson to Northumberland where he hitched a ride on a canal boat for the final lap to Albany. He had shown it could be done; and he has also given us, in the following narrative, the first and probably the most graphic account we possess of this wild, unlordly river of the wilderness.

HAVE YOU EVER run a rapid? Have you ever rushed through a wilderness on a torrent? . . . This challenge I accepted from the Hudson—not from the old river where it sinks into the sea, but from its roaring, turbulent youths [sic] among the mountains. The Boreas, the North, the Rocky, the Cedar, and the Indian rivers are his frolicking family.[1] They escape from the peaks of the Adirondacks, and rush with foam and tumult at the head of the Hudson. And the dignified old river you know below Albany is all confused by their antics, and obliged to join their turmoil. For twenty miles or more, down to the Glen,[2] the Hudson is a torrent over narrow, rocky beds, among bold mountains. It is so furious in a freshet that only the most reckless lumbermen venture on its rapids. Swift but somewhat smoother waters commence at the Glen, and continue ten miles, to Thurman.[3] Here still waters begin a course of fifteen miles, interrupted by

the falls at Luzern, and terminated at Jessup's Landing.[4] At this point the river enters six or seven miles of rapids among the mountains; then it flows on swiftly about fifteen miles to Fort Edward; and to Albany, about fifty miles, it pursues a quiet course, now and then interrupted by a slight fall, dam, or rapid. Thus, the river offers twenty-five or thirty miles of actual rapids among wild mountains; and also some quiet stretches among fertile plains and comfortable civilization. But the upper Hudson, though rough, is not so large as to require a pilot familiar with its eddies, rocks, and shoots.

We began our descent of the Hudson at the highest navigable waters.[5] We were two: one was the captain of the *Rosalie,* a *Nautilus* canoe of willful disposition; the other was the captain of the *Allegro,* a canoe of angelic mold and motive.[6] We had crossed the Adirondack wilderness from the Fulton chain of lakes *via* the Raquette to Blue Mountain Lake, and had carted our canoes to Fourteenth Dam, or Eldridge's, on the Hudson. As we drove past the hotel to the shed, our advent brought everybody to the doors and windows, and enlisted a straggling regiment of men and boys, who came after us through the rain for a nearer view. But we had become hardened to adulation. Our canoes were the first that had entered the wilderness. We had held, for the inquisitive, levees, *matinées, soirées, séances, conversaziones,* at all times of day and night, on beaches, roads, bogs, and logs, till we were inured to admiration and curiosity. So the crowd made but little impression on us at first. But when our intention to run the rapids was avowed, and the possibility and impossibility of the enterprise were delivered at us, all at once the crowd became very interesting. After hearing their chorus of conflicting statements, we systematically button-holed the most intelligent by-standers, and pried into their secret thoughts. One old log-driver, who had run rafts every freshet for thirty years,

34. *Little Falls at Luzerne,* acquatint engraved by J. R. Smith from the painting by W. G. Wall, 1821–1822; courtesy of The New-York Historical Society.

"Swift but somewhat smoother waters commence at the Glen, and continue ten miles to Thurman. Here still waters begin a course of fifteen miles, interrupted by the falls at Luzern."

believed in his inmost soul that two funerals would end our trip. Another man of experience thought that our canoes would be distributed in jackstraws as relics of metropolitan insanity. Still another thought that we could go down if we "carried" around the Spruce Mountain rift, the Horse Race, and the other rough places. On the other hand, some believed we could succeed. We questioned these minutely about the falls, the rifts, and the most dangerous localities along the way. Then, after the shower had passed, we drove off a short distance down the river. Men in wagons and on foot followed us to see the launch. But as the day was nearly spent, we disappointed them by camping for the night. They returned early next morning, however, and waited an hour or two for our departure. One man, who had arrived after our launching, pursued us two miles, and then followed three miles farther, to see us run the rapids. We stowed most of our cargo in the after-hatch, that the bow might be light, and to steer easily, and avoid catching on rocks and swinging around. It was a bright September morning, fresh with a strong west wind. So we began our running of the rapids with inspiriting weather, with a good depth of water under the dancing ripples, and with hearty good wishes from our interested companions on the shore.

The scene was quite striking to any one who had the time to see it. As for ourselves, we were at once too much occupied to give more than a glance at the surroundings. High mountains rise on each bank, wild, dark, and inhospitable. The forest is scarcely broken, excepting by a few bald peaks. The narrow gorge of the river is hardly touched with civilization, notwithstanding the railroad and an occasional cabin.[7] The banks are lined with huge bowlders; the bed of the river is filled with great rocks; and the water is broken into countless currents, eddies, and shoots.

The two little crafts, comely and fragile, already seem castaways in that wilderness. But we have no time nor disposition for such sentiments; we begin at once our combat with the elements, and already feel the energy and daring required for the exploit.

We are at the head of the Spruce Mountain rift.[8] It is considered the most dangerous place on the river. Every year, some of the log-drivers are drowned in its furious currents. Then the waters present to view a sea of foaming waves rushing at headlong speed. Their roar drowns every other sound. The great, sharp swells then met in the swiftest water are likely to capsize or swamp a boat; but, on the other hand, the wide, deep channels between the rocks offer plenty of seaway and many chances for a safe passage. If you upset, there is generally plenty of water to swim in; and a strong man, who is cool and skillful, can save himself even in those tumultuous currents. At the present time, with average water, navigation is much more difficult, and, perhaps, as dangerous as in a freshet. Now, the rift is a course of bare rocks and foaming shoots. The high rocks are half out of water, and many of the low ones are scarcely covered. The bowlders are often but a few yards apart, and sometimes but a few feet. Consequently, the channels are very narrow and crooked, and in some places too narrow even for a boat only twenty inches wide. If the current were gentle, it would still be very easy to pick your way among these passages; for you would have time to choose a route and to follow it. But the current of the Spruce Mountain rift, and of the Horse Race below, is not less than ten or twelve miles an hour in a freshet. In this ordinary water the average speed is much less, perhaps half; but the velocity of the shoots and narrow channels is fully as great. Whitecapped waves roll up below every rock under water, and foaming currents shoot right and left from every bowlder that divides the water. Therefore, the opportunities for capsizing or smashing the boat are so numerous that you wonder if she can possibly go through. The dangers from an upset into this kind of water are that you might get your limbs broken by catching between the bowlders, you might be caught on a rock and held under by the pressure of the current, or you might be knocked senseless by hitting your head on the rocks. The water is much more wicked for being too shallow for swimming and too deep for wading. Nevertheless, there are many favorable circumstances to aid you. If you manage your boat well, you will probably go through without breaking her or upsetting. The bowlders are large and smooth, and therefore not likely to punch through the planks; every swell is not able to capsize or fill the boat; and a quick eye and a steady hand will save her from nearly all the worst places. If you are spilled out you have many chances to swim ashore, or else drift there. Certainly, you will prefer to float; and certainly, also, the effort to do it in these waters will kindle your whole being to a white heat. But we often live by luck; why not here? As some German of practical experience has observed, it's a dangerous thing to live, any way.

The waters ahead are narrow shoots between rocks. Some of the bowlders, high above water, are easily seen; others quite low are shown by a foaming wave rolling out from each side as the waters divide; others, again, just covered, are marked by a white-capped swell below them. The deepest, clearest water is known by the high, sharp, and regular swells on its surface. The channels between the rocks are from three to ten feet wide; and, at intervals of a few yards, they turn right or left in swift, tortuous shoots. We are drifting down a smooth stretch, but straight toward a whitecapped swell. It rolls up some feet below the rock that makes it; so, after deciding to pass it on the left, I give a stroke with the paddle, and send the canoe safely by it. But I sit so low in the water

that I cannot see far ahead, to choose a route; and we begin to go quite fast in this current. So I back water to slow her, for fear of running suddenly into some impassable place. Besides, she turns more readily at low speed, and I avoid rock after rock quite surely as we glide along. Now and then we are completely surprised. Certain smooth pieces of water in a rapid show a good channel. I took that short quiet stretch for such a place, and steered toward it; but now I find it is the eddy below a great flat rock that hides the swell. So I back water with all speed. I then turn to the right through some rougher water. Farther down I see a breastwork of rocks and breakers extending from the left shore nearly across the stream. There is no passage there: I must cross to the right bank. Safety depends on keeping the boat headed down stream; for, if she lies across the current while drifting, a rock may catch the keel and capsize her instantaneously. The current here is not the swiftest; so I back water vigorously to stop her descent on the rocks below. She gradually obeys, and soon creeps up stream a little. Then I turn her stern just a little across stream to the right, and continue backing. She thus moves slowly across the river, but never gets broadside to the current. When we have reached a point right above the clear channel, I give a stroke or two on the left to turn her straight down stream, and in a moment we go on again between the rocks and the white-caps. But we are scarcely in this channel before I see that the main body of water is in the center of the river bed, and that we cannot pass among the rocks right ahead. The current here is too swift to stem by backing. As, however, the nearest channel to be reached is not very far to the left, and is some distance below, I turn her bow somewhat across the current and make a bold rush down stream. But the channel ahead is only four or five feet wide; and if I steer badly there will be a wrecked canoe in about ten seconds. We fly past rocks, and over others just below the keel.

The water is dangerously shallow. In this critical course every stroke must be carefully calculated. I dipped my paddle too deep that time and lost a stroke; for it struck a rock and shot out of the water as if flung upward by a treacherous hand. The next stroke must take up the loss. The current is all the time bearing us toward the rocks this side of the channel, and it seems doubtful that we can cross the current far enough to enter. I turn her a little more across the stream, pray that the water may be deep enough to float her keel above rocks, while she drifts almost sidewise, and put forth all my strength in a few strokes. We dash on, and reach the head of the channel; but she lies so much across the stream that she must certainly strike her bow and stern on each side of the entrance. It is almost hopeless, but I lay all my strength on a back stroke on the right, and then a forward stroke on the left makes her just clear her bow as she darts down the shoot. It would be a good plan to rest now and get breath again. But here is where the rapids begin in earnest. The river falls very perceptibly ahead; the rocks increase; the current is swifter and more broken. Here we are on the worst rift of the Hudson. I can give but a glance at each obstacle; but that glance is my utmost effort to see and comprehend the situation. Then my mind seems supernaturally keen in deciding, and every nerve is flooded with electric power. My strokes are jerks. The canoe starts here and there as if mad. There is not an instant's pause. We turn suddenly right, then left; just miss a rock here, gain a channel there just wide enough to pass the boat like an arrow through the hole; she strikes her keel, but goes on; or she scrapes one side of her bottom on a rock, and rolls partly over as a startling admonition. We come to a line of rocks and swells too suddenly for escape; a rock just

covered with water right ahead is the lowest leap; we put on all speed and steer straight for its round crown. She rides up it on her keel; I keep my balance and sympathetically tremble for the boat while her momentum carries her over it till far past her midships; then she hangs by the stern. But she is safe, and I soon shove her off for another race. Surely such good luck cannot last all through the Spruce Mountain rift. At last we find ourselves in a channel so crooked and obstructed that I must pause to study the situation, although the hesitation may be fatal. The only issue is down a swift, narrow shoot; and a rock lies in the middle of it, about two boat-lengths below the entrance. As this is the only chance, here goes! I drive her at full speed, right down at the rock. She cannot be turned in this short distance; she flies as straight as an arrow to her destruction. But I swing my left arm across my chest and enter the port blade of the paddle diagonally into the water on the starboard side. Her high speed makes the oblique blade press against the water and haul her sideways, several feet to starboard. She shies from the rock in a single bound. I can scarcely breathe, and my blood boils with excitement. As she glides into the pool below the shoot, I let her drift about in the eddy, while the paddles rest across the combing.

Now for the first time I have an opportunity to look around. Where is the *Rosalie?* I had passed her stranded on a rock at the top of the rift, while her captain labored to get her off. As this was not an uncommon trick with her perverse nature it gave me no anxiety; I sent the captain a nod of encouragement and went on my way rejoicing in a *Shadow* canoe. Looking up the rift now from its foot, I wonder how a boat ever got through it whole; and I feel like patting the *Allegro* on the back for her success. I suppose the *Rosalie* is hidden from view by the numerous bowlders studding the bed of the river, and making it look like a barren field of rocks with foaming waves between. As the day is nearly done, I land on the beach to make camp and await the *Rosalie*. I had gathered a large pile of wood for a camp-fire, and still the *Rosalie* was not visible, even from the point above. Then I leveled a place on the sand for laying our boats, and wondered if there would really be only one to occupy it. Finally I kindled the fire; and then went into the woods to cut some poles and forked sticks for making camp. When I returned, the other captain was just wading to the beach, and pulling the *Rosalie* by the nose.

"Hurrah!" I exclaimed, as I dropped the ax and sticks, and hurried to the water. I saw at a glance that something had happened.

"There's not much hurrah here," said he, shivering with great animation.

"Why? What's the matter?"

"She struck a rock up here, and capsized quick as a wink. The water was deep and I went under. When I came up, my paddle was gone too far for me to get it. I'm v-very sorry,—but this ends *my* trip." As he said this, he hitched up his trousers with emphasis.

"Oh, well!" I replied, "I can soon make you a paddle that will answer."

"Yes, I know; but my time is about up, and it wouldn't be worth while. I guess I'll take the train on Monday, and go home."

We soon had the boats placed side by side on the beach, about two feet apart, and propped up to lie level. We then took out their cargoes, and removed the hatches and back-boards to leave the well empty for a bed. A small mattress of cork shavings and a blanket were arranged on the bottom. Then a piece of unbleached sheeting, oiled, seven feet by nine, was spread over the boats on poles, in such a way as to form a tent covering the wells. Better beds, and a better camp for storm or sunshine, need not be offered to tired men. We soon had

a good supper stowed away, and the wet cargo of the *Rosalie* hung on poles about the fire. After toasting ourselves an hour, and discussing the maneuvers of canoes in rapids, we turned in for a long night of sound sleep. As the next day was Sunday, we still prolonged the period of rest, while the *Rosalie* and her captain prepared to depart by rail. She traveled as freight the rest of the way to New York, about 200 miles, for eighteen dollars. Why railroads should make such exorbitant charges on light canoes is a matter for disgust, wonder, and war.

The *Allegro* resumed her course in good spirits on Monday morning, notwithstanding the loss of our companion. She was eager for more rapids, more exploits on the wing. We were not long in reaching the "Horse Race," below Riverside [Riparius]. That rift is the most rapid on the river. Its name suggests its motion, but not by any means its wild and tumultuous course. Perhaps Mazeppa's Race would be better, if one holds to the analogy. The mountains on each hand are bold, high, and dark with forest or with barren rocks. The scene is gloomy, inhospitable, even without the dismal voice of the torrent. As I approached the head of the rift, I cannot see the foot, for the river falls with an ominous and hidden descent. I throw off the apron in front of me and stand up in the canoe to get a view. There are plenty of rocks ahead—with white-capped swells. But the water is evidently deeper than I found it on the Spruce Mountain rift, not quite so much broken by rocks, and the channels are somewhat wider. Moreover, I see the rift has no actual falls at the lower end, but a rapid descent of foaming swells among hidden rocks. That lively place must be entered at a given point; and that point is just below a rough-and-tumble passage that may derange all my calculations. Here will be sharp work! I run her up to the shore, to stow the baggage differently, that I may kneel in the after end of the cockpit; she now raises her head more out of the water, is more easily turned, and on my knees I can see farther ahead, and also exert much more strength on the paddle. The usual difficulty of choosing the course is increased by a glare of sunlight, and by a strong head-wind. This blows the light canoe about, and makes it hard to steer just where the greatest accuracy is necessary. Moreover, it makes the surface of the water wonderfully deceptive just where the greatest dangers are concealed. You judge of rapid water by the appearance of its surface. The face of the river is full of character. Here it sleeps, while curling dimples come and go with dreams of sylvan beauties resting on its breast. There it awakens to merry life. Further on, where the combat rages, every feature is in the tumult of passion. And a practiced eye reads all this as he runs, and governs his course accordingly. The head of a rift is often smooth, with a wedge-shaped "apron" marking the course of the channel. The central, main part of the rift is a confused mass of eddies, white-capped waves, and swift shoots. The foot is a swift rush of deep water marked with high, sharp-topped swells quite regular in succession. The deep pool below is quiet, with dark eddies and flecks of foam. Besides these general features, which vary much according to the geological formations, a rapid is full of important details. Every hidden rock marks the surface in a way that shows the depth of water and the velocity of the current. A rock in a deep, slow current figures the quiet surface with delicate lines and small eddies; in water a little swifter, it makes a round, smooth hood of water over its head, and small ripples below; in a rapid, strong current, it makes a foaming, crested wave and an eddy setting upstream; and, in a steep descent, it throws the water into high tumultuous seas. Thus you estimate the nature of the water by signs, forms, and colors of waves and eddies, that are quite reliable guides. But the high wind to-day changes every-thing. On still water it rolls up waves that belong to a deep, swift channel; on swift, clear shoots it makes white-capped waves that indicate large rocks; and on rocky courses it tumbles up the water in complete confusion. The rocks thus seem to move about the stream, like sunken monsters seeking prey. So the course is full of surprises. I suddenly find a huge bowlder right ahead, where I believed there was clear water. I get to a line of breakers where I expect to strand, but glide through rough, deep water. I lie back in imagined safety while running down a uniform shoot, but all at once find a huge rock close to my side. Nevertheless, the eye soon becomes accustomed to the change of signs, and estimates the colors and forms on a new scale. But at last I am near the end of the Horse Race. I have not approached the last swift rush of water in the right place; in avoiding some heavy seas in mid-channel, I kept too near a large eddy, setting upstream below a rock, and the upward current striking the bow turned the canoe almost about, and so took her out of the course. A glance at the tumultuous breakers and high swells ahead reveals some narrow passage between two bowlders. I strike quick and hard, and, with the help of good luck, dart into the main channel. Here the rush almost takes my breath. For a moment destruction seems perfectly certain. The current is a mass of foaming waves over rocks. But the water is deeper than I thought from its broken and discolored surface. We rush on, through swells that roll the canoe from one side to the other, wash her decks, and toss us about in the most startling manner. The race was swift, though short, and we glide out at last on the still pool below with the elation and gratitude of victors.

The sentiments are strongly stirred in such a trip alone, down an unknown rapid. The feeling of danger, the isolation in wild surroundings, the intense mental and physical activity, all unite to form a very exceptional experience. There is no time for ennui and ordinary loneliness. You are too keenly sensitive, too profoundly moved, for anything commonplace. The dominant feeling is gratitude for your preservation, and for your delights. Scarcely less strong is the yearning for companionship. Pride over the achievement is not unknown, and affection for your canoe wells up again and again as you quietly paddle her through still waters or anxiously drive her through new dangers. As I shot down the rift and under the bridge at the Glen, I kept thinking: "Oh, for some one to tell it to—some boy, just in his prime!" So I landed, and, instead of cooking my solitary meal, I went to a house in search of dinner and a pair of ears. I was at once fully supplied in both regards at a full table. Then we all went down to the river to see the *Allegro*. As I narrated her exploits on the rifts, the boys' eyes dilated with wonder and hero-worship. When I reëmbarked, one of them said: "So your friend went home, eh! But you're goin' to grit her through, ain't you?" That boy would have given all his mother's cakes and kisses to go with me, and I would certainly have accepted such an offer. But I soon pushed off, and resumed my solitary yet delightful cruise. That evening, as the sun went down in a glowing sky, I wandered again through corn-fields and an orchard in search of some human being and some potatoes. An aged woman, preparing supper in a farmer's kitchen, listened to my requests for food, but gave me little encouragement. The farmer's wife at last came to the door and explained that the hens had failed, that the bread had disappeared, and that the potatoe-bug was the only responsible party in that township; but I must have had an atmosphere of canoe about me, for, after a few minutes, she kindly divided her stores and gave me six eggs, half a loaf, and five potatoes. I picked up some apples in the orchard, and returned to my boat on the bank of the river. In the evening, as I was eating my supper by the camp-fire, the farmer and his son appeared on the scene. They had been attracted by the blaze, and had come to know where it was. My explanation re-assured them, and finally we had a pleasant chat by the fire. He urged me to come to his house for the night; but, failing in this kindness, he insisted that I should come up for breakfast. So, after all, I did not spend a lonely evening. The next morning, at breakfast, our visit was still more social. The old farm-house was in neater trim and the ladies were more cordial than before. We were scarcely seated at table before I realized that I had entered no common situation.

Mine hostess, in the kindness of her heart, had prepared a bountiful, excellent, and varied breakfast. I had come to it with the greatest zest of social and physical hunger. Every condition, therefore, promised one of those phenomenal meals that are the joy of the canoeist and the pride of any healthy man. Now mine host was a man of sound sense and quite miscellaneous reading. He had a head and face of the Andrew Jackson type, showing keen perceptions and a persistent will. We commenced with broiled chicken, and the comfortable silence of serious minds. But soon he said:

"Well, now, you follow books, and know how to judge them; and I'd like to find out just the truth on one thing: Isn't Pope the greatest poet that ever lived?"

I had to relinquish my succulent second joint, and venture on the most perilous passage of my cruise. For I know more of rocks and rapids, and care more for them, than for books. So my opinion could scarcely fulfill my host's expectations in regard to its infallibility. Yet how could I disappoint his literary interest? I did not.

"Wont you have some more baked potatoes? Now I want a poet to teach me something new. That's why every line of Pope satisfies me. What do you think of Homer? I can't get much interested in him. Perhaps he's too big—like them big trees in California, it takes two men and a boy to see to the top of him."

I never before was so devoted to a bare chicken-bone. I nibbled and scraped so assiduously that I found time for only a word or two.

"Have some more baked potatoes. Now, really, Shak-spere, he is no doubt a great genius; but I can't find so much real sense in his plays as in Pope's works. What do you think of him?"

The steaming buckwheat cakes gave me a momentary diversion; but the feast of reason soon resumed its supremacy. We had Burns and Pope, Byron and Pope, Longfellow and Pope. Then came Darwinism, predestination, Beecher, the Southern questions, the new political party, and Edison's inventions. But I struggled manfully through it all, and at the end I felt a full measure of success. The family accompanied me to the shore to see the *Allegro,* and get a glimpse of her independent, roaming life. My interesting visit ended with their best wishes, as I stowed in the locker potatoes, apples, and green corn, and regretfully shoved off for further adventures. These haphazard peeps through back-doors are one of the most entertaining features of a canoe cruise. You have the keenest relish for the companionship and the hospitality; and you see characters in their plain realities, without the mask of ceremony.

The Hudson about Thurman [9] changes from a wild mountain torrent to a stream of charming pastoral character. The valley here and there expands a little, and gives room for bits of cultivation among varied hills and dales. The gloom of the forest is broken by a few fields and a farm-house that are very welcome to the eye. The hills often shut the course of the river from view with bold points and narrow passes, quite like a miniature of the grander Highlands. The islands in the broad stream are picturesque with arching elms. The shores are varied with mossy rocks under golden beeches; with fields where brown stouts of buckwheat peep over the bank; or with green pastures and orchards near a home. The placid river was a long gallery of autumnal pictures. I floated a day through its gorgeous halls of crimson, gold, and green, flooded with sunlight; I drifted as idly and as quietly as the fleets of leaves that came and went with the zephyr. After the rush and nervous combat on the rapids, these tranquil beauties and these dreamy hours were inexpressibly delightful.

The roar of Hadley's Falls [10] broke the spell, and announced one of the most interesting episodes in the cruise. As I paddled down the rift to the head of the falls, a number of ladies in the boarding-houses along the shore caught sight of the *Allegro,* and came down to see her. A young man helped me to carry her around the falls, and launch her in an eddy or little bay behind a point of rocks just at their foot. The gorge of the river here is very narrow, crooked, and walled in with precipitous rocks. The current is swift, tortuous, and turbulent. Just below the foot of the fall is a steep plunge or shoot, where the water almost falls over some rocks, and rolls up crested waves of quite formidable appearance. A few yards below this is a second plunge, rather rougher than the first. Elsewhere the current is deep, and safe enough if it does not dash you against the cavernous walls of rock. The best channel is in the center of each shoot. The ladies watched my operations with close attention while I embarked. I tried to turn her bow toward the middle of the river, and avoid dashing against the left bank of the shoot. But the current bore her bow toward the shore, and pointed her ominously to the rocks. After many vain efforts, I landed and examined the water again at the shoot. Some of the ladies seemed quite pale and agitated; one of them asked me why I did not put my boat in below the "bad places." I answered that I

35. *Rapids above Hadley's Falls,* engraving by John Hill,
1821–1822; courtesy of The New-York Historical Society.

"The gorge of the river here is very narrow, crooked, and
walled in with precipitous rocks."

liked the fun of running such water. This made the black eyes of one dance with excitement. Another then asked with some sarcasm why I did not go. I explained the difficulties to be met. Then they were silent while I reëmbarked. I had concluded to risk a passage on the left side of the shoot, in the shallow water. So I tried again to turn her bow out from the rocks. But the current bore her in. I backed up till the stern was at the very point of the rocks by which the swift current rushed, and then tried to turn the bow out. But I backed too far, for the current caught her, and bore her away sidewise. The ladies exclaimed. For a moment the current seemed to have its own way; but I soon got control of the canoe, and, with a few sharp strokes, brought her back into the eddy below the point. There I watched the whirl of currents a while, and finally availed myself of their movements to get her bow pointed downstream. I gave her a shove, and we started. The ladies clasped their hands together. The canoe went straight to the left side of the shoot, close to the rocks; but she cleared them, and plunged down with a strange motion, as of falling. She struck her keel a sharp blow on the rock at the foot of the shoot, but she did not capsize. She ran all under the crested wave and gave me a shower on the chest and face. I had just time to get breath again, and clear my eyes, when I found her running with the current against the side of the narrow gorge. A sharp struggle ensued, and I finally got her head turned down-stream again. The second shoot was close at hand. Each side of the gorge throws a sharp wave from the bank toward the center of the shoot. These two waves meet at an acute angle, and form two crested walls of water thrown upward with great force. The shoot plunges steeply down, and passes under these waves. Now the only safe passage is directly through the center of this angle. There the boat stands some chance of being lifted equally on each side by each wave, instead of being raised on one side only by one wave, and thus capsized. As we came into the shoot, I saw that she was too far to the left, and, quickly passing the port blade to starboard, I slid her sidewise to the right. She went down the steep, swift, smooth "apron" of the shoot like a flash. In an instant she dived all under the crested wave, and shook with many sudden turnings and swayings in the strong currents. She passed not quite in the center of the angle of waves; for she rolled up one side with a jerk that startled me, but fortunately did not throw me off my balance. A moment later she floated quietly on the pool below the bridge, and turned around with the current while I took breath. Some people on the bridge peered over the railing,[11] and the ladies at the falls waved their handkerchiefs. The passage was short, but swift, and exciting; and its successful termination was not the worst of it.

The Hudson returns, at Jessup's Landing, to the ways of its youth, by plunging down a great fall and then running seven miles as a wild rapid between high mountains. I unwisely followed the counsel of the most prudent villagers instead of the most enterprising, and had my canoe carted four miles down the river to New Bridge.[12] This mistake lost me over three miles of strong, swift water, deeper and safer than the rifts about Riverside [Riparius] and the Glen. But I made up the loss by camping here several days and hunting gray squirrels. The mountains about are delightful hunting-grounds. Every peak commands an extensive view—of the deep gorge where the river foams and roars, of the wide valley of the Hudson rolling through the plain from Glen's Falls to Troy, and of the Green Mountains along the eastern horizon. Every evening the neighbors collected about my camp-fire for stories. They brought me combs of wild honey and sweet apples to roast. These bright fall days in the woods, and the jovial hours of the eve-

36. *Bridge and Hudson River near Luzerne,* anonymous lithograph, 1828–1829; courtesy of the Eno Collection, Prints Division, New York Public Library.

"Some people on the bridge peered over the railing."

ning were some of the pleasantest of the trip. But finally I launched on the last rapids, and soon left the mountains and the rifts for the plain and the still waters of every-day life.

The quiet Hudson below Glen's Falls offered no exciting passages, but this part of my trip was quite as delightful as any other, for the peaceful scenery, the rest on smooth water, and the presence of civilization, were all exceedingly welcome after the rough wilderness. Doubtless they were the more enjoyable because the *Allegro* awakened, all along the route, amusing expressions of curiosity and many acts of kindness. At Glen's Falls, a man who passed me on the canal [13] took me for an Indian, and whooped, grimaced, and grunted in the most cordial and savage manner. But I maintained the taciturnity of my tribe, and gravely worked my paddle without replying. Three men in a wagon stopped their oxen, after much hallooing, to look at me and discuss whether I was an Indian or a negro. I concluded that I had become somewhat tanned. Everybody stopped his work to stare. One man, just opening the hatch of a canal-boat, let the hatch-cover right down on his toes, and stood, quite unmindful of the pain, until I had passed out of sight.

At Northumberland [14] I left the Hudson and followed the canal on its west bank, to avoid some dams in the river; and at the same time to follow a more elevated route for the better views. The canal offered also a new phase of life, and many pleasant civilities. Toward sundown I paddled up to a canal-boat loaded with lumber, and rested from a long day's pull by towing alongside. The captain chatted to me while he manned the long tiller; his wife came up from the cabin to look at the canoe; and their two children leaned over the rail as near as possible to the *Allegro,* and almost devoured her with curiosity. The mother and daughter soon returned to the cabin, and then the rattle of dishes almost drove me distracted. In a few minutes the deck-hand was called to supper; then the captain went down; then the driver on the tow-path was taken aboard and went below into that heaven of feed. But an angel was watching over me all that time. She had suddenly appeared above my head with a tray nicely spread with a steaming supper. She was very pretty, with her little hands weighed down with her load, her matronly bearing, and her evident pleasure in extending her hospitality. I was too much overcome to refuse such an offer. So I set the tray before me on the deck, and between bites told her stories of the rapids. The boat and its people seemed so attractive that I chartered them all to take the *Allegro* on board for the night. She was soon placed in a hollow between the piles of lumber, covered with the tent, and opened to receive calls from all hands. Then the family took me still more into their circle. As we went into their cabin, and I inspected their diminutive but neat quarters, I thought it compared favorably with the cabin of the *Allegro;* for the beds, stove, stores, and furniture were all within reach of a central seat. After a chat I bade them goodnight, and went on deck to turn in. The silence of a misty night was scarcely broken by the tread of the horses on the tow-path. Now and then the men at the helm called out to the driver in a slow, sleepy voice. The boat, as well as everything else, seemed in perfect rest; but when the head-light glared on a bridge or a tree it seemed as if Nature were on a silent march to the rear. I soon fell asleep, after a long day of labor at the paddle; but the night seemed almost a dream; for I knew that we traveled, yet felt not the slightest motion; that some one watched over our progress, although he rarely spoke; and, more than all, I enjoyed again the delightful feeling of home in the little floating world that had received me.

37. *Glenns Falls*, acquatint engraved by J. Hill after the painting by E. G. Wall, 1821–1822; courtesy of The New-York Historical Society.

"The quiet Hudson below Glen's Falls offered no exciting passages."

A modern automobile bridge now connects Glens Falls and South Glens Falls at this point. A cavern in the rock at the foot of the falls is the scene of a dramatic episode in Fenimore Cooper's *Last of the Mohicans.*

I turned out just before sunrise, to enjoy every minute of the last day of my cruise. The scene was entirely veiled by fog. But this soon formed into large clouds that rolled about the great valley, and finally ascended the eastern hills, and let the sun pour down. Thus the knolls and plains were full of pretty lights and shadows on fields of corn and pumpkins, orchards bending with fruit and cozy farm-houses. Blue peaks stood up around the horizon; and a clear sky at last vaulted as bright a world and as happy a day as ever the sun shone on. The little girl sat close beside me with her patch-work, and mingled her musical babble with her womanly ways and serious pleasure. And thus we floated slowly and idly through a charming country, while watching the various operations of locking and weighing the boat, and other peculiar scenes of canal life. As we advanced, the country became still fuller of human interests. The sound of flails floated over the banks, the hum of villages grew louder and more frequent. Then the smoky breath of Troy rang with shrill whistles, and the heavy toils of commerce! Here I launched again, bade good-bye to my kind hosts, and regretfully ran my last course down to Albany. In that quiet scene, where man and his unromantic life of labor have whitewashed nature, the rush, the roar of the rapids, and the isolation of the wilderness, all seemed a dream. I had run the rapids in an egg-shell, as it were. But now it was not without apprehension that I confided myself to a smoking, steaming palace to go down the river. I had to see the *Allegro* ignominiously swung up to beams, above the reach of curious passers, and descend from my halcyon life to the humdrums of existence. Wondering men looked up at her and speculated on her voyage, and praised her beauty. I thought: "You admire only her comely form; but I love her lightsome mastery over waves, her free runs with the wind, her confiding intimacy with sea or lake, river or torrent, and with all this, her intrepid spirit, ready for any adventure, and her staunch friendship tried in flood and field, by night and by day."

PART VI *The Age of the Railroad*

The Hudson Valley

The Age of the Railroad, 1851–1905

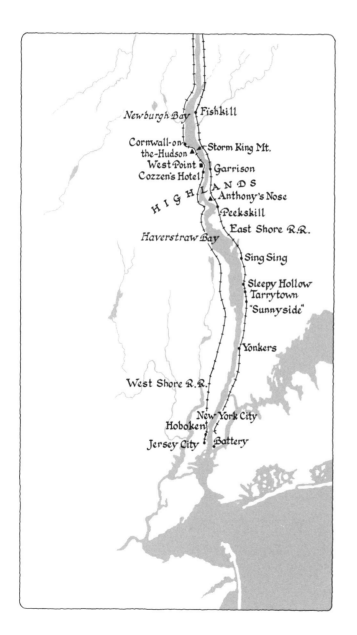

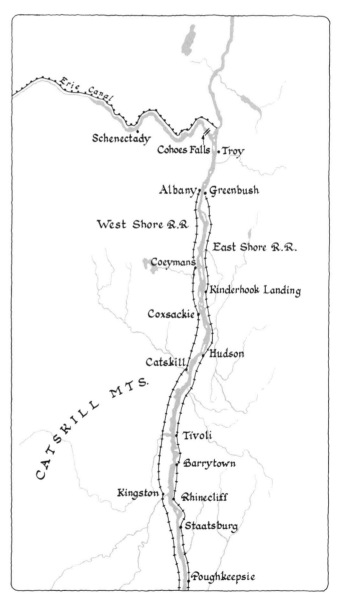

ON THE MORNING of October 8th, 1851, the first train of the Hudson River Railroad sped from New York City to Greenbush, opposite Albany, in three hours and fifty-five minutes at the unprecedented rate of forty miles an hour. The new means of swift travel and transport marked the advent of the most colorful and frenetic decades in the history of the Hudson Valley. By 1883, when the West Shore Railroad was built between Jersey City and Albany, the Hudson River and its adjacent banks teemed with almost every type of transport known to man, from sloops and yachts to canal-boat flotillas, tugs, ferries, magnificent "floating palaces," and thundering freight and passenger trains. It was a spectacle that could not be duplicated along any other river of similar length in the continental United States.

The pageantry of travel and transport in the second half of the nineteenth century was also accompanied by a new upsurge of economic life and a veritable golden age in the social life of the valley. Towns flourished as never before; untold thousands of vacationers flocked to the expanding resorts of the Highlands, Catskills, and Adirondacks; the east bank of the Hudson from Riverdale to Greenbush became the favorite retreat of famous writers, generals, inventors, statesmen; a new class of bewilderingly wealthy entrepreneurs—the Astors and Vanderbilts, the Rockefellers, Goulds, and Morgans—created great landed estates and transformed the banks of the Hudson into one of the most highly-groomed landscapes in all America. It was a time of fruition in the life of the valley, the final flowering and climax of three hundred years of history.

But a time of fruition is also a time of impending change and dissolution, and this process was hastened in the Hudson Valley by a paradox that accompanied each new stage of transportation. Each new stage added impetus to the development of the valley, yet each also subtracted from the river as a *natural* means of transportation. This was even illustrated in the Age of the Steamboat when the introduction of the steam-engine made man less dependent upon the winds, tides, and currents of the river. The railroad was another great advance in this technological liberation: transportation now dispensed with the river itself and merely utilized the valley that had been cut through the Appalachian barrier. The end of this process has awaited the twentieth century, when the development of the internal combustion engine and our modern highway system have permitted millions of people to travel up and down the Hudson Valley without once being aware of the river itself or of the teeming life and history of the past. Today many more millions of people live along the banks of the Hudson than during the last decades of the nineteenth century, yet the traffic on the river is only a fraction of what it was in former years, waterfront facilities languish and decay, and the river itself barely enters into the life of its nearby inhabitants. A major change is now hopefully in the offing, anticipating a future time when the river may be restored to the people at least as a means of recreation and aesthetic pride and joy. But now in the seventh decade of the twentieth century the Hudson River is a neglected gem of the national domain, defiled and polluted throughout most of its tidal length by human and industrial wastes, unfit for drinking, swimming, or fishing; a great natural resource awaiting the deliberations of a more enlightened society.

The paradox, as we have suggested, resides in the very dynamics of technological advance. Throughout the seventeenth and eighteenth centuries when sailing vessels provided the only means of transportation, the trip from New York to Albany commonly required four days to a week, depending upon tides and winds and possible encounters with the shifting sand bars of the upper river. Trips were planned well in advance, great care was taken in the selection of boat and captain, the day of farewell was full of concern. A major change occurred in 1807 with the first primitive steamboat. The *Clermont* made its first scheduled runs in thirty to thirty-six hours at an average speed of five to six miles per hour. By 1825 the time had been cut in half, and in the 1840's the "floating palaces" made scheduled runs in seven or eight hours at an average speed of twenty miles per hour. Then in 1851 came the railroad: time was again cut in half, and a trip that once required a minimum of four days was now performed in four hours. The quality of travel on the Hudson changed proportionately. As Washington Irving said, "before steamboats and railroads had annihilated time and space," a voyage to Albany "was equal to a voyage to Europe at present, and took almost as much time. We enjoyed the beauties of the river in those days; the features of nature were not all jumbled together, nor the towns and villages huddled one into the other by railroad speed as they are now." [1] The following chronicles, which are shorter than their predecessors and often lose sight of the river altogether, amply support that conclusion. The steamboat and the railroad had helped to make the Hudson River Valley one of the busiest and most populous regions in America, but they had also destroyed the necessary balance between remoteness and intimacy that is the prerequisite of any great experience of travel. By the time Henry James visited the Hudson in 1905 an epoch had come to an end. As we have learned since that time, "travel, for the most part, is no longer travel; it is a process which has a beginning and an end but virtually no middle. Travel is not an experience so much as a suspension of experience." [2]

The twentieth century has also seen the end of the Hudson Valley as the strategic corridor of American expansion and development. By the time New York State commemorated the 300th anniversary of Henry Hudson's discovery of the Hudson River, and the 100th anniversary of Robert Fulton's voyage on the *Clermont,* in the great Hudson-Fulton Celebration of 1909, the American Frontier Movement had come to an end and the United States had become a full continental power. The phenomenon of a national civilization stretching from sea to sea, united in part and whole by the sophisticated communications and transportation facilities of a highly developed urban-industrial society, spelled the end of the former regional thrust and glory of the Hudson River Valley. The great celebrations of 1909 were a farewell to history.

17.
Opening of the Hudson River Railroad 1851*

INTRODUCTION: The first railroad to be built in New York State was the Mohawk and Hudson, which ran between Albany and Schenectady in 1831. The following year the New York and Harlem began to be built between New York City and Albany by way of the easternmost counties, but it did not reach Greenbush, opposite the capital, until 1852, the year after the completion of the Hudson River Railroad which connected the same two cities by means of the more strategic route along the eastern bank of the Hudson. Cornelius Vanderbilt later acquired control of both railroads and then joined them to the lines that had been built in the Mohawk Valley to form one continuous railroad under the New York Central system from New York City to Buffalo; but the important development, as far as the coming of the Age of the Railroad to the Hudson Valley was concerned, was the completion of one line along the river's edge between the port of New York and the city of Albany in the fall of 1851. It was this line—appropriately called the Hudson River Railroad— that provided the first means of transportation to circumvent the seasonal limitations of river travel, and it foretold the ultimate demise of the Age of the Steamboat. This was already evident when the railroad reached Poughkeepsie in 1849 and some steamboats began terminating services at that point. But it was the completion of the railroad through to Greenbush in 1851 that impressed upon all beholders the profound influence the new means of transportation would exert upon the traditional modes of travel in the valley, and, as the following brief newspaper account of the inaugural trip attests, the event was celebrated with appropriate joy and ceremony.

* From "Hudson River Railroad; Opening of the Road to Albany," *New-York Daily Times* (Thursday, Oct. 9, 1851).

THE OPENING OF THE Hudson River Railroad to Albany was celebrated yesterday, according to the programme published several days since. At 6 o'clock in the morning a long train of cars started from the Chambers-street Dépôt for the Greenbush terminus of the road,[1] stopping at the various stations. At 7 o'clock, A.M., the Board of Directors, the stockholders in the Company, and a number of invited guests, took another train, filling seven commodious and comfortable cars. Among the latter party we noticed His Honor the Mayor,[2] a fair representation of the Common Council, Judge Oakley,[3] Mr. E. Brooks, [4] Mr. Bigelow [5] of *The Post,* and a number of other representatives of the New-York Press, together with many individuals who have been identified with the interests of the road, whose names are not familiar to us. A few minutes brought us to the upper dépôt, at Thirty-Fourth-street, where the *New York,* a new and powerful locomotive, took the train in charge, and soon we were flying over the country at a rapid rate. The day was remarkably fine. The heavy dew of the night had laid the dust so effectually that the company experienced no inconvenience from that greatest discomfort of railroad traveling.

Everything around promised enjoyment, and all seemed disposed to improve the occasion. Not a breath of air rippled the glassy surface of the beautiful Hudson as it flowed majestically on its silent course. Never was Nature's mirror seen to better advantage, and its vivid reflection of every object which cast a shadow upon its bosom was occasion of enthusiastic remark to the lovers of the beautiful in the works of Creation. On, on the iron horse sped; now winding around the rocky base of some rugged hill, then breaking the stillness of the quiet vale,—now following the shore of the noble stream, and again, rushing over its late domain, upon the narrow causeway which had subverted its long maintained su-

38. *Hudson River Railroad, Anthony's Nose,* anonymous woodcut, 1853; courtesy of The New-York Historical Society.

"On, on the iron horse sped . . . dashing through the tunneled mountain with an exultant roar of strength and triumph, or perforating St. Anthony's Nose with confident impunity."

premacy,—then dashing through the tuneled mountain with an exultant roar of strength and triumph, or perforating St. Anthony's Nose [6] with confident impunity, and anon leaving the peaceful scene of the smooth waters for the more favorable inland route, thus cutting an occasional frowning point, and with them many an old and familiar acquaintance of river travelers.

The scene along the river was exceedingly picturesque. Old Autumn, it is true, has dimmed the lustre of the velvety carpet which nature spreads during the summer months, and robbed the forest of its green and heavy foliage; but richly has he remunerated the towering subjects of his despoliation, by giving them a brilliancy and variety of hue, to the taste of many, far superior in beauty to their plain, though glorious, summer garb. It has been objected that pleasure travelers will always take the steamers on the river, in preference to the railroad, for the sake of viewing the scenery on either hand. If such make a single trip upon the road, and thus secure a view of the west side of the river from the cars, they will witness beauties in the distant landscape, never discovered from the steamer's deck, and in such a manner, too, that the company may safely leave the recollections of the traveler to induce him to repeat the trip.

But we must on to the narrative of the incidents of the occasion. There was little of ornament or decoration on the line of the road, but much—very much comfort and security. The track seems to have been laid in the most substantial manner, and even when running at the rate of forty miles an hour, the motion was so perfectly easy that reading was almost as easy as riding, and writing not very difficult to those whose professional duties occasionally require the practice of chirography under such disadvantages. The excellent flag system established upon this road renders an accident almost impossible, and gives a feeling of security to the traveler not ordinarily included in the pleasures of a railroad journey. It may not be generally known to our readers that flag men are stationed upon every mile of the road, generally at the curves, or upon a slight acclivity where the view of the track may be extended for some distance. Upon the approach of each train it is their duty to signalize the engineer whether he may go ahead confidently, or must slacken his speed, or stop because of danger, etc. During the intervals between the passages of the trains, these flag men examine the road to see if all is secure, and to repair, or procure the repair, of the slightest damage, and the removal of the least obstruction. Thus the entire road is kept under a system of vigilant police. The advantage of compelling the flag men to report at the approach of *every* train, over the system of signalizing only when there is danger, will be apparent at a glance. While they are compelled *always* to report something, or lose their situations, there is little danger of a careless failing to give notice of danger when it *is* ahead.

Of the work accomplished in the construction of the road, we have neither time nor space to speak properly here. When Fulton reached Albany on his first trip by the aid of steam-power, the friends who had reluctantly accompanied him—trembling the while lest they would be compelled to share the disgrace and scorn which a failure would entail—shook their heads, and while they acknowledged the success so far, gravely doubted whether the thing could be done again! Could the men of that day shake off the sleep of death, and look in upon the operations just completed *preparatory* to the march of the steam-horse over the iron course, they would undoubtedly feel it their first duty to warn the doubting and hesitating, how they load with chains of apathy and distrust the genius which sees new attainments in the future, and seeks to grasp them for the benefit of the human race. It is to be hoped that the lights of the past will make ours a wiser generation, and enable us as a people to escape errors which have held back the car of progress, especially when it was turned towards the proposed construction of works of internal improvement.

As the trains passed through the various towns on the line of the road, they were met by large companies of people, who hailed their arrival in the rear of artillery, and cheered them on the way to the terminus. As we passed through Hudson, the children from the Orphan Asylum were drawn up on an acclivity to the left of the road, where they displayed banners containing the inscription,

"James Boorman and the Hudson River Railroad,—the Orphans' Friend." [7]

So regular was the motion of the cars, that the rapidity of travel was hardly noticed; yet the long and crowded train reached the dépôt at Greenbush about 11 o'clock, having made the entire distance of one hundred and forty-three and a quarter miles in three hours and fifty-five minutes.

At Greenbush we found an immense circular car-house arranged for the reception of the Company and its guests. The centre was occupied by a long table, arranged in a circle, sufficient to seat at least two hundred persons. Within the circle was the table designed for the Committee of Arrangements, the officers of the Company, and the most prominent public men present, while outside the ring thus formed, about twenty tables radiated on every side. Thus arranged, the tables were spread with an excellent cold collation, to which about two hundred and fifty persons took seats. Among the guests seated with the officers of the Company, we noticed His Excellency Gov. Hunt,[8] ex-Governor Marcy,[9] Hon. John C. Spencer,[10] and a number of the officers of the State

Government. All seated, the champagne artillery soon drowned the clatter of knife and fork, playing strange variations to the music of a band in attendance; and, dinner having been disposed of with appetites rendered keen by the early ride, Edward Jones, Esq., Chairman of the Committee of Arrangements, took the chair, supported on either side by Gov. Hunt and James Boorman, Esq. Mr. J., in leading off the exercises of the occasion, briefly addressed the assemblage in substance as follows:

Gentlemen: we have met here to commemorate an event of great public interest. The great work in which we have so long labored, amid difficulties and doubt, has been pushed on to completion. That grand idea which not long since, was laughed at in New-York, and many other places, as visionary and chimerical, is to-day a fixed fact. (Cheers.) And now the work is completed, and all admit that it is eminently useful. The location of a railroad on the line of the river, even though commanding the greatest depot of commerce in the western world, was indeed a bold project. It was indeed in advance of the age when projected and commenced; yet it was necessary even then, as events have fully proved. Notwithstanding the natural advantages afforded by the noble river which rolls along almost beneath our feet, the time will soon come, if it has not come already, when New-York will no longer be satisfied with her natural advantages, but will understand the importance of adding to them all other available resources of wealth and prosperity. . . . There is a time coming, and speedily, when this enterprise will be appreciated as it deserves, as will be the judgment, zeal, energy and perseverance of its projectors. In conclusion permit me, on behalf of the Directors, to offer their hearty congratulations to the Stockholders that the great purpose of their association has been accomplished; to the cities of New-York and Albany and all the cities on the line of the work, that they have secured the benefits this new avenue confers upon them; and to the State of New-York, that another great work of public improvement has been accomplished. Permit me to give you—

The State of New-York—Unrivaled in her natural position, she now stands preëminent in her internal works.

39. *Cozzens Dock, West Point,* engraving by Currier & Ives, after 1851; courtesy of The New-York Historical Society.

"The scene along the river was exceedingly picturesque."

The Hudson River Railroad is barely visible on the east bank, opposite the new Cozzens Hotel, three miles below West Point.

18.
N. P. Willis 1854*

INTRODUCTION: Speaking about a great change that had occurred in the life of the Hudson Valley after the advent of the steamboat, Nathaniel Parker Willis (1806–1867), the renowned writer of the Knickerbocker School, noted in 1843 that "there is a suburban look and character about all the villages on the Hudson which seems out of place among such scenery. They are suburbs, in fact; steam has destroyed the distance between them and the city." † This development, however, was restricted before 1851 to the seasonal periods of travel on the Hudson; during the winter months when no form of travel was possible the towns and villages of the Hudson reverted to rural communities in states of semi-isolation. The full development of a suburban pattern with year-round living and daily commutation to and from New York City—and all the consequent changes in the life of the valley—awaited the perfection of the high-powered steam locomotive and the standard-gauge railroad.

A beginning, however, was made with the first primitive railroad of 1851, as we learn from the following account by N. P. Willis.

Willis decided to settle down at present-day Cornwall-on-the-Hudson in 1853, just two years after the completion of the Hudson River Railroad. "Idlewild," the name of the rural retreat that he soon made famous in weekly letters to the *Home Journal,* became the familiar haunt of such notable guests as Bayard Taylor, Charles A. Dana, and Washington Irving. Thanks to the fame of Idlewild and Willis's seductive literary talents, the region around Storm King and the northern gateway to the Highlands became a favorite retreat of summer residents from New York City.

And not only summer residents. By 1854—the year in which the following account was written—businessmen as well as writers were living year round on the banks of the Hudson, and daily commuting to and from the metropolis had become something of an established way of life. The railroad, despite the delays and hazards that still disrupted its winter schedules, had liberated man from the seasonal restrictions of steamship travel, and inaugurated a social revolution.

LIVING IN THE COUNTRY all the year round, has its occasional misgivings. . . . There are "spells of weather," as the country people call them, which, for a day or two at a time, in this northern climate, make all out-doors intolerable. The "sloshy going" is discouraging enough—when the snow is just so much melted with a raw east wind as to hold water six or eight inches deep on a side hill—but this, though it makes an island of the house, imprisons only those vintager snails,[1] the women and children. There is a worse stage of winter which imprisons also man and horse—the cold after a thaw, when the roads are an impassable slough of false mud, and the animal that you ride plants one foot safely on the surface, but can scarcely extricate the other from the stiffening mud in which he "slumps" to the knee. There is no exercise to be got by riding, and walking is out of the question. The lungs pine for expansion. Blood runs slow. Sidewalks and omnibuses begin to loom up with a forgotten glory.

In watching the railway trains from my library window[2] I find I have no feeling of *being-left-behind,* except in the un-get-aboutable weather. Happily at rest

* Excerpt from N. P. Willis's *Out-Doors at Idlewild* (New York: 1855), pp. 321–327.
† Quoted in the Rev. Charles Rockwell's *The Catskill Mountains and the Region Around* (New York: 1873), p. 219.

while others are wearily urged onward—or tiresomely on a shelf while others have liberty to change the scene— are two impressions receivable from the same smoke of a flying locomotive in the distance. I should often start for a week in the city, with the latter feeling, if it were not for the horse in the stable, and the chance of out-doors freedom to-morrow; but, last week, the winter's "protracted agony" got the upper hand, and, with my "7,000,000 pores" voting for a change of air, I gave in. And, of some of my experiences in getting to the city, I may as well make a passing chronicle—adding, as it will, to an understanding of that life *here-abouts* which it is the object of these sketches to illustrate.

We usually speak of the city as about two hours dis-tant; and, though a snow-storm came on in the night, after my preparations to go, I thought it would be such a ploughing as I had frequently seen to offer little or no impediment to the trains during the winter, and started from home at daylight to meet the cars, in full faith of a noon in the city. As I did not reach my hotel till the following midnight, and did not get my baggage for still eighteen hours more, the reader will see what slovenly service it is, after all, spoken of so grandly by the phi-losopher:—"Man is a world, and hath another world to attend on him." A pocket full of crackers may be a very comfortable addition to such a couple of worlds.

Missing the Newburgh-and-Erie train, which goes down upon our side of the Hudson, and then driving four miles in an open wagon against a snow-storm of pow-dered needles, and crossing the river to Fishkill by a ferry made doubtful by the ice, I got seated in the cars somewhere between nine and ten o'clock, thinking that, for this trip of pleasure, the Compensation Office must have taken the payment in advance. We started well enough out of the village. The rails had been cleared by the brakemen. A little farther on, among the rocks,

however, the drifts began to look formidable, and I soon saw that we had been reached, in the Highlands, by only a thin skirt of the storm of the night before. The drifts grew deeper and deeper—our headway slower and slower—and finally, in a rocky gorge, just opposite Coz-zen's Summer Hotel,[3] we came to a stand still for the day—a tall snow-bank on each side (neither of them "a bank whereon the *wile-time* grows") our only prospect from the windows. We found afterwards that the stop was partly from a dread of meeting an up-train and running the noses of the two locomotives together under the snow; and that the delay of the up-train was owing to the breakdown of an engine—but our several halts chanced to be in spots where the demand for "pies and coffee" had not been anticipated, and the cause of the delay was less thought of than the famishing conse-quences. At one place, I believe, a passenger or two waded back a long distance to a country grocery of which they had got a glimmer in passing, and found biscuits and gingerbread; but the remaining stomachs of our own train, and those which kept accumulating behind us from the West, "bore on" with unassisted resignation till midnight.

We Americans are a patient and merry people under difficulties. I do not think travellers have sufficiently given us credit for this national quality of *jolly indomi-tableness*. The successive additions to our long line of trains stretched to very near a mile, by sundown, and a mile of more gay and cheerful people—hungry as they all were—could not be found on a French holiday. A footpath was soon tracked through the snow, along one side of the cars, at each stopping-place, and merriment resounded under all the windows—everybody apparently acquainted with everybody, and no sign of the fretful grumbler that would have abounded in such a disap-pointed multitude in Europe. Yet most of those five

40. *American Railroad Scene—Snowbound,* engraved by
Currier & Ives, 1871; courtesy of the Harry T. Peters collection,
Museum of the City of New York.

"The drifts grew deeper and deeper—our headway slower and
slower—and finally . . . we came to a stand still for the day."

AMERICAN RAILROAD SCENE.

SNOW BOUND

hundred jokers were business men, to whom the delay was a serious inconvenience.

One of our long halts was under "Sunny Side," Irving's residence.[4] It was long after dark, and the car was double-filled—the passengers had been condensed into the forward trains, to detach as many trains as possible, and so save weight. As many persons were standing up as sitting down. Conversation was general, and whoever "had the floor" was heard by all. One man announced that we were but a stone's-throw from Washington Irving's. "Well," said a rough-looking fellow from the corner, "I would rather lay eyes on *that man* than any man in the world." "I have seen him," said another; "he looks like a gentleman, I tell you!" And then they went into a discussion of his various works—two "strong-minded" ladies who were on the front seat taking a lively and very audible part in it. [Chancing to meet Mr. Irving, two days after, at the Astor Library,[5] and finding he was at home at the time, I inquired whether his ears had burned, about eight o'clock on a certain evening; but, as he said "no," there is less magnetism in a car-full of compliments than would be set down, for that quantity of electric influence, probably, by the Misses Fox.][6]

The only ill temper that I discovered, during the fourteen hours of unfed delay, was between those who cared for fresh air, and those who preferred the allowance of about the ventilation they would get in a coffin. With the standing and sitting passengers, and the cars motionless, the atmospheric vitality within was exhaustible in five minutes at furthest; and, strangely enough, most of those sitting at the windows after dark refused to open them. I suffered painfully myself from the foulness of the atmosphere, all day. Then the stove was kept almost red-hot, and with the snow brought in by the feet of the passers to and fro, the bottom of the car was a pool of water. Like others, probably, who had not foreseen this, I was not provided with India rubbers, and of course sat with damp feet all the way—a dangerous addition to an empty stomach and a pestilent atmosphere. Ah, Messrs. Presidents and Directors of railways, is it not possible to have the ventilation of cars independent of those who do not know the meaning of fresh air?

We arrived at Thirty-first street [7] in the neighborhood of eleven o'clock; but, as no announcement was made of that happy fact, we sat fifteen or twenty minutes in the cars, wasting our resignation on a supposed snow-bank. With the discovery that the snow in the streets would prevent the cars from going farther, and that the baggage had so accumulated with the numerous trains that it could not be delivered till morning, the next query was how to travel the three miles to our various homes and hotels in the city.[8] There was one four-horse sleigh in waiting, and probably between five and eight hundred passengers. Not sorry, myself, to stir my blood with a walk for that distance before taking my lungs to bed, I gave my check to an Express agent (who brought my trunk to me at seven in the morning), and with hundreds of men, women, and children, started down-townwards. With a long stumble over the unshovelled sidewalks of slumbering and ill-lighted suburbs, I found myself, towards midnight, in the neighborhood of Union Square, and, over a venison steak which I found smoking on the supper-table at the Clarendon, vowed never again to make even a two hours' pilgrimage in a rail-car without provision against accident—say a cracker or two and some shape of fluid consolation.

19.

Isabella B. Bishop 1854 *

INTRODUCTION: Mrs. Isabella Bird Bishop (1832–1904), world traveler, author, and the first lady Fellow of the Royal Geographical Society, arrived in Albany in early November 1854, after an extensive tour of Canada, and boarded a train for New York City on the first lap of a journey through America. The narrative of this journey confirmed Washington Irving's complaint that "railroad speed" had telescoped the distance between the towns and villages of the Hudson and obscured the features of nature. Yet the narrative also reveals, for this very reason, a new tension and excitement that is distinctly modern in tone and that anticipates the grand climax of Hudson Valley travel in the vigorous decades of the late nineteenth century.

WE CROSSED THE Hudson River, and spent the night at Delaval's,[1] at Albany. The great peculiarity of this most comfortable hotel is, that the fifty waiters are Irish girls, neatly and simply dressed. They are under a coloured manager, and their civility and alacrity made me wonder that the highly-paid services of male waiters were not more frequently dispensed with. The railway ran along the street in which the hotel is situated. From my bedroom window I looked down into the funnel of a locomotive, and all night long was serenaded with screams, ringing of bells, and cries of "All aboard" and "Go ahead."

Albany, the capital of the State of New York, is one of the prettiest towns in the Union. The slope on which it is built faces the Hudson, and is crowned by a large state-house, the place of meeting for the legislature of the Empire State. The Americans repudiate the "centralization" principle, and for wise reasons, of which the Irish form a considerable number, they almost invariably locate the government of each state, not at the most important or populous town, but at some inconsiderable place, where the learned legislatures are not in danger of having their embarrassments increased by deliberating under the coercion of a turbulent urban population. Albany has several public buildings, and a number of conspicuous churches, and is a very thriving place. The traffic on the river between it and New York is enormous. There is a perpetual stream of small vessels up and down. The Empire City receives its daily supplies of vegetables, meat, butter, and eggs from its neighbourhood. The Erie and Champlain canals here meet the Hudson, and through the former the produce of the teeming West pours to the Atlantic. The traffic is carried on in small sailing sloops and steamers. Sometimes a little screw-vessel of fifteen or twenty tons may be seen to hurry, puffing and panting, up to a large vessel and drag it down to the sea; but generally one paddle-tug takes six vessels down, four being towed behind and one or two lashed on either side. As both steamers and sloops are painted white, and the sails are perfectly dazzling in their purity, and twenty, thirty, and forty of these flotillas may be seen in the course of a morning, the Hudson river presents a very animated and unique appearance. It is said that everybody loses a portmanteau at Albany: I was more fortunate, and left it without having experienced the slightest annoyance.

On the other side of the ferry [across the Hudson in Greenbush] a very undignified scramble takes place for the seats on the right side of the cars, as the scenery for 130 miles [2] is perfectly magnificent. "Go ahead" rapidly succeeded "All aboard," and we whizzed along this most extraordinary line of railway, so prolific in accidents that,

* Excerpt from Isabella Bird Bishop's *An Englishwoman in America* (London: 1856), pp. 328–333.

41. *Albany, New York,* detail of a lithograph by John W. Hill, c. 1850; courtesy of The New-York Historical Society.

"Albany, the capital of the State of New York, is one of the prettiest towns in the Union."

when people leave New York by it, their friends frequently request them to notify their safe arrival at their destination. It runs along the very verge of the river, below a steep cliff, but often is supported just above the surface of the water upon a wooden platform. Guidebooks inform us that the trains which run on this line, and the steamers which ply on the Hudson, are equally unsafe, the former from collisions and "upsets," the latter from "bustings-up"; but most people prefer the boats, from the advantage of seeing both sides of the river.

The sun of a November morning had just risen as we left Albany, and in a short time beamed upon swelling hills, green savannahs, and waving woods fringing the margin of the Hudson. At Coxsackie the river expands into a small lake, and the majestic Catsgill [*sic*] Mountains rise abruptly from the western side. The scenery among these mountains is very grand and varied. Its silence and rugged sublimity recall the Old World: it has rocky pinnacles and desert passes, inaccessible eminences and yawning chasms. The world might grow populous at the feet of the Catsgills, but it would leave them untouched and unprofaned in their stern majesty. From this point for a hundred miles the eyes of the traveler are perfectly steeped in beauty, which, gathering and increasing, culminates at West Point, a lofty eminence jutting upon a lake apparently without any outlet. The spurs of mountain ranges which meet here project in precipices from five to fifteen hundred feet in height; trees find a place for their roots in every rift among the rocks; festoons of clementis and wild-vine hang in graceful drapery from base to summit, and the dark mountain shadows loom over the lake-like expanse below. The hand wearies of writing of the loveliness of this river. I saw it on a perfect day. The Indian summer lingered, as though unwilling that the chilly blasts of winter should blight the loveliness of this beauteous scene. The gloom of autumn was not there, but its glories were on every leaf and twig. The bright scarlet of the maple vied with the brilliant berries of rowan, and from among the tendrils of the creepers, which were waving in the sighs of the west wind, peeped forth the deep crimson of the sumach. There were very few signs of cultivation; the banks of the Hudson are barren in all but beauty.[3] The river is a succession of small wild lakes, connected by narrow reaches, bound for ever between abrupt precipices. There are lakes more beauteous than Loch Katrine,[4] softer in their features than Loch Achray,[5] though like both, or like the waters which glitter beneath the blue sky of Italy. Along their margins the woods hung in scarlet and gold—high above towered the purple peaks—the blue waters flashed back the rays of a sun shining from an unclouded sky—the air was like June—and I think the sunbeams of that day scarcely shone upon a fairer scene. At mid-day the Highlands of [the] Hudson were left behind—the mountains melted into hills—the river expanded into a noble stream about a mile in width—the scarlet woods, the silvery lakes, and the majestic Catsgills, faded away in the distance; and with a whoop, and a roar, and a clatter, the cars entered into, and proceeded at slackened speed down, a long street called Tenth Avenue, among carts, children, and pigs.

True enough, we were in New York, the western receptacle not only of the traveller and the energetic merchant, but of the destitute, the friendless, the vagabond, and in short of all the outpourings of Europe, who here form a conglomerate mass of evil, making America responsible for their vices and their crimes. Yet the usual signs of approach to an enormous city were awanting—dwarfed trees, market-gardens, cockney arbours, in which citizens smoke their pipes in the evening, and imagine themselves in Arcadia, rows of small houses, and a murky canopy of smoke. We had steamed down Tenth Avenue for two or three miles, when we came to a standstill where several streets met. The train was taken to pieces, and to each car four horses or mules were attached, which took us for some distance into the very heart of the town, racing apparently with omnibuses and carriages, till at last we were deposited in Chambers Street.

20.

Jacques Offenbach 1876*

INTRODUCTION: The following account of a trip on the Hudson River Railroad taken in 1876 by Jacques Offenbach (1819–1880), the French composer of "The Tales of Hoffmann," is remarkable for its almost total absence of reference to the surrounding scenery and landscape.

Offenbach had come to the United States to visit the Philadelphia Exposition and to enhance his reputation and gain new converts among the music lovers of America. Sometime in 1876, however, he decided to make the "grand tour" to Niagara Falls, and boarded a train for Albany and Buffalo. After a few desultory remarks about the scenery of the Hudson he devoted all his attention to the novel habits and manners of his fellow travelers and the wonderful speed and elegance of the American railroad. To a European it was all a striking confirmation of American ingenuity and technological superiority.

In the twenty-year interval after Mrs. Bishop's ride on the Hudson River Railroad, the American railroad underwent a remarkable evolution. Narrow gauge yielded to standard gauge, locomotives grew to the gargantuan size of 70 tons, trunk lines enveloped every part of the nation, and from 1867 to 1876 the sleeping, dining, and chair cars of the Pullman Company revolutionized American railway travel. All this Jacques Offenbach encountered for the first time on his trip up the Hudson in 1876. His interest and enthusiasm were therefore concentrated on the new mode of transportation rather than the land through which he traveled. The following brief account therefore presaged the day when even Americans would ascend the Hudson on speedy trips to the cities of the Great Lakes or the Pacific coast without once giving thought to the erstwhile glories of the Hudson River Valley.

* Excerpt from Jacques Offenbach's *Offenbach in America: Notes on a Travelling Musician* (New York: 1877), 160–165, 172–177.

THE ROAD FROM NEW YORK to Niagara is very fine. The landscape, as far as Albany, is truly marvellous along the splendid river Hudson. I do not know to what river in Europe I could compare the American river. There are places which remind me of the most beautiful parts of the Rhine; there are others which surpass in beauty all that I had ever seen. The voyage is made in the most agreeable manner; the Pullman cars are a precious institution.[1] The great problem is realized by these wonderful carriages of being on a railway and having none of the unpleasantness of travelling by rail. One is not, as with us, packed in narrow compartments, nor exposed to the tingling sensation which passes in one's limbs after some hours of immobility. One has not to fear ankylosis of the fatigued limbs from keeping the same position for too great a length of time. In the American train you can walk about from one car to another all the way from the baggage-car to the buffer of the last carriage. When tired of walking, you can rest in an elegant saloon, upon excellent arm-chairs. You have at hand all necessary comforts to make life agreeable. I cannot better sum up my admiration for American railways than by saying that they are really—a cradle on wheels.

I do not, however, like the continual bell which accompanies you all along the journey with its funeral knell; but it is, perhaps, only a matter of habit, and one should not have too delicate an ear when travelling in America, for one is constantly persecuted by unpleasant sounds.

At Utica [?], where we stopped a few minutes to lunch, I saw (and heard, alas!) a large negro beating a tam-tam. He was evidently playing music of his own composing, for he beat sometimes loud and with astonishing quickness, sometimes with measured slowness. I forgot to lunch while watching this peculiar musician. During his last piece of music—for so he doubtless considered it—I was all ears and eyes. He began by a *fortissimo* which deafened you, for the negro was a powerful fellow, and applied all his strength. After this brilliant opening, his music continued *decrescendo, piano, pianissimo,* then silence.

At the same moment the train started. I had just time to jump on, and we were again at full speed.

At Albany we stopped to dine.[2] I found another great negro before the hotel, who resembled the first, and who was also playing the tam-tam. This must certainly be a country exceedingly fond of the tam-tam.

A hungry belly has no ears, says the proverb. I am grieved in this case at being unable to agree with the wisdom of nations, for, notwithstanding my appetite, the negro's music tormented me during all the meal. He played exactly like his colleague at Utica [?]—the same repetition of *forte, piano,* and *pianissimo.* I was on the point of asking if the negroes really considered the solo on the tam-tam to be music, and if this was their national air, when one of my friends addressed me.

"This negro puzzles you," he said; "you will see one just like him at every station on the line."

"Is it an attention on the party of the company?" I asked.

"No, it is the hotel-keepers who engage them. The negroes play all the time the train is at the station; their music warns the travellers who are inside the hotel. While the tam-tam is loud, you can remain quiet; when the sound decreases, you had better hurry; when it is at the lowest, the travellers know that they must jump into the cars, which, like Louis XIV, do not wait, and, worse still, give no warning. So much the worse for those who lose the train."

I do not know whether I prefer the American style to that employed by the hotel-keeper at Morcenz, between Bordeaux and Biarritz. Having no negro, the landlord

himself shouts, in a stentorian voice: "Five minutes more! four minutes more! three minutes more!"

The two systems are alike; the only difference is that one deafens you with his voice inside the establishment, while the other stuns you with his music in the open air. . . .

On the way [back] from Niagara I took the night train. I was glad of an opportunity to try in person the sleeping-cars of which I had heard so much.

I entered the car, which seemed arranged, as usual, with large easy-chairs on each side of the passage-way—special rooms for smokers, and all the convenience which I had so much admired on my first trip. Nothing indicated, in the arrangement of the cars, that one could sleep there in a bed, and I began to believe in some mystification, so utterly impossible did it seem that all the ladies and gentlemen who sat in this fine saloon could be supplied with sleeping accommodations.

Nevertheless, at about nine o'clock, when it began to get quite dark, two servants of the company appeared and commenced the arrangements. In the twinkling of an eye our seats were transformed into beds, and in the most simple manner. Upon the seats joined together by a board, they placed first a mattress, sheets, and blankets. The saloon, thus turned into a dormitory, would not have been sufficient for the number of travellers without another expedient. Above each of the beds is a little apparatus, which drops down, and which proves to be a sort of folding-bed. There are thus two stories of beds in each compartment—the ground floor and the entresol. But, before retiring, there is a preliminary operation, which people are not generally fond of performing in public. The men, were they alone, could easily undress before each other; but the ladies, it will readily be understood, cannot undress before all the travellers. The inventor of the sleeping-cars was therefore obliged to find some means of reassuring the modesty of the fair sex. This he has succeeded in doing by making of each pair of beds —the upper and lower ones—a complete bed-room. Two large curtains, drawn parallel the whole length of the car, form a long corridor in the centre, in which the travellers can walk, if so disposed. Between each of these curtains and the side of the wagon are smaller curtains. A person in bed is thus in a little room, which at the head has a wooden wall, and on the three other sides a curtain partition. I have known hotels where the walls were less discreet than those of the sleeping-car.

All the preparations being finished, an amusing scene begins. Each one chooses his bed, and selects the little compartment which appears most advantageous to him. Then for some minutes is heard in the adjoining rooms the noise of boots falling on the floor, or the pleasant rustling sound which reveals the removing of a skirt.

When a husband travels with his wife, he has a perfect right to occupy the same compartment with her. This fact was revealed to me by an extremely interesting conversation, held in a low tone, which took place in the next berth to mine on the right side. However discreet one may be, one is always a little curious to know what neighbors, chance has given you. On the left, the occupant of the cabin was a charming young lady. She had retired to her room as soon as the transformation of the saloon had taken place, and, to her honor be it said, her presence was revealed only by the most discreet motions. Then when the curtain ceased to stir, the sound of a bed receiving a light body informed me that she had at last lain down for the night. A few minutes elapsed. I had also

stretched myself upon my bed, but not being accustomed to this kind of travelling hotel, and being kept awake by my old Parisian habit of going to sleep very late, I lay with my eyes open, thinking of the strange aspect of this American dormitory. In the passage at my feet, formed by the two long curtains of which I have spoken, I heard the sound of people walking to and fro. Who could they be? I cast a glance upon the corridor, and saw—*horresco referens*—ladies in night jackets (it is true they were not the prettiest) who were going . . . I know not where. I saw also a good-looking Yankee who came out of his room. After ascertaining that the road was clear, he walked to the platform and lit a cigar. A moment later he threw away his fragrant Havana, and returned inside the car; but instead of going straight to his cabin, he directed his steps—you have already guessed it—to that of my pretty neighbor on the left.

His irruption into the sanctuary of the pretty American lady provoked a series of exclamations, uttered in a low voice, so as not to arouse the general attention of the dormitory, and the invader retired, making some excuse for his mistake. The night passed without any further incident.

Scarcely had rosy-fingered morn appeared, than the servants appeared also. Ladies and gentlemen tumbled out of their beds, and made their toilets as best they could behind their respective curtains. The agents of the company then restored everything to its usual order in the twinkling of an eye. After our night's sleep, therefore, we met again in the saloon as fresh and as well as though we had spent the night in a hotel.

21.
Emile De Damseaux 1877*

INTRODUCTION: The following account by the French traveler, Emile De Damseaux, presents the Hudson Valley of 1877 under the twin guises of railway and steamship travel. Like his compatriot, Jacques Offenbach, Damseaux visited Niagara Falls during his tour of America, but fortunately for us he took a day-train on his final lap from Albany to New York, and we therefore gain a fresh impression of the Hudson Valley. Some days later, Damseaux re-ascended the valley as far as West Point on a one-day excursion steamer. Here we gain an even fuller impression of the thriving, populous valley of the last quarter of the nineteenth century; but it is a scene typical of what Damseaux calls "the feverish life of the Americans," and we know that for all the pageantry of trade and traffic, the possibility of a genuine experience of travel has been permanently submerged in the frenetic tourism of an urban-industrial civilization.

FOLLOWING THE AMERICAN CUSTOM, I most often traveled at night: sleeping on a train or sleeping at home is all the same to me, but in America sleeping while traveling is saving time, and "time is money." After having admired the absolutely unrivalled splendors of Niagara Falls, I caught the night train to New-York at Suspension Bridge, on the American side, and plunged again into the curtains of the "Sleeping-Car" and the next day at day-break I found myself in Albany.

Albany, a city of 70,000 inhabitants, is the seat of the New York State government. Like all the cities in the United States, the greatest growth of population has only

* Excerpt from Emile De Damseaux's *Voyage dans l'Amerique du Nord* (Paris: 1878), Chapter XI, 158–171. Translated by Leona T. Van Zandt.

occurred since the beginning of the century; it is chiefly since 1807, the date of the first appearance of the steamboat on the Hudson, built by Fulton, that this city has had a great development; at that time, it had only a few thousand inhabitants. It was also between Albany and New-York that the first railroad line in the State was established in 1831.[1]

Albany does a big business in beer, grain, and cattle; it has numerous industrial establishments, and its port is very important. Albany has, among other numerous educational institutions, an academy and a seminary for women. Albany is also the home of the Dudley Observatory, one of the beautiful buildings of America. It was named after a woman who donated a million [francs] for its construction.[2] . . .

In leaving Albany the train crosses the Hudson on an iron bridge which is almost fourteen hundred metres long. This time I had taken a seat in a day-train and installed myself in a revolving arm-chair in the *Parlor Car,* a magnificent carriage, all in velvet and gold and sparkling mirrors, and containing such appurtenances as smoking rooms, dressing rooms, private compartments, etc., all of which are essential parts of the American idea of comfort. Though I was in the train for several hours over a distance of 125 miles, only the ubiquitous presence of the American spittoon—and its constant use by the male members of the car—reminded me that I was not throughout the journey in a *salon.* The luxury of the carriage was incomparable: ladies in elegant attire occupied a number of arm chairs, constantly coming and going, chatting, making frequent visits to the cooler to get ice-water; innumerable venders invaded the car to sell fruits, lemonade, and ices. At every station there was a great stir and bustle; people rose to greet each other, to nod to acquaintances, or chat; and I realized that such behavior was a routine matter on this train, for

42. *American Express Train,* engraving by F. F. Palmer for
Currier & Ives, 1864; courtesy of the Harry T. Peters Collection, Museum of the City of New York.

"The railroad follows the left bank of the Hudson, never
leaving the edge of the river."

AMERICAN EXPRESS TRAIN.

many people who live along the line of this railroad have business which often takes them to New York. I made the acquaintance of a gentleman in that city, the head of a great corporation, who has a country-seat on the banks of the Hudson. Commuting each day to and from the city, he spends a total of six hours traveling on this railroad. But don't imagine that this is all lost time: this gentleman has his own private compartment and spends the time preparing his business transactions. The railroad follows the left bank of the Hudson, never leaving the edge of the river; indeed, in many places where there is not room for the rails and the train has been shunted onto long artificial embankments, one has the pleasure of appearing to ride across the water itself in the very middle of a flotilla of boats.

The Hudson is the Rhine without the latter's ruins, legends, and vestiges of an heroic past; it is the Rhine in all its *natural* splendors—its mountains, valleys, and hills—but on a more sublime and majestic scale, with far broader and more distant horizons. In place of ruins the Hudson has factories, cities, and villages: it is, in fact, one of the most populous regions of America. Here one sees chalets, reminiscent of Switzerland; houses coquettishly tucked in the hills, their flat roofs bedecked with a cornice, as in Italy; and in the summer the sky above these houses is every bit as fine as in Italy. On a distant mountain a red brick building, capped with towers, reminds one of England. Many of these houses, whose white walls reflect the brilliant light of the sun and whose green awnings are lowered against the heat of the day, belong to the sons of Holland, the descendents of the original founders of this State who represent the aristocracy of the country.

Americans love to place their summer homes on the sides of these picturesque wooded hills and along the banks of this beautiful river; certain specific areas, known far and wide for the salubrity of their climate as well as the beauties of their landscape, abound in country houses.

The railway follows all the capricious meanderings of the river, now hugging the base of huge outcroppings of rock, and now even encroaching upon the river-bed itself. It would seem that in constructing this railroad the builders had been guided by the principle of never letting the traveler lose sight of the glorious landscape that constantly unrolls before his eyes.

This river, with its broad and deep waters, is covered throughout its length with every conceivable type of boat or vessel: we see huge gilt-encrusted "ferries," several stories high; large wooden rafts; small canoes; enormous barges bulging with all kinds of merchandise and being pushed or pulled by powerful tugboats; gigantic ice-boats of most peculiar construction transporting a most precious and useful commodity to the sweltering masses of the great metropolis.

On both sides of the river one sees great numbers of monolithic ice-houses which border, during the wintertime, those fields of ice that furnish such an abundant harvest. During the summer the stored ice is transported by the ice-boats to the neighboring cities. After arriving at the various docks, the cargo is transferred to "ad hoc" carts which supply each American household with its daily supply of ice.

The landscape, always magnificent, changes its aspect with every curve and bend of the railroad. Beyond the nearby hillsides that roll gently and graciously down to the river's edge and are covered with gardens, rise the mountain-peaks in successive ridges reminiscent of the Dauphiné; [3] beyond these the mountains subside into little round hills like the beautiful terrain of the Ardennes around Bouillon. [4] Then come some steep rocky escarpements, some wild gorges, then meadowland, next

43. *The "Mary Powell" passing the Gate of the Highlands,* anonymous engraving, 1875; courtesy of The New-York Historical Society.

"This river, with its broad and deep waters, is covered throughout its length with every conceivable type of boat or vessel."

THE MARY POWELL PASSING THE GATE OF THE HIGHLANDS.

The **MARY POWELL,** Capt. ANDERSON, will leave Vestry St., **Pier 39, N. R.,** (adjacent to Jersey City Ferry,) EVERY AFTERNOON, Sundays excepted, **at 3.30 o'clock,** landing at Cozzens' Hotel, West Point, Gov't Dock, Cornwall, Newburgh, New Hamburgh, Milton, Poughkeepsie, Rondout and Kingston.   *Connects with evening train at Poughkeepsie for the North.*
RETURNING—will leave Rondout at 5.30 A.M.; Poughkeepsie, 6.30; Milton, 6.45; New Hamburgh, 7; Newburgh, 7.30; Cornwall, 7.45; West Point, 8.05; Cozzens', 8.10; arriving in NEW YORK at 10.45 A.M.
MEALS SERVED AT ALL HOURS.

some houses hidden in thick foliage from which the pointed roofs of churches or the façade of a temple emerges. There is no lack of churches and temples in this country. No community, however small, is without its innumerable altars belonging to a multitude of religious sects—sects which have been produced by religious freedom yet are divided from each other by a mutual intolerance that is unknown in Europe, and that acts to the advantage of Roman Catholicism which is growing daily stronger and more prosperous.

The train stops across from West Point which is beautifully located along the opposite bank of the river. West Point, the seat of the United States Military School, is on a high pleateau sixteen [hundred] metres long. The plateau is covered with numerous buildings and military installations of the school. . . .

But alas! here as elsewhere in America nature is sullied by advertising: along lofty crags and cliffs picturesquely rising from the banks of the river, or on small rocky islands lapped by little waves in a circle of foam, one sees forever and everywhere the mutilations "Sozodout," "Gargling Oil," "Sapolio." The first is the name of a manufacturer—if one can call him that—who sells a toothpowder. "Gargling Oil" is the name of a product which one could only wish had the power to contract esophagi and keep Americans from spitting. The third, "Sapolio," advertises a product that cleans pots, mirrors, and other products. But there is no poetry in all this, no poetry whatsoever.

A little farther along we see a waterfall that plunges from the high crags into the river below: [5] it is very pretty, but after Niagara it can only appear paltry. We pass Peekskill, another charming spot. Here the river widens into the imposing proportions of Haverstraw Bay; we can hardly make out the opposite bank at this place, and so extensive are the surrounding horizons that we can find no sign of where the river takes leave of this veritable lake. Farther along we come upon Sing-Sing, the principal establishment of which is the State House of Detention: it is an immense building with a numerous population.

The banks of the Hudson are not without ruins and history. These ruins and their many associations spring from the period of the American Revolution. This beautiful countryside was once the scene of numerous battles, many of which became famous for the courage and heroism with which Americans finally freed themselves from foreign domination. Each remnant of some old fort along the Hudson is associated with the name of a hero; every mile of the way bespeaks some bloody military event.

On nearing the big metropolis one finds more activity along the river: houses, towns, and villages become more numerous. The river suddenly becomes hemmed in by towering cliffs, huge perpendicular crags, naked and gray: they are the "palisades." The railway line then quits the banks of the river, runs through the city of Hoboken [Yonkers?], a suburb of New-York, enters a series of tunnels beneath the city, then terminates at the principal station located at 42nd Street.[6]

The feverish life of the Americans creates a counterdesire for repose and distraction; the people find their greatest pleasure in occasionally taking excursions into the environs of New York and especially along the banks of the Hudson. There are many favorite places for these excursions, but next to Coney Island (a beach where there is sea bathing), West Point is the most popular. New York City is full of workers' associations whose only purpose is the organization of outings and excursions. The people rent a big boat, embark with their provisions and a hired group of musicians, and take a ride.

Excursions are also organized for the general public. I saw an advertisement for an excursion going to West

Point by means of the *Plymouth Rock,* a boat which, besides being recently renovated, magnificently redecorated, and superlatively run by the finest captains, was the biggest, most beautiful and magnificent boat—according to the poster—in all the world.[7] The advertisement also assured me that a concert would be given during the voyage by a famous group of musicians especially engaged by the company, that there would be interludes of "musical chimes" and the entertainment of the Mozart Choral Society; that the buffet and restaurant couldn't be better; and that the cost of the trip was "50 cents" (2.50 francs).

This excursion was scheduled for a Sunday, departure time one o'clock in the afternoon. I went to the Battery, the place of departure, and got my "ticket." The *Plymouth Rock* is a huge gold and white boat several stories high; on the lowest level is the engine room, the refreshment room (in the bow), the dining room (astern), and a 360 degree gallery; the next level is taken up completely by a magnificent *salon* that runs the whole length of the boat, lavishly decorated with mirrors, and richly furnished with a thick carpet, arm-chairs, and beautiful and comfortable seats; the upper level is composed of the pilot's house, the officers' cabins, and a kind of huge terrace; each level has a covered promenade deck furnished with benches, seats, and deck chairs.

When I arrived at the dock the scene looked as if I had arrived at a carnival: the musicians were making a racket like a circus band; a half dozen bells were summoning the people with a monotonous, strident chiming; and the boat was soon filled with a throng of passengers. In no time we were underway, majestically leaving the dock, heading for the middle of the channel, and ascending the river.

The spectacle at that moment was magnificent: on the right, the huge city, its docks crowded with the ships of all nations; on the left, "Jersey City," a suburb of the metropolis, the wide river with all its maritime activity, its barges, its gay "ferry boats"; and in the center of all this there was a flotilla of Russian boats composed of four magnificent frigates, one of which, the *Svetlana,* was commanded by the Grand-Duke Alexis. All these vessels, with all their flags and banners of every shape, size, and color flying in the wind, made an imposing and unique spectacle.

Arriving at the foot of 23rd street we see an enormous crowd waiting at the dock to board the approaching *Plymouth Rock.* A gangplank is lowered and three or four thousand people try to beat each other over that narrow bridge. Only two "Policemen" are present to maintain order; but they are enough: at a gesture from the guardians of the public peace, the crowd calms down and the embarkation goes on in an orderly fashion. The dock empties little by little; the boat is soon overflowing with people, and one no longer knows where to go to stand. When the *Plymouth Rock* finally gets underway, it is carrying ten thousand passengers!

This crowd of excursionists does not belong to the elite of the population: there are petty merchants and their families; working-men and women; a crowd of young people, fourteen to seventeen years old, all wearing shapeless caps and knickers tucked in below the knee with high stockings—all shouting, running, jostling, the men spitting in all directions at once, covering the decks, the carpets, the *salons* with a sea of tobacco juice, a sea that, like the ocean, rises and engulfs everything.

New-York unrolls in front of us; we pass all the wharves which are not picturesque: they extend out over the river on embankments or in the form of wooden bulwarks, and are poorly constructed: things are very dilapidated; they seem to totter and give way. At right-angles to these wharves stand a row of docks, built upon pilings and covered with a host of wooden sheds, warehouses, and buildings. Everything looks exceedingly shabby except the iron pier and immense warehouse of the French Transatlantic Company. This imperfect and rather dirty part of the city is partially hidden by the crowd of boats that line its shores.

The Hudson reveals itself in all its splendor when viewed this way from the deck of a steamer. The right bank is congested with the houses that form an extension of "Jersey City," all made of wood and adorned with balconies and "verandas." They are all built on top of each other and have very little garden-space, for everyone wants a house with a river-view and space is at a premium. Most of the larger buildings are "Boarding Houses" where several families live together and fancy themselves living in the country. Here and there we see a more significant building, an imitation of a chateau or some shapeless architectural experiment in gothic-tudor style. Now and then, however, we see a genuinely beautiful house overlooking a vast park with attractive out-buildings: one knows that this proprietor is wealthy and has taste. Such buildings, however, are still made only of wood. At different points we see groups of houses congregated into villages, and here, as throughout America wherever the location is favorable, the individual houses have much more elbow room.

Since it is Sunday, we see many pleasure boats upon the river. During this one day of the week all commercial shipping comes to a halt, just as almost everything else does, including the railroads, factories, and even omnibuses. The inhabitants along the banks of the river watch the boat pass and cry hurrah! and wave their handkerchiefs and shout and whistle; all the passengers aboard the steamer reply to these demonstrations, the captain blows the ship's whistle, the musical bells begin to chime, the band joins in, and it is all one abominable uproar.

At every other moment the passengers rush from one side of the boat to the other to observe the passing sights or to watch the many boats being overtaken and left behind. This indulgence of curiosity leads to a tilting of the boat and threatens disaster. In such a position the water in the ship's boilers rolls to one side and exposes the remaining side to the intense heat; the consequent re-leveling of the boat throws the water against the heated portion and threatens to produce enough steam to explode the boilers. This kind of accident is, in fact, a frequent occurrence,[8] and one can easily imagine what the consequences would be if it happened aboard such a ship as the *Plymouth Rock* with its thousands of passengers. To obviate such a possibility, enormous chests mounted on small wheels, and heavily weighted with bars of lead, have been placed on the lower deck; at a signal from an officer these chests are manipulated according to the movement of the passengers and are rolled in opposite directions to maintain the balance of the vessel.

The crowd aboard the vessel constantly moves in and out of the buffet and restaurant; the gayety becomes more and more strident as the day advances; drunkenness appears; at seven o'clock the boat arrives at West Point, pauses for just a moment, and then immediately sets out for the return voyage to New-York. Night falls, and with the night comes the evening cold. Everyone wants to go inside and take refuge in the *salons:* the overcrowding is impossible to imagine. The magnificent chandeliers which decorate the *salon* are now illuminated, and the resulting scene is worthy of the pencil of Callot.[9] In the midst of all this luxury a veritable mob gradually settles down for the return voyage; children fall asleep in the arms of their mothers (who themselves end by suc-

44. *Up the Hudson,* drawing by A. E. Emslie, 1870; courtesy of the Magazine Collection, New York Public Library.

"At every other moment the passengers rush from one side of the boat to the other to observe the passing sights or to watch the many boats being overtaken and left behind."

UP THE HUDSON.—Drawn by A. E. Emslie.—[See Page 489.]

cumbing to fatigue); husbands, long-since lost in drunk-enness, are stretched out full length on the carpet, their clothes in complete disarray; over there a woman lies asleep in the arms of a man; whole groups of men, women, and children, unable to find seats, lie pell-mell on the carpeted floor; elsewhere one sees drunkards lying crosswise on the decks; the galleries, the passageways, are all encumbered with slumbering forms; even the dining-room tables, long-since cleared for this purpose, serve as beds. In this incredible pell-mell there are no longer any sexes: it is all a compact mass of weary, drunken peo-ple. Yet in the midst of it all a die-hard group of "Yan-kees," thoroughly inebriated, run about yelling, jostling, fighting; the band plays on; the choir—and my God, what a choir!—continues to rend the air in faithful fulfillment of its contract; the giant paddle-wheels beat the water with monotonous regularity; and the ship's whistle lets out an occasional blast of piercing shrillness.

At one o'clock in the morning I disembarked, able to breathe at last, and happy beyond words to have escaped that hellish bedlam.

22.
Henry James 1905 *

INTRODUCTION: Something had come to an end in America, Henry James discovered while journeying down the Hudson Valley by train in 1905, something that had been destroyed by the new age of the railroad and all it symbolized—"a felicity forever gone."

James had decided to revisit his homeland in the summer of 1904 during his sixty-second year. He had not seen America for nearly a quarter of a century, and he was eager to gain one final impression—one more confrontation with his youth—before returning to England to end his days. He arrived in America in early September, and after spending the fall in New England, returned to New York to spend Christmas in the city of his birth and then pushed on to Florida and California. At the end of April he journeyed back to New York and returned to England in August 1905. It had been a year of revelation for this great expatriate, but of all the experiences that illuminated his final years of reflection about his native land none were more "telling" than his rediscovery of the Hudson Valley from a fast-moving train while returning from the West in the spring of 1905.

In the following account, which was originally written for the *North American Review* and the *Fortnightly Review* under the title of "New York and the Hudson: A Spring Impression," James records his discovery that in the Hudson Valley at least America had achieved "a ripe old civilization." It was a dramatic revelation to a man who had predicated his career upon the assumption that such a civilization could be found only in Europe, but James could not deny the evidence of "a preposterous ecstacy" that arose in him as he viewed the passing scene. The lesson was also reenforced by a second trip to West

Point and Irving's "Sunnyside" before he returned to Europe. Looking now "through the glaze of all-but-filial tears" he discovered that the Hudson Valley partook of "the geography of the ideal," however much the railroad had put him in "a false position" for doing "justice to the scenery." The railroad, indeed, was an ugly intrusion upon this ideal landscape of the past: it represented a new and feverish America that was intrinsically inimical to the "great romantic stream" and all its historical associations. The Hudson Valley of Irving and the Hudson River School of painting, of leisurely travel and the white pillared mansion on the brow of the hill, were now forever gone. James's "Spring Impression" is at once a song of discovery and an eulogistic farewell to three hundred years of history.

IT IS STILL VIVID to me that, returning in the springtime from a few weeks in the Far West, I re-entered New York State with the absurdest sense of meeting again a ripe old civilization and traveling through a country that showed the mark of established manners. It will seem, I fear, one's perpetual refrain, but the moral was yet once more that values of a certain order are, in such conditions, all relative, and that, as some wants of the spirit *must* somehow be met, one knocks together any substitute that will fairly stay the appetite. We had passed great smoky Buffalo in the raw vernal dawn—with a vision, for me, of curiosity, character, charm, whatever it might be, too needfully sacrificed, opportunity perhaps forever missed, yet at the same time a vision in which the lost object failed to mock at me with the last concentration of shape; and history, as we moved Eastward, appeared to meet us, in the look of the land, in its overwrought surface and thicker detail, quite as if she ever

* Excerpt from Henry James's *The American Scene* (New York: 1907), "New York and the Hudson: A Spring Impression," 142–152.

consciously declined to cross the border and were aware, precisely of the queer feast we should find in her. The recognition, I profess, was a preposterous ecstacy: one couldn't have felt more if one had passed into the presence of some seated, placid, rich-voiced gentlewoman after leaving that of an honest but boisterous hoiden. It was doubtless a matter only of degrees and shades, but never was such a pointing of the lesson that a sign of any sort may count double if it be but artfully placed. I spent that day, literally, in the company of the rich-voiced gentlewoman, making my profit of it even in spite of a second privation, the doom I was under of having only, all wistfully, all ruefully, to avert my lips from the quaint silver bowl, as I here quite definitely figured it, in which she offered me the entertainment of antique Albany. At antique Albany, to a certainty, the mature matron involved in my metaphor would have put on a particular grace, and as our train crossed the river for further progress I almost seemed to see her stand at some gablewindow of Dutch association, one of the two or three impressed there on my infantile imagination, to ask me why then I had come so far at all.

I could have replied but in troubled tones, and I looked at the rest of the scene for some time, no doubt, as through the glaze of all-but-filial tears. Thus it was, possibly, that I saw the River shine, from that moment on, as a great romantic stream, such as could throw not a little of its glamour, for the mood of that particular hour, over the city at its mouth. I had not even known, in my untravelled state, that we were to "strike" it on our way from Chicago, so that it represented, all that afternoon, so much beauty thrown in, so much benefit beyond the bargain—the so hard bargain, for the traveller, of the American railway-journey at its best. The ordeal was in any case at its best here, and the perpetually interesting river kept its course, by my right elbow, with such splendid consistency that, as I recall the impression, I repent a little of having just now reflected with acrimony on the cost of the obtrusion of track and stations to the Riverside view. One must of course choose between dispensing with the ugly presence and enjoying the scenery by the aid of the same—which but means, really, that to use the train at all had been to put one's self, for any proper justice to the scenery, in a false position. That, however, takes us too far back, and one can only save one's dignity by laying all such blames on our detestable age. A decent respect for the Hudson would confine us to the use of the boat—all the more that American river-steamers have had, from the earliest time, for the true *raffiné*, their peculiar note of romance. A possible commerce, on the other hand, with one's time—which is always also the time of so many other busy people—has long since made mince-meat of the rights of contemplation; rights as reduced, in the United States, to-day, and by quite the same argument, as those of the noble savage whom we have banished to his narrowing reservation. Letting that pass, at all events, I still remember that I was able to put, from the car-window, as many questions to the scene as it could have answered in the time even had its face been clearer to read.

Its face was veiled, for the most part, in a mist of premature spring heat, an atmosphere draping it indeed in luminous mystery, hanging it about with sun-shot silver and minimizing any happy detail, any element of the definite, from which the romantic effect might here and there have gained an accent. There was not an accent in the picture from the beginning of the run to Albany to the end—for which thank goodness! one is tempted to say on remembering how often, over the land in general, the accents are wrong. Yet if the romantic effect as we know it elsewhere mostly depends on them, why *should* that glamour have so shimmered before me in their absence?—how should the picture have managed to be a constant combination of felicities? Was it just *because* the felicities were all vagueness, and the "beauties," even the most celebrated, all blurs?—was it perchance on that very account that I could meet my wonder so promptly with the inference that what I had in my eyes on so magnificent a scale was simply, was famously, "style"? I was landed by that conclusion in the odd further proposition that style could then exist without accents—a quandary soon after to be quenched, however, in the mere blinding radiance of a visit to West Point. I was to make that memorable pilgrimage a fortnight later—and I was to find my question, when it in fact took place, shivered by it to mere silver atoms. The very powers of the air seemed to have taken the case in hand and positively to have been interested in making it transcend all argument. Our Sunday of mid-May, wet and windy, let loose, over the vast stage, the whole procession of storm-effects; the raw green of wooded heights and hollows was only everywhere rain-brightened, the weather playing over it all day as with some great gray water-color brush. The essential character of West Point and its native nobleness of position can have been but intensified, I think, by this artful process; yet what was mainly unmistakable was the fact again of the suppression of detail as in the positive interest of the grand style. One had therefore only to take detail as another name for accent, the accent that might prove compromising, in order to see it made good that style *could* do without them, and that the grand style in fact almost always must. How on this occasion the trick was played is more than I shall attempt to say; it is enough to have been conscious of our being, from hour to hour, literally bathed in that high element, with the very face of nature washed, so to speak, the more clearly to express and utter it.

Such accordingly is the strong silver light, all simplifying and ennobling, in which I see West Point; see it as a cluster of high promontories, of the last classic elegance, overhanging vast receding reaches of the river, mountain-guarded and dim, which took their place in the geography of the ideal, in the long perspective of the poetry of association, rather than in those of the State of New York. It was as if the genius of the scene had said: "No, you *sha'n't* have accent, because accent is, at the best, local and special, and might here by some perversity—how do I know after all?—interfere. I want you to have something unforgettable, and therefore you shall have *type*—yes, absolutely have type, and even tone, without accent; an impossibility, you may have hitherto supposed, but which you have only to look about you now really to see expressed. And type and tone of the finest and rarest; type and tone good enough for Claude or Turner, if they could have walked by these rivers instead of by their thin rivers of France and Italy; type and tone, in short, that gather in shy detail under wings as wide as those which a motherly hen covers her endangered brood. So there you are—deprived of all 'accent' as a peg for criticism, and reduced thereby, you see, to asking me no more questions." I was able so to take home, I may add, this formula of the matter, that even the interesting facts of the School of the Soldier which have carried the name of the place about the world almost put on the shyness, the air of conscious evasion and escape, noted in the above allocution: they struck me as forsaking the foreground of the picture. It was part of the play again, no doubt, of the gray water-color brush: there was to be no consent of the elements, that day, to anything but a generalized elegance—in which effect certainly the clustered, the scattered Academy played, on its high green stage, its part. But, of all things in the world, it massed, to my vision, more mildly than I

had somehow expected; and I take that for a feature, precisely, of the pure poetry of the impression. It lurked
there with grace, it insisted without swagger—and I could
have hailed it just for this reason indeed as a presence of
the last distinction. It is doubtless too much to say, in
fine, that the Institution, at West Point, "suffers" comparatively, for vulgar individual emphasis, from the over-
whelming liberality of its setting—and I perhaps chanced
to see it in the very conditions that most invest it with
poetry. The fact remains that, both as to essence and as
to quantity, its prose seemed washed away, and I shall
recall it in the future much less as the sternest, the
world over, of all the seats of Discipline, than as some
great Corot-composition of young, vague, wandering figures in splendidly classic shades.

I make that point, for what it is worth, only to remind
myself of another occasion on which the romantic note
sounded for me with the last intensity, and yet on which
the picture swarmed with accents—as, absent or present,
I must again call them—that contributed alike to its interest and to its dignity. The proof was complete, on this
second Sunday, with the glow of early summer already in
possession, that affirmed detail was not always affirmed
infelicity—since the scene here bristled with detail (and
detail of the importance that frankly *constitutes* accent)
only to the enhancement of its charm. It was a matter
once more of hanging over the Hudson on the side opposite West Point, but farther down; the situation was
founded, as at West Point, on the presence of the great
feature and on the consequent general lift of foreground and distance alike, and yet infinitely sweet was
it to gather that style, in such conditions and for the
success of such effects, had not really to depend on mere
kind vagueness, on any anxious deprecation of distinctness. There was no vagueness now; a wealth of distinctness, in the splendid light, met the eyes—but with the
very result of showing them how happily it could play.
What it came back to was that the accents, in the delightful old pillared and porticoed house that crowned the
cliff and commanded the stream, were as right as they
were numerous; so that there immediately followed
again on this observation a lively recognition of the
ground of the rightness. To wonder what this was could
be but to see, straightway, that, though many reasons had
worked together for them, mere time had done more
than all; that beneficence of time enjoying in general,
in the United States, so little even of the chance that so
admirably justifies itself, for the most part, when inter-
ference happens to have spared it. Cases of this rare
mercy yet exist, as I had had occasion to note, and their
consequent appeal to the touched sense within us comes,
as I have also hinted, with a force out of all proportion,
comes with a kind of accepted insolence or authority.
The things that have lasted, in short, whatever they may
be, "succeed" as no newness, try as it will, succeeds, inasmuch as their success is a created interest.

There we catch the golden truth which so much of
the American world strikes us as positively organized to
gainsay, the truth that production takes time, and that
the production of interest, in particular, takes *most* time.
Desperate again and again the ingenuity of the offered,
the obtruded substitute, and pathetic in many an instance its confessed failure; this remark being meanwhile
relevant to the fact that my charming old historic house
of the golden Sunday put me off, among its great trees,
its goodly gardens, its acquired signs and gathered memo-
ries, with no substitute whatever, even the most specious,
but just paid cash down, so to speak, ripe ringing gold,
over the counter, for all the attention it invited. It had
character, as one might say, and character is scarce less

precious on the part of the homes of men in a raw medium than on the part of responsible persons at a difficult crisis. This virtue was there within and without and on every face; but perhaps nowhere so present, I thought, as in the ideal refuge for summer days formed by the wide north porch, if porch that disposition may be called—happiest disposition of the old American country-house—which sets tall columns in a row, under a pediment suitably severe, to present them as the "making" of a high, deep gallery. I know not what dignity of old afternoons suffused with what languor seems to me always, under the murmur of American trees and by the lap of American streams, to abide in these mild shades; there are combinations with depths of congruity beyond the plummet, it would seem, even of the most restless of analysts, and rather than to try to say why my whole impression here melted into the general iridescence of a past of Indian summers hanging about mild ghosts half asleep, in hammocks, over still milder novels, I would renounce altogether the art of refining. For the iridescence consists, in this connection, of a shimmer of association that still more refuses to be reduced to terms; some sense of legend, of aboriginal mystery, with a still earlier past for its dim background and the insistent idea of the River as above all romantic for its warrant. Helplessly analyzed, perhaps, this amounts to no more than the very childish experience of a galleried house or two round about which the views and the trees and the peaches and the pony seemed prodigious, and to remembrance of which the wonder of Rip Van Winkle and that of the "Hudson River School" of landscape art were, a little later on, to contribute their glamour.

If Rip Van Winkle had been really at the bottom of it all, nothing could have furthered the whole case more, on the occasion I speak of, than the happy nearness of the home of Washington Irving, the impression of which I was thus able, in the course of an hour, to work in—with the effect of intensifying more than I can say the old-time charm and the general legendary fusion. These are beautiful, delicate, modest matters, and how can one touch them with a light enough hand? How can I give the comparatively coarse reasons for my finding at Sunnyside, which contrives, by some grace of its own, to be at once all ensconced and embowered in relation to the world, and all frank and uplifted in relation to the river, a perfect treasure of mild moralities? The highway, the old State road to Albany, bristling now with the cloud-compelling motor, passes at the head of a deep, long lane, winding, embanked, overarched, such an old-world lane as one scarce ever meets in America; but if you embrace this chance to plunge away to the left you come out for your reward into the quiet indefinable air of the little American literary past. The place is inevitably, to-day, but a qualified Sleepy Hollow—the Sleepy Hollow of the author's charming imagination was, as I take it, off somewhere in the hills, or in some dreamland of old autumns, happily unprofanable now; [1] for "modernity," with its terrible power of working its will, of abounding in its sense, of gilding its toy-modernity, with its pockets full of money and its conscience full of virtue, its heart really full of tenderness, has seated itself there under pretext of guarding the shrine. What has happened, in a word, is very much what has happened in the case of other shy retreats of anchorites doomed to celebrity—the primitive cell has seen itself encompassed, in time, by a temple of many chambers, all dedicated to the history of the hermit. The cell is still there at Sunnyside, and there is even yet so much charm that one doesn't attempt to say where the parts of it, all kept together in a rich conciliatory way, begin or end—though indeed, I hasten to add, the iden-

45. *Sunnyside from the Hudson,* anonymous oil painting, after 1851; courtesy of Sleepy Hollow Restorations, Tarrytown, N.Y.

"It has taken *our* ugly era to thrust in the railroad at the foot of the slope."

tity of the original modest house, the shrine within the gilded shell, has been religiously preserved.[2]

One has, in fact, no quarrel whatever with the amplified state of the place, for it is the manner and the effect of this amplification that enabled us to read into the scene its very most interesting message. The "little" American literary past, I just now said—using that word—(whatever the real size of the subject) because the caressing diminutive, at Sunnyside, is what rises of itself to the lips; the small, uncommodious study, the limited library, the "dear" old portrait-prints of the first half of the century—very dear to-day when properly signed and properly sallow—these things, with the beauty of the site, with the sense that the man of letters of the unimproved age, the age of processes still comparatively slow, could have wanted no deeper, softer dell for mulling material over, represent the conditions that encounter now on the spot the sharp reflection of our own increase of arrangement and loss of leisure. This is the admirable interest of the exhibition of which Wolfert's Roost [3] had been, a hundred years before the date of Irving's purchase, the rudimentary principle—that it throws the facts of our earlier "intellectual activity" into a vague, golden perspective, a haze as of some unbroken spell of the same Indian summer I a moment ago had occasion to help myself out with; a fond appearance than which nothing could minister more to envy. If we envy the spinners of prose and tellers of tales to whom our American air anciently either administered or refused sustenance, this is all, and quite the best thing, it would seem, that we need do for them: it exhausts, or rather it forestalls, the futilities of discrimination. Strictly critical, mooning about Wolfert's Roost of a summer Sunday, I defy even the hungriest of analysts to be: his predecessors, the whole connected company, profit so there, to his rueful vision, by the splendor of their possession of better conditions than his. It has taken *our* ugly era to thrust in the railroad at the foot of the slope, among the masking trees; the railroad that is part, exactly, of the pomp and circumstance, the quickened pace, the heightened fever, the narrowed margin expressed within the very frame of the present picture, as I say, and all in the perfect good faith of collateral piety. I had hoped not to have to name the railroad—it seems so to give away my case. There was no railroad, however, till long after Irving's settlement [4]—he survived the railroad but by a few years, and my case is simply that, disengaging *his* Sunnyside from its beautiful extensions and arriving thus at the sense of his easy elements, easy for everything but rushing about and being rushed at, the sense of his "command" of the admirable river and the admirable country, his command of all the mildness of his life, of his pleasant powers and his ample hours, of his friends and his contemporaries and his fame and his honor and his temper and, above all, of his delightful fund of reminiscence and material, I seemed to hear, in the summer sounds and in the very urbanity of my entertainers, the last faint echo of a felicity forever gone. That is the true voice of such places, and not the imputed challenge to the chronicler or the critic.

NOTES

Part I · Seventeenth-Century Beginnings

1. Robert Juet 1609

1. *R.V.Z.* The *Half Moon* had grounded upon a series of sand bars that were to become famous in the history of Hudson River navigation. Located just south of the city of Albany, they soon became known as the "Overslaugh" and remained a major impediment to navigation until the second half of the nineteenth century when engineers of the federal government finally succeeded in removing them.

2. *R.V.Z.* This was probably just above the present site of Kingston.

3. *R.V.Z.* The term "reach" from the earliest years of the sixteenth century meant that portion of a river, channel, or lake which lies between two bends and may therefore be seen in one view and navigated on one tack or compass heading. The Hudson soon became known for about fourteen specific reaches between New York and Albany (*cf.* note 7 in De Laet's narrative of 1625), and Juet herein designates the first and one of the most famous of them all. The "Long Reach" extended from Wappingers Creek (where the *Half Moon* anchored on September 29th) near New Hamburg, north to Crum Elbow Point, two miles south of Hyde Park; a distance of about thirteen miles.

4. *R.V.Z.* The northern entrance of the Highlands near Cornwall or Storm King Mountain.

5. *R.V.Z.* The episode probably occurred while at anchor in some part of Haverstraw Bay.

6. *R.V.Z.* Somewhere along the Palisades, perhaps off the mouth of Spuyten Duyvil Creek.

7. *R.V.Z.* Paul Wilstach, author of *Hudson River Landings* (Indianapolis: 1933), asserted that the *Half Moon* was anchored "in the lee of the rock now known as Stevens Point, Hoboken" (p. 43).

2. Johannes De Laet 1625

Notes by J. F. Jameson are preceded by the initials J.F.J.

1. *J.F.J.* The versions of 1633 and 1640 [Latin and French editions of the *New World*] mention also the name Nassau River, but say that Great River and North River (the latter

by distinction from the South River, our Delaware) are the most usual. Port May, they say, is named from Captain Cornelius May.

R.V.Z. Further references to the problem of the early names of the Hudson may be found in note 41 of Chapter 3.

2. *R.V.Z.* Lower New York Bay or perhaps Raritan Bay.

3. *R.V.Z.* Possibly Sandy Hook.

4. *R.V.Z.* Governor's Island.

5. *J.F.J.* The Latin version of 1633 adds, "Yet our people have bought from them the island separated from the rest of the land by the Hellgate, and have there laid the foundations of a fort, and of a town called New Amsterdam." So also the French.

6. *J.F.J.* Three or four, say the later versions. Bedloe's Island, Ellis Island, and Black Tom, we may assume. 40°28′ is the latitude of Sandy Hook.

7. *R.V.Z.* De Laet goes on to describe twelve of the fourteen reaches by which the Hudson became known. The reach he designates as the "first," where "the land is low" and there "dwells a nation of savages, named Tappaans," actually became the second or the Tappan Reach. The first was the reach along the Palisades called the Great Chip Rock Reach. The other significant omission is that of Long Reach, already referred to by Juet in 1609. Otherwise De Laet's list is an accurate reflection of what became the standard designations: Haverstroo became Haverstraw Reach; Sailmaker's the Seylmakers; Cook's became Crescent Reach; Foxes' became Vorsen Reach; Fisher's remained the same; Klaverack became the Claverack or Clover Reach; Baker's the same or Bacerach; Playsier's the same; Vasterack the same or Vaste Reach; Hart's the Hunter's Reach.

8. *R.V.Z.* Upper New York Bay.

9. *R.V.Z.* Kingston.

10. *J.F.J.* The margin adds, "At latitude 41°58′ [latitude of Kingston and Rhinebeck] Hudson found the variation of the compass nine degrees N.W."

11. *J.F.J.* Bear's Island.

R.V.Z. Bear Island is five miles south of Albany. De Laet could also be referring to Berren (or Barren) Island which is located just south of Coeymans.

12. *J.F.J.* Old Anchorage.

13. *R.V.Z.* This is in the area where the *Half Moon* became grounded on the sand bars or the region known as the Over-

slaugh. The fort in question, as De Laet goes on to say, was built by Hendrick Christiaensz (or Christiaensen) in 1614. The site was on Castle Island, which is now under water just across from the city of Albany. The fort was named Nassau in honor of William the Silent's son Maurice, Prince of the House of Nassau and Stadtholder of Holland; but it only lasted three years, having been destroyed by a freshet in 1617. Seven years later (1624) another fort was built on the present site of Albany and was named Fort Orange. This one took.

14. *R.V.Z.* The Adirondacks.

15. *R.V.Z.* The natives, of course, *did* reach the fort from Canada, but they did so via Lake Champlain and Lake George and ten or twelve miles of portage.

16. *J.F.J.* The Mohawks.

17. *J.F.J.* In March 1614, the States General of the United Netherlands promised by a general ordinance that discoverers of new lands should, if they reported their discoveries promptly, have for the period of four voyages a monopoly of trade to the new-found regions. On October 11 a group of merchants of Amsterdam and North Holland, who for three years had been sending trading-ships to the region about the North River, and under whose auspices Block, Christiaensen, and May had made their explorations, asked and obtained from the States General, under the ordinance named, a monopoly of trade in the region from 40° to 45°N. latitude, to continue during four voyages, or three years. The charter gives to the region the name of New Netherland.

18. *J.F.J.* Maize or Indian corn.

19. *R.V.Z.* This was on September 13, 1609, off present-day 129th Street, Manhattan.

20. *R.V.Z.* Where the Kinderhook Creek flows into the Hudson just north of the city of Hudson.

21. *J.F.J.* Addition in the edition of 1630.

3. *Jasper Dankers 1680*

Notes by B. B. James are preceded by the initials B.B.J.

1. *R.V.Z.* Presumably not to trade.

2. *R.V.Z.* Sir Edmund Andros, who became governor of New York in 1674, had instituted a policy of prohibiting all but residents of the state of New York from trading with the Indians at Albany.

3. *B.B.J.* Schenectady, Rensselaerswyck, Esopus.

4. *B.B.J.* William Dyer had been commissioned by the Duke of York in 1674 as collector of the port of New York, and was still acting as such. The next year, 1680–1681, he was mayor of the city.

5. *B.B.J.* Pemaquid.

6. *R.V.Z.* In the vicinity of Stony Point, about forty miles north of New York City.

7. *B.B.J.* Dominie Schaet's son-in-law was Thomas Davidtse Kekebel or Kieckebuls. His wife had been sent away from Albany by the magistrates. In 1681 she and her husband came into a final concord; *Doc. Hist.* N.Y., quarto ed., III, 534.

8. *R.V.Z.* Esopus or Kingston.

9. *R.V.Z.* Bartlett B. James identifies this as "Cats Kill." He is undoubtedly correct, since Noorman's Kill (or Norman's Kill) is located just south of Albany, and Dankers did not arrive at that place until the following day. James is in error, however, when he calls the "two high falls" mentioned in the following sentences "Kaaterskill Falls." The latter are located twelve miles to the west of Catskill on the eastern escarpment of the Catskill Mountains. The falls that Dankers describes are probably those of the Kaaterskill Creek just to the west of Catskill village.

10. *R.V.Z.* Delaware River.

11. *B.B.J.* The garden at the Thetinga State, the manor-house at Wieuwert. The tree is the arbor-vitae.

12. *B.B.J.* The *fuyck* is a hoop-net used for catching fish. Its shape is that of a truncated cone. The ground-plan of Albany . . . had that shape.

13. *B.B.J.* Robert Sanders of Albany was a prominent Indian trader, skilled in Indian languages.

14. *R.V.Z.* La Grange was a merchant of New York.

15. *B.B.J.* Mohawk River.

16. *B.B.J.* The falls of Niagara had been mentioned by Cartier and by Champlain, but the first full description of them, that of Hennepin in his *Description de la Louisiane*, was not published till 1683.

R.V.Z. The falls at Cohoes, located about seven miles north of Albany where the Mohawk empties into the Hudson, are about 75 feet high and 900 feet long. In a short time, other falls in the Hudson Valley began to attract considerable attention, most notably the aforementioned Kaaterskill Falls which are at least 175 feet higher than the Cohoes Falls. In spite of this, however, and because of their proximity to the Hudson, the Cohoes Falls remained a prime tourist attraction until the middle of the nineteenth century.

17. *B.B.J.* Peanuts.

18. *B.B.J.* No Frederick Pieters seems to be known. It was perhaps Philip Pieterse Schuyler, progenitor of a distinguished family, who lived on a large farm at the flats below West Troy.

19. *B.B.J.* Schenectady, of which Dankaerts tried to make Dutch words, *quasi* "beautiful section."

20. *B.B.J.* Probably Adam Vrooman, who at that time of the general massacre by the Indians, 1690, defended his house with great courage and success.

21. *B.B.J.* The patroonship of Rensselaerswyck was founded in 1630 by Kiliaen van Rensselaer of Amsterdam. It was a great manorial estate, extending along the west bank of the Hudson from Beeren Island to the Mohawk and running so far back from the river as to embrace about the same area as the present Albany County, though Albany itself was not a part of it. The first patroon had died in 1646, the second, his oldest son Johannes, had also died, and the present heir was the latter's son Kiliaen. The lady here described was Maria, the widow of Jeremias van Rensselaer, the original patroon's third son, who had ruled the colony from 1658 to 1674. She was a daughter of Oloff Stevensz van Cortland, and lived till 1689. Her husband's youngest brother Richard had lived at the colony from 1652 to 1672, but was now in Holland, treasurer of Vianen, and never came to America again.

22. *B.B.J.* Ninety bushels.

23. *B.B.J.* Rev. Gideon Schaets (1608–1694) was minister of Rensselaerswyck from 1652 to 1657, and of Fort Orange (Beverwyck, Albany) from 1657 to 1694.

24. *R.V.Z.* This is the same fort mentioned by Johannes De Laet (see Chapter 2, note 13), built on Castle Island near Albany in 1614. Since 63 years had passed between the time of the flood (1617) that wiped out the fort, and the date of Danker's visit, we are perhaps not surprised at the ignorance of the natives regarding the history of the fort. It *is* surprising, however, that the natives should associate the ruins with Spanish origins. The French rather than the Spanish had been constant visitors to the upper Hudson Valley from the end of the sixteenth century, and Castle Island was probably the scene of

some French fortifications as early as 1540 (Maud Esther Dilliard, *An Album of New Netherland* [New York: 1963], p. 19). It is this remote fact that the natives were probably confusing with Spanish origins.

25. *R.V.Z.* A reference to a local episode regarding the conversion of an Indian to Christianity.

26. *B.B.J.* *Wild,* savage, is the word commonly used by the Dutch of that time to denote the Indians.

27. *B.B.J.* Rev. Bernhardus Arensius had since 1674 ministered to these two Lutheran congregations, and continued till his death in 1691.

28. *R.V.Z.* This was either present-day Stuyvesant, formerly Kinderhook Landing, or the site of a yet older landing two miles north of Stuyvesant at the mouth of Mill Creek.

29. *B.B.J.* This was one Frans Pieterse Clauw, who had come out to Beverwyck (Albany) in 1656.

R.V.Z. The waterfall described in the following sentences was probably along the aforementioned Mill Creek, two miles north of Stuyvesant.

30. *B.B.J.* "Clover Reach," now Claverack.

31. *R.V.Z.* The manufacture of lime remained an important occupation of the people of Hysopus (Kingston) until recent times, and it was in the nearby community of Rosendale that some of the most famous cement deposits in America were discovered in 1828.

32. *R.V.Z.* Dankers is right about the east bank affording some of the best views of the Catskills. Magnificent views, for instance, may be obtained today from the Taconic State Parkway.

33. *R.V.Z.* The shad had ascended the Hudson from the sea to spawn, a spring ritual on the river, and the basis of an important local industry, until the present century, when irresponsible water pollution destroyed the breeding grounds.

34. *B.B.J.* Gerrit Duyckinck.

35. *R.V.Z.* A new stone church, 45 x 60 feet, was built in Kingston on what is now the northeast corner of Main and Wall Streets in 1679 and dedicated in January 1680.

36. *R.V.Z.* The term "flats" is still used (1971) in reference to this rich land of alluvial soil along the banks of the Esopus Creek on the western edge of Kingston. Used from ancient times by the Indians for the cultivation of maize, this rich bottom land had the reputation throughout the seventeenth and eighteenth centuries of being some of the most valuable

farm acreage in the Hudson Valley. It has yielded today, however, to the demands of modern transport, and a good deal of it lies under the concrete cloverleaf of the Kingston exit of the New York Thruway.

37. *R.V.Z.* The Esopus war occurred intermittently between the years 1658 and 1664.

38. *B.B.J.* Willem Hellekers.

39. *R.V.Z.* Present-day Roundout Creek.

40. *R.V.Z.* Cornwall or Storm King Mountain.

41. *B.B.J.* The Figurative Map of 1616 gives the name Riviere van den Vorst Mauritius (River of Prince Maurice). Wassenaer (1624) speaks of the river as "called first Rio de Montagnes, now the River Mauritius." De Laet, in his *Nieuwe Wereldt* (1625), gives "Manhattes River" and "Rio de Montaigne," but says that "the Great River is the usual designation." In his Latin version of 1633, and French of 1640, he adds a mention of the name Nassau River. As Dr. Johannes la Montagne did not come to New Netherland until 1637, the derivation here given cannot hold. River of the Mountains is an obvious enough name, to anyone who had sailed up through the Highlands of the Hudson.

R.V.Z. The present editor always heard his father, who lived all his life in New Jersey and was descended from the original Dutch settlers of the state, refer to the Hudson as the North River. Generally speaking, however. the name North River is currently used only by the people of Manhattan (though not universally so) and this in reference only to that part of the river that flows by the city of New York. The name Hudson River became the universal cognomen in the 1850s when the "Hudson River Railroad" was built between New York and Albany.

42. *R.V.Z.* The East River may be said to "separate" from the North River only if we assume it is an extension of the Harlem River. The Kill achter Kol or Hackensack River, however, does not separate from the North River by any definition of the term, for it flows southward out of northern New Jersey parallel to the North River and empties into Upper New York Bay by way of Newark Bay and Kill Van Kull.

43. *B.B.J.* Greenwich, a district of New York.

R.V.Z. The more common designation today (1971) is the Upper Bay and the Lower Bay.

44. *R.V.Z.* The tides of the Hudson extend all the way to Troy, where the level of the water is only five feet higher than the level of the Narrows.

45. *B.B.J.* At the cove in the north part of the town of Newburgh.

46. *R.V.Z.* Now called Storm King, thanks to the persuasive charms of N. P. Willis.

47. *B.B.J.* As if like a clover-leaf. Noten Hoeck was opposite Coxsackie, Potlpels (now Polopel's) Island opposite Cornwall. Kock Achie or Coxsackie is probably Koeksrackie, the cook's little reach, to distinguish it from the Koeks Rack, cook's reach, the name which the early voyagers gave to the reach far below, near present Peekskill.

48. *B.B.J.* Referring, but of course mistakenly, to Lake Champlain, or Lakes Champlain and George.

49. *R.V.Z.* A remarkable prophecy brilliantly fulfilled in 1825 with the opening of the Erie Canal.

Part II · Frontier and Battleground

4. *Peter Kalm 1749*

Notes by A. B. Benson are preceded by the initials A.B.B.

1. *R.V.Z.* The population of New York City in 1749 was 13,294.

2. *R.V.Z.* Probably Haverstraw Bay.

3. *R.V.Z.* Geology was still an unknown science in the first half of the eighteenth century. Lacking a scientific theory of water erosion, which did not appear until 1795 when the Scot James Hutton published his findings, Kalm naturally fell back upon the traditional doctrine of Providential intercession. It is interesting in this context to read the comments of Sir Charles Lyell who traveled by steamboat up the Hudson in 1841 (eight years after the publication of the *Principles of Geology*): "The Hudson is an arm of the sea or estuary, about

twelve fathoms deep, above New York, and its waters are inhabited by a curious mixture of marine and fresh-water plants and mollusca. At first on our left, or on the western bank, we had a lofty precipice of columnar basalt from 400 to 600 feet in height, called the Palisades, extremely picturesque. . . . On arriving at the Highlands, the winding channel is closed in by steep hills of gneiss on both sides, and the vessel often holds her course as if bearing directly on the land. The stranger cannot guess in which direction he is to penetrate the rocky gorge, but he soon emerges again into a broad valley, the blue Catskill Mountains appearing in the distance. The scenery deserves all the praise which has been lavished upon it, and when the passage is made in nine hours it is full of variety and contrast." (*Travels in North America, in the Years 1841–2; with Geological Observations on the United States, Canada, and Nova Scotia,* 2 vols. [New York, 1845], pp. 12–13.)

4. *R.V.Z.* After the discovery of the sources of the Hudson in the early 1830s the total length of the river was found to be a little over 300 miles. The navigable part of the river between New York and Albany is halfway or about 145 miles.

5. *R.V.Z.* The Hudson is 175 feet deep at West Point. Kalm would have been surprised to learn that in pre-glacial times the river was another 700 to 1,000 feet deeper in the great gorge of the Highlands.

6. *A.B.B.* Here presumably southern parts of the Catskill mountain system. The name in Kalm's day was probably loosely descriptive, and applied to the whole eastern chain of mountains.

7. *R.V.Z.* Now called Storm King, thanks to efforts of the nineteenth-century American writer, N. P. Willis.

8. *R.V.Z.* The American mountain laurel which Kalm discovered during his American tour and to which he gave his name.

9. *R.V.Z.* Near the present city of Cornwall at the northern entrance to the Highlands.

10. *R.V.Z.* Newburgh Bay.

11. *R.V.Z.* The reader will recall that Jasper Dankers pointed out as early as 1680 that some of the best limestone deposits are found at Esopus or Kingston.

12. *R.V.Z.* Danskammer Point, five miles above Newburgh.

13. *R.V.Z.* Probably Esopus Island, seven miles below Kingston.

14. *R.V.Z.* The Shawangunk and Catskill (or Blue) Mountains.

15. *R.V.Z.* Staatsburg, five miles below Rhinebeck, was named after Dr. Samuel Staats, one of the earliest landholders. The area abounded in Palatine Germans who arrived 1,800 strong in 1710 to make tar on Livingston Manor and, after the failure of that enterprise, dispersed throughout the countryside to found such communities as East and West Camp, Germantown, and Rhinebeck.

16. *R.V.Z.* A Dutch contraption. The roof moved up and down as the hay increased or decreased in volume. The New-York Historical Society has a painting by George Harvey of such a haystack.

17. *A.B.B.* From the French *bateaux* (boats).

18. *R.V.Z.* Probably an exaggeration, though we possess considerable evidence that the winters of two centuries ago were much colder than today.

19. *R.V.Z.* Possibly present-day Cabbage Island, though the configuration of the various islands below Albany has been changed by the erection of dikes and dams since the eighteenth century.

20. *A.B.B.* Now called Cyclops, a genus of minute crustaceans. They have one median eye (though a double one), hence the name.

21. *R.V.Z.* The Helderbergh Mountains.

22. *R.V.Z.* New Jersey.

23. *A.B.B.* British commissioner to New England in 1664. With Nicolls he took New Amsterdam from the Dutch. . . .

24. *A.B.B.* Sir Richard Nicolls (1624–1672), chief military director in the capture of New Amsterdam, and the first English colonial governor of New York.

25. *R.V.Z.* Kalm's castigation of the Albany Dutch is impressive, to say the least. A clue to a possible exaggeration in his indictment may be found in his previous comments about the ruthlessness of the Dutch in driving the Swedes out of the Delaware Valley: he deemed this a crime against his compatriots. His statements about the composition of the population are even more difficult to appraise. Though the historian John Fiske held that as late as 1638 Manhattan "was still a waterside population of sailors, wharf-keepers, and longshoremen, including a fair proportion of rough and shiftless characters," and that "the thrifty and respectable people of Holland had not yet begun to come in any considerable num-

bers to the New World," they *did* start to arrive shortly thereafter, and it is difficult to take Kalm's point seriously that the configuration of the population of 1749 was still being determined by its configuration before 1638. (John Fiske, *The Dutch and Quaker Colonies in America* [Cambridge, 1899], vol. I, p. 169.)

26. *R.V.Z.* It is historically true that throughout most of the French and Indian wars Albany traders maintained a brisk trade in furs with merchants in Montreal and favored neutrality in the various conflicts between the French and the English colonies. The trade was carried on with the connivance of French officials in Canada and in defiance of attempts of English officials to suppress it. English goods from Albany arrived in Montreal to be exchanged for furs that had been collected by the French-Indians; the furs, in turn, ended up in Albany storehouses. Some of the English goods probably included guns, and it was during the early phases of Queen Anne's War (1702–1713) that New Englanders were particularly convinced that they were being killed with guns from Albany.

27. *R.V.Z.* Kalm originally published this portion of his *Travels* during the Seven Years' War (1754–1763), the last of Colonial Wars.

28. *R.V.Z.* These periodic conferences determined the role of the powerful Iroquois League during the Colonial Wars and made Albany one of the most important towns in America prior to the American Revolution. The first was held in 1689 and was composed of representatives from the colonies of Massachusetts, Plymouth, and Connecticut. In 1745 a congress of colonial governors was convened by Governor Clinton of New York. Two years after Kalm passed through Albany, Clinton called another conference (1751) which was attended by representatives from Massachusetts, Connecticut, and South Carolina. The most famous conference occurred in 1754 when seven colonies sent representatives and Benjamin Franklin presented his auspicious plan of federal union. One of the delegates to this conference, Isaac Norris of Pennsylvania, kept a diary of his experiences which was published in Philadelphia in 1867 as *The Journal of Isaac Norris.* It contains a description of his voyage by sloop from New York to Albany, but it is too sketchy to warrant publication in this anthology.

29. *R.V.Z.* Fort. St. Frédéric or Crown Point (its present designation) is located on a promontory on Lake Champlain

near present-day Port Henry and 110 miles north of Albany. Its history will be noted in subsequent references.

30. *A.B.B.* This must have been a hazardous method. Today, of course, the navigators of a canoe generally sit while propelling the boat.

31. *R.V.Z.* Opposite present-day Troy which was still farmland when Kalm passed through.

32. *R.V.Z.* Lewis Evans (c. 1700–1756) was a geographer and cartographer and friend of Benjamin Franklin who had traveled extensively throughout the Middle Colonies gathering material for his authoritative work, "A Map of Pennsylvania, New-Jersey, New-York, and the Three Delaware Counties." The map was published the very year Kalm went up the Hudson.

33. *A.B.B.* Water plants, probably of the filamentous green alga type.

34. *R.V.Z.* Fort Ann at the head of the Woodcreek, nine miles from Hudson Falls and eleven miles from Fort Edward on the Hudson River, along present-day route 4. This was one of the classic routes from the Hudson to Lake Champlain and Canada. The other was from Fort Edward via the "Great Carry" to Lake George. Subsequent narratives feature both routes.

35. *R.V.Z.* Probably in the vicinity of Mechanicville, fifteen miles north of Albany.

36. *R.V.Z.* Between Mechanicville and Stillwater.

37. *R.V.Z.* The arbor-vitae or white cedar.

38. *R.V.Z.* This is Old Saratoga or present-day Schuylerville which was settled in 1689. The fort mentioned by Kalm was built in 1709. Four years before Kalm visited the scene (as noted in greater detail in subsequent paragraphs) both the community and the fort were destroyed by the French and Indians. Settlers did not return to rebuild until 1760. The name of Saratoga was changed to Schuylerville in 1831 in honor of General Philip Schuyler.

39. *R.V.Z.* The episode that Kalm describes in this and the following paragraph occurred on June 30, 1747. According to Howard H. Peckham (*The Colonial Wars 1689–1762* [Chicago, 1964], pp. 113–114), when the French and their Indian allies appeared in the vicinity of the fort, the garrison thought they were merely a scouting party. A hundred men went out to dislodge the enemy and discovered that they amounted to five or six hundred soldiers and Indians. Fifteen of the garrison

were killed and forty-nine captured. Colonel Peter Schuyler, nephew of Albany's late mayor, arrived with a force to relieve the fort, but it was seen to be indefensible and was burned down. Kalm does not mention that this was the second of three forts on or near the same site. The original fort, together with the pioneer settlement around it, was burned in 1745 when it was attacked by a force of 500 French and Indians. The fort was not garrisoned at that time; sixty to a hundred inhabitants, many of whom were negro slaves, were captured and thirty settlers killed. The destruction of the fort exposed Albany to attack, and it was quickly rebuilt, only to be destroyed (as noted) by the English in 1747. The third and last fort was built in September 1757, to protect Albany during the final phases of the French and Indian wars.

40. *R.V.Z.* The fort of 1757 was built near, though not on, this island.

41. *R.V.Z.* Probably at present-day Northumberland.

42. *R.V.Z.* Fort Nicholson, which Kalm soon describes in greater detail, was renamed by Sir William Johnson "Fort Edward," the name by which the community is known today. It is located five miles south of Glens Falls. As previously noted, the fort was the point of departure of two classic routes from the Hudson to Canada.

43. *R.V.Z.* Probably at present-day Fort Miller.

44. *R.V.Z.* Kalm is anticipating himself. He first had to go, as stated previously, to Fort Nicholson; then east to Fort Ann on the Woodcreek. Assuming he left his canoe as present-day Fort Miller ("the upper falls") on the Hudson, he had to travel overland about eight miles to Fort Nicholson (Fort Edward), then about another ten miles to Fort Ann, a total of eighteen statute miles rather than the "forty-three to fifty English miles" he mentions.

45. *A.B.B.* Probably John Henry Lydius, an Englishman.

46. *R.V.Z.* Sir Francis Nicholson (1655–1728), a British colonial administrator who captured Port Royal in 1710 and led an unsuccessful attempt to capture Quebec in 1711. The fort was rebuilt in 1755 and under the name of Fort Edward played an important role in the concluding years of the French and Indian wars. Its importance, as previously noted, was due to the fact that it controlled the site where two Indian routes (and later, roads) from Canada—one via Lake George and the other via the Woodcreek and the upper end of Lake Champlain—formed a junction on the Hudson River.

47. *R.V.Z.* The term "punky" is still used in New York State in respect to these troublesome creatures. They abound in the Adirondacks and Catskill Mountains. Kalm was traveling through the woods when they are most plentiful, the month of June.

48. *R.V.Z.* The Hudson abounds in rapids and falls between Fort Edward and Glens Falls. The specific falls, however, that Kalm undoubtedly heard were those in the vicinity of Hudson Falls, for it is at this point where the trail that he was following turned away from the Hudson River and headed northeast to Fort Ann.

49. *R.V.Z.* Kalm's statement about "the conclusion of the war against the French" refers of course to the end of Queen Anne's War (1702–1713). Fort Ann (as Fort Nicholson and Fort Saratoga) was later rebuilt to serve in the French and Indian War (1754–1763) and the American Revolution. During the Revolution an engagement took place here between the rear guard of the retreating American army and the advance guard of Burgoyne's invading army (July 8, 1777). The retreating Americans destroyed Fort Ann before falling back upon Fort Edward.

50. *R.V.Z.* This was probably in the vicinity of present-day Comstock.

51. *R.V.Z.* These are the famous passenger pigeons that once blanketed North America. They were ruthlessly slaughtered until they finally became extinct, the last known specimen dying in the Cincinnati Zoological Garden in 1914.

52. *R.V.Z.* The same tactics were later used by General Philip Schuyler when he delayed the advance of the British army under Burgoyne along the Woodcreek, an action that contributed to the American victory at Saratoga.

53. *R.V.Z.* Probably in the vicinity of present-day Whitehall, where the river widens.

54. *R.V.Z.* This episode undoubtedly occurred on the Poultney River, which heads north out of Whitehall for several miles and then turns directly south.

55. *R.V.Z.* These mountains form the eastern border of Lake George.

56. *R.V.Z.* They had reached a point on Lake Champlain where, six years later, Fort Ticonderoga was built to command the approaches to Lake George as well as the Woodcreek.

57. *R.V.Z.* Kalm is undoubtedly more right than wrong, for we now know that virgin forests make very poor habitats for

deer and that the State of New York now has a deer population far greater than that of the seventeenth and eighteenth centuries.

58. *R.V.Z.* Crown Point, as previously noted, lies on a commanding promontory of Lake Champlain 110 miles north of Albany and about 75 miles south of the Canadian border. Here in 1731 the French built a great citadel with projecting stories, hoping to make it the capital of all their possessions between Lake Ontario and the Connecticut River. Upon the advance of Sir Jeffery Amherst in 1759, however, the garrison blew up the fort and retreated into Canada. Amherst immediately started to build another and larger fortress, planning to make it one of the key strongholds in British America. The work was abandoned when the English realized the French would never again pose a threat to this part of America. In 1775, two years after the fortress was almost totally destroyed by fire, the Green Mountain Boys under the leadership of Col. Seth Warner captured the remains in the name of the American Republic. The last military action at the fort occurred in 1777 when the Americans in turn abandoned the site at the approach of General Burgoyne. Since 1910 the site has been maintained as a State Park.

59. *R.V.Z.* Paul-Louis Lusignan, a French army officer (1691–c. 1752).

5. Richard Smith   1769

Notes by F. W. Halsey are preceded by the initials F.W.H.

1. *F.W.H.* Now Jersey City.

2. *F.W.H.* Burns's Tavern, or Burns's Coffee House, stood on the west side of Broadway just north of the present Trinity Building [a few doors from Trinity Church]. It was formerly the DeLancey homestead. At various times it bore different names—including the Province Arms, New York Arms, York Arms, and City Arms. Several men had been its proprietors—Burns being one of them. Here in 1765 was signed the Non-Importation Agreement. During the Revolution, it was a favorite resort of military men, being near the fashionable promenade, or mall, in front of Trinity Church. In 1793, the building was taken down, and on its site was erected the City Hotel, which in turn long remained a famous hostelry.

3. *R.V.Z.* Sir Henry Moore (1713–1769) was Governor of New York from 1765 to his death. He died four months after Smith saw him in Burns's Tavern.

4. *F.W.H.* Now known as the Palisades.

5. *F.W.H.* Now written Spuyten Duyvil. The origin of the term has been much discussed. In a deed to Van Der Donck in 1646 the Indian name is given as Papirinimen—"called by our people," adds the deed, "Spytden Duyvel, in spite of the Devil."

6. *R.V.Z.* The Connecticut border was then as now some miles to the east of the Harlem River.

7. *R.V.Z.* Kingsbridge was located at the northeastern tip of Manhattan Island (Broadway and 230th St.) and in 1769 was the only bridge that connected the island with the mainland.

8. *F.W.H.* The Philipse Manor lands comprised "all the hunting grounds" between Spuyten Duyvil and the Croton River. In 1693 parts of them were erected into a Manor which included the present town of Yonkers. In 1682 was built the Manor House which still stands in Yonkers and is now the City Hall. Mr. Philipse's possessions included Fredericksborough, since better known as Sleepy Hollow, above Tarrytown, which with other lands comprised 240 square miles. Here in 1683 he built Castle Philipse, a stone structure, and also built the church which still stands there, the oldest religious edifice in New York State.

R.V.Z. The manor house in Yonkers was used as the City Hall until 1908 when it fortunately passed into the hands of the American Scenic and Historic Preservation Society. Philipse Castle was acquired by the Tarrytown Historical Society in 1940 through the beneficence of John D. Rockefeller, Jr., and it is now being restored to its original seventeenth-century condition. The church "which still stands there" is the famous Sleepy Hollow Church, built in 1699 by Frederick Philipse, the first Lord of the Manor.

9. *F.W.H.* The first of the Van Cortlands was Oliver. It was his son, Stephanus, who in 1697 had his landed estates erected into a manor. The manor house he built is still standing at Croton Bay. It was meant to be a fort as well as a home, the walls being three feet thick and pierced with holes for use in defense.

R.V.Z. The manor house, which originally owned 87,000 acres lying between the Croton River and Anthony's Nose in the Highlands, is now under the jurisdiction of the Sleepy Hollow Restorations, and is open to the public. The house entertained such famous personages as Benjamin Franklin, George and DeWitt Clinton, George Washington, Lafayette, Von Steuben, Cadwallader Colden, Bishop Asbury, George Whitefield, John Jay, Joseph Brandt, and Citizen Genet.

10. *R.S.* The name of a creek of the river Susquehanna whereon, and in the vicinity, we afterwards formed a settlement.

F.W.H. Otego Creek flows into the Susquehanna from the north a few miles west of Oneonta, and about 25 miles below Cooperstown.

11. *F.W.H.* This rock no longer exists.

12. *F.W.H.* Now written Polopel's Island. According to local tradition, it was called originally Polly Pell's Island. [See Chapter 14, note 15.]

13. *F.W.H.* Now Break Neck Mountain.

14. *F.W.H.* By this is meant the stream known on the maps as Moodna Creek, which enters the Hudson at Cornwall. Murderer's Creek, however, still survives as a colloquial term for it. Below Albany, near Castleton, flowing in from the east, there is another stream called Murderer's Creek.

15. *F.W.H.* This point is now Marlborough.

16. *R.V.Z.* The distance between Newburgh (where pioneers from New England crossed the Hudson) to present-day Port Jervis in the heart of the Minisink Indian country. This was known as the Minisink Trail, and led to the headwaters of the Susquehanna by way of the Delaware Valley.

17. *R.V.Z.* Probably Esopus, seven miles below Kingston. Esopus Island, which is located in the middle of the river at this point, would be halfway between New York and Albany if we assumed with Richard Smith that the total distance between those two points was 164 miles. Peter Kalm also designated this island as the halfway point (see Chapter 4, note 13).

18. *R.S.* This town has since been burned by the British General Vaughan.

F.W.H. The burning of Kingston occurred on Oct. 16, 1777. Vaughan was accompanying Gen. Clinton northward to reinforce Burgoyne, but arrived too late. Burgoyne capitulated the day after Kingston was burned.

19. *F.W.H.* So called, although the Beekmans were not properly Patroons.

20. *F.W.H.* Robert R. Livingston, the judge, who had been an energetic member of the Stamp Act Congress, was described by Sir Henry Moore, the Governor of New York, as "A man of great ability and many accomplishments, and the greatest landholder, without any exception, in New York." By "greatest" Sir Henry may have meant the richest: in actual acres Sir William Johnson is understood to have been the largest. Livingston's daughter married General Richard Montgomery, who fell at Quebec, and lies buried in St. Paul's Churchyard at Broadway and Vesey Street, New York City. His son, also Robert R. Livingston, was the Chancellor who administered the oath of office in Federal Hall, Wall Street, to George Washington at his inauguration as the first president of the United States.

R.V.Z. The house is "Clermont," on the border of Dutchess and Columbia Counties, just north of Tivoli. It was erected in 1729–1730 by the Judge's father, Robert Livingston (1688–1775). The Judge's son, third lord of Clermont, financed Robert Fulton who named his first steamboat after the estate.

21. *R.V.Z.* Cherry Valley is in the upper Susquehanna Valley near Cooperstown, about thirty miles west of Schoharie, the latter being in turn about forty miles northwest of Catskill. In 1778 Cherry Valley was the scene of a famous massacre perpetrated by the Indian leader, Joseph Brandt.

22. *R.V.Z.* Sopus or Esopus Creek empties into the Hudson at present-day Saugerties, ten miles below Catskill.

23. *R.V.Z.* Kingston.

24. *R.V.Z.* Now a part of Germantown, nine miles below Hudson on the east bank. As noted in Peter Kalm's narrative (Chapter 4, note 15), it was originally settled by the remnants of 1,800 Palatine Germans who had been brought to America by Governor Hunter to make tar and other naval stores on the lands of Robert Livingston. In 1712, after two years of failure, the government abandoned its support of the enterprise and the Germans scattered to Rhinebeck and the Schoharie and Mohawk Valleys. Some accepted Livingston's terms and settled at German Camp.

25. *R.V.Z.* Located at the mouth of Roeleff Jansen's Kill, about two miles below Catskill on the east bank. The house was erected by the first lord of the manor and dismantled about 1800 by Robert Thong Livingston, grandson of the last lord of the manor.

26. *R.V.Z.* This road is the present-day state highway 145.

27. *R.V.Z.* Now Rogers Island.

28. *R.V.Z.* It was another twenty years before Catskill began to develop as a town.

29. *R.V.Z.* Just south of present-day Athens.

30. *F.W.H.* Staats Long Morris belonged to the family of that name of Morrisania, and was a brother of Lewis Morris, one of the signers of the Declaration of Independence. He was an officer in the British army, who had served in India, where he was present at the seige of Pondicherry. Having adhered to the royal cause in the Revolution, he lost title to his patent on the Susquehanna; but these lands were granted to his brothers Lewis and Richard after the war, as compensation for losses due to depredations committed by the British at Morrisania.

31. *R.V.Z.* Freehold is about fifteen miles from Catskill along present-day route 32. The road follows the Catskill Creek around the northern flank of the Catskill Mountains and thus provided, when it was first built, a pioneer route to the rich farmlands of the upper Susquehanna. From 1800 on it was known as the Susquehanna Turnpike. Cherry Valley, the destination of Col. Morris and his party, was close to Richard Smith's own destination. Smith, however, adhered to his original plan of reaching that destination by way of Albany and the Mohawk River.

32. *R.V.Z.* Also spelled Barren Island. It is located at Coeymans (or "Cojemans").

33. *F.W.H.* Now Schodack, but originally Shotag, an Indian word, meaning the fire place, or the place where the councils are held. This island by the action of the water has since been divided in two, known as Upper and Lower Schodack Islands.

34. *R.V.Z.* Peter Kalm, as we might recall, used the word "battoes" for "Batteaux." According to *F.W.H.* the French word used by Richard Smith is the correct one, for the boats in question were introduced by the French to replace the much lighter Indian canoes, which were not found to be very serviceable in the fur trade.

35. *F.W.H.* Philip Schuyler, when only 23 years old, had served with Bradstreet at Oswego, and in 1758 had become Bradstreet's deputy commissary. In 1761 he went to England as Bradstreet's agent in settling his accounts with the home government. A few years later he became an acknowledged leader of the patriotic party in New York, during the controversies that preceded the Revolution.

Major General John Bradstreet, whose rank had been won in the French War, had title to an extensive tract of land, some 300,000 acres, on the Susquehanna River near the mouth of the Unadilla, which, after his death, became a subject of litigation, unprofitable alike to his heirs and to the settlers, many of whom were ruined by the expenses involved in the contest.

R.V.Z. We shall hear much more about Philip Schuyler and his "Grand House" at Albany in later narratives. We may point out at this time, however, that he participated in an unsuccessful campaign against Crown Point five years after Peter Kalm visited the fortifications, and in 1755 saw a good deal of service at Fort Edward. His Revolutionary War activities at Ticonderoga, Crown Point, Saratoga, etc., are featured in later narratives.

36. *R.V.Z.* In 1680 when Jasper Dankers visited Rensselaerswyck it was in the hands of Maria Van Rensselaer, the widow of Jeremias, the third lord of the manor. The "young man" mentioned by Richard Smith was Stephen Van Rensselaer, the eighth patroon (1764–1839). He was five years old in 1769 and had only recently acquired ownership of the manor (his father had died only a few months before Smith arrived in Albany). Philip Livingston, the boy's grandfather, acted as guardian until he came of age. In 1783 he married Margaret Schuyler, the daughter of the aforementioned Philip Schuyler of Albany, and two years later moved to Rensselaerswyck to assume active command of the manor.

6. Charles Carroll of Carrollton 1776

1. *R.V.Z.* The sloop probably came to anchor off the mouth of the Harlem River at Spuyten Duyvil.

2. *R.V.Z.* The "Asia" was a formidable British warship stationed in New York harbor. On June 6, 1775, it was used to transport British soldiers from the rebellious island of Manhattan to Boston. Two months later it was back in New York and fired upon the city's militia when the soldiers removed the guns from Fort George on the tip of Manhattan. In October of 1775 Governor William Tryon (1729–1788) fled to the ship in fear of his life and remained there until August 1776, when Lord Howe arrived with a British expeditionary force. He was thus on the ship on the night of April 2nd when Franklin and Carroll were awakened by the cannon fire.

3. *R.V.Z.* Bedloe's (or Bedlow's) Island, famous since 1886 as the site of the Statue of Liberty, is located in Upper New York Bay one-half mile west of the Battery. It was named after its original owner, an Englishman by the name of Bedlow, who had a commission from Lord Edward Hyde Cornbury, Governor of New York from 1702 until 1708, for victualling the English fleet. Bedlow used the island as a convenient base of operations where he could store supplies and outfit British ships without the necessity of the ships tying up at the wharves along the East River.

4. *R.V.Z.* Frederick Philipse, the third and last lord of the manor of Philipsburgh. A brief history of this manor, originally erected in 1682, appears in note 8 of Chapter 5 (Richard Smith's tour of the Hudson). The third lord, "Colonel Phillips," was arrested and placed on parole as a tory in 1775. Five months after Carroll passed his manor house, Philipse fled to New York City to secure the protection of the British army, the recent victors of the battles of Long Island and Harlem Heights. This fact, together with Philipse's frequent communication with his two tory sons-in-law, Beverly Robinson and Roger Morris, led to the confiscation of all his property by the Americans in 1779. Upon the evacuation of New York by the British in 1783 Philipse fled with his family to England. His property was sold to a New York merchant in 1785, the very year of Philipse's death. In 1868 the manor house was bought by the city of Yonkers and used as the city hall until 1908, when it came under the custody of the American Scenic and Historic Preservation Society.

5. *R.V.Z.* This church was built in 1752 by the second lord of Philipsburgh and was used until 1870, when it was replaced by a much larger structure.

6. *R.V.Z.* At Stony Point, the southern portal of the Highlands.

7. *R.V.Z.* Anthony's Nose, as it soon came to be called, is opposite Bear Mountain at the northern end of the "Race" or "Rack," the most dangerous part of the river for sailing vessels. Within days after Carroll and his party passed this point construction was begun on two forts at the base of Bear Mountain. Their fate, together with that of the famous chain that was also placed at this point, is featured in later narratives.

8. *R.V.Z.* Thunder Hill was another name for Dunderberg Mountain. The latter, however, is about two and a half miles south of Anthony's Nose, and it is difficult to tell from Carroll's

statements exactly where he was anchored on April 4th. The only "bay" about "half a mile" from Anthony's Nose is Doodletown Cove on the northern edge of Iona Island.

9. *R.V.Z.* Probably the series of cascades that form the lower reaches of Poplopen's Kill (or in later times, Montgomery Creek), opposite Anthony's Nose. It was at this place that Forts Montgomery and Clinton were erected later in 1776.

10. *R.V.Z.* These fortifications were erected during the fall of 1775 and the following winter on a rocky promontory on the east or left bank of the Hudson, and were the first such fortifications to be built in the area of West Point. The promontory is now known as Constitution Island, but in Carroll's day was called "Martelaer's Rock" (not "Marbler's," as Carroll put it). These fortifications (together with Forts Montgomery and Clinton erected later in 1776) failed to stop the British advance up the Hudson in 1777; for this reason Washington ordered the erection of new fortifications based upon a central citadel at West Point, opposite Constitution Island.

11. *R.V.Z.* This is one mile below West Point on the right bank of the river in the present community of Highland Falls.

12. *R.V.Z.* "Gravel Hill" is unknown to this editor, but it presumably refers to "Fort Montgomery" in the following sentence. The battery "a little below" Anthony's Nose is Fort Clinton.

13. *R.V.Z.* Presumably the Appalachian Mountains; if so, Carroll is correct.

14. *R.V.Z.* This is a water wheel driven by water passing over from above (opposed to an undershot wheel where the water approaches from the bottom).

15. *R.V.Z.* These were probably the frigates "Montgomery" (24 guns) and "Congress" (28 guns), both of which were built at or near Poughkeepsie. Both frigates were lost in October, 1777, when Sir Henry Clinton swept up the Hudson. The "Congress" was lost on the flats near Fort Constitution and the "Montgomery" was lost at Fort Clinton.

16. *R.V.Z.* General William Heath (1737–1814), who had been appointed a brigadier-general during the seige of Boston, had recently been transferred to New York to ready the defenses of that city against an expected invasion of Lord Howe. Washington arrived from Boston to take charge of defense on April 13th.

17. *R.V.Z.* There are several inaccuracies here. The Patroons —or in English, Patrons (not "Patrones," as Carroll has it)—

were the Dutch landlords of the system of Patroonships established by the West India Company in 1629. When the English conquered New Netherland in 1664 they confirmed these Patroonships under the English manorial system and established several new manors. An owner of such a tract was called lord of the manor. Technically, in other words, before 1664 there were only Patroons and Patroonships; after 1664, only Lords and Manors. In popular speech, however, the various terms were often used interchangeably.

18. *R.V.Z.* This would be Stephen Van Rensselaer (1764–1839) whom we first encountered when he was five years old (Richard Smith's tour, 1769, Chapter 5, note 36). The reader will also recall that Jasper Dankers visited Rensselaerswyck (p. 27) on his tour of 1680 when the patroonship was fifty years old.

19. *R.V.Z.* Robert R. Livingston (1746–1813), whom we first heard of in connection with Richard Smith's tour (Chapter 5, note 20) will be encountered again in later narratives. Under the original grant of Livingston Manor in 1686 the estate occupied ten miles of riverfront, or 160,000 acres, about thirty miles south of Albany.

20. *R.V.Z.* In point of fact, there were probably only four *permanent* manors in the history of the Hudson Valley: Rensselaerswyck, the first and largest (1630), Livingston Manor (1686), Philipse Manor (1693), and Van Cortland Manor (1697).

21. *R.V.Z.* The statement is highly misleading. The manorial history of the Hudson is very complex and involves constant litigation, division of land, transfer of titles, and even outright failure and loss. By the end of the Dutch period, for instance, all but two of the original patroonships of New Netherland had been repurchased by the Dutch West India Company.

22. *R.V.Z.* This is an early instance of the use of this word. Formerly, during the early years of the seventeenth century, the famous obstructions to navigation below Albany were usually referred to as "a shoald" (Juet, 1609, Chapter 1, p. 12), or "shoals," or simply "sand bars." Gradually, however, the obstructions came to be called "the overslaw" or, more commonly, "overslaugh." The term, in this sense, is an Americanism, and probably derives from the Dutch word, "overslag," meaning a place of transfer of goods from one ship to another. Since such transfers became common along the sand bars south of Albany, the word came to refer to any shoals or sand bars that obstructed navigation.

23. *R.V.Z.* General Philip Schuyler, who was at this time in command of the American forces in the province of New York and was busily engaged in sending supplies to General Benedict Arnold's army on the St. Lawrence, had been forewarned of the arrival of the commission from Philadelphia. On March 11, 1776, Franklin wrote to Schuyler: "Sir:—The Congress have appointed three commissioners to go to Canada, of which number I have the honor to be one. We purpose setting out some day this week. I take the liberty of mentioning this, as possibly a little previous notice may enable you more easily to make any preparation you shall judge necessary to facilitate and expedite our journey, which I am sure you will be kindly disposed to do for us. A friend with us will make our company four, besides our servants. We shall either go in carriages directly to Albany, or by water if the river is open from New York. Hoping soon for the pleasure of seeing you, I now only add that I am, with the sincerest respect and esteem, sir, etc., B. Franklin."

24. *R.V.Z.* Betsey (Elizabeth Schuyler) married Alexander Hamilton in the Albany mansion in December, 1780. Peggy (Margaret) became the wife of General Stephen Van Rensselaer, the patroon.

25. *R.V.Z.* Albany, which had a population of about 3,000 in 1776, was considerably larger than Annapolis. As late as 1860, when Albany had a population of 57,333, Annapolis had only 4,529.

26. *R.V.Z.* Catherine Schuyler (1735–1803) married Philip Schuyler in 1755; she was the daughter of Colonel Johannes Van Rensselaer, the patroon of the Greenbush manor.

27. *R.V.Z.* General John Thomas (1724–1776) was on his way to take command of the American forces at Quebec, having been ordered there by Congress after the death of Montgomery (Jan. 10, 1776) and the ensuing debacle under the command of General David Wooster. After arriving at Quebec on May 1st, Thomas ordered a retreat to Sorel where he died of the smallpox on June 2nd while Carroll and his party were returning to New York and Philadelphia.

28. *R.V.Z.* This house, which was located just outside the present town of Schuylerville, was used by General Burgoyne as his headquarters in 1777 just before the battle of Saratoga. Three days after the battle and one week before he surrendered to Gates, Burgoyne burned the house to the ground. Schuyler

rebuilt the house about 1783, and it is now an historic site administered by the National Park Service.

29. *R.V.Z.* On the Richelieu River about 25 miles north of the American border. These rapids are now circumvented by the locks of the Chambly Canal.

30. *R.V.Z.* The week spent at Saratoga due to bad weather must have been a godsend to Benjamin Franklin. On April 15th, the day before the resumption of his journey, Franklin wrote a letter to Josiah Quincy in which he said in part: "I am here on my way to Canada, detained by the state of the lakes, in which the unthawed ice obstructs navigation. I begin to apprehend that I have undertaken a fatigue that at my time of life may prove too much for me; so I sit down to write to a few friends by way of farewell." As noted in the Introduction, Franklin was indisposed throughout the journey and finally had to cut short his stay in Canada and return home with Charles Carroll's brother. The day after arriving back in New York (May 26) he wrote to the remaining commissioners in Canada saying: "I shall be glad to hear of your welfare. As to myself, I find I grow daily more feeble, and think I should hardly have got along so far, but for Mr. Carroll's friendly assistance and tender care of me. Some symptoms of the gout now appear, which makes me think my indisposition has been a smothered fit of that disorder, which my constitution wanted strength to form completely. I have had several fits of it formerly."

31. *R.V.Z.* This is where present route U.S. 4 crosses the Hudson between Northumberland and Thomson.

32. *R.V.Z.* Carroll undoubtedly refers here to the village of Fort Miller, still in existence eight miles below Fort Edward on the left bank of the Hudson. The village was named after the fort that had been erected about 1755 on the opposite bank of the river.

33. *R.V.Z.* This is probably William Duer (1747–1799) who came to America from England in the 1760s to purchase timber for the British navy. Upon the advice of Philip Schuyler he purchased an extensive tract of timberland near Fort Miller and established the saw mills that Carroll mentions in the following sentences. Duer subsequently adopted New York province as his permanent home and became a leading patriot in the Revolution.

34. *R.V.Z.* These falls were a major obstacle during the con-

struction of the Champlain Canal, but were finally circumvented in a series of well-built locks and dams.

35. *R.V.Z.* Fort Edward, as previously noted, was located at a bend in the Hudson where two major routes to Canada diverged to Lake George and Skenesborough (Whitehall). It had been allowed to fall into decay after the conclusion of the French and Indian wars (1763). Built originally in 1709 and named Fort Nicholson after the Lieutenant-Governor of New York who was in charge of military operations against Montreal, the fort had completely disappeared by the time Peter Kalm visited the area in 1749. In 1755 the fort was rebuilt by General Phineas Lyman who was leading an expedition against the French on Lake Champlain. It was called Fort Lyman after the battle of Lake George but was changed shortly after to Fort Edward by Sir William Johnson in honor of Edward, Duke of York, the grandson of King George II. Shortly after Carroll's visit it was rebuilt once again by the Americans, but was abandoned by General Schuyler in July, 1777, as Burgoyne's army approached along the Woodcreek. After the American victory at Saratoga, the fort was lightly garrisoned until the end of the Revolution. We shall encounter it again in the following narrative when the Marquis De Chastellux visited it in 1780.

36. *R.V.Z.* These are undoubtedly the same falls that Peter Kalm heard, but did not see, when he traveled along the same route on June 27, 1749. Carroll, however, appears to have been misinformed about their name. They were called Bakers Falls after one Albert Baker who was one of the original settlers of the Kingsbury Patent (granted 1762) that embraced 26,000 acres of this area. After the Revolution the community that grew up near the falls was called Sandy Hill, a name which was retained until the present century, when it was changed to Hudson Falls.

37. *R.V.Z.* Charlotte County, which was named after Princess Charlotte, eldest daughter of George III, was formed in 1772. In 1784 its name was changed to Washington in honor of the father of his country. In 1813 part of Washington County was absorbed into the new Warren County, and that part now embraces the present city of Glens Falls which was the site of Wing's tavern. The tavern in question was owned by Abraham Wing, one of the original settlers of the area, who also owned the famous falls on the Hudson. The community was known as Wings Falls from 1759 to 1788 when, as tradition says, Colonel

John Glen won the right to call the community in his name when he threw an elaborate dinner party in Wing's tavern.

38. *R.V.Z.* The construction of Fort George was begun (though never completed) by Jeffery Amherst (1717–1797) in 1759. Amherst had been appointed commander-in-chief of all the British forces in North America after his victory at Louisburg (1758), and he started the erection of a fort at the southern tip of Lake George to cover his advance into Canada. During the same campaign he seized Crown Point and Ticonderoga from the French, and in 1760 his capture of Montreal added all Canada to British America. Though, as Carroll says, the fort was in ruinous condition in April, 1776, it was soon repaired and garrisoned by American forces until the advance of Burgoyne forced its abandonment in 1777. After the battle of Saratoga it was reoccupied by American forces and then finally abandoned for all time after it was captured by Sir John Johnson in 1780. After the Revolution local farmers dismantled most of the walls to manufacture lime, and nothing remains of the fort today except a hundred-foot mound and a few sections of stone.

39. *R.V.Z.* Fort William Henry, named in honor of the Duke of Cumberland, brother of the heir apparent, afterward George III, was built in 1755 by Sir William Johnson to protect the strategic portage between Lake George and the Hudson. The "action with Dieskau" mentioned by Carroll, however, occurred in early September, 1755, just before Johnson built the fort. General Braddock had ordered Johnson to proceed from Albany with a force of about 2,000 militia and 200 or 300 Indians to attack the French at Crown Point. Arriving at Lake George, Johnson discovered that the French under Baron Dieskau had fortified Ticonderoga and were arriving in force from the vicinity of South Bay (Whitehall) to attack his rear. A battle ensued in which Dieskau was taken prisoner and the French thoroughly routed. Johnson then decided that his forces were too weakened to pursue the remaining French and Indians back to Lake Champlain and contented himself with building Fort William Henry during the remainder of the season.

40. *R.V.Z.* This final action at Fort William Henry occurred on August 10, 1757. The blame for the defeat of English-American arms is today ascribed to General Daniel Webb, probably the most incompetent English officer to serve in America during the Seven Years' War. Though Webb com-

manded 4,000 troops at Fort Edward, only 15 miles from Lake George, and was repeatedly urged by the commander of Fort William Henry to come to his assistance, Webb refused to act and finally advised the commander (Col. Munro) to surrender. In spite of Carroll's view of the matter, Munro had no alternative but to comply with his superior officer's decision, for his force of 2,000 men was besieged by 9,000 French and Indians. The ensuing massacre by the Indians was played up as an "atrocity story" and has often been considered a blot on Montcalm's record. Before retiring to Lake Champlain, Montcalm burned Fort William Henry to the ground. The restoration of the fort was started in 1953 by a private corporation and became the prized attraction of the State-owned Lake George Battleground and Campsite. A recent fire (Sept. 18, 1967), said to look "like a scene out of the French and Indian War," destroyed about one-third of the ill-fated fort.

41. *R.V.Z.* The state of New York now owns, and maintains public campsites on, 48 islands in Lake George.

42. *R.V.Z.* One of the narrowest sections of Lake George, today called Sabbath Day Point, about 20 miles north of Fort George.

43. *R.V.Z.* "Below" means toward the mouth of the lake, or north.

44. *R.V.Z.* Carroll is here confusing the "south end" with the bottom of the lake. As he says in the very next sentence, however, Lake George runs north and south. Going by the compass, therefore, the landing place is at the north end of the lake.

45. *R.V.Z.* The French and Indian wars and the American Revolution delayed the settlement of Lake George until the 1790s (Bolton, in 1792; Caldwell, or the present town of Lake George, about 1790). By the time of the Civil War, Lake George had become a popular summer resort, and it is today one of the most congested vacation lands in the state of New York. The rugged east bank, however, is still thinly settled compared to the crowded centers along route 9N on the west bank.

46. *R.V.Z.* Lake George is 36 miles long and one to three miles wide. The widest point is near the southern or upper part of the lake, not, as Carroll says, "nearest the north end." The narrowest contraction is at the aforementioned Sabbath Day Point, a few miles north of the center of the lake.

47. *R.V.Z.* The outlet of Lake George descended 150 feet in a mile and a half and provided, as late as 1860, water-power for some of the most extensive milling operations in the state.

48. *R.V.Z.* Lord Howe, the brother of Sir William Howe and Admiral Howe, British commanders during the Revolution, was killed July 6, 1758, while acting as second in command during General James Abercromby's disastrous attempt to storm French-held Fort Ticonderoga.

49. *R.V.Z.* Agitation for a system of canals linking Lake Champlain and the Hudson began in earnest after the Revolution, but the route along the Woodcreek to Whitehall (fulfilled in 1823) was always favored over the route via Lake George, and the latter was never incorporated into the canal system.

50. *R.V.Z.* A dubious point: an all-water route from Canada to the Hudson would certainly benefit an invading army as much as a defending force. Lake Champlain, of course, saw a great deal of naval action throughout the French and Indian wars as well as the American Revolution and the War of 1812. Six months after Carroll passed over the lake (October, 1776) Benedict Arnold fought a naval battle with the British that delayed an invasion of New York until the following summer.

51. *R.V.Z.* Contemporary historians place Abercromby's losses at 1,944 (out of at least 15,000) as against 377 (out of 3,600) for the French under Montcalm. The battle has been judged one of the bloodiest in the history of British arms. Abercromby, a general as incompetent as D. Webb, immediately lost favor with both the Americans and the British and was recalled by Pitt three months after the battle. The extent of the tragedy may be measured by the fact that Montcalm had decided to retreat and abandon Ticonderoga and Crown Point until Abercromby recklessly assaulted the makeshift abatis without the aid of artillery.

52. *R.V.Z.* Carroll missed seeing Sabbath Day Point on April 20th, as the reader will recall, because the heavy ice along the western shore forced his party to descend the lake along the opposite coast. The point was named, according to legend, when General Amherst landed there on a Sabbath during his advance upon Ticonderoga in July, 1759.

53. *R.V.Z.* As previously noted, the "ruinous condition" of Fort Ticonderoga may be attributed to the fact that in 1759 it was blown up by the French upon Amherst's approach and that the fort lay idle from the end of the French and Indian War until the opening stages of the American Revolution. When Ethan Allen and Benedict Arnold seized the fort in May 1775, it was commanded by only 45 to 48 men and officers.

54. *R.V.Z.* Carroll seems to be unaware that only four months prior to his visit most of the armament of the fort (14 mortars and coehorns, 2 howitzers and 43 cannon) was removed by Colonel Henry Knox and dragged overland to Cambridge, Mass., to help persuade the British to vacate the city of Boston. The omission seems all the more remarkable in the light of Carroll's knowledge (in the following sentences) of the cannon that were removed from the "four vessels" he saw at Ticonderoga.

55. *R.V.Z.* That the American army would probably be forced out of Canada was already obvious by the time Carroll wrote this. Although St. Johns, Fort Chambly, and Montreal had all fallen to General Montgomery during the previous winter, the assault on the final bastion of Quebec had failed (Dec. 31) and the besieging army knew it must retreat from Canada as soon as the St. Lawrence was open to navigation and a British army appeared from across the Atlantic (May 5, 1776). Of the "four vessels" mentioned by Carroll, the sloop was probably captured at Skenesborough (Whitehall) in May, 1775, when Arnold was on his way to Canada. Two of the schooners, as Carroll says, were taken at St. Johns when Montgomery seized that fort on Nov. 2, 1775. All four vessels, plus eleven more that were hastily constructed at Skenesborough in the summer of 1776, did magnificent service in the naval battles of October of that year, when Arnold, though defeated by a superior British fleet of 25 sails, compelled the British to retreat to Canada, thus saving New York from invasion until the following summer. The remains of the *Royal Savage,* one of the vessels lost by Arnold off Valcour Island, were still visible in the clear waters of Lake Champlain as late as 1860.

56. *R.V.Z.* *Isle aux Noix,* now called Port Henry, is about halfway between the American border and St. Johns on the Richelieu River.

57. *R.V.Z.* The historian James Truslow Adams lays the victory to General Montgomery, a New Yorker, and gives a somewhat different picture of the composition of his troops: "His troops, largely New Englanders, were poor military material. They were lacking in discipline, were constantly deserting, and at times practically mutinous. Montgomery deserves the highest praise for working them into shape for the expedition" (*Dic-*

tionary of American Biography, Centenary Edition, vol. XIII, p. 99). The well-provisioned garrison of St. Johns required a siege of 55 days before it succumbed (Sept. 17–Nov. 2). Fort Chambly, 10 miles to the north on the Richelieu River rapids, was captured on Oct. 20. The transfer of provisions, ammunition, and batteries from Chambly to St. Johns finally gave Montgomery the strength to force the surrender of the lower fort.

58. *R.V.Z.* Crown Point, as the reader will recall from Peter Kalm's narrative of 1749 (see Chapter 4, note 58), was built in 1759 by Sir Jeffrey Amherst to replace Fort St. Frédéric, a French bastion built in 1731 and demolished by the French themselves upon the approach of Sir Jeffrey. Crown Point, as Carroll says, was indeed "a considerable fortress," for Amherst planned to make it a permanent British stronghold and had almost completed the work when the French and Indian wars came to an end. An accidental fire (noted by Carroll in the following sentences) destroyed most of the fort in 1773. One year after Carroll's visit the fort was abandoned by the Americans during the approach of Burgoyne's expeditionary force. The ruins of both Fort St. Frédéric and Crown Point are now within the state-owned Crown Point Reservation.

59. *R.V.Z.* This deep ditch, about one-half mile in circumference, still surrounds the ruins of the fort.

60. *R.V.Z.* This barracks is undoubtedly the one that is still in a remarkable state of preservation. It faces the entrance of the present ruins of the fort.

61. *R.V.Z.* The narrow passage between Crown Point and Chimney Point is only about 1,800 feet wide and is spanned today by the Lake Champlain Bridge.

62. *R.V.Z.* Probably located at present-day Barber Point, about three miles south of Westport.

63. *R.V.Z.* Located between Split Rock Point on the north and North West Bay on the south.

64. *R.V.Z.* Undoubtedly a little cove called today Grog Harbor.

65. *R.V.Z.* Split Rock is a slab 30 feet high with a surface of half an acre and is located on a point of the same name opposite Thompson's Point in Vermont. The rock was the traditional boundary between the Mohawk and Algonquin tribes; it marked the northern limits of British possessions by the Treaty of Utrecht (1713); and from 1760 to 1776 it marked the boundary between New York and Canada.

66. *R.V.Z.* Perhaps in the present town of Essex.

67. *R.V.Z.* Located opposite Shelburne Point, Vermont. The "point of land" to the south of the Four Brothers where Carroll spent the night was probably Ligonier Point on the New York side.

68. *R.V.Z.* Schuyler Island lies halfway between Port Douglas and Port Kent. Six months after Carroll passed the island Benedict Arnold's badly battered naval force escaped the British trap at Valcour Island and stopped to make repairs at Schuyler Island before continuing the battle the following day (October, 1776).

69. *R.V.Z.* Cumberland Bay provides a sheltered harbor for the present city of Plattsburg. On September 11, 1814, it was the scene of an American naval victory under the command of Thomas Macdonough that halted a British invasion of the Champlain Valley.

70. *R.V.Z.* Opposite the island of North Hero and just north of Treadwell Bay.

71. *R.V.Z.* Monty Bay.

72. *R.V.Z.* Opposite the present town of Chazy and now belonging to the state of Vermont.

73. *R.V.Z.* Carroll and his party lay in at least 30 feet of water; had they had time to sail a mile or so north along the west coast of the island they could have come to anchor in six feet of sheltered water.

74. *R.V.Z.* An island in the Richelieu River, about ten miles north of the American border, and the site of the Fort Lennox National Historic Park.

75. *R.V.Z.* Three miles south of Rouse's Point at present-day King Bay.

76. *R.V.Z.* Windmill Point is opposite Rouse's Point, and is two miles south of the present international boundary.

77. *R.V.Z.* In point of fact it is a little over a mile.

78. *R.V.Z.* Possibly what is called today Bloody Island, about half a mile south of the Canadian Customs and Immigration Office on Ash Island.

79. *R.V.Z.* It is now called the Richelieu River, and modern maps place its beginning at Windmill Point where Carroll noted that "the lake begins to contract itself."

80. *R.V.Z.* Carroll is of course referring to the Adirondacks on the west, the highest of which is Mt. Marcy (5,344'), and the Green Mountains on the east, the highest of which is Mt. Mansfield (4,393').

7. *Marquis de Chastellux 1780*

Notes by G. Greive are preceded by the initials G.G.

1. *R.V.Z.* Griffin's Tavern still stands (1971) about two and a half miles from present Hopewell Junction and has a roadside marker saying it was "frequented by Washington, La-Fayette, Putnam, Steuben, Continental and French soldiers."

2. *R.V.Z.* General William Heath (1737–1814) was appointed commander of West Point when Benedict Arnold's treason was discovered in late September, 1780, just two months prior to Chastellux's visit. The French officer, however, had met General Heath in Newport, R.I., the previous July when the French army arrived under the command of Rochambeau. Heath had been appointed by Washington to receive the army. Both Washington and Lafayette had instructed the new commander of West Point to receive Chastellux with all military honors.

3. *R.V.Z.* Chastellux, who had been traveling south along present route 9, had turned west toward the river in the vicinity of present McKeel Corners. The heights in this area still afford the same magnificent view of West Point.

4. *R.V.Z.* Chastellux learned more about the purpose of this foraging expedition when he talked with General Heath later that evening. The expedition was evidently part of a general plan, later abandoned, of taking New York City from the British. General John Stark (1728–1822) defeated the British at Bennington on August 16, 1777.

5. *R.V.Z.* This was Benedict Arnold (1741–1801). His activity as a horse dealer gains amplification later in the narrative (p. 109).

6. *R.V.Z.* The officers are John Lamb (1735–1800), Sebastian Bauman, Nicholas Fish (1758–1833), and David S. Franks (1740–1793).

7. *R.V.Z.* Fort Putnam was probably named after Colonel Rufus Putnam (1738–1824) whose regiment built the fort in 1778. It was partly restored in 1907–1910 and is located on Mount Independence, 451 feet above the Hudson. Fort Wallis (or Wyllis) was named after Colonel Samuel Wyliss and together with Fort Webb, which Chastellux does not name, was located on the first ridge of the mountains to the west of the river. The lower battery nearer to the river was probably Fort Meigs.

8. *R.V.Z.* The French officers had arrived in Newport with Rochambeau and, like Chastellux, were taking advantage of the usual cessation of hostilities during the winter to see the sights of the country.

9. *R.V.Z.* King's Ferry connected Stony Point and Verplanck's Point eleven miles below West Point and was a major link in the north-south military line of communications between New England and the South.

10. *R.V.Z.* Sir Henry Clinton, of course, never did join forces with Burgoyne, for the latter was defeated at Saratoga at the time Clinton was burning Kingston. Fort Clinton, named after the American George Clinton (1739–1812), was located five miles below West Point at the mouth of Popolopen Creek, on the west bank of the Hudson, opposite Anthony's Nose. The Bear Mountain Bridge now spans the Hudson at this point. The fort was captured by the English Clinton on October 6, 1777.

11. *R.V.Z.* A heavy steel chain had also extended across the river at Fort Clinton, and was easily cut by Sir Henry Clinton during his sweep up the Hudson in October 1777.

12. *R.V.Z.* The Clove is a valley formed by the Ramapo River and extends from Suffern, N.Y. to Newburgh and New Windsor on the Hudson. It therefore outflanks the Highlands on the west; during the Revolution it permitted a safe inland route for Washington's armies from the interior of New England to northern New Jersey and the South. The New York Thruway, the Erie Railroad, and highway 17 still make use of this convenient passage around the western flank of the Highlands.

13. *R.V.Z.* The statement is highly misleading, for the Americans never took Verplanck's Point until it was abandoned by the British on October 21, 1779. The facts regarding the military action at these two points are as follows: Sir Henry Clinton captured both Stony Point and Verplanck's Point between May 31st and June 2nd, 1779; Wayne captured Stony Point on July 16th, but failed to take Verplanck's Point when an attempt was made the following day. The arrival of British reinforcements forced the Americans to retire from the field on July 18th, leaving both points in the hands of the British (occupied July 20th). The two fortifications were not regained by the Americans until the British in turn abandoned the posts in October, 1779. The famous storming of Stony Point was thus devoid of military significance, though it was a timely moral victory.

14. *R.V.Z.* This is James Livingston (1747–1832) who was placed in command of Fort Lafayette on Verplanck's Point after it was abandoned by the British in October, 1779.

15. *R.V.Z.* The "immense lake" is Haverstraw Bay which lies to the south of Stony Point.

16. *R.V.Z.* The *Vulture* was waiting at a "sort of promontory" called Teller's Point, five miles below Stony Point on the east bank of the Hudson.

17. *R.V.Z.* The site of the former homestead of Joshua Hett Smith, two miles below the village of Stony Point, is now occupied by the New York State Reconstruction Home.

18. *R.V.Z.* Chastellux is correct in saying that André "found the gibbet" on the right or west bank: the specific place was in the village of Tappan on the New York–New Jersey border. However, André had previously crossed the river to the left or east bank, for he was captured at the northern end of the village of Tarrytown.

19. *R.V.Z.* Lafayette's army occupied the left flank of Washington's army along the Totowa (now Passaic) River just north of present-day Paterson, N.J. Washington's own headquarters were at nearby Preakness. The armies remained in that area from October 9 to November 27, 1780.

20. *R.V.Z.* General Henry Knox's headquarters is still maintained as an historic site. It is located southwest of New Windsor near present Vails Gate. Washington's own headquarters were closer to the village of New Windsor, but are no longer standing. Washington maintained his winter quarters here from December 6, 1780, to June 25, 1781.

21. *R.V.Z.* Colonel William Stephens Smith (1755–1816) was rewarded for distinguished military service by being appointed Washington's aide in July, 1781. In 1786 he married Abigail Amelia Adams, daughter of John and Abigail Adams, and lived for a time in New York City on an estate purchased from one Peter Praa Van Zandt, an ancester of the present editor.

22. *R.V.Z.* Colonel David Humphreys (1752–1818).

23. *R.V.Z.* As the narrative soon explains, General Schuyler had agreed to take Chastellux and his companions on a guided tour of the Saratoga battlefields.

24. *R.V.Z.* Since Chastellux had traveled twenty-three miles after leaving Pride's Tavern three miles north of Poughkeepsie, and he was following present route US 9, Thomas' Inn must have been located in the vicinity of Upper Red Hook.

25. *R.V.Z.* The story is possibly true, for Arnold did in fact personally conduct a horsetrading business between Quebec and the West Indies while maintaining a residence in New Haven.

26. *R.V.Z.* The Claverack Creek flows into the Hudson at Stockport, three miles north of the present city of Hudson. Chastellux's "approach" to the Hudson was only temporary, for as he soon says, he turned northeast again to enter the village of Claverack, three miles west of Claverack Landing (now Hudson).

27. *R.V.Z.* This is possibly a reference to Captain Abraham Van Buren, the father of the President, Martin Van Buren, who kept an inn on Hudson Street in Kinderhook.

28. *R.V.Z.* Mrs. Carter was one of General Schuyler's daughters whom Chastellux first met in Newport.

29. *R.V.Z.* Hamilton had married Elizabeth Schuyler, the second daughter of the general, just ten days before Chastellux arrived at the house.

30. *R.V.Z.* The reader will recall that Charles Carroll also found the Schuyler children very attractive when he met them four years prior to Chastellux's visit (p. 83).

31. *R.V.Z.* Half Moon is the present Waterford. This route, of course, permitted the bypassing of the Mohawk.

32. *R.V.Z.* Either Green or Van Schack Islands located to the south of Peobles Island which was being fortified.

33. *R.V.Z.* The figures roughly correspond to those mentioned by Jasper Dankers (p. 24), Peter Kalm (p. 58), and Charles Carroll (p. 83).

34. *R.V.Z.* Saratoga here and following means Old Saratoga, now Schuylerville. Stillwater is three miles above Mechanicville, the site of the aforementioned "Anthony's Kill."

35. *R.V.Z.* The evacuation occurred in July 1777, upon the advance of Burgoyne's army.

36. *R.V.Z.* A reference to Fish Creek at Schuylerville.

37. *G.G.* The name given in America to horsedealers as well as to those who take care of horses.

38. *R.V.Z.* The battle of Saratoga had occurred three years before Chastellux's visit.

39. *R.V.Z.* Glens Falls.

40. *R.V.Z.* Jane McCrea's death on July 27, 1777, gave rise to a great deal of American propaganda as well as poetry and song, and it materially influenced the number of enlistments who rushed to support Gates and Arnold before the battle of Saratoga. The house in Fort Edward from which she departed

on her fatal interview, and the site of her grave in the local Union Cemetery, are still pointed out to tourists.

41. *R.V.Z.* The newer fort ("a large redoubt") was built shortly after Charles Carroll's visit of 1776. Details of the history of Fort Edward may be found in Chapter 6, note 35.

42. *R.V.Z.* Fort Stanwix, located on the present site of Rome, N.Y., was originally built in 1758. Abandoned after the French and Indian War, it was rebuilt during the American Revolution and named Fort Schuyler in honor of Chastellux's guide and host. The recent devastation that Chastellux describes occurred only two months before his visit, when a large party of tories and Indians invaded New York from Canada.

43. *G.G.* Two of the most melancholy garrisons in France.

44. *R.V.Z.* George Grieve, the translator, has a footnote to the effect that these birds cannot be classified as either quails or partridges. Terminology is still very confused about this species of game bird, but it seems likely that Chastellux was describing a Bob-white.

45. *R.V.Z.* The house was rebuilt, in all probability, between 1780 and 1783. It is now a central attraction of the Saratoga National Historical Park.

46. *R.V.Z.* Burgoyne published a bombastic proclamation calling upon the people of New York to surrender to his irrepressible armies just before taking Ticonderoga on June 29, 1777.

47. *R.V.Z.* This occurred on "The Field of Grounded Arms" in the center of the present Schuylerville.

Part III · Peacetime Travel by Sloop

8. John Maude 1800

Notes by J. Maude are preceded by the initials J.M.

1. *R.V.Z.* Jan Willem De Winter (1750–1812) was in command of a Dutch fleet on October 11, 1797, when it was defeated off Camperdown by an English fleet commanded by Admiral Duncan. He was subsequently exonerated by a Dutch court-martial and went on to accumulate a distinguished record under the Emperor Napoleon.

2. *R.V.Z.* Timothy Pickering was Secretary of State from 1795 to May, 1800. His son Octavius later wrote the first volume of a four-volume biography of his famous father.

3. *J.M.* I recognized in the Bluff (Teller's-point) separating Tappan from Haverstraw-bay, the original of a sketch done by Major André, with pen and ink, the night before his capture.

4. *R.V.Z.* Possibly Phillips Pond on the east bank just south of Verplanck's Point.

5. *R.V.Z.* Maude slept that night where the Bear Mountain Bridge now spans the Hudson.

6. *R.V.Z.* Maude was something of an artist, and several of his charming sketches, including one called "Entrance to the Highlands of the Hudson River," were printed in the 1826 edition of *Visit to the Falls of Niagara*.

7. *J.M.* On the 6th of October, 1777, three thousand men, conveyed by some Ships of War under Commodore Hotham, landed at Verplanck-Point, forty miles from New York; of these, two thousand one hundred were transported without artillery across the Hudson to Stoney-Point, and from thence proceeded by a very difficult pass over the Donderberg to the attack of Fort Montgomery, and Fort Clinton, which were both stormed at the same moment!

8. *R.V.Z.* Probably Iona Island which is separated from the west bank by a marshy inlet. This island later became the site of an arsenal and supply depot of the federal government. It is now (1971) the home of the Hudson River Valley Commission dedicated to the enhancement of "the river's recreational, industrial, historic, scenic, cultural, residential and esthetic values."

9. *R.V.Z.* Windermere is a town on the eastern shore of the largest lake in England. The view Maude has in mind is one looking west from the town across the lake of the same name to the various mountains named in the following sentence.

10. *R.V.Z.* Esopus Meadows, as they are now called, and Vanderberg Cove, are located just south of Kingston.

11. *R.V.Z.* Morgan Lewis (1754–1844), soldier, jurist, and Governor of New York, married the daughter of Robert R. and Margaret Beekman Livingston of Clermont and helped to manage the Livingston estates.

12. *R.V.Z.* Possibly today's Magdalen and Cruger Islands.

13. *R.V.Z.* The name Esperanza was used between 1790 and 1840 at the instigation of several Livingstons who owned a great deal of land in the area and proposed to develop a large trading center. These plans failed to materialize, and the town is now known as Athens. The reference to Algiers alludes to the famous pirates of the Barbary Coast who from 1785 to 1815 preyed upon American shipping in the Mediterranean and reduced sailors and civilians to slavery. The practice was terminated in 1815 when Commodore Stephen Decatur destroyed the pirate fleet and forced the Bey of Algiers to accede to American terms.

14. *R.V.Z.* Sixty years later New Baltimore still only had a population of 709.

15. *R.V.Z.* Present-day Bethlehem Center is located on route 9W four miles below the center of Albany. Along the opposite (or east) bank of the Hudson stretches Papscanne Island, John Maude's "Highhill Island."

16. *R.V.Z.* Charles Williamson (1757–1808), a British officer and land promoter, came to America about 1791 to manage Sir William Pulteney's tract of 1,200,000 acres in Steuben County. John Maude visited him two years after Williamson had laid out the town square of Bath. The Cuylers were descended from an old Dutch family that settled in Albany as early as 1664.

17. *R.V.Z.* The Le Roys were some of the most distinguished merchants of New York City during the post-Revolutionary period.

18. *R.V.Z.* Dykes and dams were, in fact, used by the engineers of the federal government when they solved the problem of the Overslaugh after the Civil War. (See also Chapter 1, note 1, and Chapter 6, note 22.)

19. *J.M.* As the New York Currency is eight shillings the dollar, £4,800 is 12,000 dollars, or £2,700 sterling.

20. *R.V.Z.* See Chapter 8, note 13.

21. *R.V.Z.* John Livingston (1750–1822) built this house in 1793 along the northern boundary of the Livingston Manor after the death of his father, the third and last Lord of the Manor. The house is still standing in the present town of Oak Hill opposite the town of Catskill and has never been outside the Livingston family. It is presently (1971) owned by Henry H. Livingston.

22. *R.V.Z.* The Old Manor House was the so-called "Upper Manor" and was erected at the mouth of Roelif Jansen's Kill (now Ancram Creek) in the present town of Linlithgo. It was demolished the very year John Maude saw it.

23. *R.V.Z.* This is the famous "Clermont" built by Margaret Beekman Livingston opposite the present town of Malden. It replaced an earlier "Clermont" that had been burned by the British in 1777. The Chancellor, Robert R. Livingston (1746–1813), was born in the first Clermont (often called the "Lower Manor") and lived there with his widowed mother until he came of age when he built his own mansion (also called "Clermont" according to Benson J. Lossing) within a stone's throw of his mother's. The British also burned the Chancellor's house, and he built another that in turn burnt down in the early part of the present century.

24. *R.V.Z.* This may be the John Swift Livingston who built a mansion at Upper Red Hook (Tivoli) before the Revolution. It was acquired by Col. J. L. De Peyster.

25. *R.V.Z.* Isaac Weld (1774–1856), a young Irish "topographical" writer and illustrator, sailed up the Hudson in July, 1796, while on the way to see the sights of Canada. The picture in question, Weld's "View of the Hudson," appeared with other illustrations in the first edition of Weld's *Travels through the States of North America, and the Provinces of Upper and Lower Canada,* in 1799. The book enjoyed an immediate and sustained success, went through a second edition in 1799, and a third the following year while Maude was in America.

26. *R.V.Z.* See Chapter 6, note 9, and p. 81 of the Charles Carroll text.

27. *R.V.Z.* Just north of Nyack.

9. John Lambert 1807

1. *R.V.Z.* This sloop was undoubtedly named after the famous "Experiment" that was built in Albany in 1780 and that Captain Stewart Deane sailed to China and back in 1785–87. Only 60 feet long and with a displacement of 80 tons (as against 130 tons for the sloop taken by Lambert), the first "Experiment" was sold to new owners after its incredible voyage to the Orient and used in the Albany–New York City run. It undoubtedly had ceased to exist by the time the second

"Experiment" was built in 1807. The Museum of the City of New York has a scale model of this most famous of all Hudson River sloops.

2. *R.V.Z.* Mrs. Montgomery was the former Janet Livingston, daughter of Robert R. Livingston (1718–1775). She married General Richard Montgomery (1738–1775) in 1773. The estate in question could be "Grassmere," the first Montgomery mansion built at Rhinebeck; or "Montgomery Place," built in 1805 by Janet Montgomery near Tivoli. (See Chapter 5, note 20.)

3. *R.V.Z.* Political passions were at their height during this period of the Napoleonic Wars, and the bitter conflict between Federalists and Jeffersonians was to come to a near breaking-point when Jefferson inaugurated his ill-fated embargo policy in December, 1807.

Part IV · The Age of the Steamboat

Introduction

1. *R.V.Z.* Fulton, of course, did not invent the steamboat. At least fifteen steamboats had been built in America by eight different inventors prior to the *Clermont*. John Fitch of Connecticut conducted experiments in the 1780s and 1790s (a famous one occurring on the Collect Pond in New York City in 1796). John Evans *almost* had a steamboat in operation on the Mississippi in 1802, claiming that he had failed only because he lacked Fulton's capital and a state monopoly. But Fulton was successful, and it was the voyage of 1807 that, as Donald C. Ringwald said, marked "the beginning of the unbroken development of steam navigation in America" (*Hudson River Day Line* [Berkeley, California, 1965], p. 1).

2. *R.V.Z.* Dionysius Lardner (1793–1859), the author of this statement, has of course erred in this date. The maiden voyage of the *Clermont,* as noted above, was in the summer of 1807,

and the boat was put into regular packet service between New York and Albany in September of the same year.

3. *R.V.Z.* Dionysius Lardner, *Railway Economy* (London: 1851), p. 312.

4. *R.V.Z.* James Silk Buckingham, *America, Historical, Statistic, and Descriptive* (London: 1841), vol. II, pp. 265–266.

5. *R.V.Z.* Alice Cary Sutcliffe, *Robert Fulton and the "Clermont"* (New York: 1909), p. 219.

6. *R.V.Z.* Martha J. Lamb and Burton Harrison, *History of the City of New York* (New York: 1896), vol. III, p. 532.

7. *R.V.Z.* Sutcliffe, *Fulton,* p. 234.

8. *R.V.Z. Ibid.,* p. 248.

9. *R.V.Z. Ibid.,* p. 252.

10. *R.V.Z.* Paul Wilstach, *Hudson River Landings* (Indianapolis: 1933), p. 155.

11. *R.V.Z.* Ringwald, *Day Line,* p. v.

10. Lafayette 1824

Introduction

1. *R.V.Z.* Levasseur, A., *Lafayette in America, in 1824 and 1825; or, Journal of Travels, in the United States* (New York: 1829), vol. I, p. 96.

2. *R.V.Z.* Dumas Malone, ed., *Dictionary of American Biography* (New York: 1946), vol. IX, p. 538.

3. *R.V.Z.* Harriet A. Weed, ed., *Autobiography of Thurlow Weed* (Boston: 1883), p. 185.

Text

1. *R.V.Z.* The *James Kent* had been chartered by the City of New York for this occasion. It was under the command of Commodore Samuel Wiswall. The North River Steam Boat Company first put this steamboat in service during the summer of 1823. It became one of the most celebrated of the early steamboats on the Hudson. On May 12, 1824, it made the run to Albany in 15 hours and 30 minutes—a new record.

2. *R.V.Z.* The "number of others" listed by Thurlow Weed in his *Autobiography* are as follows: Mr. Levasseur, Lafayette's secretary; Generals Morgan Lewis, Simeon DeWitt, Anthony Lamb, and Philip Van Cortland; Colonels Marinus Willett,

Nicholas Fish, Robert Trout, and E. S. Duncombe; Majors Popham, Fairlee, and [J. Taylor] Cooper; Captains [Jedediah] Rogers and Halsey, and Lieutenant Gregory of the Society of Cincinnati; Alderman [Philip] Hone; Colonel Francis K. Huger of South Carolina; General [James] Tallmadge; Colonels A. M. Muir and William L. Stone; Edward Livingston of Louisiana; and Miss Francis Wright, authoress of *Manners and Society in America.*

3. *R.V.Z.* Sylvanus Thayer (1785–1872) was superintendent of West Point from 1817 until 1833. He is truly known as the "Father of the Military Academy," for when he took charge, the Academy was hardly more than a secondary school, and in a few years' time he made it one of the best in the world.

4. *R.V.Z.* General Jacob Jennings Brown (1775–1828), hero of the battle of Niagara during the War of 1812, was in command of the United States Army from 1821 until his death.

5. *R.V.Z.* General Winfield Scott (1786–1866), a hero of the War of 1812 and one of the greatest military figures in American history between the time of Washington and Grant, was also to be at West Point to receive the Prince of Wales when the latter made his celebrated trip up the Hudson in 1860.

6. *R.V.Z.* "Mr. Cozzen's" (*sic*) was the name of a proprietor of a hotel which was maintained under government auspices at West Point and which will be mentioned in subsequent narratives. After 1849, when Cozzens built a much larger hotel one mile south of West Point, General Scott still used it as his headquarters during "the four or five warmer months of the year" (Benson J. Lossing, *The Hudson from the Wilderness to the Sea* [New York, 1866], p. 251).

7. *R.V.Z.* Levasseur's account (*Lafayette in America*, vol. I, pp. 104–105) of this late dinner in Newburgh includes the following remarkable episode: "While we were at table, the report was circulated through the town, that the General was to depart immediately. At this news the whole population assembled in a tumultuous manner under the windows of the hotel, and a thousand confused voices were raised, to declare that it was cruel to tear away from the inhabitants of Newburgh, the friend they had so long and so ardently desired; that the darkness which had enveloped him on his arrival had permitted no one to see him; that they would be greatly disappointed if unable to do him honour by the arrangements they had made for his reception; and finally that they would not allow him to depart before the sun should have shone upon him in their town, and he had bestowed his blessing on the children of Newburgh. This noise was soon increased by a conflict that took place between the militiamen who kept the door of the hotel, and the crowd that wished to get in and greet General Lafayette. For a few minutes the mayor of the town, who was at table with us, seemed to pay little attention to what was passing in the street, but some one coming in to inform him that the disorder seemed likely to become serious, the militia and police officers beginning to be weary of resisting the multitude, he rose, took General Lafayette by the hand, and preceded by two lights, conducted him to a balcony that looked out upon the street. At the sight of General Lafayette, shouts and plaudits were raised on all sides; but a signal from the mayor restored silence, while he addressed the people as follows: 'Gentlemen!' (for there all magistrates use polished phrases in addressing the people,) 'Gentlemen! Do you wish to give offence to the Guest of the Nation?' 'No, no, no!' 'Do you wish that Lafayette should be deprived of his liberty, in the land that owes him its emancipation?' 'No, no!' 'Well then, listen to what I am going to say, and do not oblige me to resort to the law to reduce you to order.' There was then a profound silence. 'Your friend is expected at Albany. He has promised to be there to-morrow before night. He has already been delayed by an unforeseen accident, by which he lost three hours on his route. If you should keep him here until to-morrow, you deprive him of the pleasure of visiting all the other towns, where also he is looked for, and make him break all his engagements. Do you wish to cause him such chagrin?' 'No, no, no!' And the air resounded with cries of applause and huzzas. General Lafayette then addressed to the crowd a few words of thanks, which were received with great enthusiasm. The people, however, who were now silent, still remained crowding the street, but without pressing at the door of the hotel."

8. *R.V.Z.* The *Chancellor Livingston*, a 494-ton vessel built in 1816, was to play a leading role in the ceremonies marking the opening of the Erie Canal in the following season (1825).

9. *R.V.Z.* Francis Wright (1795–1852) and her sister Camilla had first visited America in 1818–1820 when they gathered material for Francis' *Views of Society and Manners in America*, published in 1821. This book led to a warm friendship with Lafayette, and the two sisters planned their next visit to

America to coincide with that of Lafayette. They arrived in New York in September 1824 and accompanied Lafayette during most of his tour, including his visit to Jefferson and Madison.

10. *R.V.Z.* Thomas Jackson Oakley (1783–1857) was a lawyer and judge of the Supreme Court of New York who represented New York in the famous case of *Gibbons vs. Ogden* that broke the Fulton-Livingston monopoly and opened steamboating to general competition.

11. *R.V.Z.* James Tallmadge (1778–1853) was a lawyer and statesman who became lieutenant-governor of New York in 1825. He owned a large farm in Dutchess County, had been in command of the troops in defense of New York City during the War of 1812, and was one of the founders of the University of the City of New York (now New York University).

12. *R.V.Z.* James Emott (1771–1850) was a lawyer and judge who represented Dutchess County in the state legislature.

13. *R.V.Z.* Colonel Francis K. Huger (1773–1855) was the son of Benjamin Huger, a friend of Lafayette with whom the General spent his first night in America after arriving from France in April 1777. The son was educated in Europe and in 1794 while on a continental tour heard of Lafayette's imprisonment for political reasons at Olmütz, Austria, and resolved with Dr. Justus Eric Bollman to effect his rescue. The melodramatic attempts miscarried at the last moment, Lafayette was wounded and returned to prison, and Col. Huger and Dr. Bollman themselves imprisoned. Huger returned to America after a confinement of eight months, but Lafayette (who spent a total of five years in prison for his political convictions) was not released until 1797 when Napoleon arrived with his victorious armies in Austria and peremptorily demanded his liberation. The story was told by Huger himself, at Lafayette's invitation, as the *James Kent* sailed north of Kingston.

14. *R.V.Z.* General Philip Van Cortlandt (1749–1831) was the son of Pierre Van Cortlandt, the first lieutenant-governor of New York, and a great-grandson of the Stephanus Van Cortlandt who in 1697 erected the manor at Croton (see Chapter 5, note 9). General Philip Van Cortlandt, who served at Saratoga during the Revolution and later was elected to the United States Congress, came out of retirement in 1824 to honor Lafayette and to accompany his friend on a large part of his tour.

15. *R.V.Z.* General Nicholas Fish (1758–1833) was a part of Lafayette's military command in the years 1780–1781 and was Alexander Hamilton's second-in-command during the battle of Yorktown. He accompanied Lafayette to Virginia after finishing the Hudson tour, and on October 19, 1824, during the ceremonies at Yorktown, received a wreath from Lafayette in commemoration of his services.

16. *R.V.Z.* General Morgan Lewis (1754–1844), who served in both the Revolution and the War of 1812, became governor of New York in 1804–1807. He played host to Lafayette on his estate on the Hudson the afternoon after leaving Poughkeepsie (see note 18 below).

17. *R.V.Z.* Henry A. Livingston was probably Col. Henry Alexander Livingston (1776–1849), a grandson of Philip Livingston, a signer of the Declaration of Independence.

18. *R.V.Z.* General Morgan Lewis's estate is now the Ogden Mills and Ruth Livingston Mills Memorial State Park, located just north of Staatsburg on route 9. Lewis acquired the estate in 1782 through marriage to Gertrude, sister of Chancellor Livingston and daughter of Robert R. and Margaret Beekman Livingston of Clermont. The house that Lafayette visited was almost destroyed by fire in 1832, but some of the masonry walls were incorporated in a new house built by Lewis soon after. This house was in turn acquired by Ruth Livingston Mills, great-granddaughter of General Lewis, who married Ogden Mills, Sr. (heir of Darius Ogden Mills, 1825–1910, who made a fortune in California). Ruth L. Mills and Ogden Mills, Sr., enlarged the house into the present mansion in 1895 under the direction of the architect Stanford White. After the death of Ogden L. Mills (1884–1937), son of Ruth L. and Ogden Mills, Sr., his sister, Mrs. Henry Carnegie Phipps, the great-great granddaughter of General Lewis and Gertrude Livingston Lewis, gave the property to the state in memory of her parents. The mansion, which now contains the offices of the Taconic Park Commission, is open to the public and possesses, among far more valuable treasures, a picture of the house Lafayette visited.

19. *R.V.Z.* Colonel Henry Beekman Livingston (1750–1831), brother to Chancellor and Edward Livingston.

20. *R.V.Z.* The incident was described by Thurlow Weed in the following manner: "As the steamer was approaching Esopus, on the second day, I observed a small boat pulling out from the west shore with a signal, and called the attention of

Commodore Wiswall to the circumstance. The commodore immediately directed the pilot to steer in that direction. It proved to be a skiff, with an old gentleman seated in the stern, with his bandana handkerchief fastened to his cane as a signal. As we approached the skiff, the commodore remarked, 'I know him,' and then directed the steamer to be stopped, and the steps lowered. The commodore received the old gentleman, and walked with him to the promenade deck, where General Lafayette, surrounded by his old comrades, was seated. No word was spoken. As we approached, Commodore Wiswall leading the old gentleman by the hand, General Lafayette rose, as did the other officers, but still no word was spoken. The stranger offered both his hands, which the general received, and each looked the other steadily in the face. It was evident that General Lafayette was taxing his memory severely, and, after a profound silence of more than a minute, the general exclaimed, 'My old friend, Colonel Harry Livingston!' and then, after a few words of mutual congratulation, he added, 'Do you remember when I reviewed your regiment of infantry on Rhode Island?' " (Weed, *Autobiography of Thurlow Weed,* pp. 191–192.)

21. *R.V.Z.* Chancellor Robert R. Livingston died in 1813 and Clermont then passed into the hands of Robert L. Livingston. (See Chapter 5, note 20.)

22. *R.V.Z.* Edward P. Livingston was the grandson of Philip Livingston (1716–1778) and a lieutenant-governor of the state of New York.

23. *R.V.Z.* The *Richmond* was built for the New York–Albany run in 1814.

24. *R.V.Z.* Jacob Rutsen Van Rensselaer was well known in New York State as an early champion of the Erie Canal.

25. *R.V.Z.* Edward Livingston (1764–1836) was the brother of Chancellor R. Livingston and the youngest son of Robert R. Livingston the elder (1718–1775). One of the most famous of the Livingstons, Edward represented Louisiana in Congress from 1823 to 1829, was a United States Senator from 1829 to 1831, Secretary of State from 1831 to 1833, and minister to France from 1833 to 1835. His codification of the penal laws of both Louisiana and the United States gave him enduring fame as one of the finest legal minds of the nineteenth century. He died where he was born, at the "Clermont" of this narrative.

26. *R.V.Z.* Peter R. Livingston was the son of Robert Livingston (1708–1790), the third lord of the Livingston Manor.

27. *R.V.Z.* Mrs. Montgomery was Janet Livingston, sister of Robert R. Livingston, the Chancellor. Her husband, General Richard Montgomery, fell in the assault on Quebec in 1777 (as noted in Chapter 5, note 20). In 1805 Mrs. Montgomery built "Montgomery Place" at Annandale, midway between Tivoli and Barrytown. Lafayette visited her at this place on his return voyage down the Hudson (see note 46 below). The estate was left to her brother, the above Edward Livingston (1764–1836), upon her death in 1828.

28. *R.V.Z.* Levasseur (*Lafayette in America,* I, p. 106) gives the additional information that "we had hardly left Clermont, when we saw the fine mountains of the Catskills, which, rising a few miles from the river, beautifully form the western horizon with their brown bulk, exhibiting an amphitheatre, in the center of which is the *Pine Orchard House* [or the Catskill Mountain House], situated 2500 feet above the level of the Hudson. The building is an object of curiosity for the traveller; and of pleasure excursions to the inhabitants of the vicinity." This famous landmark of the Hudson Valley was in existence until the winter of 1963 when it was burned down by the Conservation Department of the state of New York.

29. *R.V.Z.* Solomon Van Rensselaer (1774–1852) was the son of Henry Kiliaen Van Rensselaer and fifth in descent from Kiliaen Van Rensselaer, the first patroon. He saw military service under General Anthony Wayne at the battle of Fallen Timbers, distinguished himself during the War of 1812, was elected to Congress during the period of the Missouri Compromise, and served several terms as Adjutant-General of New York and Postmaster of Albany.

30. *R.V.Z.* The episode is described by Levasseur (*Lafayette in America,* I, p. 108) in the following terms: "It was not until night that we got opposite Albany, on the borders of the river, which was to be crossed before we could enter the city, which stands upon the right bank. A large flying bridge called a horseboat, received both our carriages at once, although drawn by four horses each, with about 30 of our mounted escort, and more than 150 pedestrians, and carried us with ease to the other shore, which echoed with the acclamations of a multitude, and the uninterrupted sound of artillery."

31. *R.V.Z.* Nathan Sanford (1777–1838) became chancellor of New York upon the retirement of James Kent in the summer

of 1823. Sanford also served in both the federal and state congresses throughout a long career of public service.

32. *R.V.Z.* Probably Henry Inman (1801–1846), who set up shop as a genre and portrait painter in New York City in 1823 and painted a portrait of Lafayette.

33. *R.V.Z.* Ambrose Spencer (1865–1848), one of the most powerful politicians in the state of New York during the years 1800–1830, was mayor of Albany in 1824 and 1825.

34. *R.V.Z.* Joseph C. Yates was governor of New York for the one term of 1822–1824.

35. *R.V.Z.* De Witt Clinton had been governor in 1822–1823 and was to be re-elected for another two-year term in November, 1824. (See note 37 below.)

36. *R.V.Z.* Robert Morris (1734–1806), the financier of the Revolution.

37. *R.V.Z.* Lafayette here alluded to De Witt Clinton's father, James Clinton (1733–1812), a major-general in the Revolution; and to De Witt Clinton's uncle, George Clinton (1739–1812), soldier and first governor of the state of New York. De Witt Clinton (1769–1828) was himself twice governor of New York as well as a United States senator and a mayor of New York City. He was co-founder of the New York Literary and Philosophical Society and served as its president from 1816 until his death. His greatest claim to fame, however, stems from his championship of the Erie Canal, of which we will presently hear more.

38. *R.V.Z.* The easternmost section of the Erie Canal going along the Hudson from Albany to Cohoes Falls with a lateral canal leading into the river itself at Watervleit opposite the city of Troy was completed in October, 1823.

39. *R.V.Z.* Stephen Van Rensselaer (1764–1834), the eighth patroon, and one of the chief advocates and architects of the Erie Canal. His great manor house, built in 1765 (and disassembled in 1897 and re-erected in Williamstown, Massachusetts), stood on Broadway on the north end of Albany. The "second lock" mentioned in the text stood just to the north of the mansion.

40. *R.V.Z.* Located halfway between Albany and Troy.

41. *R.V.Z.* Located about eight miles to the west or roughly halfway between Albany and Schenectady.

42. *R.V.Z.* Now called Watervliet. The arsenal was established to produce arms for the War of 1812 and has continued to produce munitions for every subsequent war in American history. In the summer of 1967 the arsenal was designated a national historical landmark by the National Parks Service, and it is now open to the public. The present grounds of the arsenal extend over 136 acres, providing space for 81 buildings and a working staff of 4,000 people.

43. *R.V.Z.* This is the famous Troy Female Seminary founded in 1821 by Emma Willard, one of the great educators of the nineteenth century. The Seminary was one of the first institutions in the world to be devoted to the higher education of women. The buildings Lafayette visited are located on the corner of Second and Ferry Streets and are presently a part of the Russell Sage College, founded in 1916. The present Emma Willard School is located on the western side of Troy on Pawling Avenue.

44. *R.V.Z.* The "great work" is, of course, the Erie Canal which was not completed and officially opened until the fall of 1825.

45. *R.V.Z.* As noted previously (notes 34 and 35 above). Joseph C. Yates was the incumbent governor during Lafayette's visit, though De Witt Clinton had been governor in 1822–1823 and was to be re-elected again in November 1824.

46. *R.V.Z.* See note 27 of this chapter and Chapter 9, note 2.

11. *Opening of the Erie Canal 1825*

1. *R.V.Z.* Elisha W. King had been Alderman from 1810 to 1815 and from 1818 to 1824. He was a member of the Common Council in 1825.

2. *R.V.Z.* The Lieutenant-Governor, James Tallmadge (1778–1853), was a lawyer and statesman who had been in command of the troops for the defense of New York City during the War of 1812. He served as Lieutenant-Governor from 1825 to 1827.

3. *R.V.Z.* The New York Delegation included Governor Clinton, Lieutenant-Governor James Tallmadge, Stephen Van Rensselaer (the patroon), General Solomon Van Rensselaer, Jacob Rutsen Van Rensselaer, and Colonel William L. Stone, the author of the narrative.

4. *R.V.Z.* Located, as the reader will recall, twenty miles south of New York City off the Atlantic Highlands and marking the entrance to Lower New York Bay. Fortifications had existed on the tip of Sandy Hook from the time of the War of 1812.

5. *R.V.Z.* George Catlin (1796–1872) later became the celebrated painter of the American Indian.

6. *R.V.Z.* One of these kegs is now in the collection of the New-York Historical Society.

7. *R.V.Z.* Black Rock in 1825 was a village located on Lake Erie two miles north of the mouth of Buffalo Creek where the present city of Buffalo first came into being. Termination of the canal at the mouth of Buffalo Creek gave the advantage to the community of Buffalo, and the latter soon grew northward to absorb the town of Black Rock (officially recognized as a part of the city of Buffalo in 1853). The Erie Canal ran from the mouth of Buffalo Creek along Lake Erie to Black Rock, then parallel to the Niagara River to the mouth of Tonawanda Creek ten miles north of Buffalo. At that point the canal followed the Tonawanda Creek as the present Barge Canal does.

8. *R.V.Z.* About fifteen miles northeast of the present city of Buffalo.

9. *R.V.Z.* Named after William C. Bouck (1786–1859), Governor of New York from 1842 to 1846. He was appointed a canal commissioner in 1821 and was in charge of the construction of the most difficult section of the canal—that from Brockport to Lake Erie.

10. *R.V.Z.* Holley is located six miles west of Brockport along present-day route 31.

11. *R.V.Z.* Brockport is located about twenty miles west of Rochester.

12. *R.V.Z.* General Vincent Matthews was head of the bar in Western New York. He died in Rochester in 1846.

13. *R.V.Z.* John Canfield Spencer (1788–1855) was a lawyer and congressman who also served as the Secretary of War and Secretary of the Treasury under President Tyler.

14. *R.V.Z.* The Inland Lock Navigation Company was an early attempt by private enterprise to build a canal along the Mohawk. Chartered in 1792 under the direction of General Philip Schuyler, it had completed a canal around the obstructions at Little Falls (1793) when it was forced to suspend all further efforts because of financial as well as engineering troubles.

15. *R.V.Z.* The people of Schenectady perhaps anticipated the fact that the construction of the Erie Canal would all but destroy the advantage the city had enjoyed as a transshipment center for goods brought overland from Albany as long as the Cohoes Falls blocked navigation.

16. *R.V.Z.* A college founded in 1795 through the efforts of Philip Schuyler of Albany and the Reverend Dirck Romeyn of Schenectady.

17. *R.V.Z.* The Half-Way House has been mentioned in connection with Lafayette's visit of 1824 (p. 168).

18. *R.V.Z.* The reader will recall that Lafayette paid a visit to the arsenal at Gibbonsville (now Watervliet) during his tour of 1824 (see Chapter 10, note 42).

19. *R.V.Z* See Chapter 10, note 39.

20. *R.V.Z.* Philip Hone (1780–1851), whose fame today rests upon the secret diary he kept from 1828 to 1851, was an early projector of the Delaware and Hudson Canal as well as the Erie Canal. He became mayor of New York in January 1826.

21. *R.V.Z.* This is probably George Horton Barrett (1794–1860), a famous actor of the period who was once considered the best light comedian in America.

22. *R.V.Z.* The *Chief Justice Marshall* was a bright new steamboat of 300 tons. Five years later the boat exploded her boiler and killed eleven people.

23. *R.V.Z.* The reader will recall that the *Chancellor Livingston* (see Chapter 10, note 8) was first encountered at Newburgh in 1824 when it took off some of the passengers from Lafayette's overcrowded *James Kent*.

24. *R.V.Z.* Charles Rhind (d. 1845) was a merchant and a diplomatic agent for President Jackson who had also played a role in Lafayette's reception in New York in 1824.

25. *R.V.Z.* The *Constitution* was a 276-ton steamboat built early in 1825.

26. *R.V.Z.* The *Constellation* was another new vessel of 276 tons.

27. *R.V.Z.* The *Swiftsure,* a steamboat of 270 tons with a capacity of 60 passengers, was built in the summer of 1825 by the Steam Navigation Company to pull the first safety barge on the Hudson, the *Lady Van Rensselaer.*

28. *R.V.Z.* The *Olive Branch* was a steamboat of 265 tons built in 1815.

29. *R.V.Z.* The reader will recall that the *Richmond,* a steamboat of 370 tons built in 1814, brought many notables from Albany and Hudson to the festivities for Lafayette at Clermont in 1824 (see Chapter 10, note 23).

30. *R.V.Z.* The *Saratoga* was another new but small steamboat (250 tons) built in 1825.

31. *R.V.Z.* The scene occurred on "Parade Hill," a public park and place of promenade that was built in 1795 on a bluff overlooking the Hudson. It is still (1971) a conspicuous feature of the city of Hudson and is located at the foot of Warren Street, which in turn runs due east to the eminence called "Prospect Hill," 500 feet above the Hudson.

32. *R.V.Z.* This could be either Upper Red Hook Landing (present-day Tivoli) or Lower Red Hook Landing (present-day Barrytown).

33. *R.V.Z.* James D. Livingston (1786–1837), son of Robert C. Livingston, lived at "The Locusts," about six miles north of Hyde Park.

34. *R.V.Z.* The *Commerce* was a twin of the aforementioned *Swiftsure*, built by the Steam Navigation Company in 1825 to pull the safety barge, *Lady Clinton*.

35. *R.V.Z.* The *Lady Clinton* together with the *Lady Van Rensselaer*, as noted above, were the first safety barges to ply the waters of the Hudson. The purpose of these barges is revealed by an advertisement of 1825: "Passengers on board the Safety-Barge, will not be in the least exposed to any accident which may happen by reason of the fire or steam on board of the Steam-Boat; the noise of the machinery, the trembling of the boat, the heat from the furnace, boilers, and kitchen, and every thing which may be considered as unpleasant or dangerous on board a Steam-Boat, are entirely avoided in the Safety-Barge." The *Lady Clinton* was fitted exclusively for passengers (i.e. not for freight), had a dining cabin nearly 90 feet in length, a range of staterooms for private families, a reading room, a promenade deck more than 100 feet in length, furnished with settees and covered with an awning, "and all the usual accommodations found in the best steam boats."

36. *R.V.Z.* De Witt Clinton married Catharine Jones, the daughter of a New York physician, on May 8, 1819. She was the governor's second wife. The first, Maria Franklin De Witt, died in 1818.

37. *R.V.Z.* The Brooklyn Navy Yard, on Wallabout Bay along the East River opposite Corlears Hook, Manhattan, was acquired by the federal government in 1801 and steadily expanded until it became the largest naval industrial establishment in America.

38. *R.V.Z.* Opposite the Brooklyn Navy Yard on the eastern shore of Manhattan Island.

39. *R.V.Z.* Named after Oliver Ellsworth (1745–1807), the Chief Justice of the United States before John Marshall.

40. *R.V.Z.* The Castle in question is "Castle William," erected on Governor's Island off the tip of Manhattan shortly after the federal government acquired the island in 1800. It was a fortress on the northwestern corner of the island named after Jonathan Williams (1750–1815) who was the first superintendent of West Point, a brigadier-general of the New York militia, and the engineer in charge of the construction of the defenses of New York harbor during the first decade of the nineteenth century.

41. *R.V.Z.* Fort Tompkins was located close by present-day Fort Wordsworth on Staten Island and guarded the southern entrance to the Narrows of New York harbor. Fort Lafayette was located 200 yards off Fort Hamilton on a small island called "Hendricks Reef" on the Long Island side of the Narrows. Fort Lafayette was called "Fort Diamond" when it was first built in 1812.

42. *R.V.Z.* This is, of course, the famous Duncan Phyfe (1768–1854) who lived and worked in New York City and designed some of the best furniture in American history.

43. *R.V.Z.* Samuel Latham Mitchill (1764–1831), a physician, United States senator and representative, and a promoter of science, was an early enthusiastic supporter of the Erie Canal. He is also distinguished by the fact that he accompanied Fulton on the first voyage of the *Clermont,* and as early as 1796 conducted a mineralogical survey of the banks of the Hudson River that became a pioneer work of geological research.

12. Fanny Kemble 1832–33

Notes by Fanny Kemble are preceded by the initials F.K.

1. *R.V.Z.* Barclay Street was the location of the main pier of the North River Steamship Line. A picture of this pier as it looked at the time of Fanny Kemble's trip may be found on page 135 of John A. Kouwenhoven's *The Columbia Historical Portrait of New York* (New York: 1953).

2. *F.K.* Of course the captain is undisputed master of the boat, and any disorders, quarrels, etc., which may arise, are settled by his authority. Any passenger, guilty of misbehaviour,

is either confined, or sent immediately on shore, no matter how far from his intended destination. I once saw very summary justice performed on a troublesome fellow who was disturbing the whole community on board one of the North River steamers. He was put into the small boat with the Captain and a stout looking sailor, and very comfortably deposited on some rafts which were floating along shore, about twenty miles below West Point, whither he was bound.

3. *F.K.* The quantity of one's companions in these conveyances is not more objectionable than their quality sometimes. As they are the only vehicles, and the fares charged are extremely low, it follows, necessarily, that all classes and sorts of people congregate in them, from the ragged Irish emigrant, and the boorish back-countryman, to the gentleman of the Senate, the Supreme Court, and the President himself.

4. *R.V.Z.* The reader will recall that the Palisades range in height from 300 to 500 feet.

5. *R.V.Z.* Fanny's "three companions" were undoubtedly the unnamed Colonel and two other admirers she met on the voyage. Her father and Aunt Dall were unacquainted with the history of the river.

6. *R.V.Z.* A little later Fanny Kemble says that "Mr. Cozzens" is the proprietor of the hotel. We have already encountered this hotel in Lafayette's visit of 1824 (see Chapter 10, note 6). Six years after Fanny's visit when James Silk Buckingham visited West Point (1838, Chapter 14) the hotel had been closed by the government because it interfered with the "good discipline" of the students. Cozzens later (in 1849, according to Benson J. Lossing) built a larger hotel one mile south of West Point (at present-day Highland Falls) that became one of the most famous hostelries of the Hudson Valley. Known for years simply as "Cozzens," it subsequently enjoyed a distinguished history as "Cranston's Hotel and Landing" and finally became in 1900 the home of a Catholic order under the name of Lady Cliff Academy.

7. *R.V.Z.* It was not "the Americans," but the Dutch who called this mountain Butter Hill. N. P. Willis, as the reader will recall, renamed the mountain Storm King. Fanny Kemble is also somewhat less than accurate on other counts. As early as 1816, for instance, Joseph Rodman Drake, Washington Irving, Fitz-Greene Halleck, and James Fenimore Cooper—writers all—were on a walking tour of the Crows Nest when Drake was in-

spired to write "The Culprit Fay," a poem that was long considered one of the finest in American literature.

8. *R.V.Z.* The reader will recall that Sylvanus Thayer (1785–1872), who was superintendent of West Point from July 1817 until July 1833, had also been on hand to greet Lafayette during the visit of 1824 (see Chapter 10, note 3). Thayer was recently honored as "The Father of the Military Academy" by being elected to New York University's Hall of Fame (October 1965).

9. *R.V.Z.* Fort Putnam has been mentioned in connection with the Marquis de Chastellux's visit of 1780 (see Chapter 7, note 7). A visit to the ruins still provides one of the most rewarding experiences of the Hudson Valley and the modern tourist can drive to within a short walk of the impressive walls and battlements.

10. *R.V.Z.* Gouverneur Kemble (1786–1875) was the proprietor of the famous iron works at Cold Spring. Fanny and her father visited him the following spring on their second voyage up the Hudson (see notes 12 and 14 below).

11. *R.V.Z.* Edward John Trelawny (1792–1881), a friend, as Fanny soon notes, of Shelley and Byron, was present at Leghorn when Shelley died by drowning. In 1858 Trelawny wrote a book about his acquaintanceships entitled *Records of Shelley, Byron and the Author.* He was somewhat famous by the time he met Fanny on the Hudson, having written in 1831 the popular *Adventures of a Younger Son,* a Byronic tale of adventure based for the most part on the incidents of his own life.

12. *R.V.Z.* William Kemble, the brother of Gouverneur Kemble, was the New York representative of the Cold Spring Iron Foundry and apparently in charge of the factory at the foot of Beach Street that manufactured many of the engines for the steamboats of the Hudson as well as the engine of the *Merrimac* (of Civil War fame) and of the *De Witt Clinton* (New York's first locomotive, used on the Mohawk and Hudson River Railroad).

13. *R.V.Z.* This marsh forms the southeastern boundary of Foundry Cove (or what Fanny calls the extension of the "main current" of the Hudson) and separates Constitution Island from the mainland. Gouverneur Kemble's house did not long survive his death in 1875. The buildings of the "West Point Foundry" clustered along the edge of the Cove at the mouth of Foundry Creek. (See note 15 below.)

14. *R.V.Z.* Called Indian Falls, and located on a small stream (Indian Brook) that flows into the Hudson just south of Constitution Island. Fanny's visit to the falls was to terminate in a notable experience that was later commemorated, according to Edgar M. Bacon (*The Hudson River,* 1909, 385), in renaming the falls "Fanny Kemble's Bath."

15. *R.V.Z.* Fanny had every reason to be impressed. The West Point Foundry was established in 1817 under the following circumstances: The War of 1812 had revealed a paucity of cannon foundries in the United States. The only two foundries in existence, Havre de Grace and Georgetown, had been rendered ineffective by the blockade of the British fleet. President Madison therefore ordered the erection of four foundries in different parts of the country. Cold Spring was chosen as one site because it could be protected by the guns of West Point in case of another foreign invasion of the Hudson Valley. Gouverneur Kemble, a friend of most of the outstanding men of his age, received the commission for the Cold Spring foundry because of his friendship with James Kirke Paulding, at that time Secretary of the Board of Naval Commissioners. The foundry became one of the major sources of northern ordnance during the Civil War, employing at various times as many as 700 men. One of the directors was Robert P. Parrott, who invented the famous "Parrott gun" and thereby helped materially in the victory of the Union. The foundry maintained a fleet of seven sloops shuttling material and finished products between New York City and Cold Spring. One of these sloops, the *Victorine,* was the fastest such vessel on the Hudson. The foundry made and launched the first iron vessel in America, the revenue cutter *Spencer.* President Lincoln once visited the foundry and called on its owner. So famous had the establishment become after the Civil War that Jules Verne chose the foundry as the manufactory of the projectile that was used in his *Trip to the Moon.* By 1884, however, the foundry could no longer keep abreast of the technological changes in the industry and was compelled to shut down.

Gouverneur Kemble, who turned out to be only a distant relative of Fanny Kemble, was one of the most remarkable men of his age. It was his early home in Newark, N.J. (Crockloft Hall) where Washington Irving and his friends composed the *Salmagundi Papers.* Irving was a frequent visitor to Cold Spring, as was about every other famous American of the mid-nineteenth century. Kemble created a social life (centered about his famous "Saturday Night Dinners") that was one of the most illustrious in the history of the Hudson Valley. Nearby West Point was an indissoluble part of that life. "Cold Spring and West Point were two halves of a whole. The commandant, the professors, the visiting notables were all part of the Cold Spring social and professional life" (Margaret Lente Raoul, "Gouverneur Kemble and the West Point Foundry," *Americana,* vol. XXX, Jan.–Dec. 1936, p. 470).

The Putnam County Historical Society now (1971) runs a Foundry School Museum, located at 63 Chestnut Street in Cold Spring. It is opened to the public on Wednesdays and Sundays and contains many items pertaining to the foundry plus a painting by John Ferguson Weir depicting Kemble and Mr. and Mrs. Parrott watching a tense moment at the factory when molten iron is being poured into a cannon mold. ("Hudson Valley Showcase," *New York Times,* Sunday, May 14, 1967.)

16. *R.V.Z.* Indian Brook. Present-day route 9D passes over the stream, and the falls Fanny visited are accessible by a road and path along the edge of the ravine.

17. *R.V.Z.* Margaret Lente Raoul says that the test-guns were often fired across the river at the wall of Storm King Mountain, putting big holes in the rock that were still visible in 1936 (Raoul, "Gouverneur Kemble," *Americana,* vol. XXX, Jan.–Dec. 1936).

18. *R.V.Z.* A French historian and poet of the fourteenth century.

13. Harriet Martineau 1835

1. *R.V.Z.* The reader will recall that Lafayette visited this hotel (see Chapter 10, note 6) and that when Fanny Kemble visited West Point (see Chapter 12, note 6) the hotel was closed for the season, but she was able to stay at its proprietor's own house. We will encounter the hotel again in the following narrative when James Silk Buckingham visits West Point.

2. *R.V.Z.* The 1,396-foot peak on the west bank of the Hudson between West Point and Storm King Mountain.

3. *R.V.Z.* Irving, as we noted during Fanny Kemble's visit to West Point, was an old friend of Gouverneur Kemble, the proprietor of the foundry.

4. *R.V.Z.* Probably George P. Morris (1802–1864) and his

wife. Morris, who owned a famous country home in the area ("Undercliff" near Cold Spring), was the founder of the *New-York Mirror,* the organ of the Knickerbocker school of writers, and also enjoyed a minor reputation as a poet.

5. *R.V.Z.* Details about the history of Fort Putnam may be found in the narrative of the Marquis de Chastellux's visit (see Chapter 7, note 7). The reader will also recall that Fanny Kemble made a notable visit to the fort (see Chapter 12, note 9).

6. *R.V.Z.* Thaddeus Kosciusko (1746–1817) was a Polish patriot who came to America during the Revolution with the French expeditionary force and was appointed by Washington to supervise the erection of fortifications at West Point. A monument was erected in his honor in 1828 at the site of Fort Clinton (see Chapter 14, note 13).

7. *R.V.Z.* The "two long reaches" are Vorsen Reach (between Constitution Island and Storm King Mountain) and Crescent Reach (between Montgomery and West Point).

8. *R.V.Z.* The party has rowed around Constitution Island to the mouth of Indian Brook. The reader will recall that two or three years earlier Fanny Kemble and her hosts walked the distance between Cold Spring and Indian Brook.

9. *R.V.Z.* The reader will recall that Fanny Kemble almost fell at this point when she successfully climbed the falls in 1832 or 1833 (see Chapter 12, p. 204).

10. *R.V.Z.* We first encountered Edward Livingston aboard the steamboat *James Kent* during Lafayette's triumphal tour of 1824 (see Chapter 10, note 25). He was appointed minister to France on May 29, 1833 by President Jackson just to negotiate the difficult matter that Harriet Martineau describes in the following paragraph. He resigned that commission and returned to "Montgomery Place," his home on the Hudson, in the late summer of 1835 when this encounter with Harriet Martineau took place.

The Englishwoman's appraisal of Livingston's attempt to "manage the temper of his own potentate as well as baffle the policy of the European monarch" is undoubtedly correct. The French government had agreed by treaty in 1831 to pay American citizens 150,000,000 francs over a period of six years for damages and spoliations incurred during the Napoleonic Wars. When no payment was made during the next two years, Livingston was sent to France to see what could be done. A year of failure (1834, when Harriet Martineau heard about Mr.

Livingston "almost daily") thoroughly angered President Jackson and in a message to Congress in December, 1834, he suggested that the American government ought to take reprisals against French property. The recommendation undermined Livingston's tact and diplomacy, but in spite of French anger Livingston was able to mollify the French to the extent of getting the Chamber of Deputies to assent to the payment of the spoliations-claims, provided some apology was made for the offensive message of 1834. Livingston then decided he had done all he could and returned home. In January 1836 he argued his case before the Supreme Court and counseled the President about further negotiations with the French. The affair, which had become notorious on both sides of the Atlantic, finally ended amicably due to the friendly mediation of Great Britain.

11. *R.V.Z.* Fanny Kemble had also been disappointed when she passed the estate on the way to Albany in July, 1833: "As we came up the river we passed Dr ——'s place, Hyde Park, which has the reputation of being the best kept private estate in America; the situation of the house, on the edge of the ridge, appeared to me, from the river, rather too much exposed" (*Journal,* II, p. 174). The beauties of the place, as Harriet Martineau discovered, could only be appreciated by visiting the site of the house itself.

The history of this superlative estate runs from the early eighteenth century to the present day, and is one of the most distinguished in the Hudson Valley. The Hyde Park estate (which antedates the town of the same name by more than a century and gave its name to the latter) was acquired by Dr. David Hosack in 1828. The name of the estate dates back to the original owner, Peter Fauconnier, who was the private secretary of Edward Hyde, Viscount Cornbury, later third Earl of Clarendon and Governor of New York from 1702 to 1708. Fauconnier, a collector and receiver-general in the colony of New York, acquired ownership about the time Queen Anne granted the original patent in 1705. After Fauconnier's death in 1746 Dr. John Bard, noted physician and pioneer hygienist, purchased the entire Hyde Park patent, and about 1772 moved from New York City and started the first improvement of the land. After the Revolution, Dr. Bard returned to New York City to resume his medical practice and assisted his son, Dr. Samuel Bard, as attending physician to George Washington during the latter's first term as President of the United States. He returned to Hyde Park in 1798 to resume the improvement of the estate, but died only a year later. The son, Dr. Samuel Bard, then acquired ownership, built a mansion overlooking the Hudson, conducted experiments in horticulture and farming, and continued to make extensive improvements on the property. When the young Dr. Bard and his wife died within a day of each other in 1821, the property passed to their only surviving son, William Bard. The latter, however, only lived there until 1828 when, as we have already noted, the eminent Dr. Hosack (a former partner of Dr. Samuel Bard) acquired ownership. As Harriet Martineau indicates, Dr. Hosack had a botanist's as well as a landscape designer's interest in plants, flowers, and trees. The remarkable specimens of exotic trees and shrubs that may still be seen on the estate undoubtedly date from the years 1828–1830 when Dr. Hosack revived horticultural experimentation at Hyde Park and employed André Parmentier, a Belgian landscape designer, to lay out the paths, roads, and the fine scenic vistas that Harriet Martineau romantically attributes to Providence. To go beyond the date of the Englishwoman's visit and bring the history of this magnificent estate up to the present, John Jacob Astor bought the estate from the heirs of Dr. Hosack in 1840, five years after the death of the latter. Astor immediately gave the property to his daughter, Dorothea Astor Langdon. Her son, Walter Langdon, Jr., became sole owner in 1853. From then until his death in 1894 Langdon continued to improve the property. In 1895 it was bought by Frederick W. Vanderbilt, a grandson of the Commodore Cornelius Vanderbilt who founded the family fortune. The new owner tore down the old Langdon house and built in 1898 the ostentatious Italian Renaissance structure (designed by the famous architectural firm of McKim, Mead, and White) that is now permanently preserved as a national historic site in conjunction with the nearby estate of Franklin Delano Roosevelt. The estate thus spans the history of the Hudson Valley from the era of the original land grants to the period of the affluent mansions of the American Gilded Age and the *fin de siècle*. To visit the estate today (it is open to the public) is to see the same magnificent setting that is pictured in the popular nineteenth-century print, "View from Hyde Park" (1837).

12. *R.V.Z.* This road, which Harriet Martineau mentions earlier as separating the farming from the residential or "pleasure-grounds" of the estate, is the present-day U.S. route 9. To drive along this highway today is to confirm the division noted by the English writer a century and a quarter ago. Estate after estate in this fashionable section of the valley placed their barns and service buildings on the eastern side of the turnpike. On the western side of the road stand the fine old mansions that proudly face the Hudson and ignore the bustling commercialism some distance to the rear.

13. *R.V.Z.* Eleven years after this was written another writer, born and raised on the Hudson, returned to even greater fame as a result of a sojourn among the "savages" of the South Sea Islands. Herman Melville's account, however (*Typee,* 1846; and *Omoo,* 1847), contained severe indictments of the "bad effects" of such missionaries as the Rev. Charles Stewart. The indictments led to counter-charges, and Stewart's *Visit to the South Seas* (c. 1831) often entered the public debate. The orthodox voices of the period held that Stewart's account was more accurate than Melville's. Dispassionate opinion now gives the whole case to Melville.

14. *R.V.Z.* Dr. David Hosack (1769–1835) was indeed one of the most illustrious figures of nineteenth century New York. He studied medicine under the noted Dr. Benjamin Rush; became a professor of botany at Columbia University; was attending surgeon at the Burr-Hamilton duel; was the first physician in America to use the stethoscope and to advocate vaccination; was a professor of medicine in the new College of Physicians and Surgeons; one of the founders of the Bellevue Hospital as well as the New-York Historical Society; a substantial author and lecturer; and one of the most prominent figures in the cultural life of his period.

15. *R.V.Z.* Harriet Martineau had determined to visit the Catskill Mountain House when she had espied it as a tiny white speck on a distant mountain-peak while on a previous voyage up the Hudson. After visiting it she decided it was the "noblest wonder" of the Hudson Valley and wondered why "European travellers," who universally "seem to agree in their love of the Hudson," never mentioned this remarkable feature of the valley. With an enthusiasm which perhaps derived from the fact that she thought she had personally discovered this unknown wonder, she held that she would rather "have missed the Hawk's Nest, the Prairies, the Mississippi, and even Niagara, than this" (*Retrospect,* pp. 57–58).

The Mountain House was indeed remarkable, but it was far from being unknown—even to her own compatriots—by the time she visited it in 1835. Built in 1823–24 (see Roland Van

Zandt, *The Catskill Mountain House,* New Brunswick: 1966) as the pioneer hotel of the Catskill Mountains (and probably the first mountain resort in American history), the Mountain House was in continuous operation until the year 1942; and it did not cease to exist until its decaying ruins had to be burned down by the Conservation Department of the State of New York in January, 1963. From the time it opened its doors until well into the 1880s and '90s when literally hundreds of hotels and boarding houses catered to thousands of vacationers in every region of the Catskills, the Mountain House attracted the foremost figures of American society and became a "must" on the itinerary of any foreign visitor to the United States. By the time Harriet Martineau visited it the hotel had already become familiar to such representative personages as Capt. Basil Hall (1827), the Irish actor Tyrone Power (1833), Aaron Burr (1823), Washington Irving (1832), Thomas Cole (1825), and had become a standard feature of all the guide books and picture books of the era. Beginning with Cole's visit in 1825, it became a favorite subject of the Hudson River School of painting and was familiar to such diverse English and American artists and illustrators as Asher B. Durand, Jaspar F. Cropsey, Frederick E. Church, S. R. Gifford, B. B. G. Stone, W. H. Bartlett, W. Bennett, Thomas Nast, G. Harvey, Winslow Homer, George Inness, and Currier and Ives. Writers also flocked to the romantic hotel on the mountain: James Fenimore Cooper, William Cullen Bryant, Willis Gaylord Clark, Park Benjamin, N. P. Willis, Bayard Taylor, and hosts of others. Jenny Lind is reputed to have sung there; Oscar Wilde put on a skit; Alexander Graham Bell personally installed the first telephone; Ulysses S. Grant and William Tecumseh Sherman came to bask in the warmth of their fame; President Chester A. Arthur sought relaxation from the cares of office. Statesmen, diplomats, foreign dignitaries, people of fame and fashion—they all visited the Mountain House during the post-Civil War era. At the turn of the century when the hotel was at the height of its fame and glory it maintained miles of trails and carriage roads, a 3,000-acre park along the eastern escarpment of the mountains, a farm with a dairy and its own herd of cows, a golf course, bowling alleys, boathouses and beaches (it owned two lakes), and a railroad (complete with rolling stock, depots, warehouses, etc.) that ran all the way from the Hudson to the top of the Catskill Mountains. Though the Mountain House had not become this formidable

when Harriet Martineau visited it in 1835, it was already what she called with pardonable exaggeration "the noblest wonder" of the Hudson Valley. We shall visit this great mecca of nineteenth-century travel again in the following narrative by James S. Buckingham.

16. *R.V.Z.* In a later period a small inn was built at this place halfway up the mountain (two miles from the beginning of the ascent) and it became popularly known as "The Rip Van Winkle House," the presumed site of the famous encounter between Irving's hero and the "odd-looking personages playing at nine-pins."

17. *R.V.Z.* The view from the Mountain House elicited many exaggerations, but none as extreme as this. The "right extremity" terminated in the Highlands of West Point, a good fifty miles from the sea. Even so, however, the view from the Mountain House embraced at least fifty linear miles of the Hudson River and has been justly categorized by the American Geographical Society as "one of the most inspiring views of the national domain east of the Rocky Mountains."

18. *R.V.Z.* A visit to these falls was a standard outing for patrons of the Mountain House. Higher than Niagara, they were considered at this time one of the scenic wonders of the American landscape. Cooper described them at length in the first of the Leatherstocking stories; Bryant wrote a long poem about them; and they were painted by such artists as Thomas Cole (in several versions), Winslow Homer (showing the gigantic cavern behind the falls), W. H. Bartlett, John F. Kensett, Jervis McEntee, Sanford R. Gifford, and many others. For over a century the falls were part of the property of the nearby Laurel House, but they recently (1965) passed into the hands of the New York State Conservation Department which also now owns all the former property of the Catskill Mountain House.

14. James S. Buckingham 1838

1. *R.V.Z.* Buckingham traveled with his wife and son.

2. *R.V.Z.* It was not until after the Civil War and the coming of the big luxury liners that the "larger vessels" took over the piers of the North River.

3. *R.V.Z.* The dueling ground was a narrow ledge or terrace of open land at the base of the cliffs that was later effaced by

the construction of the West Shore Railroad and that was located opposite the end of 42nd Street in New York City. The Hamilton-Burr duel occurred on July 11, 1804. Hamilton's son, Philip, was killed in a duel at the same place in late 1801. Other famous duelers included De Witt Clinton (1802) and Capt. Oliver Hazard Perry (1818), the naval hero of Lake Erie. Duels continued to be fought there as late as 1843.

4. *R.V.Z.* The former sites of Forts Lee and Washington are demarcated today (1971) by the opposite ends of the George Washington Bridge. The last remnants of Fort Washington succumbed to bulldozers and apartment houses in the 1930s. The British destroyed Fort Lee soon after taking it in November, 1776. The area which contained the outworks of Fort Lee on top of the Palisades is still free of buildings and other encumbrances and may still have a chance of being preserved as an historic site.

5. *R.V.Z.* The remains of André were removed to Westminster Abbey in 1821.

6. *R.V.Z.* The "Horse Race" is a narrow, swift, and deep part of the river that runs from Dunderberg Mountain opposite the town of Peekskill to the present Bear Mountain Bridge. The reader will recall that Benjamin Franklin came to grief here while on his way to Canada in 1776 (see Chapter 6, note 7).

7. *R.V.Z.* Forts Montgomery and Clinton were located on either side of Poplopen Creek at the western terminus of the present Bear Mountain Bridge opposite Anthony's Nose. The remains of Fort Clinton, on the south side of Poplopen Creek, can be seen close by the traffic circle at the entrance to the bridge. The few remains of Fort Montgomery are located at the water's edge on the north side of the creek.

8. *R.V.Z.* Benson J. Lossing (*The Hudson*, New York: 1966, pp. 262–264) has an extended description of the capture of these forts; and the reader will recall that the Marquis de Chastellux mentions their capture during his visit of 1780 (Chapter 7, note 10). Sir Henry Clinton captured the forts on October 6, 1777, while on the way north to relieve Burgoyne. After capturing the forts and cutting the chain and protective log boom that had been placed across the river at this point, Clinton then seized Fort Constitution (opposite present-day West Point on Constitution Island) and ascended the river as far north as Kingston. This was the first and last time the British threatened the Hudson during the Revolution. The withdrawal of Sir Henry Clinton was followed by the erection of stronger fortifications under the direction of Kosciusko at West Point (plus additional chains and booms between the Point and Constitution Island); but these fortifications were never challenged.

9. *R.V.Z.* "Bloody Pond" has also been known as Lake Sinnipink (Lossing, *The Hudson*, p. 263). It is now (1971) called Hessian Lake and borders present-day route 9W between the traffic circle at Bear Mountain Bridge and the Bear Mountain Lodge.

10. *R.V.Z.* This statement, of course, pays more tribute to Buckingham's Whig prejudices than to historical fact. Fort Putnam, as we have seen, was not erected until after Sir Henry Clinton retreated from the northern Hudson in 1777, and it was never tested in battle. The fort was dismantled in 1787 and its guns sold for old iron. Other references to Fort Putnam may be found in the narratives of the Marquis de Chastellux (p. 102), Fanny Kemble (p. 199) and Harriet Martineau (p. 211).

11. *R.V.Z.* The hotel has been mentioned in connection with the visits of Lafayette (1824, Chapter 10, note 6), Fanny Kemble (1832, Chapter 12, note 6), and Harriet Martineau (1835, Chapter 13, note 1).

12. *R.V.Z.* The reader will recall that Sylvanus Thayer, "The Father of West Point," was on hand to greet Lafayette during his visit of 1824 (Chapter 10, note 3) and that Fanny Kemble encountered him while visiting the ruins of Fort Putnam (Chapter 12, note 3).

13. *R.V.Z.* The reader will recall that Harriet Martineau visited this garden during her stay at West Point in 1835 (p. 211). He has been mentioned in Chapter 13, note 6. Kosciusko came to America at the age of twenty to serve under Washington after seeing Franklin in Paris. Besides building Fort Clinton at West Point (in 1778), he served with General Greene in the southern campaigns. After the Revolution he returned to Poland and in 1794 led an abortive revolution against Russia. He revisited the United States in 1797 in enforced exile from his native Poland and received a grant of land from Congress in recognition of his services. He died in Switzerland in 1817. In 1824 the cadets of West Point erected the famous monument in his memory, placing it within the ruins of Fort Clinton, where it became one of the most familiar landmarks of passing steamboats.

14. *R.V.Z.* Buckingham has his facts wrong. The monument was erected *by* General Jacob Brown in memory of his friend, Colonel E. D. Wood, who fell in an attack on Fort Erie on September 17, 1814.

15. *R.V.Z.* Pollopel (or Palopel) Island, a conspicuous landmark at the northern gateway to the Highlands, was mentioned by Richard Smith during his voyage of 1769 (Chapter 5, note 12). In 1905 Francis Bannerman, a dealer in munitions and second-hand military materials, built an arsenal and warehouse in the shape of a massive castle, complete with towers, turrets, and battlements. Since that time the island has been known as Bannerman's.

16. *R.V.Z.* This is the venerable "Hasbrouck House," the first building to be preserved as an historic site by any state in the Union. It served as Washington's headquarters from April 1, 1782, until August 18, 1783. It was from this house that Washington refused to consider the possibility of establishing a monarchy in America, and in which he also ordered the establishment of the "Order of the Purple Heart" and announced the cessation of hostilities on April 10, 1783. The museum also contains some sections of the chain and boom which spanned the Hudson at West Point.

17. *R.V.Z.* About 1910 an inclined railway was built up the western side of Mount Beacon (or North Beacon Mountain) which is still in use and affords easy access to one of the finest views of the Hudson Valley.

18. *R.V.Z.* In 1882 the difficulties of this road were overcome when the proprietor of the Mountain House erected a railroad from Catskill to the base of the mountains, and in 1892 he built an elevating railroad up the face of the mountain to the very doors of the hotel.

19. *R.V.Z.* The place was known throughout most the nineteenth century as "Saxe's Farm" and was also the site of a toll house maintained by the proprietor of the Mountain House.

20. *R.V.Z.* There are a dozen peaks in the Catskills higher than 3,000 feet, and two (Slide and Hunter) rise over 4,000 feet.

21. *R.V.Z.* The statement is somewhat misleading. The "depth of only 24" refers to a wing that was built in 1825 and placed at right angles to the original structure that fronted the Hudson Valley and that contained a piazza of 140 feet. By 1880, when the Mountain House reached its maximum size, it had a frontage of 280 feet with two additional great wings placed at right angles to that section, one of which was 192

feet long. By that time the hotel also contained 313 rooms and could accommodate four to five hundred paying guests.

22. *R.V.Z.* Though the Mountain House is gone, the view that first inspired its erection is, of course, still accessible to the public. The modern motorist may drive to within a short walk of the edge of the mountain by following the signs that direct him from Haines Falls to the public campsite on North Lake.

23. *R.V.Z.* Ararat is an isolated mountain peak in the eastern extremity of Turkey that was the legendary landing place of Noah's Ark.

Part V · The Upper River

15. William C. Redfield 1836–37

Introduction

1. *R.V.Z.* The Adirondack State Park, which was established in 1892 to protect the watershed of the Hudson, contains five separate mountain ranges, 1,345 lakes, and embraces two-thirds of all the northern lobe of the state of New York between Lake Champlain and Lake Ontario. Embracing more than five million acres over an area of more than four thousand square miles, the Park is larger than any other state or national park in the Union. The Adirondack Forest Preserve comprises more than two million acres that "shall be kept forever as wild forest land" within the Park; it is, with a single exception, the largest forest preserve in the United States. The region is so wild that there is still today a 35-mile stretch of the Hudson that is without any road or path winding along its banks.

2. *R.V.Z.* The story of this enterprise is told in Harold K. Hochschild's *The MacIntyre Mine—From Failure to Fortune*, a publication of the Adirondack Museum, Blue Mountain Lake, N.Y., 1962. The enterprise failed in the year 1858 due to transportation and other insoluble problems. At the advent of

World War II when America's supply of titanium—a necessary element in the manufacture of pigment—could no longer be imported from India, the National Lead Company acquired ownership of the titanium-bearing ore of the old MacIntyre property and built a thriving enterprise (complete with factories, town, and railroad) that is today one of the economic glories of the Adirondacks. The present editor remembers the inception of this enterprise with particular interest, for he happened to be visiting the new "MacIntyre Development" on December 7, 1941, when the Japanese attacked Pearl Harbor.

3. *R.V.Z.* Redfield invented the "safety barges" that were once towed behind the steamboats of the Hudson River for the safety of women passengers, and he was an early advocate of the New York to Albany railroad. Emmons considered Redfield's narrative of the MacIntyre expeditions "a valuable document" that precluded the necessity of a fuller account ("Report of E. Emmons, Geologist of the 2d Geological District of the State of New-York," *New York State Natural History Survey,* 1837, p. 240).

Text

1. *R.V.Z.* Archibald McIntyre (or MacIntyre, as it was later spelled), who lived from 1772 to 1858, was a Scotch immigrant who resided in New York and later moved to Albany from whence he directed his mining operations and also served four terms in the State Senate. Judge [Duncan] McMartin was McIntyre's brother-in-law; he died in 1836. David Henderson, who soon assumed a commanding position in the mining operations, was a friend of the McIntyre family; he was killed in 1845 in a hunting accident that gave its name to "Calamity Pond" near Lake Sanford (a monument now marks the spot along the trail to Marcy). David C. Colden was a prominent New Yorker and close friend of Henderson's who tried to interest English capitalists in the Adirondack enterprise; a lake and a mountain in the nearby area now carry his name. James Hall (1811–1891) had undoubtedly been appointed Ebenezer Emmons's assistant because he had been a pupil of Emmons's at the Troy School (now Rensselaer Polytechnic Institute). The association proved most unsatisfactory and both men acquired an enmity that was to last for the rest of their lives. Hall went on to a brilliant career as director of the New York State Museum, state geologist (1893), vice president of several inter-

national conferences of geology, a charter member of the National Academy of Sciences, and the first President of the Geological Society of America.

2. *R.V.Z.* This road was first surveyed in 1828 at the instigation of Judge McMartin, then a state senator. According to one of Emmons's geological reports on the area (c. 1840), the road ran forty miles from Port Henry to the lower end of Lake Sanford. The owners of the MacIntyre mine then built a connecting road along the west side of Lake Sanford to the site of their mine near Lake Henderson. This must have occurred, however, after the summer of 1826, for Redfield says a little later that there was only a "path" between those two points at that time (Hochschild, *The MacIntyre Mine,* p. 4). When the present editor walked over this road in the fall of 1941 it was still little more than a dirt track in the wilderness. It was subsequently paved, however, by National Lead Company.

3. *R.V.Z.* The "Main Northern Branch of the Hudson" mentioned by Redfield is today known as the "Opalescent River." That which he calls a little later "the north fork of the Hudson" is today the Hudson proper. This change subsequent to Redfield's narrative has caused considerable confusion, for by general consensus of opinion "Lake Tear of the Clouds" at the head of the Opalescent River is today the exact source of the Hudson. Yet the waters from the lake flow into a river which in turn does not encounter the Hudson until it meets the main stream falling out of Lake Sanford, or what Redfield calls "the north fork of the Hudson." The confusion, it is needless to add, could be eliminated if contemporary usage could revert to the first reports of the geologists and the Opalescent River once again became the Hudson proper.

4. *R.V.Z.* The proprietors of the MacIntyre mine reprinted a section of Emmons's report to Governor William H. Seward on January 1, 1840 under the title of *Papers and Documents relative to the Iron Veins, Water Power and Wood Land, etc., etc., in and around the Village of McIntyre in the Town of Newcomb, Essex County, State of New York* (Hochschild, *The MacIntyre Mine,* p. 4).

5. *R.V.Z.* But alas, it is no more! In returning to the scene during the summer of 1967 the editor was disturbed to discover that Lake Sanford had completely disappeared beneath the tailings of the titanium mills of National Lead Company.

6. *R.V.Z.* A stone blast furnace, built in 1854 and measuring 60 feet high and 160 feet around its base, still exists at the site

of the original iron works. Remnants of the nearby village of McIntyre or Adirondack—preserved since the 1870s as a sportsman's club—were seen by the present editor during his visit of 1941 and again in 1967.

7. *R.V.Z.* Redfield and his party followed the present route of the Opalescent River trail from Sanford to Marcy. The modern hiker and mountain climber can retrace the exact path of the historic expedition of 1836–37 by following the excellent directions and maps provided by the Conservation Department of the State of New York in A. S. Hopkins's *The Trails to Marcy,* Recreation Circular 8. The only section of the original hike that is not today covered by well-marked trails is the section between the Feldspar leanto and the upper regions of the Opalescent to Little Marcy. The present yellow trail follows the Feldspar Brook to the top of Marcy, whereas Redfield and his party chose to follow the Opalescent to its source.

8. *R.V.Z.* The party probably made camp at the junction of the Opalescent (or East) River and Upper Twin Brook where the modern hiker may find a leanto, 5.10 miles from Lake Sanford. The type of shelter erected by Redfield's woodsmen was the ancestor of the now famous "Adirondack leanto" used throughout the state of New York.

9. *R.V.Z.* The expedition was on what is today the red trail from the Twin Brook leanto through the gorge of the Opalescent River (p. 19 of aforementioned Circular 8).

10. *R.V.Z.* Between Calamity Mountain on the west and Cliff Mountain on the east.

11. *R.V.Z.* Now called "Hanging Spear Falls." A picture of these falls may be found on p. 20 of the aforementioned Circular 8.

12. *R.V.Z.* Now called "Flowed Land." It is near this place where a monument marks the site of the tragic death of David Henderson (1845).

13. *R.V.Z.* The Opalescent River (or what Redfield calls the Hudson) turns abruptly southeast (facing upstream) at this place and heads straight for the still-undiscovered base of Mt. Marcy. Today's blue and red trails intersect at this point.

14. *R.V.Z.* The mountain on the east was also later named Mt. Colden (4,714'). Archibald McIntyre and David Henderson were undoubtedly responsible for naming the lake and mountain after their friend, David C. Colden.

15. *R.V.Z.* Leantos are again found at this point today.

16. *R.V.Z.* The expedition of the following summer proved that the elevation of Lake Sanford was *more than double* the estimated elevation of 1836. The lake is 1,718 feet above sea level (not 800, as estimated). Lake Colden and the place of encampment were actually 2,764 feet above sea level (or 1,046 feet above Sanford). The peaks around Lake Colden are four to five thousand feet high. Such discoveries profoundly altered the geographical conceptions of the whole state of New York.

17. *R.V.Z.* John Cheney was a young guide, courier, and general factotum of the McIntyre Iron Company and lived to become one of the most famous hunters in the history of the Adirondacks. He was present at David Henderson's death in 1845. A lake (Cheney Pond, on the Boreas River) and a mountain (Cheney Cobble, near the Boreas Ponds) are named after him.

18. *R.V.Z.* Redfield and Henderson were on today's red or Opalescent River trail from Lake Colden to Marcy.

19. *R.V.Z.* If this account is true, William C. Redfield and David Henderson deserve as much credit as Ebenezer Emmons for the first discovery of the highest peak in New York State.

20. *R.V.Z.* Avalanche Pass is now traversed by a well-established trail.

21. *R.V.Z.* The expedition had followed what is now the Calamity Brook (or blue and red) trail which is only half as long as the 9-mile trail to Lake Colden via the Opalescent River.

22. *R.V.Z.* Why the Indians favored this route may still be seen by glancing at any contemporary road map of the Adirondacks. The trail from Lake Placid to Lake Sanford leads directly through Indian Pass; the alternative is a 50-mile detour around the western or eastern flanks of the mountains. The prospecting party that originally discovered the McIntyre deposits in 1826 was led by an Abenaki Indian through this pass from North Elba to Lake Henderson.

23. *R.V.Z.* See note 3 above.

24. *R.V.Z.* John Torrey (1796–1873) was a botanist and chemist who taught at Princeton, Columbia, and the New York College of Physicians and Surgeons. At the time of the 1837 expedition he was professor of chemistry, mineralogy, and geology at West Point. Ingham was possibly Charles C. Ingham (1796–1863), the portrait painter. Strong was possibly Theodore Strong (1790–1869), professor of mathematics and natural philosophy at Hamilton College from 1816 to 1827. Miller was

possibly Samuel Miller (1769–1850), a founder of the New-York Historical Society and a professor at the Princeton Theological Seminary from 1816 to 1850. Emmons, Jr., was the son of Prof. Ebenezer Emmons (1799–1863). Upon completing his geological survey in 1842, Emmons, Sr., became custodian of the state collections at Albany. In 1851 he was appointed state geologist of North Carolina. His enmity with James Hall, previously noted, was based upon professional as well as personal differences. He prepared a geological map of New York State which was severely criticized by Hall because of its inaccuracies, and a three-volume work on *American Geology* (1854–57) aroused similar criticism from many other geologists.

25. *R.V.Z.* Notes on Ticonderoga may be found in Chapter 6, note 53; notes on Crown Point may be found in Chapter 4, note 58, and in Chapter 6, note 58.

26. *R.V.Z.* The same route was followed during the first expedition. Clear Pond is located four or five miles west of the present village of Schroon River on route 9.

27. *R.V.Z.* As noted previously by the editor, this beautiful lake has been completely filled in by the tailings of the titanium factory of National Lead Company.

28. *R.V.Z.* Judge Duncan McMartin died the previous October. The name of this mountain was subsequently changed to Colden in honor of Henderson's close friend.

29. *R.V.Z.* The party was following the present red trail from Lake Colden up the Opalescent River. Redfield and Henderson, as the reader will recall, followed this route on August 19 of the previous summer when they first discovered the Great Dyke Falls (see p. 243).

30. *R.V.Z.* The present yellow trail from Lake Sanford intersects the red trail at this point, and another leanto may also be found here.

31. *R.V.Z.* If Redfield and his party had turned right (where there is today a leanto on the yellow trail) and ascended this tributary, they would have arrived in a little more than a mile at a picturesque small pond that is today universally conceded to be the exact source of the Hudson River. The tributary is "Feldspar Brook," and it issues from "Lake Tear of the Clouds" 4,293 feet above sea level on the southwestern slopes of Mt. Marcy. Redfield and his party, however, did not see this phenomenon; they were determined to pursue the main bed of the Opalescent (or what they called the Hudson River) to where it disappeared on the northern slopes of Marcy at an estimated

elevation of 4,700 feet. This they called the source of the Hudson. The issue here is at best academic. The sources of a great river like the Hudson involve a multiplicity of interlocking streams and rivulets, and the choice of any one of them as a specific source is a rather arbitrary matter. Lakes Sanford and Henderson and all the springs and brooks that flow into them (and especially Indian Pass Brook, 2,800 feet high) are certainly major sources of the Hudson. Contemporary opinion supports the early geologists, however, in pitching upon the slopes of Mt. Marcy as the location of the source of the river. The fact that Marcy is the highest mountain in the area makes this a logical choice, for the ultimate source of any river that rises in a mountainous area must be its highest vanishing point. This, according to Redfield and his party, was in the "High Valley" (a name that has not been perpetuated) where what we today call the Opalescent River first appears from the earth. Contemporary opinion, however, says that "Lake Tear of the Clouds" is the specific source. Several factors favor our modern opinion. Recent survey maps attest that the Opalescent River first appears at an elevation of about 4,050 feet—not at 4,700 feet, as believed by the early geologists. And "Lake Tear of the Clouds" is firmly established at 4,293 feet. Furthermore, this little pond is the highest known source in the state of New York from which water flows continuously to the Atlantic Ocean. The fact would seem to favor our more modern opinion regarding the source of the Hudson. When all is said and done, however, such "facts" are of little moment in deciding such an issue. The issue belongs to the realm of poetry and romance, rather than science. Who in the last analysis can resist a secluded tarn on the slopes of a high mountain peak that immortalizes itself under the name of "Lake Tear of the Clouds"?

32. *R.V.Z.* The name "High Meadow fork" has not been perpetuated, and its possible location is difficult to designate. It probably refers to a point where the present blue trail from Lake Arnold intersects the Opalescent River. The "tributary from the north" is not depicted on contemporary survey maps. The elevation at the aforementioned point is 3,400 feet. Redfield and his party continued their ascent of the "mountain valley" from that point and thus pursued the diminishing waters of the Opalescent River rather than the route that goes up the Feldspar to "Lake Tear of the Clouds." No trail has therefore ever been built along this portion of the track of the 1837 expedition.

33. *R.V.Z.* This change in course probably occurred where the Opalescent River reaches an elevation of 3,700 feet (U.S. Geological Survey Map, Mount Marcy Quadrangle, 1953).

34. *R.V.Z.* This camp was probably made where the Opalescent River all but disappears as a spring at about an elevation of 4,100 feet (i.e. on present survey maps, as noted above).

35. *R.V.Z.* Redfield and his party had arrived at or near the top of "Little Marcy" at an elevation of 4,765 feet. Johns Brook, a tributary of the Ausable River that flows northward into Lake Champlain (and subsequently into the St. Lawrence), has its source within three-quarters of a mile of this spot. Just north of the area the Hopkins trail (or yellow trail) intersects the north (or blue) trail to Mt. Marcy.

36. *R.V.Z.* Redfield is obviously basing his computations on the northeastern Catskills which rise to elevations of 3,500 feet (e.g. North Mountain) and 3,640 feet (e.g. High Peak). Later, when the southwestern Catskills became more familiar, Slide Mountain was discovered to rise to 4,204 feet. Assuming that Redfield was at 4,700 feet, we must conclude that he was only 496 feet above the highest peak in the Catskills. The general truth of his observation, however, need not be questioned: Redfield and his party had indeed established the fact that the Adirondacks are a much more formidable mountain-range than the Catskills. Yet legends die hard, and it was not until after the Civil War when the Adirondacks first became a popular vacationland that the general public gave up the notion that the Catskills were the highest in the state.

37. *R.V.Z.* This is roughly the same course as the present northern trail to Marcy from the Adirondack Lodge.

38. *R.V.Z.* The Franconia range is now considered one segment of the White Mountains.

39. *R.V.Z.* By modern survey Mt. Marcy is 477 feet higher than Whiteface (4,867') and 1,140 feet higher than Slide Mountain (4,204'). The five highest mountains of the eastern United States are: Mitchell in North Carolina (6,684), Clingmans Dome in Tennessee (6,642), Washington in New Hampshire (6,288), Rogers in Virginia (5,729), and Marcy in New York (5,344).

40. *R.V.Z.* Redfield and his party seemed to have again missed Lake Tear of the Clouds and Feldspar Brook on their descent of the mountain.

41. *R.V.Z.* Mt. Colden is 4,714 feet high.

42. *R.V.Z.* Avalanche Lake, which is mostly spring fed, is not much more than a mile north of the headwaters of the Opalescent. The present editor assumes that the tributary that flows into Lake Henderson from Wallface Pond is the northernmost source of the Hudson. It is two miles farther north than the northernmost point of the Opalescent.

43. *R.V.Z.* There are several small lakes in the immediate vicinity that are considerably higher, including, as we have seen, Lake Tear of the Clouds. The highest lake in the United States is Tulainyo in California (12,802).

44. *R.V.Z.* The genesis of this change in spelling is unknown to this editor. Harold K. Hochschild, author of the aforementioned *The MacIntyre Mine,* merely says that "the 'a' was inserted many years after its christening" (p. 3). Archibald McIntyre was state controller from 1806 to 1821.

45. *R.V.Z.* The modern trail to MacIntyre takes advantage of another ravine a half mile to the north of the more difficult one used by Redfield and his party. The name of the "small stream" is Cold Brook. Modern trails converge on Lake Colden, as we have noticed, from every direction of the compass. The lake also features a ranger station and a cluster of leantos.

46. *R.V.Z.* As becomes clear a little later on, Redfield here refers to the upper or northern end of Indian Pass as "the valley of the west branch of the Au Sable." The small body of water is today called "Indian Pass Brook," a branch of the West Branch of the Ausable River that flows into the latter stream near North Elba. The actual valley of the West Branch of the Ausable, according to modern cartographers, lies north-northwest of Mount MacIntyre. This river rises on the northern slopes of MacIntyre, skirts Lake Placid, and falls into Lake Champlain fifteen miles south of Plattsburgh.

47. *R.V.Z.* Redfield is correct about MacIntyre being the second highest mountain in the Adirondacks. However, this mountain (known as "Algonquin" at its highest peak) and Mt. Marcy are the only two mountains above 5,000 feet. The three peaks "lying eastward of the main source of the Hudson" are Basin (4,827), Skylight (4,926), and Haystack (4,960). The only peak of a commensurate size "lying in a westerly direction," however, is Santanoni (4,607), but this mountain cannot be included in the ten major peaks of the Adirondacks. Nor can Mount McMartin (or Colden). The ten major peaks, in order of height, are: Marcy, Algonquin (on the MacIntyre range), Haystack, Skylight, Whiteface, Dix, Boundary, Gray, Iroquois

(also on MacIntyre), and Basin (the last being the smallest at 4,827). Redfield is therefore substantially correct in saying there are "ten" peaks that are close to 5,000 feet. His last statement is also substantially correct: there are twenty-one peaks in the Adirondacks that exceed the height of Slide Mountain in the Catskills. The Catskills have only two peaks above 4,000; the Adirondacks have forty-five.

48. *R.V.Z.* As previously noted, Wallface Pond from which a tributary flows into Indian Pass Brook and thence into Lake Henderson is 3,100 feet high.

49. *R.V.Z.* The trail now ascends MacIntyre from the headwaters of the Ausable. It cannot, of course, be compared to the scenic wonders of some of the trails of the Sierras and Rockies, still unappreciated at this time.

16. Charles Farnham   1880

1. *R.V.Z.* These are all small tributaries of the Hudson near the sources of the river in the central Adirondacks.

2. *R.V.Z.* The Glen is in the heart of Warren County on present auto route 28, a few miles north of Warrensburg.

3. *R.V.Z.* Thurman was named after one John Thurman who owned extensive tracts of land in the area and also founded the village that bears his name in the 1780s.

4. *R.V.Z.* Luzern or Luzerne is on the border of Warren and Saratoga Counties. Jessup's Landing is a few miles south, in the town of Corinth.

5. *R.V.Z.* As becomes clear in the following sentences, Farnham and his friend embarked upon the Hudson at the present town of North River, on the border of Warren and Essex Counties, along present-day route 28. They had entered the Adirondacks by way of the lakes of Hamilton County and "carted" their canoes from Blue Mountain Lake to "Fourteenth Dam" (or "Fourteenth Station," as the village was known before being named North River). A new road of about twenty miles connecting these two points had been built about 1872. "Eldridge's" was a hotel that existed in North River (or Fourteenth Station), also as early as 1872 (see E. R. Wallace, *Descriptive Guide to the Adirondacks*, New York, 1872).

6. *R.V.Z.* Both canoes were fourteen feet long with a twenty-eight inch beam on deck and looked something like a heavier version of our modern kayaks. The *Allegro* had a flatter bottom than the *Rosalie,* and this together with other structural differences gave it, in Farnham's opinion, greater buoyancy and maneuverability in violent rapids. Farnham never once names the captain of the *Rosalie.*

7. *R.V.Z.* Farnham is not exaggerating. In 1880 the Adirondacks were still an undeveloped wilderness. People first became aware of the Adirondacks as a sportsman's paradise in 1869 with the publication of the Rev. William H. H. Murray's *Adventures in the Wilderness,* and it was not until 1879 that Thomas C. Durant and son built the first elaborate hunting lodge in the mountains.

8. *R.V.Z.* A map of 1876 by W. W. Ely (that may be consulted in the Map Room of the New York Public Library) places "Spruce Mountain" just east of The Glen. This is the only reference to "Spruce Mountain" that the editor has been able to find. Farnham, however, is here talking about a "Spruce Mountain rift" that presumably exists someplace between North Creek and Riverside [Riparius]. Rifts exist in both places, and it is possible that Farnham is confusing the more southern one at The Glen (and near "Spruce Mountain") with the unnamed rift near North Creek.

9. *R.V.Z.* Farnham is referring to the area halfway between The Glen and Warrensburg along present route 28.

10. *R.V.Z.* Hadley, or Luzerne Falls as the falls are called today, are located between the twin villages of Hadley and Luzerne where the Hudson separates the counties of Warren and Saratoga. In 1860 J. H. French described them in the following terms: "The water flows in a series of rapids for three-fourths of a mi. over a declining rocky bottom, and is then compressed into a narrow gorge for 80 rods, at the bottom of which it shoots down a nearly perpendicular descent of 60 ft." (*Gazetteer of the State of New York,* Syracuse, New York, 1860, p. 670.)

11. *R.V.Z.* The bridge was undoubtedly located where in 1860 J. H. French said that "a few rods above the last leap of the water, and where it is rushing with the greatest velocity, the river is spanned by a single plank 13 ft. in length." (*Gazetteer,* p. 670.)

12. *R.V.Z.* New Bridge is halfway between present-day Corinth and Glens Falls.

13. *R.V.Z.* In 1829 a canal was built around the falls at Glens Falls to act both as a feeder for the Champlain Canal (Albany

to Lake Champlain) and a navigable watercourse between that canal and the town of Glens Falls.

14. *R.V.Z.* Northumberland is located on the Hudson fifteen miles below Glens Falls. The Champlain Canal was constructed in conjunction with the Erie Canal and passed Northumberland on the way to Fort Edward where it left the Hudson and followed the course of the Woodcreek to Whitehall on Lake Champlain.

Part VI · The Age of the Railroad

Introduction

1. *R.V.Z.* Wallace Bruce, *Along the Hudson with Washington Irving* (Poughkeepsie, N.Y.: 1913), p. 9.

2. *R.V.Z.* Howard Gossage, "Understanding Marshall McLuhan," *Ramparts* (April, 1966), Vol. 4, No. 12, p. 38.

17. *Opening of the Hudson River Railroad 1851*

1. *R.V.Z.* Located on the east bank of the Hudson opposite Albany. The transit of the river was made by ferry until the erection of a bridge a few years later.

2. *R.V.Z.* Ambrose C. Kingsland was mayor of New York from 1851 to 1853.

3. *R.V.Z.* Judge Thomas Jackson Oakley (1783–1857) supported the Erie Canal project as well as the Hudson River Railroad, and he acquired some fame as the attorney for the state of New York in the case of *Gibbons vs. Ogden* (see p. 152).

4. *R.V.Z.* Probably Erastus Brooks (1815–1886), a well-known journalist of the period who ran the *New York Express*.

5. *R.V.Z.* John Bigelow (1817–1911), editor, writer, and diplomat, joined William Cullen Bryant on the *Evening Post* in 1848.

6. *R.V.Z.* A good view of this tunnel may be seen from the present Storm King Highway.

7. *R.V.Z.* James Boorman (1783–1866) was a merchant and philanthropist who also helped to found the Hudson River Railroad and later became its president.

8. *R.V.Z.* Washington Hunt (1811–1867) was governor from 1850 to 1852.

9. *R.V.Z.* We have already encountered Governor William L. Marcy (1786–1857) in connection with the discovery of the sources of the Hudson (see p. 239). He was governor for three terms, 1833–1838.

10. *R.V.Z.* We have already encountered John C. Spencer (1788–1855) in connection with the opening of the Erie Canal (Chapter 11, note 13).

18. *N. P. Willis 1854*

1. *R.V.Z.* A species of snail that hibernates in the winter by retiring into the earth and closing the opening in its shell.

2. *R.V.Z.* Willis could probably see either the East Shore Line across Newburgh Bay or the trains of the Newburgh extension of the Erie Line that ran along the west shore (built 1850).

3. *R.V.Z.* The reader will recall encountering this hotel in previous narratives (see Chapter 13, note 1). The train had come to a halt just below present-day Garrison, ten miles out of Fishkill.

4. *R.V.Z.* Sunnyside is twenty-five miles north of New York City. As anyone may discover who visits Irving's home, the tracks of the railroad are but a few feet away from his parlor windows.

5. *R.V.Z.* The Astor Library—the cultural showplace of New York City when it was opened in January 1854—was located on Lafayette Street. In 1911 its collection was moved to 42nd Street when it became part of the New York Public Library. The building was the first structure to be saved under New York's Landmarks Preservation Law (Jan., 1966), and it is now the permanent home of the New York Shakespeare Festival.

6. *R.V.Z.* This is an allusion to Margaret, Katherine, and Leah Fox who conducted seances and established the vogue of spiritualism in 19th century America.

7. *R.V.Z.* The railroad station on Tenth Avenue between 31st and 34th Streets was the end of the line for the trains that were drawn by steam locomotives. South of this point the cars were drawn by a "dumb engine" to the terminal at Chambers Street and West Broadway.

8. *R.V.Z.* As late as 1865 the population of New York was still concentrated below Union Square—Willis's destination at 14th Street.

19. *Isabella B. Bishop   1854*

1. *R.V.Z.* Delaval's Hotel was a popular stopover for passengers waiting to make train connections in Albany. Abraham Lincoln stayed there in February 1861, on his way from Springfield to Washington for his first inaugural.

2. *R.V.Z.* The actual distance was 143 miles.

3. *R.V.Z.* The observation is only comprehensible when we remember that it was made on a November day from a fast-moving train.

4. *R.V.Z.* Loch Katrine is the famous lake in Scotland that is featured in Sir Walter Scott's "Lady of the Lake." It is 9½ miles long.

5. *R.V.Z.* Loch Achray is a small and beautiful lake 1¼ miles long that connects with Loch Katrine.

20. *Jacques Offenbach   1876*

1. *R.V.Z.* The Pullman car, the invention of George Mortimer Pullman (1831–1897), dates from the year 1859 when the first three cars were put into service by the Chicago and Alton Railroad. General use, however, dates from 1867 when the inventor established the Pullman Palace Car Company.

2. *R.V.Z.* The New York Central (of which the Hudson River Railroad had become a part of by 1876) had apparently not started using the new dining cars by this time.

21. *Emile de Damseaux   1877*

1. *R.V.Z.* As we have noted elsewhere, the first railroad was the Mohawk and Hudson which was opened in 1831 between Schenectady and Albany.

2. *R.V.Z.* Mrs. Blandina Dudley, wife of a wealthy Albany merchant, contributed $76,000 to the observatory. The building was dedicated in 1856.

3. *R.V.Z.* This is a province in southeastern France that contains the Dauphiné Alps.

4. *R.V.Z.* A town in Belgium located on the Semois River.

5. *R.V.Z.* Possibly Buttermilk Falls on the western bank.

6. *R.V.Z.* The first Grand Central Station was built in 1871.

7. *R.V.Z.* The *Plymouth Rock* was built by Cornelius Vanderbilt in 1854. It was 330 feet long and had water wheels 37 feet in diameter. It had been thoroughly remodeled about 1870 when it was taken off the New York-Stonington run and placed in service on the Hudson. Its career ended in 1886 when it was taken to Boston and sold as junk.

8. *R.V.Z.* The most serious accidents due to exploding boilers occurred in the period prior to 1852 when steamboat racing was not prohibited by law. The *General Jackson,* the *Reindeer,* the *Alexis,* and the *Aetna* are the names of some of the steamboats that were destroyed by bursting boilers with considerable loss of life. The disaster of the *Henry Clay,* which caught fire during a race with the *Armenia* in 1852 and killed such notable people as Andrew Jackson Downing and the sister of Nathaniel Hawthorne, led to the enactment of a rigid Steamboat Inspection Act by the New York legislature. Disasters were less frequent after that date.

9. *R.V.Z.* Jacques Callot (1592–1635), the great French engraver.

22. *Henry James   1905*

1. *R.V.Z.* It is no wonder James is confused about the location of "Sleepy Hollow." The famous Sleepy Hollow of the nineteenth century, the one known to all Irving's public, was located in the Catskill Mountains on the approach to the Catskill Mountain House (see Chapter 13, note 16). This was the presumed site of Rip Van Winkle's long sleep. Today,

however, the public associates "Sleepy Hollow" with Ichabod Crane and *The Legend of Sleepy Hollow* located near Irving's home in Tarrytown. The loss of interest in the Catskill site coincided with the decline of the famous Catskill Mountain House.

2. *R.V.Z.* John D. Rockefeller, Jr., bought "Sunnyside" from the collateral descendents of Irving in 1945, and the accretions which had been added after Irving's day were eliminated. The house was opened to the public in 1947 and is now in the condition in which Irving left it. It is now owned and administered by the Sleepy Hollow Restorations, a non-profit educational corporation that also owns the Van Cortlandt Manor and the Philipsburg Manor. On Sept. 23, 1966, it was designated a National Historic Landmark.

3. *R.V.Z.* This was the name Irving gave to the house. It derives from one Wolfert Ecker who about 1690 built the original little Dutch house, the ruins of which Irving incorporated into his additions. Irving purchased the estate in 1835.

4. *R.V.Z.* Irving lived at Sunnyside for about 14 years before the Hudson River Railroad was put through (c. 1849). He died in 1859, thus surviving the railroad by 10 years.

INDEX